Computer Accounting
with
QuickBooks® Pro 2006

Eighth Edition

Donna Ulmer, MBA, PhD, CPA, CITP
Webster University

QuickBooks 2006, QuickBooks Pro 2006,
QuickBooks Premier 2006
QuickBooks Premier 2006: Accountant Edition

 Irwin

Boston   Burr Ridge, IL   Dubuque, IA   Madison, WI   New York   San Francisco   St. Louis
Bangkok   Bogotá   Caracas   Kuala Lumpur   Lisbon   London   Madrid   Mexico City
Milan   Montreal   New Delhi   Santiago   Seoul   Singapore   Sydney   Taipei   Toronto

McGraw-Hill Irwin

COMPUTER ACCOUNTING WITH QUICKBOOKS PRO® 2006
QuickBooks 2006, QuickBooks Pro® 2006, QuickBooks Premier 2006, QuickBooks Premier 2006: Accountant Edition
Donna Ulmer

Published by McGraw-Hill/Irwin, a business unit of The McGraw-Hill Companies, Inc., 1221 Avenue of the Americas, New York, NY 10020. Copyright © 2007 by The McGraw-Hill Companies, Inc. All rights reserved.

QuickBooks, QuickBooks Pro and Quick Books Premier are registered trademarks of Intuit Inc. in the United States and other countries. Computer Accounting with QuickBooks has not been reviewed, approved, or endorsed by Intuit. Intuit expressly disclaims any responsibility for its content.

Turbo Tax is a registered trademark of Intuit Inc.

Microsoft, Windows, and Excel are registered trademarks of Microsoft Corporation.

1 2 3 4 5 6 7 8 9 0 QPD/QPD 0 9 8 7 6
ISBN-13: 978-0-07-313114-6
ISBN-10: 0-07-313114-8

Editorial director: *Stewart Mattson*
Senior sponsoring editor: *Steve Schuetz*
Editorial assistant: *Megan McFarlane*
Lead project manager: *Pat Frederickson*
Production supervisor: *Debra R. Sylvester*
Designer: *Cara David*
Executive marketing manager: *Rhonda Seelinger*
Media producer: *Greg Bates*
Media project manager: *Lynn M. Bluhm*

www.mhhe.com

ABOUT THE AUTHOR

Donna Ulmer, CPA, CITP (Certified Information Technology Professional), has provided computer software training to college students, faculty, businesses, and non-profit organizations. Donna is an Associate Professor of Accounting at Webster University in Saint Louis, Missouri.

Five times nominated to Who's Who Among America's Teachers, Dr. Ulmer earned her B.S. from Southern Illinois University at Edwardsville where she also earned an MBA with an emphasis in accounting and information systems. She obtained her Ph.D. from Saint Louis University where she conducted doctoral research on the effectiveness of instructional techniques for the computer classroom.

Donna is a member of the American Institute of Certified Public Accountants, Missouri Society of CPAs, American Accounting Association, Missouri Association of Accounting Educators, and American Association of University Women.

Donna loves to hear from other professors teaching QuickBooks and accounting software, so feel free to email her at donna.ulmer@charter.net.

QUICK REFERENCE GUIDE

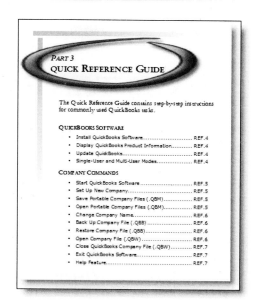

To save you time....

Computer Accounting with QuickBooks Pro 2006 features a convenient Quick Reference Guide.

Now you can have it all....

Computer Accounting with QuickBooks Pro 2006 gives you both chapter tutorials for experiential learning *and* a handy resource manual for quick reference. The Quick Reference Guide provides step-by-step instructions for the most frequently used customer, vendor, and employee tasks in a user-friendly resource.

NEW THIS EDITION....

New, easy way to save QuickBooks files....

Now *Computer Accounting with QuickBooks Pro 2006* features a convenient new way to save your QuickBooks files using Portable company files.

More end-of-chapter exercises....

New exercises in Chapters 8, 9, and 10 give you practice setting up new QuickBooks company files.

Streamlined Home Page navigation....

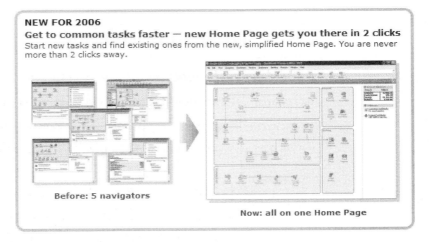

Convenient, new Information Centers....

PREFACE

Computer Accounting with QuickBooks Pro® 2006 makes learning QuickBooks software convenient and easy.

What distinguishes this book is quite simple: while software training materials usually focus on the software, this text focuses on the learner—incorporating sound pedagogy and instructional techniques that make learning software as effortless as possible.

Using a hands-on approach, the text integrates understanding accounting with mastery of the software. Each chapter builds on the previous chapter as you progress from entering simple transactions to using QuickBooks' advanced features. The text provides both the "big picture" overview ("Where am I going?") and step-by-step instructions ("Where do I click?").

Designed for flexibility in meeting the learner's needs, the text can be used either in a QuickBooks course or by an individual who wants to learn QuickBooks at his or her own pace. The text can be used with QuickBooks® 2006, QuickBooks Pro® 2006, QuickBooks Premier® 2006, or QuickBooks Premier® 2006: Accountant Edition.

The text begins with a vignette describing the realistic travails of a software user. Subsequent chapters continue the case that runs throughout the text. The case approach requires the learner to apply both software skills and problem-solving skills. End-of-chapter exercises and virtual company projects offer additional practice using the software.

Online assignments in each chapter provide web sites with useful information for small business accounting. A real world project walks students through the design and development of a QuickBooks accounting system for a real company.

Feel free to email me with questions, tips, suggestions, comments, and ideas at donna.ulmer@charter.net.

Have fun learning QuickBooks!

Donna Ulmer

TEXT OVERVIEW

A virtual company case runs throughout the text, enabling students to better understand how various transactions and activities are interrelated.

Part 1 of the text, Exploring QuickBooks with Rock Castle Construction, focuses on learning the basics of entering transactions and generating reports. Part 2, Small Business Accounting with QuickBooks 2006, covers the entire accounting cycle including setting up a new company as well as using advanced features of QuickBooks software.

Part 1 includes:

- **Chapter 1: Quick Tour of QuickBooks Pro 2006.** This chapter provides a guided tour of the software using QuickBooks Navigation tools and the QuickBooks sample company, Rock Castle Construction. Other topics include how to save and open portable company files.

- **Chapter 2: Chart of Accounts.** This chapter introduces the chart of accounts and how to customize the chart of accounts to suit specific business needs. Other topics include creating passwords and using the Reminders List.

- **Chapter 3: Banking.** This chapter focuses on the checking account and check register for a small business. Topics include making deposits, writing checks, and reconciling a bank statement.

- **Chapter 4: Customers and Sales.** Chapter 4 demonstrates how to record customer transactions. Topics include how to create invoices, record sales, record customer payments, and print customer reports.

- **Chapter 5: Vendors, Purchases, and Inventory.** This chapter focuses on recording vendor transactions, including creating purchase orders, paying bills, and printing vendor reports.

- **Chapter 6: Employees and Payroll.** Chapter 6 covers how to use the time tracking feature, how to transfer tracked time to customer invoices, and how to process payroll using QuickBooks.

- **Chapter 7: Reports and Graphs.** In this chapter, you will complete the accounting cycle by creating a trial balance and entering adjusting entries. In addition, you will learn how to create a number of different reports and graphs using QuickBooks, including how to export reports to Microsoft® Excel® software.

Part 2, Business Accounting with QuickBooks Pro 2006, builds upon the basics covered in Part 1. Fearless Painting Service, a case that runs throughout the second part, starts out as a sole proprietor service business, then expands to become a merchandising corporation. Using a building block approach, the text gradually introduces advanced features while maintaining continuity and interest.

Part 2 includes:

- **Chapter 8: Creating a Service Company in QuickBooks.**
  Chapter 8 covers how to use the EasyStep Interview feature to set
  up a new company in QuickBooks. You also learn how to create
  customer, vendor, and item lists.

- **Chapter 9: Accounting for a Service Company.** Chapter 9
  records transactions for an entire year using the company created in
  Chapter 8. New in this edition is a short exercise for setting up a
  new company and entering transactions. Project 9.1 provides an
  opportunity to integrate all the QuickBooks skills covered in a more
  extensive and comprehensive case.

- **Chapter 10: Merchandising Corporation: Sales, Purchases, and
  Inventory.** After learning how to set up a merchandising
  corporation with inventory, you record transactions for the first
  month of operations. Project 10.1 is a comprehensive case for a
  merchandising corporation.

- **Chapter 11: Merchandising Corporation: Payroll.** Chapter 11
  covers how to set up payroll for a company and how to record
  payroll and create paychecks using QuickBooks. Project 11.1 is a
  continuation of Project 10.1.

- **Chapter 12: Advanced Topics.** This chapter covers the advanced
  features of QuickBooks software including budgets, estimates,
  progress billing, credit card sales, accounting for bad debts,
  memorized reports, and the audit trail. Using the advanced features
  of QuickBooks, Project 12.1. is a continuation of Project 9.1.

PEDAGOGY:
THE ART AND SCIENCE OF TEACHING

This text is based on sound pedagogy for learning software effectively. The pedagogy's strengths include:

- Experiential Learning

- Quick Reference Guide

- Virtual Company Cases

- Real World QuickBooks Project

- Page-Referenced Learning Objectives

- Unique Annotated Screen Captures

- Online Exercises

- Instructor's Resource Manual, including Instructional Techniques for the Computerized Classroom

EXPERIENTIAL LEARNING

Experiential learning and constructivist instructional methodology is increasingly recognized as an effective approach to computer software training. Based on theories of educator John Dewey, the constructivist approach is student-directed using realistic, practical applications to aid learners in constructing a deeper understanding with improved retention.[1]

---

[1] R.Cwiklik, "Dewey Wins!: If the "New" Teaching Methods Pushed by High-Tech Gurus Sound Familiar, It Isn't Surprising," *The Wall Street Journal*, (November 17, 1997), R19.

Utilizing a constructivist instructional design, the training materials presented here use a two-step approach:

- Each chapter is a hands-on guided instructional tutorial that familiarizes the student with software tasks. The guided instruction portion of the chapter may be used by students individually or the instructor can demonstrate the tasks with students completing the tasks at individual workstations. Realistic company cases are used in the guided instruction sessions.

- End-of-chapter assignments provide practical applications to gain mastery. The assignments use a problem-solving case approach and consist of both exercises and projects. Each exercise contains multiple tasks that ask students to apply what they learned in the guided instruction session. Comprehensive projects review and integrate the various topics.

QUICK REFERENCE GUIDE

To save you time, Part 3 of the text is a convenient Quick Reference Guide. Now you can have it all: chapter tutorials for hands-on experiential learning *and* a handy resource manual for quick reference. The Quick Reference Guide provides step-by-step instructions for the most frequently used customer, vendor, and employee tasks in a user-friendly resource.

VIRTUAL COMPANY CASES

Each section of the text uses a virtual company case that runs throughout the section. Part 1 focuses on Rock Castle Construction, while Part 2 sets up Fearless Painting Service that grows from a sole proprietorship service company into a merchandising corporation. The use of Rock Castle and Fearless Paint provides a real world context to enhance understanding of how various tasks are related.

REAL WORLD QUICKBOOKS PROJECT

The Real World QuickBooks Project (Appendix A) guides you through the development of a real world QuickBooks application. Integrating and applying the skills learned in the course, real applications provide learners with the most effective software training.

The Real World QuickBooks Project can be used in several different ways. The project can be assigned as a capstone project for the course. The project can also be used as a service learning project where students learn while providing community service using their computer accounting skills. Finally, the small business user who is creating a QuickBooks accounting system can use the Real World QuickBooks Project as a development tool.

PAGE-REFERENCED LEARNING OBJECTIVES

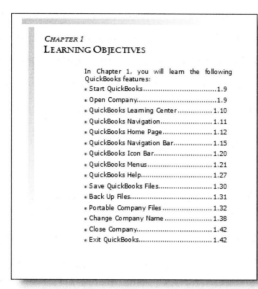

Learning objectives at the beginning of each chapter are page-referenced. The page references allow the instructor and students to easily focus on areas of interest. In addition, the page-referenced learning objectives are an efficient way for students to locate information needed to complete end-of chapter exercises and projects.

ANNOTATED SCREEN CAPTURE SYSTEM

Screen captures are an essential tool for helping learners bridge the gap between printed page and computer screen. The text provides concise, easy-to-follow instructions.

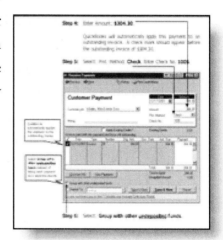

ONLINE EXERCISES

> **NOTE:** The websites in the exercises are subject to change due to web page updates.

Web Quests appear at the end of each chapter. From the IRS website (www.irs.gov) to Intuit's website (www.intuit.com), online exercises provide an opportunity to learn useful information about small business accounting.

INSTRUCTOR'S RESOURCE MANUAL

The Instructor's Resource Manual is a valuable resource for faculty. In addition to providing complete solutions for all assignment material in the text, the Instructor's Resource Manual offers successful teaching strategies for computer accounting with QuickBooks, including instructional techniques for the computerized classroom.

ACKNOWLEDGMENTS

Many thanks to the McGraw-Hill team who made this text possible, especially Steve Schuetz and Kelly Wagner. A special thanks to Ayanna Makonnen for her sense of humor and careful copyediting, Richie McBride for his life-saving technology assistance, Gina Shea of Baltimore Community College for her work on the Instructor's Manual, and Anna Boulware of St. Charles Community College for her feedback and helpful reviewer comments.

My sincere gratitude...

To other educators who have shared ideas, comments, suggestions, and encouragement:

> *Tom Dent, St. Louis Community College*
> *Charlie Blumer, St. Charles Community College*
> *Troy Luh, Webster University*
> *David Porras, Webster University*
> *Lanny Nelms, Gwinnett Technical College*
> *Carol Thomas, West Virginia University-Parkersburg*
> *Joni Onishi, Hawaii Community College*
> *Bob Rachowicz, Midstate College*
> *George Mitchell, Forsyth Tech Community College*
> *Cathy Attebery, Black Hawk College*
> *Lynne Kemp, North Country Community College*
> *Brian Voss, Austin Community College*
> *Charles McCord, Portland Community College*
> *Baruch England, City University of New York*
> *Jeff Carper, Point Park College*
> *Lori Fuller, Widener University*
> *Edna Murugan Central Florida College*
> *Karen Taylor, Butte-Glenn Community College*

To Michael for his eye for detail and his unwavering support

Contents

CONTENTS

PART 1:
EXPLORING QUICKBOOKS WITH ROCK CASTLE CONSTRUCTION

PART 2:
SMALL BUSINESS ACCOUNTING WITH QUICKBOOKS 2006

CHAPTER 8: CREATING A SERVICE COMPANY IN QUICKBOOKS.... 8.1

CHAPTER 9: ACCOUNTING FOR A SERVICE COMPANY 9.1

CHAPTER 12: ADVANCED TOPICS *12.1*

PART 3: QUICK REFERENCE GUIDE

APPENDICES

PART 1
EXPLORING QUICKBOOKS WITH ROCK CASTLE CONSTRUCTION

CHAPTER 1:
QUICK TOUR OF QUICKBOOKS PRO 2006

CHAPTER 2:
CHART OF ACCOUNTS

CHAPTER 3:
BANKING

CHAPTER 4:
CUSTOMERS AND SALES

CHAPTER 5:
VENDORS, PURCHASES, AND INVENTORY

CHAPTER 6:
EMPLOYEES AND PAYROLL

CHAPTER 7:
REPORTS AND GRAPHS

CHAPTER 1
QUICK TOUR OF QUICKBOOKS PRO 2006

SCENARIO

Mr. Rock Castle, owner of Rock Castle Construction, called to hire you as his accountant. His former accountant unexpectedly accepted a job offer in Hawaii and Rock Castle Construction needs someone immediately to maintain its accounting records. Mr. Castle indicates they use QuickBooks to maintain the company's accounting records. When you tell him that you are not familiar with QuickBooks software, Mr. Castle reassures you, *"No problem! QuickBooks is easy to learn. Stop by my office this afternoon."*

When you arrive at Rock Castle Construction, Mr. Castle leads you to a cubicle as he rapidly explains Rock Castle's accounting.

"Rock Castle needs to keep records of transactions with customers, vendors, and employees. We must keep a record of our customers and the sales and services we provide to those customers. Also, it is crucial for the company to be able to bill customers promptly and keep a record of cash collected from them. If we don't know who owes Rock Castle money, we can't collect it.

"Rock Castle also needs to keep track of the supplies, materials, and inventory we purchase from vendors. We need to track all purchase orders, the items received, the invoices or bills received from vendors, and the payments made to vendors. If we don't track bills, we can't pay our vendors on time. And if Rock Castle doesn't pay its bills on time, the vendors don't like to sell to us.

"Also, we like to keep our employees happy. One way to do that is to pay them the right amount at the right time. So Rock Castle must keep track of the time worked by its employees, the amounts owed to the employees, and the wages and salaries paid to them.

"QuickBooks permits Rock Castle to keep a record of all of these transactions. Also, we need records so we can prepare tax returns, financial reports for bank loans, and reports to evaluate the company's performance and make business decisions.

"Your first assignment is to learn more about QuickBooks." Mr. Castle tosses you a QuickBooks training manual as he rushes off to answer a phone call.

Slightly overwhelmed by Mr. Castle's rapid-fire delivery, you sink into a chair. As you look around your cubicle, you notice for the first time the leaning tower of papers stacked beside the computer, waiting to be processed. No wonder Mr. Castle wanted you to start right way. Opening the QuickBooks training manual, you find the following.

CHAPTER 1
LEARNING OBJECTIVES

In Chapter 1, you will learn the following QuickBooks features:

ACCOUNTING INFORMATION SYSTEMS

QuickBooks is accounting software that provides an easy and efficient way to collect and summarize accounting information. In addition, QuickBooks creates many different reports that are useful when managing a business.

> Accounting is the language of business. Learning accounting is similar to learning a foreign language. As you use this text, you will learn terms and definitions that are unique to accounting.

The objective of an accounting system is to collect, summarize, and communicate information to decision makers. Accounting information is used to:

- Prepare tax returns to send to the IRS and state tax agencies.

- Prepare financial statements for banks and investors.

- Prepare reports for managers and owners to use when making decisions about the business. Such decisions include: Are our customers paying their bills on time? Which of our products are the most profitable? Will we have enough cash to pay our bills next month?

TRANSACTIONS

An accounting system collects information about *transactions*. As a company conducts business, it enters into transactions (or exchanges) with other parties such as customers, vendors, and employees. For example, when a business sells a product to a customer, there are two parts to the transaction:

1. The business *gives* a product or service to the customer.
2. In exchange, the business *receives* cash (or a promise to pay later) from the customer.

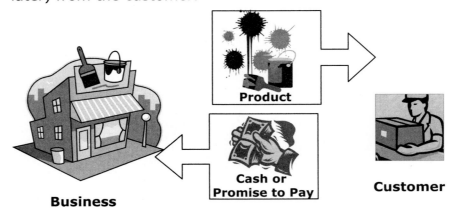

Business   **Product**   **Cash or Promise to Pay**   **Customer**

DOUBLE-ENTRY ACCOUNTING

Double-entry accounting has been used for over 500 years. In Italy in the year 1494, Luca Pacioli, a Franciscan monk, wrote a mathematics book that described double-entry accounting. At the time, the double-entry system was used by the merchants of Venice to record what was given and received when trading.

Double-entry accounting is used to record what is exchanged in a transaction:
(1) the amount *received*, such as equipment purchased, is recorded with a *debit*, and
(2) the amount *given*, such as cash or a promise to pay later, is recorded with a *credit*.

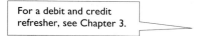

For a debit and credit refresher, see Chapter 3.

Each entry must balance; debits must equal credits. In a manual accounting system, accountants make debit and credit entries in a journal using paper and pencil. When using QuickBooks for your accounting system, you can enter accounting information in two different ways: (1) onscreen journal, and (2) onscreen forms.

1. **Onscreen Journal.** You can make debit and credit entries in an onscreen journal shown below. Notice the similarities between the onscreen journal and a manual journal.

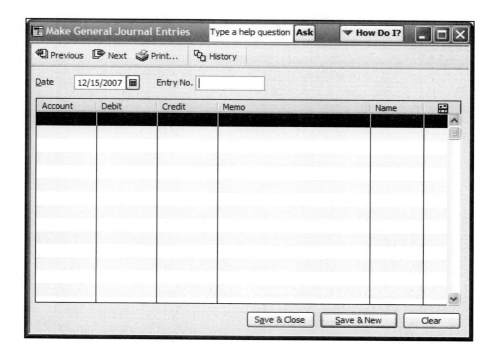

Instead of using the onscreen journal, you can use onscreen forms to enter information in QuickBooks.

2. **Onscreen Forms.** You can enter information about transactions using *onscreen forms* such as the onscreen check and the onscreen invoice shown below.

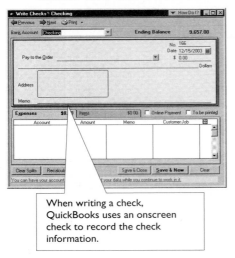

When preparing a customer's bill, record the information in an onscreen invoice.

When writing a check, QuickBooks uses an onscreen check to record the check information.

QuickBooks automatically converts information entered in onscreen forms into double-entry accounting entries with debits and credits. QuickBooks maintains a list of journal entries for all the transactions entered—whether entered using the onscreen journal or onscreen forms.

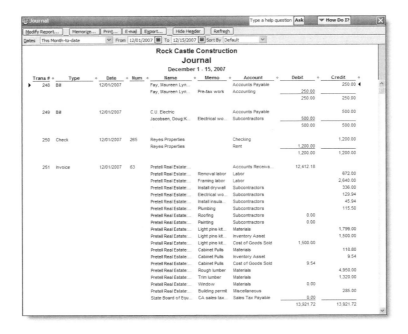

QUICKBOOKS ACCOUNTING SYSTEM

Steps to create an accounting system using QuickBooks are:

Step 1: **Set up a new company data file.** QuickBooks uses an EasyStep Interview that asks you questions about your business. QuickBooks then automatically creates a company data file for your business. In Part 1 of this text, Exploring QuickBooks, you will use a sample company data file that has already been created for you. In Part 2, you will set up a new company using the EasyStep Interview. To learn how to setup a company file, see Chapter 8.

Step 2: **Create a Chart of Accounts.** A chart of accounts is a list of all the accounts for a company. Accounts are used to sort and track accounting information. For example, a business needs one account for Cash, another account to track amounts customers owe (Accounts Receivable), and yet another account to track inventory. QuickBooks automatically creates a chart of accounts in the EasyStep Interview. QuickBooks permits you to modify the chart of accounts later, after completing the EasyStep Interview.

Step 3: **Create Lists.** QuickBooks uses lists to record and organize information about:

- **Customers**
- **Vendors**
- **Items** (items purchased and items sold, such as inventory)
- **Employees**
- **Other** (such as owners)

Step 4: **Enter transactions.** Enter transaction information into QuickBooks using the onscreen journal or onscreen forms (such as onscreen invoices and onscreen checks).

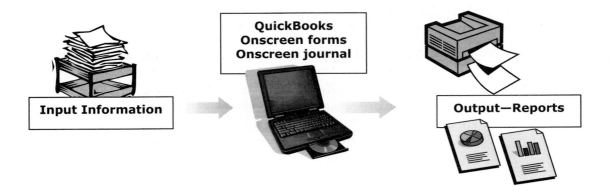

Step 5: Prepare reports. Reports summarize and communicate information about a company's financial position and business operations. Financial statements are standardized financial reports given to external users (bankers and investors). Financial statements summarize information about past transactions. The primary financial statements for a business are:

- **Balance sheet**: summarizes what a company owns and owes on a particular date.

- **Profit and loss statement** (or **income statement**): summarizes what a company has earned and the expenses incurred to earn the income.

- **Statement of cash flows**: summarizes cash inflows and cash outflows for operating, investing, and financing activities of a business.

Other financial reports are created for internal users (managers) to assist in making decisions. An example of such a report is a cash budget that projects amounts of cash that will be collected and spent in the future.

In Part 1: Exploring QuickBooks, you will learn about Step 2: creating a chart of accounts; Step 3: creating lists; Step 4: entering transactions; and Step 5: preparing reports. In Part 2: Small Business Accounting, you will learn how to set up a new company in QuickBooks as well as review Steps 2 through 5.

START QUICKBOOKS

To start QuickBooks software, click the **QuickBooks** icon on your desktop. If a QuickBooks icon does not appear on your desktop, in Microsoft® Windows®, click the **Start** button, **Programs**, **QuickBooks**, **QuickBooks Pro 2006** (or QuickBooks Premier 2006).

OPEN COMPANY

After starting QuickBooks software, the next step is to open a company data file. To open the sample company data file, Rock Castle Construction, complete the following steps:

Step 1: Select **Open a sample file**.

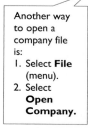

Another way to open a company file is:
1. Select **File** (menu).
2. Select **Open Company.**

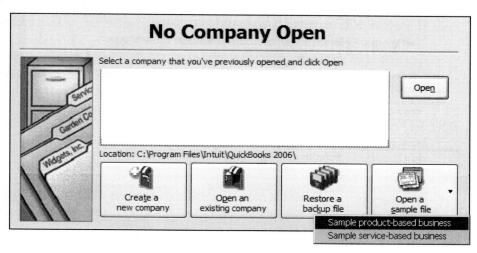

Step 2: Select **Sample product-based business**.

Step 3: The following message will appear about the sample company. Click **OK** to close the window.

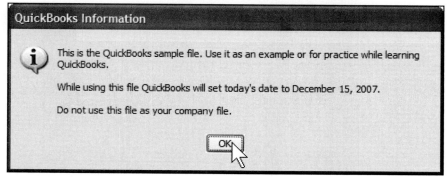

QUICKBOOKS LEARNING CENTER

The *QuickBooks Learning Center* window may appear on your screen. The Learning Center consists of tutorials divided into the following sections:

- Welcome to QuickBooks
- Understanding the Basics
- Customers & Sales
- Vendors & Expenses
- Inventory
- What's New

The Learning Center is a useful tool to review QuickBooks features.

If you want to return to the Learning Center at a later time, click **Help | QuickBooks Learning Center**. For the Learning Center to appear whenever you start QuickBooks, check the **Show this window at startup** in the lower left corner of the *Learning Center* window.

To proceed with using QuickBooks software, click the **Begin Using QuickBooks** button in the lower right corner of the window.

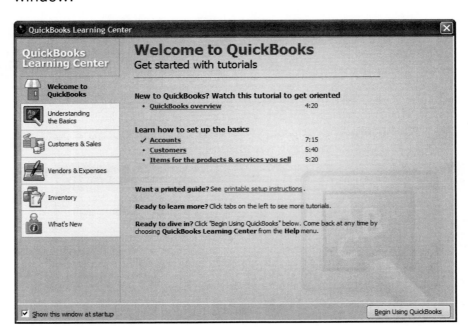

QUICKBOOKS NAVIGATION

QuickBooks offers four different ways to navigate in QuickBooks 2006 software:

- Home page
- Navigation Bar
- Icon Bar
- Menu Bar

Menus: Click on the menu to reveal a drop-down menu for each area.

Navigation Bar: Click on icons on the Navigation Bar to display customer, vendor, and employee centers.

Icon Bar: Click on icons to display frequently used windows, such as customer invoices.

Home page is a flowchart of frequently used tasks.

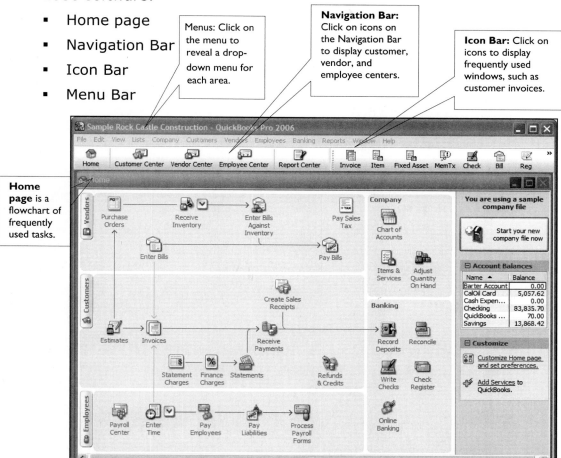

HOME PAGE

To view the QuickBooks Home page, click the Home icon. The Home page contains the main categories of transactions and tasks:

1. *Customer* or sales transactions
2. *Vendor* or purchase transactions
3. *Employee* or payroll transactions
4. *Banking* transactions
5. *Company* tasks

CUSTOMERS

The Customers section is a flowchart of the main activities associated with sales and customers. You can:

- Create estimates.

- Create invoices to bill customers.

- Record refunds and credits for merchandise returned by customers.

- Record payments received from customers (cash, check, and credit card payments).

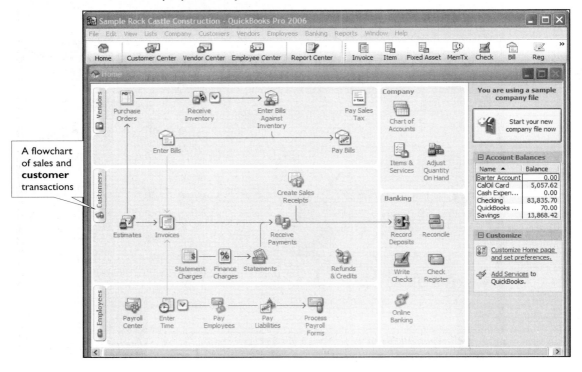

A flowchart of sales and **customer** transactions

VENDORS

From the Vendors flowchart, you can record:

- Purchase orders (orders placed to purchase items).
- Inventory received.
- Bills received.
- Bills paid.
- Sales tax paid.

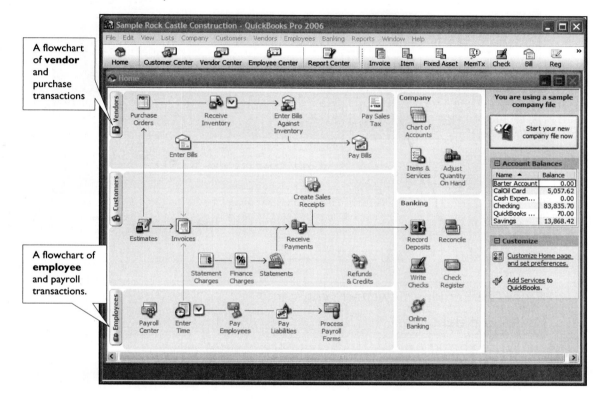

A flowchart of **vendor** and purchase transactions

A flowchart of **employee** and payroll transactions.

EMPLOYEES

From the Employees flowchart, you can:

- Enter time worked.
- Pay employees.
- Pay payroll tax liabilities.
- Process payroll forms.

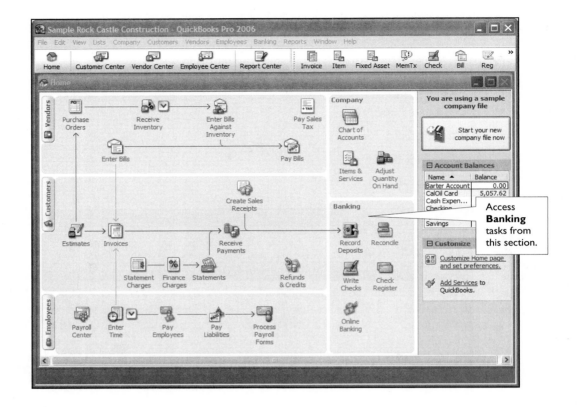

BANKING

From the Banking flowchart, you can:

- Record deposits.
- Write checks.
- Conduct online banking.
- Reconcile your bank statement.
- Open your check register.

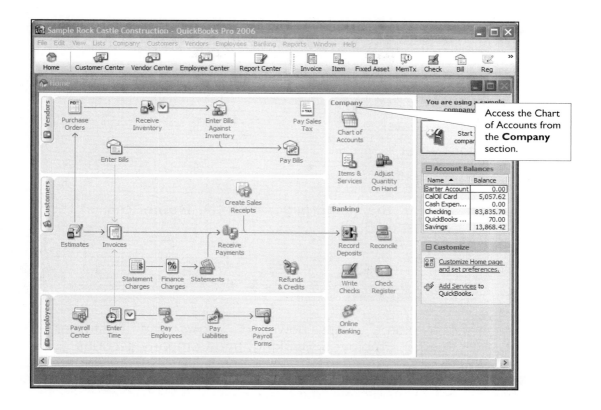

COMPANY

From the Company section, you can access:

- Chart of Accounts: a list of accounts a company uses to track accounting information.

- Items & Services: a list of items and services that a company buys and/or sells.

NAVIGATION BAR

The Navigation Bar provides access to the following:

- Home Page
- Customer Center
- Vendor Center
- Employee Center

Step 1: To view the Home page, click the **Home** icon on the Navigation Bar.

The Home page flowchart shows the Customer, Vendor, Employee, Banking, and Company sections.

Step 2: Click the **Customer Center** icon on the Navigation Bar to display the following Customer Center.

You can also access the Customer Center by clicking on the **Customer** button in the Customer section of the Home page.

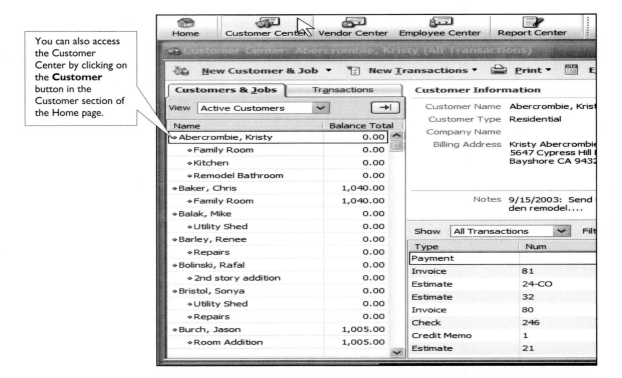

The Customer Center summarizes information about customers, jobs, and customer transactions. The information can be printed or exported to Excel or Word.

Step 3: Click the **Vendor Center** icon on the Navigation Bar to display the following Vendor Center.

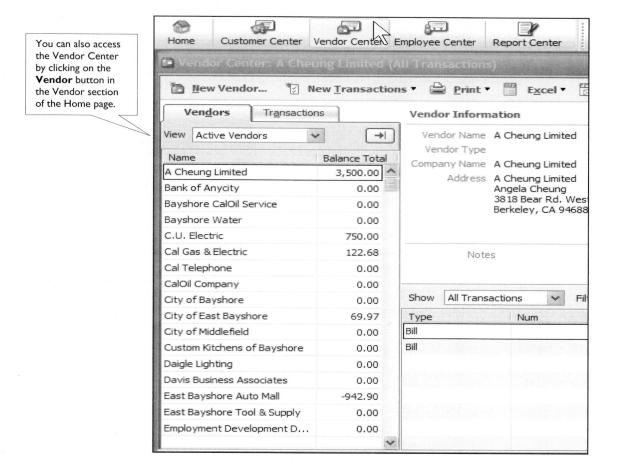

You can also access the Vendor Center by clicking on the **Vendor** button in the Vendor section of the Home page.

Step 4: Click the **Employee Center** icon on the Navigation Bar to display the following Employee Center.

You can also access the Employee Center by clicking on the **Employee** button in the Employee section of the Home page.

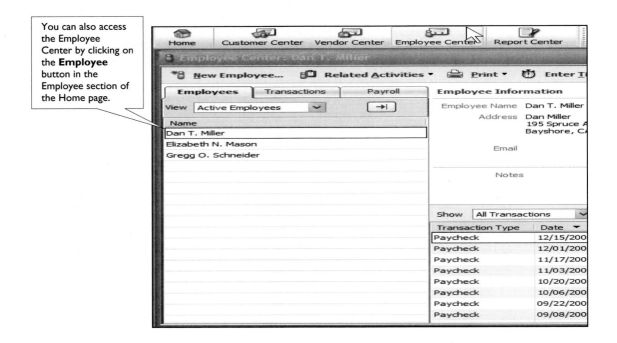

Step 5: Click the **Report Center** icon on the Navigation Bar to view the Report Center.

To prepare a report:

- Select the type of report from the report categories on the left of the window

- Select the desired report from the choices on the right side of the window.

- Select the date range.

- Select Print to print out the report.

- Select Export to send the report to Microsoft Excel.

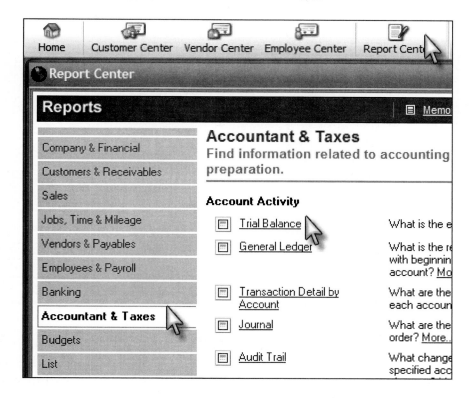

To print the Trial Balance for Rock Castle Construction:

- Select **Accountant & Taxes** from the report categories on the left of the window

- Select **Trial Balance** from the choices on the right side of the window.

- Select the date range: **11/01/2007** To **11/30/2007**.

- To identify your printout, insert your name and the chapter number in the footer as follows:

  - Click **Modify Report**.

  - Click **Header/Footer Tab**.

  - Check **Extra Footer Line**.

  - Enter **[your name] Chapter 1**.

  - Click **OK**.

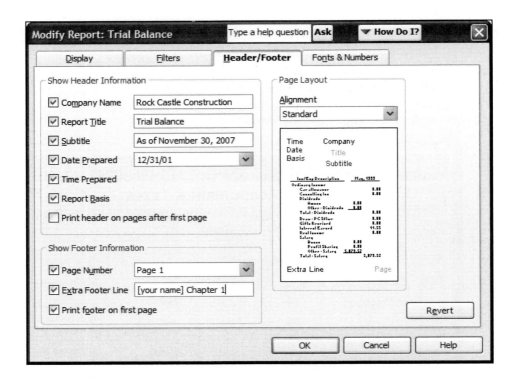

> If you are taking an online course, click the **Export** button to export the report to Excel.

- ▪ 🖨 Select **Print** to print out the report.

- ▪ Click the ☒ in the upper right corner of the *Trial balance* window to close the report window. If asked if you would like to memorize the report, click **No**.

QUICKBOOKS ICON BAR

The QuickBooks Icon Bar is a toolbar that appears beneath the Menu Bar and contains buttons for frequently used activities.

To display the Icon Bar if it does not appear on your screen:

Step 1: Click **View** on the Menu Bar.

Step 2: Select **Icon Bar**.

The Icon Bar can be customized to display the tasks that you use most frequently. To customize the Icon Bar:

Step 1: Click **View** on the Menu Bar.

Step 2: Select **Customize Icon Bar**.

Step 3: Select the tasks and order in which you would like them to appear on the Icon Bar, and then click the **OK** button.

QUICKBOOKS MENUS

You can also access tasks using the Menu Bar across the top of the *QuickBooks* window.

Step 1: Click **File** on the menu bar and the following drop-down menu will appear.

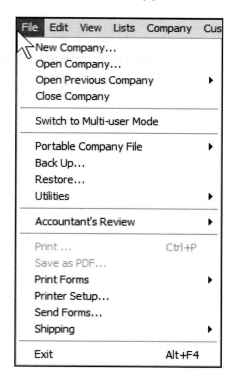

From the File drop-down menu, you can perform tasks including the following:

- Create a new company file.
- Open an existing company file.
- Close a company file.
- Switch to Multi-user mode when QuickBooks is used on a network.
- Create a portable company file.
- Back up your company file.
- Restore a company backup file.
- Use utilities such as importing and exporting files

Print tasks include:

- Print Forms permits you to print forms such as invoices, sales receipts, and tax forms.
- Printer Setup permits you to select a printer as well as fonts and margins.
- Send Forms permits you to e-mail various QuickBooks forms, such as sending invoices to customers.

To remove the File drop-down menu from the screen, click anywhere outside the drop-down menu or press the **Esc** (Escape) key.

Step 2: Click **Edit** on the menu bar and the following drop-down menu appears:

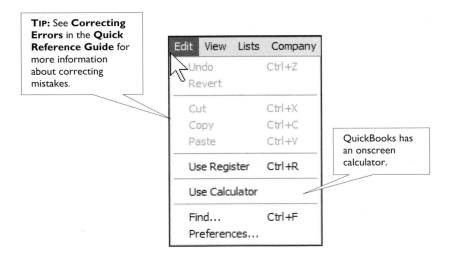

TIP: See **Correcting Errors** in the **Quick Reference Guide** for more information about correcting mistakes.

QuickBooks has an onscreen calculator.

From the Edit drop-down menu, you can undo, cut, copy, paste, and edit information entered in QuickBooks.

The Edit menu changes based upon which windows are open. For example:

- Click **Home** icon to display the Home page, then click the **Purchase Orders** icon in the Vendor section to display the Purchase Order form.

- Click **Edit** (menu). Now the Edit menu will appear as follows:

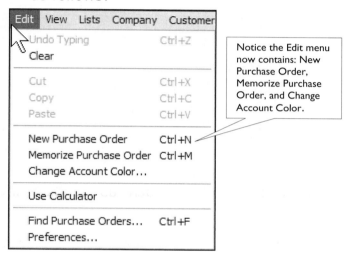

Notice the Edit menu now contains: New Purchase Order, Memorize Purchase Order, and Change Account Color.

Step 3: Click **Lists** on the menu bar to display the following drop-down menu.

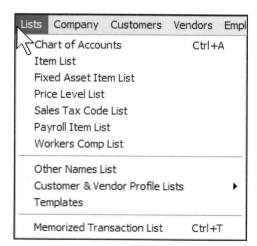

From the List drop-down menu, you can access various lists of information.

- **Chart of Accounts**: a list of accounts used to record transactions.

- **Item List**: a list of inventory items that you buy and sell or a list of services provided to customers.

- **Payroll Item List**: a list of items related to payroll checks and company payroll expense such as salary, hourly wages, federal and state withholding, unemployment taxes, Medicare, and Social Security.

- **Templates**: a list of templates for business forms, such as invoices and purchase orders.

- **Memorized Transaction List**: a list of recurring transactions that are memorized or saved. For example, if your company pays $900 in rent each month, then the rent payment transaction can be memorized to eliminate the need to reenter it each month.

Step 4: Click **Company** on the menu bar to display the drop-down menu.

From the Company menu, you can:

- Access company information and, for example, change the company name.

- Set up users and restrict access to certain parts of QuickBooks.

- Change your password.

- Set up budgets and use planning decision tools.

- Create To Do and Reminder Lists.

- Access the Chart of Accounts and onscreen journal.

Step 5: The next four items on the menu bar display drop-down menus listing various activities related to the four major types of transactions for a company:

- Customer

- Vendor

- Employee

- Banking

File   Edit   View   Lists   Company   Customers   Vendors   Employees   Banking   Reports   Window   Help

Some of the frequently used activities on these drop-down menus can also be accessed from the Home page.

Step 6: Click **Reports** on the menu bar to display the list of reports that QuickBooks can create for your company. These reports can also be accessed from the Report Center in the Navigation Bar.

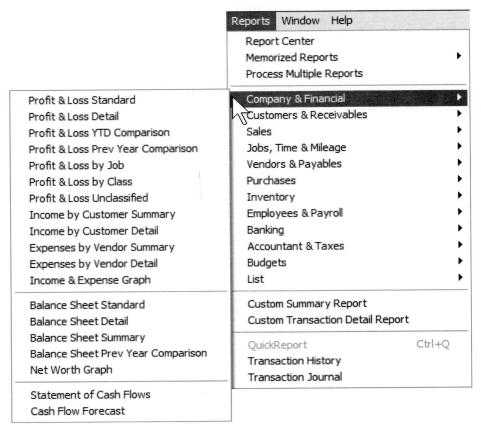

Step 7: Click **Window** on the menu bar to display the drop-down menu. From this menu you can switch between windows to display onscreen.

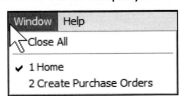

- If not already selected, select **Create Purchase Orders** from the drop-down menu.

- **Close** the *Purchase Order* window by clicking the ⊠ in the upper right corner of the window.

HELP

QuickBooks has several Help features to assist you when using QuickBooks software.

Click **Help** on the menu bar to display the drop-down menu of Help features.

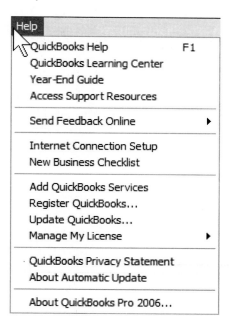

Help features that QuickBooks provides include:

- **QuickBooks Help** (located on the Help menu)
- **QuickBooks Learning Center** (provides tutorials for learning QuickBooks)
- **Access Support Resources** (includes web-based QuickBooks Support Knowledge Base and technical support plans)

QUICKBOOKS HELP

The *QuickBooks Help* window contains three tabs:

- **Contents:** lists topics contained in QuickBooks Help.
- **Index:** similar to a book index, you can look up specific terms or tasks.
- **Search:** this feature permits you to type your question and then the QuickBooks database is searched for an answer.

Next, you will use the Help Index to search for information about contact management. QuickBooks has a contact synchronization feature that permits you to transfer information from your contact management software (Symantec ACT! or Microsoft Outlook) to update your customer and vendor lists in QuickBooks 2006. This feature permits you to enter the contact information only once.

To learn more about using contact management with QuickBooks:

Step 1: Click **QuickBooks Help** on the drop-down Help menu, and the following window will appear.

Step 2: Click the **Index** tab.

Step 3: Type **contact** in the *Type in the keyword to find* field.

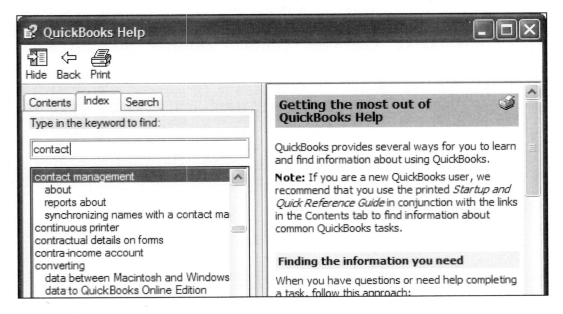

Notice that after typing only a few letters, *contact management* appears in the *Index Entry* window.

Step 4: Double-click **synchronizing names with a contact manager**, then double-click **About contact management synchronization** to learn more.

Step 5: Read the *Help* window about contact management synchronization. To print the Help information, click the 🖶 **Print** icon in the upper right corner, then select your printer and click **Print**.

Step 6: **Close** the *QuickBooks Help* window.

How Do I?

QuickBooks also provides onscreen assistance with the *How Do I?* feature. The *How Do I?* button appears in the upper right corner in many QuickBooks windows.

Step 1: Click the **Write Checks** icon in the Banking section of the Home page.

Step 2: Click on the **How Do I?** button in the upper right corner of the *Write Checks* window.

TIP: For additional assistance, you can type your questions and click the **Ask** button. For example, type in **writing checks**, then click the **Ask** button to learn more about how to write checks using QuickBooks software.

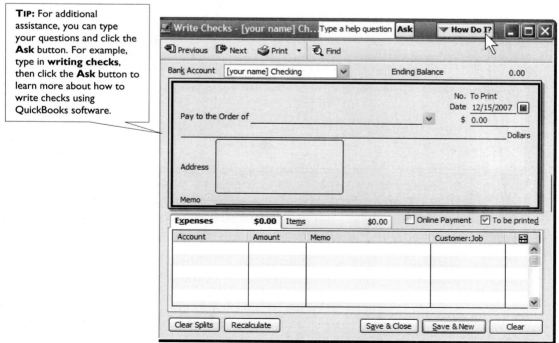

The following drop-down menu identifying various tasks associated with this window appears. If an arrow [▸] appears to the right of the task, this indicates there is yet another pull-down menu.

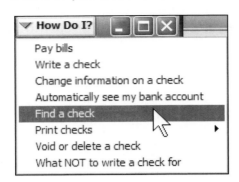

Step 3: Click **Find a check**. A *QuickBooks Help* window appears listing the steps to find a check recorded in QuickBooks.

Step 4: 🖨 **Print** the **Find a check** instructions.

Step 5: **Close** the *QuickBooks Help* window by clicking the ⊠ in the upper right corner of the *Help* window.

Step 6: **Close** the *Write Checks* window.

SAVING COMPANY FILES

There are three different types of QuickBooks files:

1. **.QBW file:** This is the regular company file that has a .QBW extension. It is a QuickBooks working file that is automatically saved to the hard drive (C:) of your computer.

2. **.QBB file:** This is a QuickBooks backup file. You can save a backup file to the hard drive or to other media such as USB drive or memory stick, a CD drive, a network drive, or floppy disk. Backup files are compressed files and used only if the working file (.QBW) file fails.

3. **.QBM file:** This is a QuickBooks moveable file, also called a portable file. These files are compressed and can be emailed or moved to another computer by saving to media such as a USB drive.

The .QBW file is the only QuickBooks file in which you can enter data and transactions. The .QBB and .QBM files are compressed and must be converted to .QBW files before they can be used.

BACKUP FILES (.QBB FILES)

QuickBooks backup files are designated by a .QBB extension. A business would use the .QBW (QuickBooks working) file to record transactions and periodically back up to a .QBB (QuickBooks Backup) file.

For example, a good backup system is to have a different backup for each business day: Monday backup, Tuesday backup, Wednesday backup, etc. Then if it is necessary to use the backup file and the Wednesday backup, for example, fails, the company has a Tuesday backup to use. Furthermore, it is recommended that a business stores at least one backup at a remote location.

The backup file is used only if the company's working file (.QBW file) fails. If the company's working file (.QBW file) fails, the backup file (.QBB file) can be restored and used. Therefore, it is important that the backup copy is as up to date as possible in case it must be used to replace lost company data.

In QuickBooks 2003 and later, you can schedule a backup every time you close a QuickBooks company file or at regular intervals.

You can backup a company file, from the File menu by clicking Back Up and then identifying the filename and location for the backup file.

Note that you cannot open a backup (.QBB) file. First, the backup file must be restored or unzipped before it can be opened and used.

To restore a company file, from the File menu, select Restore and then follow the onscreen instructions. The backup file is restored to the hard drive of the computer as a .QBW file.

PORTABLE FILES (.QBM FILES)

In this text, you will save a .QBM file at the end of each chapter, exercise assignment, or project. Portable (.QBM) files can be emailed or moved to other computers.

SAVE A PORTABLE FILE

To create a portable (.QBM) file:

Step 1: With the Rock Castle Construction company file open, click **File** on the menu bar, then select **Portable Company File** | **Create File**.

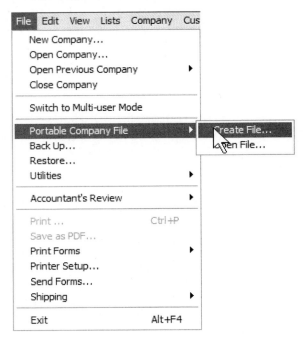

Step 2: Click **OK** when the following message appears that QuickBooks must close and reopen your company file before creating a portable company file.

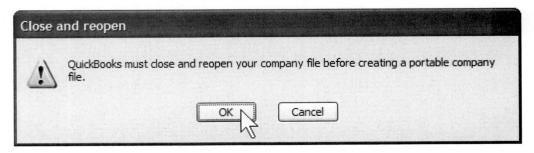

Step 3: When the following message appears, click **OK**.

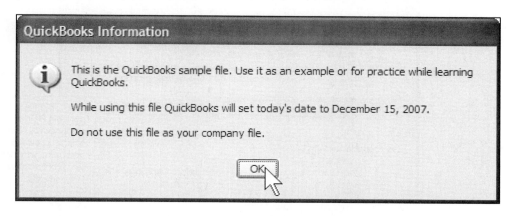

Step 4: You can save the portable company file to the hard drive or removable media, such as a USB or floppy disk. Insert USB media or other media that your instructor specifies in the appropriate drive. Note that if you are using floppy disks, it may require more than one disk.

To save the portable file, when the following *Create Portable Company File* window appears:

- Change the Filename to your **[your name] Chapter 1** as shown below. Depending upon your operating system settings, the file extension .QBM may appear automatically. If the .QBM extension does not appear, *do not type it.*

- Save the portable company file to the location your instructor specifies. To save to the hard drive of your computer, the location should as shown below. If you are saving to a removable media, change Location to the appropriate drive depending upon your media and computer.

- Click **Save**.

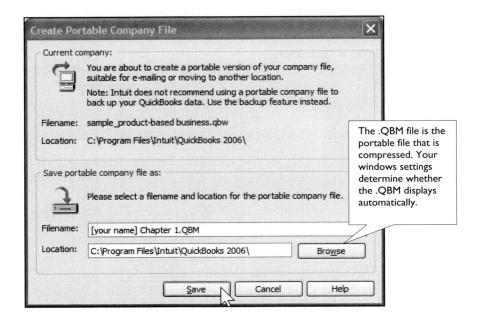

The .QBM file is the portable file that is compressed. Your windows settings determine whether the .QBM displays automatically.

Step 5: Click **OK** when the following window appears.

OPEN A PORTABLE FILE

Next, you will convert the sample company file to your data file for Chapters 1 through 7 by opening the portable company file.

To open a portable (.QBM) file on the destination computer, the portable file is converted to a regular company (.QBW) file. To open the portable (.QBM) file for Chapter 1:

Step 1: From the menu bar, click **File** | **Portable Company File** | **Open File**.

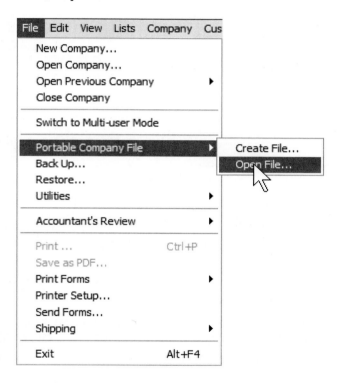

Step 2: Identify the filename and location for the portable company file:

- Click the **Browse** button to find the Location of the portable company file on the hard drive or removable media. In the example below, the portable file was saved to the hard drive. If you saved the portable company file to removable media such as USB, floppy disk, or CD, you would specify the location of the removable media.

- Click on the file: **[your name] Chapter 1**. The .QBM may appear automatically based upon your Windows settings.

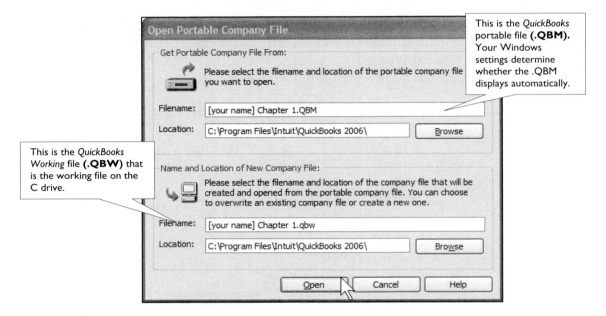

Step 3: Identify the filename and location of the new company file (.QBW) file:

- Filename: **[your name] Chapter 1**. The .QBW extension should appear automatically based upon your Windows settings. The .QBW identifies this as the QuickBooks working file.

- Location: **C:\Program Files\Intuit\QuickBooks 2006**. This is the location of the .QBW file on the hard drive of your computer. You can click the Browse button to specify the location.

Step 4: Click **Open** to open the portable company file.

Step 5: Click **Cancel** when the following *Create a Backup* window appears.

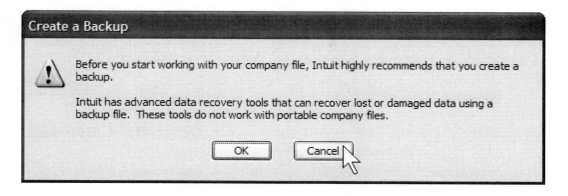

Step 6: Click **OK** when the following window appears.

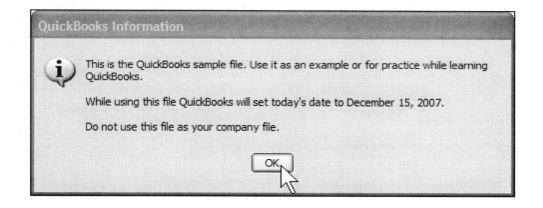

> If the *QuickBooks Learning Center* window appears, uncheck **Show this window at startup**. Then click **Begin using QuickBooks**.
>
> **NOTE:** Since you used a different filename ([your name] Chapter 1.qbw) instead of the sample company filename, the existing sample company file on the C drive was not overwritten or modified.

CHANGE COMPANY NAME

In order to identify your assignment printouts, add your name to the company name and Checking account. When you print out reports, your name will then appear on the printouts.

To change a company name in QuickBooks, complete the following:

Step 1: From the menu bar, select **Company | Company Information**.

Step 2: When the following *Company Information* window appears, enter **[your name] Chapter 1** in the *Company Name* field before Rock Castle Construction.

The company name that appears in the title bar of the QuickBooks window and on reports is different than the portable company filename.

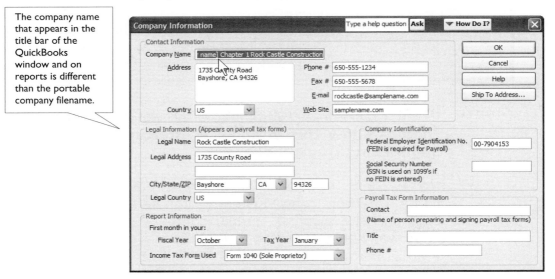

Step 3: Click **OK** to close the *Company Information* window.

To add your name to the company Checking account, complete the following:

Step 1: Click the **Chart of Accounts** icon in the Company section of the Home page.

Step 2: When the following *Chart of Accounts* window appears, select **Checking**.

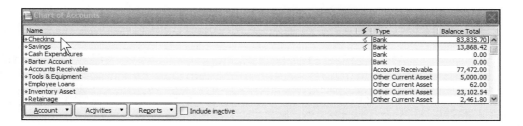

Step 3: **Right-click** the mouse to display the following pop-up menu, then select **Edit Account**.

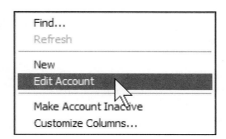

Step 4: When the following *Edit Account* window appears, enter **[your name]** in the *Name* field before the word Checking.

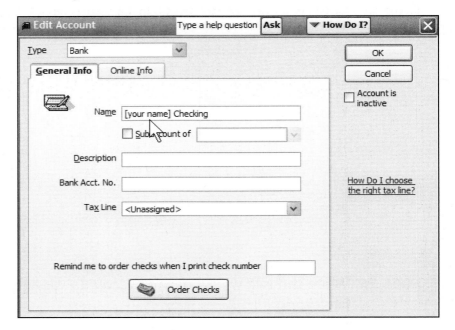

Step 5: Click **OK** to save the changes and close the *Edit Account* window.

Step 6: **Close** the *Chart of Accounts* window by clicking the ☒ in the upper right corner of the *Chart of Accounts* window.

SAVE YOUR COMPANY FILE

To save the changes you made to the company name, save the portable company file for Chapter 1 again as follows:

Step 1: If using removable media, insert the media (USB, CD, floppy disk, etc.) in the appropriate drive.

Step 2: From the menu bar, click **File | Portable Company File | Create File**.

Step 3: Click **OK** to close the *Close and Reopen* window.

Step 4: Click **OK** again to close the QuickBooks information about the sample company.

Step 5: Confirm that the filename is **[your name] Chapter 1** and the file is saved to the appropriate location. Click **Save**.

Example: if your name is Gina Shea the filename would be: Gina Shea Chapter 1.QBM. If the .QBM does not appear automatically, do **not** type .QBM.

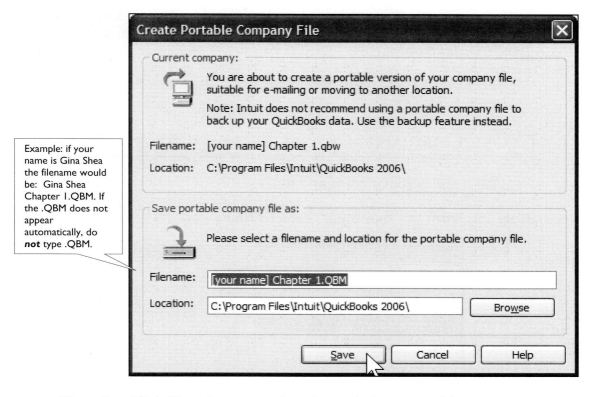

Step 6: Click **Yes** to overwrite the existing portable company file.

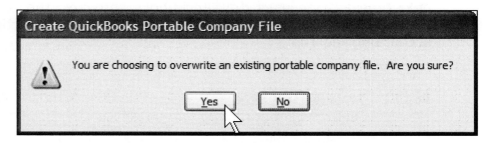

Step 7: Click **OK** when the message appears that your QuickBooks portable company file has been created successfully.

> **NOTE: In this text, you will save a portable company file with a .QBM extension at the end of each chapter, exercise, or project.**
>
> **If you are continuing your computer session, proceed to Exercise 1.1.**
>
> **If you are ending your computer session now, follow the directions below to (1) close the company file and (2) exit QuickBooks.**

CLOSE COMPANY

To close a QuickBooks company file:

Step 1: From the menu bar, select **File**.

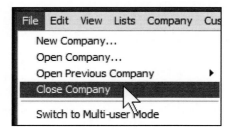

Step 2: Click **Close Company**.

If the company file is left open when you exit QuickBooks, the next time anyone uses the QuickBooks software, the company file may still be open, permitting access to your company accounting records.

EXIT QUICKBOOKS

To exit QuickBooks, click the ⊠ in the upper right corner of the *QuickBooks* window, *or* click the **File** menu, then **Exit**.

ASSIGNMENTS

NOTE: See the Quick Reference Guide in Part 3 for step-by-step instructions to frequently used tasks.

EXERCISE 1.1:
PRINTING FINANCIAL STATEMENTS

SCENARIO

While working at your computer, you notice Mr. Castle heading toward you. Adding another stack of papers to your overflowing inbox, he says, *"I need a profit and loss statement and a balance sheet for November as soon as possible. I haven't seen any financial statements since our former accountant left."*

As he walks away, Mr. Castle calls over his shoulder, *"From now on I'd like a P&L and balance sheet on my desk by the first of each month."*

TASK 1: OPEN PORTABLE COMPANY FILE

To open the portable company file (.QBM) file, convert the portable file to a regular company file with a .QBW extension as follows:

Step 1: From the menu bar, click **File | Portable Company File | Open File**.

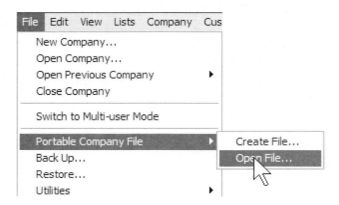

Step 2: Identify the filename and location for the portable company file:

- Click the **Browse** button to find the location of the portable company file on the hard drive or removable media. In the example below, the portable file was saved to the hard drive. If you saved the portable company file to removable media such as USB, floppy disk, or CD, you would specify the location of the removable media.

- Select the file: **[your name] Chapter 1**. The .QBM may appear automatically based upon your Windows settings.

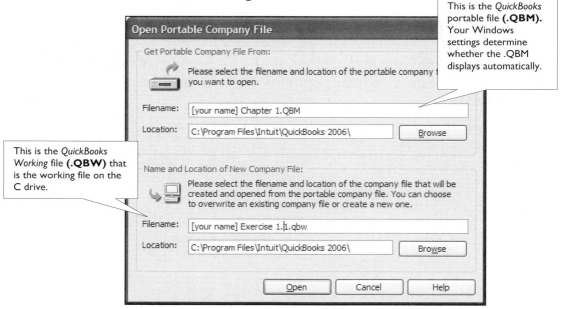

This is the *QuickBooks* portable file **(.QBM).** Your Windows settings determine whether the .QBM displays automatically.

This is the *QuickBooks Working* file **(.QBW)** that is the working file on the C drive.

Step 3: Identify the name and location of the new company file (.QBW) file to use for completing Exercise 1.1:

- Filename: **[your name] Exercise 1.1**. The **.QBW** extension should appear automatically based upon your Windows settings. The .QBW identifies this as a QuickBooks working file.

- Location: **C:\Program Files\Intuit\QuickBooks 2006**. This is the location of the .QBW file on the hard drive of your computer. You can click the Browse button to specify another location.

Step 4: Click **Open** to open the portable company file.

Step 5: Click **Cancel** when the following *Create a Backup* window appears.

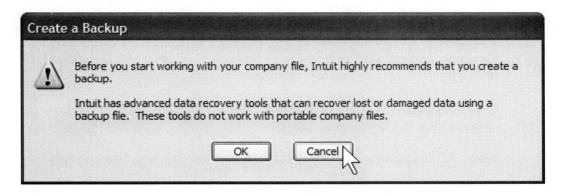

Step 6: Click **OK** when the following window appears.

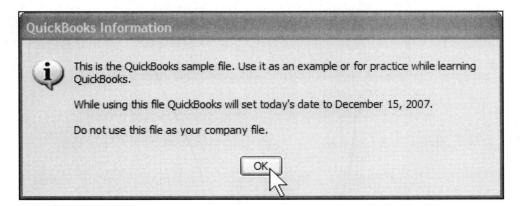

If the *QuickBooks Learning Center* window appears, uncheck **Show this window at startup**. Then click **Begin using QuickBooks**.

Step 7: Change the company name to: **[your name] Exercise 1.1 Rock Castle Construction** as follows:

> Recall that the filename is the .QBW or .QBM filename that is changed when you save the file. The company name is the name that appears on reports and is changed through the Company Information window.

- To change the company name, select **Company** (menu), **Company Information**.

- If necessary, change the Checking account title to include your name. (See Chapter 1 for instructions.)

TASK 2: PRINT PROFIT & LOSS STATEMENT

The profit & loss statement (also called the income statement) lists income earned and expenses incurred to generate income. Summarizing the amount of profit or loss a company has earned, the profit and loss statement is one of the primary financial statements given to bankers and investors.

Print the profit & loss statement for Rock Castle Construction by completing the following steps:

Step 1: Click the **Report Center** icon in the Navigation Bar.

Step 2: Select type of report: **Company & Financial**.

> Also see the **Quick Reference Guide** in **Part 3** for step-by-step directions.

Step 3: Select report: **Profit & Loss Standard**.

Step 4: Select the date range: **Last Month**. The *From* field will now be: **11/01/2007**. The *To* field will be: **11/30/2007**. Your screen should now appear as the profit and loss statement below.

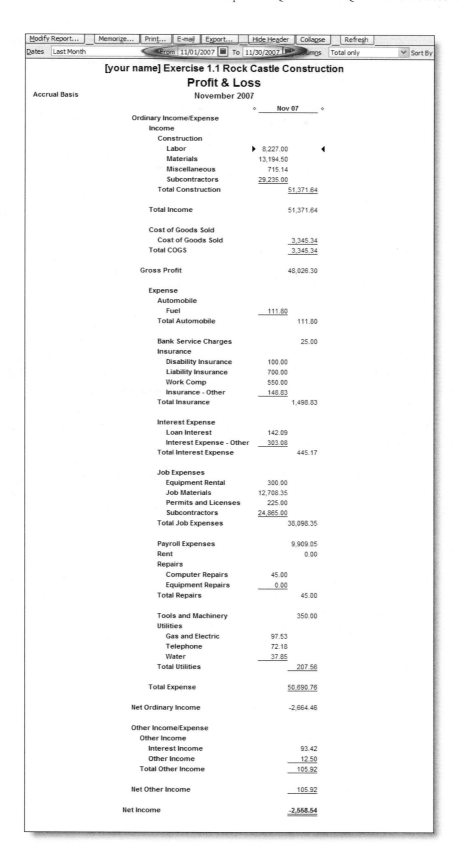

| Modify Report... | Memorize... | Print... | E-mail | Export... | Hide Header | Collapse | Refresh |

| Dates | Last Month | | From | 11/01/2007 | To | 11/30/2007 | umns | Total only | ∨ | Sort By |

[your name] Exercise 1.1 Rock Castle Construction

Profit & Loss

Accrual Basis   November 2007

	Nov 07
Ordinary Income/Expense	
Income	
Construction	
Labor	▶ 8,227.00 ◀
Materials	13,194.50
Miscellaneous	715.14
Subcontractors	29,235.00
Total Construction	51,371.64
Total Income	51,371.64
Cost of Goods Sold	
Cost of Goods Sold	3,345.34
Total COGS	3,345.34
Gross Profit	48,026.30
Expense	
Automobile	
Fuel	111.80
Total Automobile	111.80
Bank Service Charges	25.00
Insurance	
Disability Insurance	100.00
Liability Insurance	700.00
Work Comp	550.00
Insurance - Other	148.83
Total Insurance	1,498.83
Interest Expense	
Loan Interest	142.09
Interest Expense - Other	303.08
Total Interest Expense	445.17
Job Expenses	
Equipment Rental	300.00
Job Materials	12,708.35
Permits and Licenses	225.00
Subcontractors	24,865.00
Total Job Expenses	38,098.35
Payroll Expenses	9,909.05
Rent	0.00
Repairs	
Computer Repairs	45.00
Equipment Repairs	0.00
Total Repairs	45.00
Tools and Machinery	350.00
Utilities	
Gas and Electric	97.53
Telephone	72.18
Water	37.85
Total Utilities	207.56
Total Expense	50,690.76
Net Ordinary Income	-2,664.46
Other Income/Expense	
Other Income	
Interest Income	93.42
Other Income	12.50
Total Other Income	105.92
Net Other Income	105.92
Net Income	**-2,558.54**

Step 5: Click the **Print** button at the top of the *Profit and Loss* window.

- Select the appropriate printer.

- Select **Portrait** orientation.

- Select **Fit report to 1 page(s) wide**.

- 🖨 Click **Print** to print the Profit & Loss statement for November.

Step 6: QuickBooks lets you save or memorize report settings for future use. To memorize the settings for the Profit & Loss statement you prepared:

- Click the ☒ in the upper right corner of the *Profit & Loss* window to close the window.

- When the following *Memorize Report* window appears, click **Yes**.

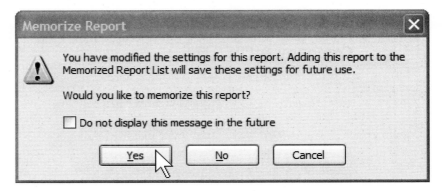

- Name the memorized report: **Profit & Loss**.

- Click **OK**.

✓   *Net loss is $2,558.54.*

Step 7: 🖊 **Circle** the single largest income item appearing on the Profit & Loss statement for the month of November.

Step 8: 🖊 **Circle** the single largest expense item appearing on the Profit & Loss statement for the month of November.

TASK 3: PRINT BALANCE SHEET

The balance sheet is the financial statement that summarizes the financial position of a business. Listing assets, liabilities, and equity, the balance sheet reveals what a company owns and what it owes.

To print the balance sheet for Rock Castle Construction at November 30, 2007, complete the following steps:

Step 1: From the *Report Center* window, select type of report: **Company & Financial**.

Step 2: Select report: **Balance Sheet & Net Worth Standard**.

Step 3: Select date range: **Last Month**.

Step 4: 🖨 **Print** the Balance Sheet.

Step 5: To memorize the settings for the Balance Sheet you prepared:

- Click the ⊠ in the upper right corner of the *Balance Sheet* window as if to close the window.

- When the *Memorize Report* window appears, click **Yes**.

- Name the memorized report: **Balance Sheet**.

- Click **OK**.

Step 6: If necessary, **close** the *Balance Sheet* window.

✓ **Total Assets equal $659,356.50.**

Step 7: ✒ **Circle** the single largest asset listed on Rock Castle Construction's November 2007 Balance Sheet.

Step 8: **Close** the *Report Center* window.

TASK 4: SAVE EXERCISE 1.1 FILE

Step 1: If necessary, insert a removable disk.

Step 2: From the menu bar, click **File | Portable Company File | Create File**.

Step 3: When the *Close and Reopen* window appears, click **OK**.

Step 4: When the following *Create Portable Company File* window appears, enter the filename: **[your name] Exercise 1.1** and the appropriate location. Then click **Save**.

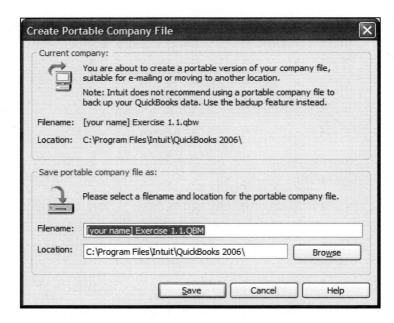

Step 5: Click **OK** after the portable file has been created successfully.

Step 6: Close the company file by clicking **File** (Menu), **Close Company**.

EXERCISE 1.2: QUICKBOOKS HELP

In this Exercise, you will use QuickBooks Help to obtain additional information about using QuickBooks.

TASK 1: BACKUP FILES AND PORTABLE FILES

Use the QuickBooks Help Index to locate information about QuickBooks Backup files and QuickBooks Portable files.

Step 1: 🖨 **Print** the information you find.

Step 2: ✏ **Circle** or highlight the information on the printout about the differences between backup files and portable files.

TASK 2: YOUR CHOICE

Use the QuickBooks Help Index to learn more about a QuickBooks feature of your choice.

Step 1: 🖨 **Print** the information.

Step 2: ✏ **Circle** or highlight the information on the printout that you find the most useful.

EXERCISE 1.3: WEBQUEST

QuickBooks provides business services to assist the small business owner and operator.

> **NOTE:** Websites are subject to change due to web page updates.

Step 1: Go to the www.QuickBooks.com web page.

Step 2: 🖨 On the QuickBooks website, locate and **print** the comparison of QuickBooks Pro and QuickBooks Premier Versions.

Step 3: ✏ On your printout, **circle** the differences in the QuickBooks versions.

CHAPTER 1 PRINTOUT CHECKLIST
NAME: _____DATE:_____

INSTRUCTIONS:
1. *CHECK OFF THE PRINTOUTS YOU HAVE COMPLETED.*
2. *STAPLE THIS PAGE TO YOUR PRINTOUTS.*

☑ *PRINTOUT CHECKLIST – CHAPTER 1*
☐ Trial Balance Printout
☐ Contact Management Printout
☐ Find a Check Instructions Printout

☑ *PRINTOUT CHECKLIST – EXERCISE 1.1*
☐ Task 2: Profit & Loss Statement
☐ Task 3: Balance Sheet

☑ *PRINTOUT CHECKLIST – EXERCISE 1.2*
☐ Task 1: Help Topic Printout
☐ Task 2: Your Choice Help Topic Printout

☑ *PRINTOUT CHECKLIST – EXERCISE 1.3*
☐ QuickBooks Product Comparison

CHAPTER 2
CHART OF ACCOUNTS

SCENARIO

The next morning when you arrive at work, Mr. Castle is waiting for you, pacing in the aisle outside your cubicle.

He looks at you over the top of his glasses, his voice tense when he asks, *"Do you have the P&L and balance sheet ready?"*

"Yes sir!" you reply, handing him the financial statements.

The creases in his brow disappear as his eyes run down the statements, murmuring to himself as he walks away, *"The banker waiting in my office should like this...."*

As he rounds the corner, he calls back to you, *"See your inbox for account changes we need to make. And password protect that QuickBooks file so every Tom, Dick and Harry can't get into our accounting records!"*

CHAPTER 2
LEARNING OBJECTIVES

In Chapter 2, you will learn the following QuickBooks features:

INTRODUCTION

In Chapter 2, you will learn about a company's chart of accounts, a list of all the accounts used by a company to collect accounting information. QuickBooks software automatically creates a chart of accounts when a new company file is created. In this chapter, you will learn how to revise the chart of accounts by adding, editing, and deleting accounts. Also, in Chapter 2, you will learn how to restrict access to your QuickBooks accounting records using passwords.

To begin Chapter 2, start QuickBooks software and then open the portable QuickBooks file.

Step 1: Start QuickBooks by clicking on the **QuickBooks** desktop icon or click **Start**, **Programs**, **QuickBooks**, **QuickBooks Pro 2006**.

Step 2: To open the portable company file (.QBM) file and convert the portable file to a regular company file with a .QBW extension, from the menu bar, click **File | Portable Company File | Open File**.

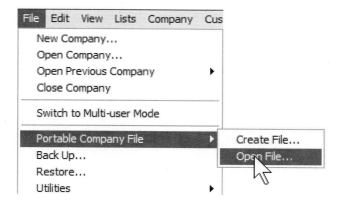

Step 3: Identify the filename and location for the portable company file:

- Click the **Browse** button to find the location of the portable company file on the hard drive or removable media. In the example below, the portable file was saved to the hard drive. If you saved the portable company file to removable media such as USB, floppy disk, or CD, you would specify the location of the removable media.

- Select the file: **[your name] Exercise 1.1**. The .QBM may appear automatically based upon your Windows settings, but if it does not appear automatically, do **not** type it.

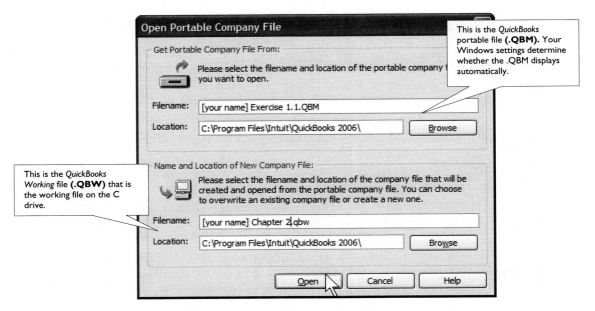

Step 4: Identify the name and location of the new company file (.QBW) file to use for Chapter 2:

- Filename: **[your name] Chapter 2**. The **.QBW** extension should appear automatically based upon your Windows settings. The .QBW identifies this as a QuickBooks working file.

- Location: **C:\Program Files\Intuit\QuickBooks 2006**. This is the location of the .QBW file on the hard drive of your computer. You can click the Browse button to specify another location.

Step 5: Click **Open** to open the portable company file.

Step 6: Click **Cancel** when the following *Create a Backup* window appears.

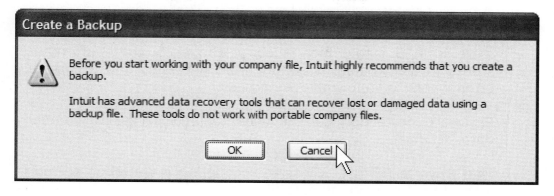

Step 7: Click **OK** when the following window appears.

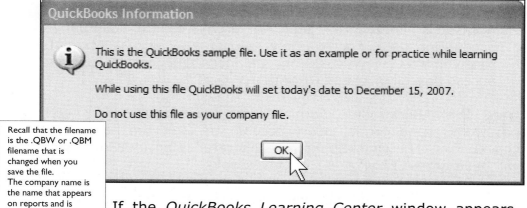

Recall that the filename is the .QBW or .QBM filename that is changed when you save the file.
The company name is the name that appears on reports and is changed through the Company Information window.

If the *QuickBooks Learning Center* window appears, uncheck **Show this window at startup**. Then click **Begin using QuickBooks**.

Step 8: Change the company name to: **[your name] Chapter 2 Rock Castle Construction**. (For step-by-step instructions, see Part 3: Quick Reference Guide.)

If necessary, change the Checking account title to include your name.

NOTE: in this text you will create a portable company file for each Chapter and Exercise to create your data files to use with the text. For a typical business, however, you would open the company .QBW file (**File, Open Company**), creating backups that would be used only if the .QBW file was damaged or destroyed.

The portable company file (Exercise 1.1.QBM) should now be converted to a regular company file (Chapter 2.QBW) that can be used to complete the assignments for Chapter 2.

PASSWORD PROTECTION

QuickBooks is an accounting information system that permits a company to conveniently collect accounting information and store it in a single file. Much of the accounting information stored in QuickBooks is confidential, however, and a company often wants to limit employee access.

Password protection can be used to limit access to company data.

Two ways to restrict access to accounting information stored in a QuickBooks company data file are:

1. The company data file can be password protected so that individuals must enter a user ID and password in order to open the company data file.

2. Access is limited to selected areas of the company's accounting data. For example, a user may access accounts receivable to view customer balances but not be able to access payroll or check writing.

Only the QuickBooks Administrator can add users with passwords and limit user access to selected areas of QuickBooks. The QuickBooks Administrator is an individual who will have access to all areas of QuickBooks.

To add a new user and password protection to a company file:

Step 1: Click **Company**, then click **Set Up Users**.

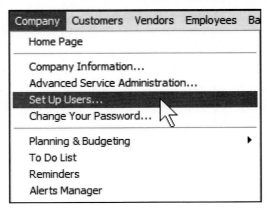

Step 2: First, set up a QuickBooks Administrator who has access to all areas of QuickBooks. The Administrator can then add new users.

- If necessary, enter Administrator's Name: **Admin**.
- Enter and then confirm a **password** of your choice.
- Click **OK**.

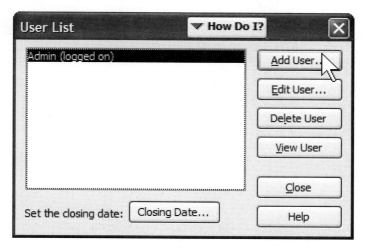

Step 3: Only the QuickBooks Administrator can add new users. To add another user, click **Add User**.

Step 4:   In the following *Set up user password and access* window:

- Enter **[Your Name]** in the *User Name* field.

- At this point, if you were adding another employee as a user, you would ask the employee to enter and confirm his or her password. In this instance, simply enter and confirm a **password** of your choice.

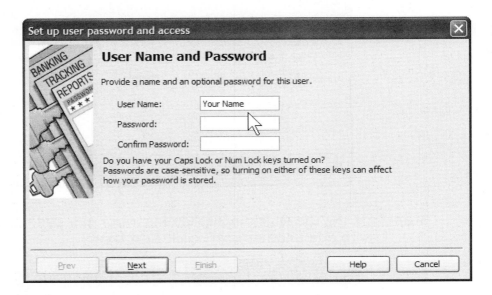

- Click **Next**.

Step 5: In the following window, you can restrict user access to selected areas of QuickBooks or give the user access to all areas of QuickBooks. Select: **All areas of QuickBooks**, then click **Next**.

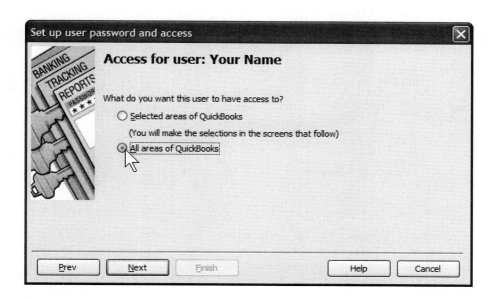

Step 6: Select **Yes** to confirm that you want to give access to all areas of QuickBooks, including Payroll, check writing, and other sensitive information.

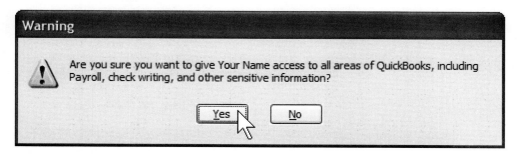

Step 7: The next window summarizes the user's access for each QuickBooks area, indicating access to create documents, print, and view reports. Click **Finish**.

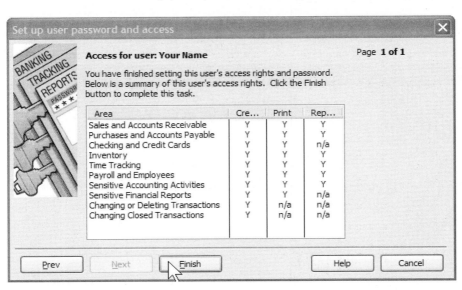

Step 8: Two names (Administrator and Your Name) should appear on the User List.

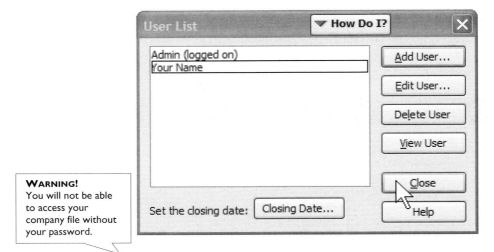

> **WARNING!**
> You will not be able to access your company file without your password.

Step 9: Click **Close** to close the *User List* window.

Now whenever you open the company file for Rock Castle Construction, you will be asked to enter your user name and password.

CHART OF ACCOUNTS

The chart of accounts is a list of accounts and account numbers. A company uses accounts to record transactions in the accounting system. Accounts (such as the Cash account or Inventory account) are a way to sort and track information.

QuickBooks will automatically create a chart of accounts when you set up a new company. Then you may edit the chart of accounts, adding and deleting accounts as necessary to suit your company's specific needs. QuickBooks also permits you to use subaccounts (subcategories) of accounts.

Accounts can be categorized into the following groups:

Balance Sheet Accounts

Assets

Liabilities

Equity

Profit & Loss Accounts

Income (Revenue)

Expenses

Non-Posting Accounts

Purchase Orders

Estimates

BALANCE SHEET ACCOUNTS

The balance sheet is a financial statement that summarizes what a company owns and what it owes. Balance Sheet accounts are accounts that appear on the company's balance sheet.

Review the balance sheet you printed in Exercise 1.1 for Rock Castle Construction. Three types of accounts appear on the balance sheet:
1. Assets
2. Liabilities
3. Owners' (or Stockholders') Equity

> **ASSETS = LIABILITIES + OWNERS' EQUITY**

> **TIP:** If unsure whether an account is an asset account, ask the question: *Does this item have future benefit?* If the answer is yes, the item is probably an asset.

1. **Assets** are resources that a company owns. These resources are expected to have *future benefit*.

   Asset accounts include:

   - Cash.

   - Accounts receivable (amounts to be *received* from customers in the future).

   - Inventory.

   - Other current assets (assets likely to be converted to cash or consumed within one year).

   - Fixed assets (property used in the operations of the business, such as equipment, buildings, and land).

   - Intangible assets (such as copyrights, patents, trademarks, and franchises).

> **TIP:** If unsure whether an account is a liability account, ask the question: *Is the company obligated to do something, such as pay a bill or provide a service?* If the answer is yes, the item is probably a liability.

2. **Liabilities** are amounts a company owes to others. Liabilities are *obligations*. For example, if a company borrows $10,000 from the bank, the company has an obligation to repay the $10,000 to the bank. Thus, the $10,000 obligation is shown as a liability on the company's balance sheet.

Liability accounts include:

- Accounts payable (amounts that are owed and will be *paid* to suppliers in the future).

- Sales taxes payable (sales tax owed and to be *paid* in the future).

- Interest payable (interest owed and to be *paid* in the future).

- Other current liabilities (liabilities due within one year).

- Loan payable (also called notes payable).

- Mortgage payable.

- Other long-term liabilities (liabilities due after one year).

> **NOTE:** The difference between a note payable and a mortgage payable is that a mortgage payable has real estate as collateral.

> **OWNERS' EQUITY = ASSETS - LIABILITIES**

3. **Owners' equity** accounts (stockholders' equity for a corporation) represent the net worth of a company. Equity is calculated as assets (resources owned) minus liabilities (amounts owed).

Three different types of business ownership are:

- Sole proprietorship (an unincorporated business with one owner).

- Partnership (an unincorporated business with more than one owner).

- Corporation (an incorporated business with one or more owners).

Owners' equity is increased by:

- Investments by owners. For a corporation, owners invest by buying stock.

- Net profits retained in the business rather than distributed to owners.

Owners' equity is decreased by:

- Amounts paid to owners as a return for their investment. For a sole proprietorship, this is called withdrawals. For a corporation, it is called dividends.

- Losses incurred by the business.

The following QuickBooks Learning Center graphic shows the relationship of assets, liabilities, and owners' equity accounts.

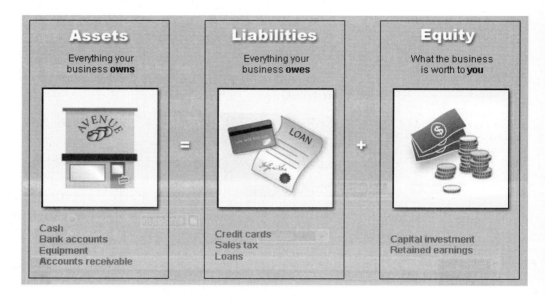

Balance Sheet accounts are referred to as *permanent accounts*. Balances in permanent accounts are carried forward from year to year. Thus, for a Balance Sheet account, such as Cash, the balance at December 31 is carried forward and becomes the opening balance on January 1 of the next year.

INCOME STATEMENT (PROFIT & LOSS) ACCOUNTS

The income statement (also called the profit and loss statement or P&L statement) reports the results of a company's operations, listing income and expenses for a period of time. Income statement accounts are accounts that appear on a company's income statement.

Review the income statement you printed in Exercise 1.1 for Rock Castle Construction. QuickBooks uses two different income statement accounts:

1. Income accounts
2. Expense accounts

1. **Income** accounts record sales to customers and other revenues earned by the company. Revenues are the prices charged customers for goods and services provided.

   Examples of income accounts include:

   - Sales or revenues
   - Fees earned
   - Interest income
   - Rental income
   - Gains on sale of assets

2. **Expense** accounts record costs that have expired or been consumed in the process of generating income. Expenses are the costs of providing goods and services to customers.

   Examples of expense accounts include:

   - Cost of goods sold expense
   - Salaries expense
   - Insurance expense
   - Rent expense
   - Interest expense

INCOME (OR REVENUE)
- EXPENSES
= NET INCOME

Net income is calculated as income (or revenue) less cost of goods sold and other expenses. Net income is an attempt to match or measure efforts (expenses) against accomplishments (revenues).

Income statement accounts are called *temporary* accounts because they are used for only one year. At the end of each year, temporary accounts are closed (the balance reduced to zero).

For example, if an income statement account, such as Advertising Expense, had a $5,000 balance at December 31, the $5,000 balance would be closed or transferred to owner's equity at year-end. The opening balance on January 1 for the Advertising Expense account would be $0.00.

The following QuickBooks Learning Center graphic summarizes the five types of accounts in the Chart of Accounts.

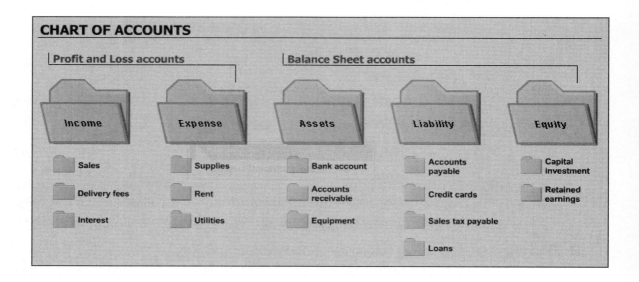

NON-POSTING ACCOUNTS

Non-posting accounts are accounts that do not appear on the balance sheet or income statement. However, these accounts are needed to track information necessary for the accounting system.

Examples of non-posting accounts include:

- Purchase orders: documents that track items that have been ordered from suppliers.
- Estimates: bids or proposals submitted to customers.

LISTS

QuickBooks uses lists to provide additional supporting detail for selected accounts.

QuickBooks lists include:

1. **Customer List:** provides information about customers, such as customer name, customer number, address, and contact information.

2. **Vendor List:** provides information about vendors, such as vendor name, vendor number, and contact information.

3. **Employee List:** provides information about employees for payroll purposes including name, social security number, and address.

4. **Item List:** provides information about the items or services sold to customers, such as hours worked and types of items.

5. **Payroll Item List:** tracks detailed information about payroll, such as payroll taxes and payroll deductions. The Payroll Item List permits the use of a single or limited number of payroll accounts while more detailed information is tracked using the Item List for payroll.

6. **Class List:** permits income to be tracked according to the specific source (class) of income. An example of a class might be a department, store location, business segment, or product line.

Lists are used so that information can be entered once in a list and then reused as needed. For example, information about a customer can be entered in the customer list. This customer information, such as address, etc., can then be entered automatically on the customer invoice.

> **TIP:** Obtain a copy of the tax form for your business at www.irs.gov. Then modify your chart of accounts to track the information needed for your tax return.

DISPLAY CHART OF ACCOUNTS

When you set up a new company, QuickBooks automatically creates a chart of accounts. Then you can modify the chart of accounts to suit your specific needs. Next, you will learn how to display the chart of accounts, then add, delete, and edit accounts.

To view the chart of accounts for Rock Castle Construction, complete the following steps:

Step 1: To display the *Chart of Accounts* window, click the **Chart of Accounts** icon in the Company section of the Home page.

For each account, the account name, type of account, and the balance of the account is listed.

The Account button at the bottom of the window displays a drop-down menu for adding, editing, and deleting accounts. Or you can right-click to display a pop-up menu to add and edit accounts.

Name		Type	Balance Total
◆ [your name] Checking	⚡	Bank	83,835.70
◆ Savings	⚡	Bank	13,868.42
◆ Cash Expenditures		Bank	0.00
◆ Barter Account		Bank	0.00
◆ Accounts Receivable		Accounts Receivable	77,472.00
◆ Tools & Equipment		Other Current Asset	5,000.00
◆ Employee Loans		Other Current Asset	62.00
◆ Inventory Asset		Other Current Asset	23,102.54
◆ Retainage		Other Current Asset	2,461.80
◆ Undeposited Funds		Other Current Asset	58,742.77
◆ Land		Fixed Asset	90,000.00
◆ Buildings		Fixed Asset	325,000.00
◆ Trucks		Fixed Asset	78,352.91
◆ Computers		Fixed Asset	28,501.00
◆ Furniture		Fixed Asset	7,325.00
◆ Accumulated Depreciation		Fixed Asset	-121,887.78
◆ Pre-paid Insurance		Other Asset	1,041.85
◆ Accounts Payable		Accounts Payable	53,780.04
◆ QuickBooks Credit Card	⚡	Credit Card	70.00
◆ CalOil Card		Credit Card	5,057.62
◆ Direct Deposit Liabilities		Other Current Liability	0.00
◆ Payroll Liabilities		Other Current Liability	7,082.68
◆ Sales Tax Payable		Other Current Liability	5,531.77
◆ Bank of Anycity Loan		Long Term Liability	19,932.65
◆ Equipment Loan		Long Term Liability	3,911.32
◆ Note Payable		Long Term Liability	3,440.83

DISPLAY ACCOUNT NUMBERS

> Account Type determines whether the account appears on the balance sheet or income statement.

Account numbers are used to identify accounts. Usually the account number also identifies the account type. For example, a typical numbering system for accounts might be as follows.

Account Type	Account No.
Asset accounts	1000 – 1999
Liability accounts	2000 – 2999
Equity accounts	3000 – 3999
Revenue (income) accounts	4000 – 4999
Expense accounts	5000 – 5999

To display both the account name and account number for Rock Castle Construction's chart of accounts, you must select a QuickBooks preference for viewing the account numbers.

To display account numbers:

Step 1: From the **Edit** menu, select **Preferences**.

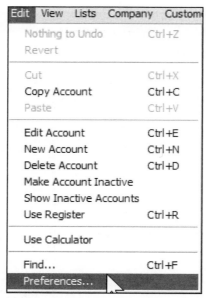

Step 2: When the *Preferences* window appears, the left scrollbar lists the different types of preferences.

- Click the **Accounting** icon in the left scrollbar.

- Then select the **Company Preferences** tab.

- Select **Use account numbers** to display the account numbers in the chart of accounts.

- Then click **OK**. (If asked if you want to set the closing date password, select No.)

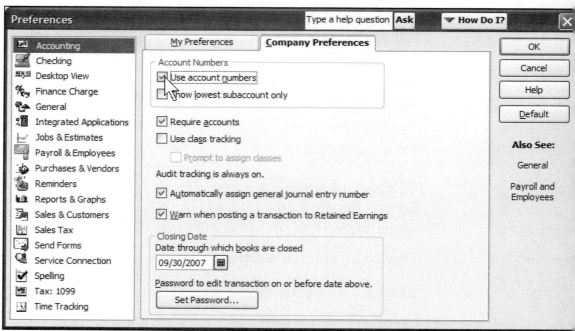

Step 3: If the chart of accounts does not appear on your screen, from the menu bar, click **Window** | **Chart of Accounts**.

The chart of accounts should now list account numbers preceding the account name.

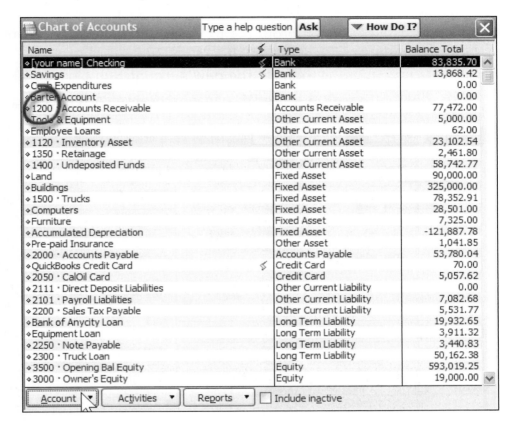

ADD NEW ACCOUNTS

You can modify the chart of accounts by adding new accounts, deleting accounts, or editing accounts as needed to suit your company's specific and changing needs.

Rock Castle Construction has decided to begin advertising and would like to add an Advertising Expense account to the chart of accounts.

To add a new account to the chart of accounts:

Step 1: Click the **Account** button at the bottom of the *Chart of Accounts* window to display a drop-down menu, then click **New**.

Step 2: Enter information in the *New Account* window.

- From the drop-down list, select Account Type: **Expense**.

- Enter the new Account Number: **6040**.

- Enter the Account Name: **Advertising Expense**.

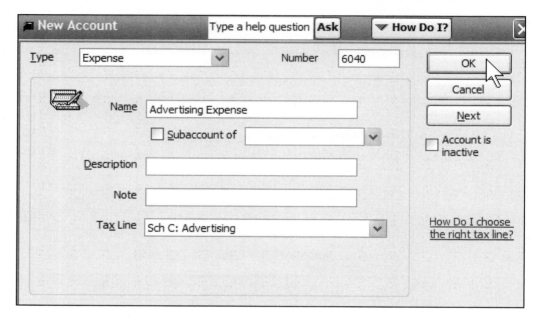

- Leave subaccount unchecked. Subaccounts are subcategories of an account. For example, Rock Castle Construction has an Automobile Expense account (Account No. 6000) and two Automobile Expense subaccounts: Repairs and Maintenance (Account No. 6010) and Fuel (Account No. 6020).

- Select Tax Line: **Sch C: Advertising**. This indicates the Advertising Expense account balance will appear on Schedule C of Rock Castle Construction's tax return.

> **IMPORTANT!** Selecting the appropriate Tax Line will ensure that your accounting records provide the information needed to complete your tax return.

Step 3: Click **OK** to save the changes and close the *New Account* window.

Notice that Account 6040 Advertising Expense now appears on the chart of accounts.

If the new account had been a Balance Sheet account (an asset, liability, or equity account), QuickBooks would ask you for the opening account balance as of your QuickBooks start date. Since Advertising Expense is an expense account that appears on the income statement and not a Balance Sheet account, QuickBooks did not ask for the opening balance.

DELETE ACCOUNTS

Occasionally you may want to delete unused accounts from the chart of accounts. You can only delete accounts that are not being used. For example, if an account has been used to record a transaction and has a balance, it cannot be deleted. If an account has subaccounts associated with it, that account cannot be deleted.

Rock Castle Construction would like to delete an account it does not plan to use, the Printing and Reproduction Expense account.

To delete an account:

Step 1: Display the *Chart of Accounts* window.

Step 2: Select the account to delete. In this case, click **6900: Printing and Reproduction**.

Step 3: Click the **Account** button at the bottom of *the Chart of Accounts* window.

Step 4: Click **Delete Account**.

Step 5: Click **OK** to confirm that you want to delete the account.

EDIT ACCOUNTS

Rock Castle Construction would like to change the name of the Advertising Expense account to Advertising & Promotion.

To make changes to an existing account, complete the following steps:

Step 1: Display the *Chart of Accounts* window.

Step 2: Select the account to edit: **6040 Advertising Expense**.

Step 3: Click the **Account** button in the lower left corner of the *Chart of Accounts* window or right-click the mouse to display the pop-up menu.

Step 4: Click **Edit Account** to open the *Edit Account* window.

Step 5: Make changes to the account information. In this case, change the account name to: **Advertising & Promotion**.

> **NOTE:** You cannot change the type of account if there are subaccounts associated with the account.

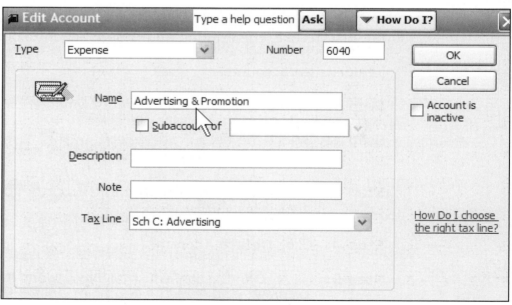

Step 6: Click **OK** to save the changes. Advertising Expense should now appear as Advertising & Promotion in the *Chart of Accounts* window.

QuickBooks permits you to rearrange the order in which the accounts appear in the chart of accounts. A chart of accounts is often arranged in numerical order by account number.

To demonstrate how to move accounts in the chart of accounts, you will move the account you just added, Advertising & Promotion, to a new location in Rock Castle Construction's chart of accounts.

To move an account within the chart of accounts:

Step 1: In the *Chart of Accounts* window, move the mouse pointer over the diamond that appears to the left of the Advertising & Promotion account.

> **TIP:** After making changes to the chart of accounts, to resort the list, click the **Account** button, then select **Re-sort List** or click the arrow by the Name button at the top of the *Chart of Accounts* window.

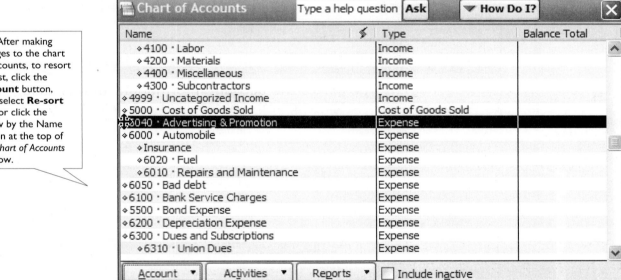

Step 2: Hold down the left mouse button and drag the **Advertising & Promotion** account to the desired location above the Bad Debt Account (Account No. 6050), then release the mouse button.

PRINT CHART OF ACCOUNTS

QuickBooks provides a Chart of Accounts printout or an Account Listing report that includes the account balances.

To print the Account Listing report:

Step 1: Display the *Chart of Accounts* window.

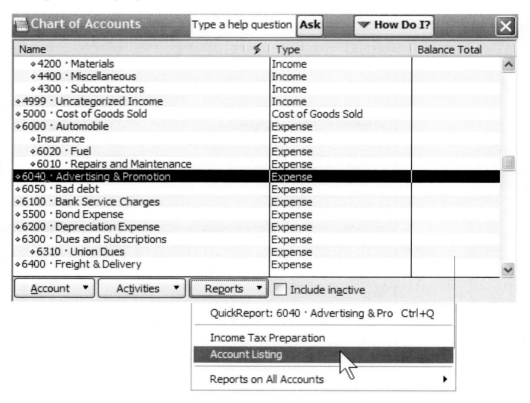

Step 2: Click the **Reports** button at the bottom of the *Chart of Accounts* window, then click **Account Listing** on the drop-down menu.

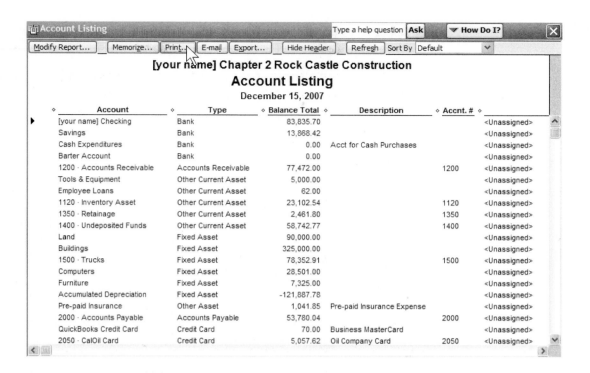

Step 3: 🖶 **Print** the Accounting Listing report as follows:

- Click the **Print** button at the top of the *Account Listing* window.

- Select orientation: **Portrait**.

- Select **Fit report to 1 page(s) wide** that appears in the lower left of the window.

- Click **Print**.

Step 4: **Close** the *Account Listing* window, saving it as a Memorized Report named Chart of Accounts. **Close** the *Chart of Accounts* window.

REMINDER LIST

QuickBooks has three features to assist you in tracking tasks to be done:

1. To Do List: tracks all tasks to be completed. You can add items to the To Do List, mark items complete, and print the list.

2. Reminders List: shows only those tasks that are currently due.

3. Alerts Manager: a listing of tasks and due dates related to taxes and regulations. These alerts will appear on the Reminders List as they become due.

To display the Reminders List and the To Do List:

Step 1: From the menu bar, click **Company | Reminders** to display the Reminders List.

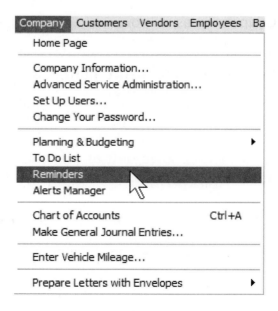

Step 2: To display the detail for the To Do Notes, click **To Do Notes** on the Reminders List.

Reminders	Type a help question	Ask	▼ How Do I?	☒

Due Date	⚡	Description	Amount
		Business Service Messages	
		Online Banking transactions ready to send.	
		To Do Notes	
12/13/2007		Call Doug about grout in the kitchen.	
12/15/2007		Finish Jacobsen poolhouse estimate	
		Money to Deposit	58,742.77
		Bills to Pay	-25,923.56
		Overdue Invoices	5,265.42
		Checks to Print	-47,951.78
		Paychecks to Print	-81,265.30
		Sales Orders to Print	1,724.00
		Purchase Orders to Print	-48,000.00
		Inventory to Reorder	
		Assembly Items to Build	
		Alerts	
		A payment to the loan Equipment Loan is due on 12/22/2007	

SAVE CHAPTER 2

Save Chapter 2 as a portable QuickBooks file to the location specified by your instructor.

Step 1: If necessary, insert a removable disk.

Step 2: From the menu bar, click **File | Portable Company File | Create File**.

Step 3: When the *Close and Reopen* window appears, click **OK**.

Step 4: When the following *Create Portable Company File* window appears, enter the filename: **[your name] Chapter 2** and the appropriate location. Then click **Save**.

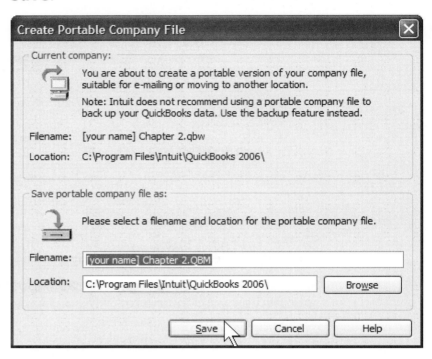

Step 5: Click **OK** after the portable file has been created successfully.

Step 6: Close the company file by clicking **File** (Menu), **Close Company**.

NOTE: In this text, you will save a portable company file with a .QBM extension at the end of each chapter, exercise, or project.

If you are continuing your computer session, proceed to Exercise 2.1.

If you are ending your computer session now, see the Quick Reference Guide in Part 3 for instructions to (1) close the company file and (2) exit QuickBooks.

ASSIGNMENTS

NOTE: See the Quick Reference Guide in Part 3 for step-by-step instructions to frequently used tasks.

EXERCISE 2.1: TO DO LIST

SCENARIO

When you return to your cubicle after lunch, you find the following note stuck to your computer screen.

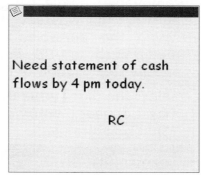

Need statement of cash flows by 4 pm today.

RC

In addition to printing out the statement of cash flows, you decide to add a task to your QuickBooks To Do List to remind you to print out the financial statements for Rock Castle each month.

TASK 1: OPEN PORTABLE COMPANY FILE

To open the portable company file (.QBM) file, convert the portable file to a regular company file with a .QBW extension as follows:

Step 1: From the menu bar, click **File** | **Portable Company File** | **Open File**.

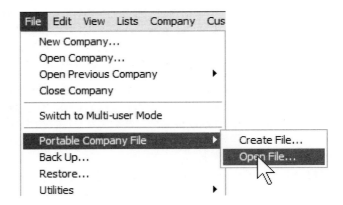

Step 2: Identify the filename and location for the portable company file:

- Click the **Browse** button to find the location of the portable company file on the hard drive or removable media. In the example below, the portable file was saved to the hard drive. If you saved the portable company file to removable media such as USB, floppy disk, or CD, you would specify the location of the removable media.

- Select the file: **[your name] Chapter 2**. The .QBM may appear automatically based upon your Windows settings.

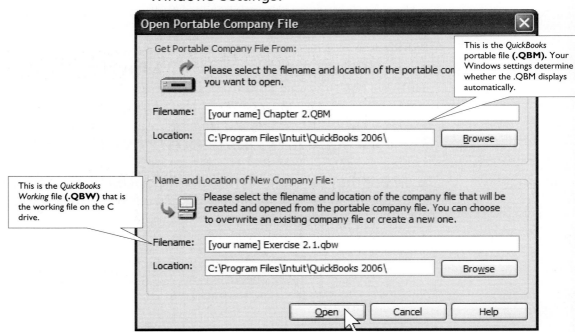

Step 3: Identify the name and location of the new company file (.QBW) file to use for completing Exercise 2.1:

- Filename: **[your name] Exercise 2.1**. The **.QBW** extension should appear automatically based upon your Windows settings. The .QBW identifies this as a QuickBooks working file.

- Location: **C:\Program Files\Intuit\QuickBooks 2006**. This is the location of the .QBW file on the hard drive of your computer. You can click the Browse button to specify another location.

Step 4: Click **Open** to open the portable company file.

Step 5: Click **Cancel** when the following *Create a Backup* window appears.

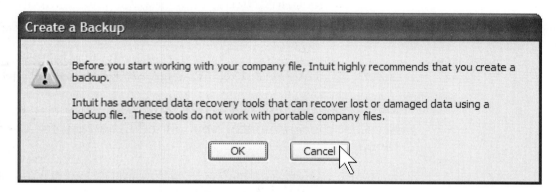

Step 6: If the following login window appears, enter your **password**, then click **OK**.

Step 7: Click **OK** when the following window appears.

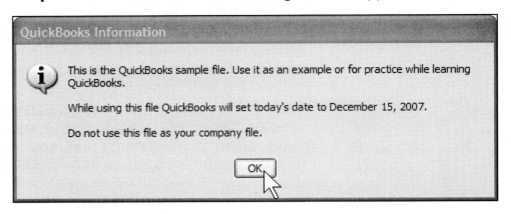

Step 8: Change the company name to: **[your name] Exercise 2.1 Rock Castle Construction**. (If you need instructions to change the company name, see Part 3: Quick Reference Guide.)

TASK 2: ADD A TASK TO THE TO DO LIST

Add a task to your To Do List to prepare financial statements for Mr. Castle each month. You will add the task for December and January.

To add a task to the To Do List, complete the following steps:

Step 1: From the menu bar, click **Company | To Do List**.

Step 2: Click the **To Do** button in the lower left corner of the *To Do List* window.

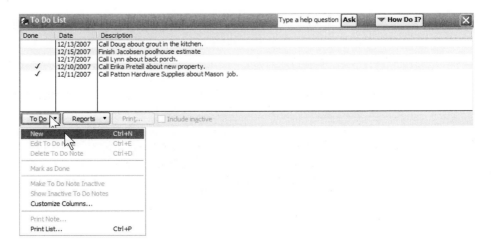

Step 3: Click **New**.

Step 4: Enter the December task: **Print financial statements for Mr. Castle**. Remind me on: **12/12/2007**.

Step 5: Click the **Next** button to add another task.

Step 6: Enter the January task: **Print financial statements for Mr. Castle**. Remind me on: **01/01/2008**.

Step 7: Click **OK** to save the task and close the window.

TASK 3: PRINT STATEMENT OF CASH FLOWS

The Statement of Cash Flows summarizes a company's cash inflows and cash outflows. The cash flows are grouped by activity:

- *Cash flows from operating activities:* Cash flows related to the operations of the business—providing goods and services to customers.

- *Cash flows from investing activities:* Cash flows that result from investing (buying and selling) long-term assets, such as investments and property.

- *Cash flows from financing activities:* Cash flows that result from borrowing or repaying principal on debt or from transactions with owners.

Print the Statement of Cash Flows for Rock Castle Construction by completing the following steps:

Step 1: Click the **Report Center** icon in the Navigation Bar.

Step 2: Select type of report: **Company & Financial**.

Step 3: Select report: **Cash Flow: Statement of Cash Flows**.

Step 4: Select the date range: **Last Month**. The *From* field should now be: **11/01/2007**. The *To* field should be: **11/30/2007**.

Step 5: ⊟ **Print** the Statement of Cash Flows as follows:

- Click the **Print** button at the top of the *Statement of Cash Flows* window.

- Select the appropriate printer.

- Select **Portrait** orientation.

- Select **Fit to 1 page(s) wide**.

- Click **Print** to print the Statement of Cash Flows.

Step 6: **Close** the *Statement of Cash Flows* window, saving the Memorized Report as Statement of Cash Flows.

Step 7: Then **close** the *Report Center* window.

✓ *Net cash provided by operating activities is $18,826.39.*

Step 8: ✐ **Circle** the net change in cash for the period on the Statement of Cash Flows printout.

TASK 4: MARK TASK COMPLETE

Mark the task to print November financial statements as completed.

To mark a task complete:

Step 1: Open the *To Do* window.

Step 2: Select the To Do task: **12/12/2007 Print financial statements for Mr. Castle**.

Step 3: With the mouse pointer on the selected task, right-click. When the onscreen menu appears, select **Mark as Done**. A ✓ should now appear in front of the task and the task drops to the bottom of the To Do List.

Step 4: 🖨 **Print** the To Do List as follows:

- Click the **Reports** button at the bottom of the *To Do List* window.
- Click **Detail List**.
- Click **Print**. Select Print to: **Printer**. Click **Print**.
- **Close** the *To Do List* window.

TASK 5: SAVE EXERCISE 2.1

Save Exercise 2.1 as a portable QuickBooks file to the location specified by your instructor.

If necessary, insert a removable disk.

Step 1: From the menu bar, click **File | Portable Company File | Create File**.

Step 2: When the *Close and Reopen* window appears, click **OK**.

Step 3: When the following *Create Portable Company File* window appears, enter the filename: **[your name] Exercise 2.1** and the appropriate location. Then click **Save**.

Step 4: Click **OK** after the portable file has been created successfully.

Step 5: Close the company file by clicking **File** (Menu), **Close Company**.

You have now saved the portable company file Exercise 2.1.QBM.

EXERCISE 2.2: EDIT CHART OF ACCOUNTS

SCENARIO

When you return to your cubicle after your afternoon break, another note is stuck to your computer screen.

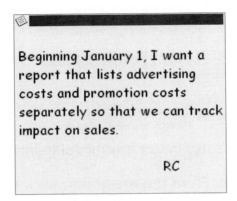

Beginning January 1, I want a report that lists advertising costs and promotion costs separately so that we can track impact on sales.

RC

In order to track advertising costs separately from promotion costs, you decide to make the following changes to the chart of accounts.

1. Rename Account 6040 Advertising & Promotion account to: Selling Expense.

2. Add two subaccounts: 6041 Advertising Expense and 6042 Promotion Expense.

After these changes, the chart of accounts should list the following accounts:

> Account 6040: Selling Expense
>
> Subaccount 6041: Advertising Expense
>
> Subaccount 6042: Promotion Expense

TASK 1: OPEN PORTABLE COMPANY FILE

To open the portable company file (.QBM) file, convert the portable file to a regular company file with a .QBW extension as follows:

Step 1: From the menu bar, click **File | Portable Company File | Open File**.

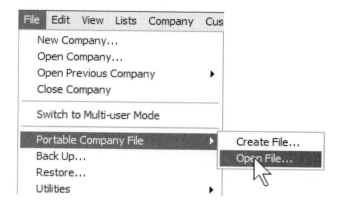

Step 2: Identify the filename and location for the portable company file (.QBM file):

- Click the **Browse** button to find the location of the portable company file on the hard drive or removable media. In the example below, the portable file was saved to the hard drive. If you saved the portable company file to removable media such as USB, floppy disk, or CD, you would specify the location of the removable media.

- Select the file: **[your name] Exercise 2.1**. The .QBM may appear automatically based upon your Windows settings.

Step 3: Identify the name and location of the new company file (.QBW file) to use for completing Exercise 2.2:

- Filename: **[your name] Exercise 2.2**. The **.QBW** extension should appear automatically based upon your Windows settings. The .QBW identifies this as a QuickBooks working file.

- Location: **C:\Program Files\Intuit\QuickBooks 2006**. This is the location of the .QBW file on the hard drive of your computer. You can click the Browse button to specify another location.

Step 4: Click **Open** to open the portable company file.

Step 5: Click **Cancel** when the *Create a Backup* window appears.

Step 6: If prompted, enter your User ID and Password.

> To change the company name, select **Company** (menu), **Company Information**.

Step 7: Change the company name to: **[your name] Exercise 2.2 Rock Castle Construction**. If necessary, change the Checking account title to include your name.

TASK 2: EDIT ACCOUNT

Edit the chart of accounts to change the name of Account 6040 from Advertising & Promotion to Selling Expense.

Step 1: Open the *Chart of Accounts* window by clicking the **Chart of Accounts** icon in the Company section of the Home page.

Step 2: Select account: **6040 Advertising & Promotion**.

Step 3: Click the **Account** button at the bottom of the *Chart of Accounts* window, then select **Edit Account** from the drop-down menu.

Step 4: Change the account name from Advertising & Promotion to: **Selling Expense**.

Step 5: Click **OK** to save the changes.

TASK 3: ADD SUBACCOUNTS

Add two subaccounts to the Selling Expense account:
(1) Advertising Expense and (2) Promotion Expense.

Step 1: Click the **Account** button at the bottom of the *Chart of Accounts* window, then select **New** to open the *New Account* window.

Step 2: Select Account Type: **Expense**.

Step 3: Enter Account Number: **6041**

Step 4: Enter Account Name: **Advertising Expense**.

Step 5: **Check** the box in front of the *Subaccount of* field.

Step 6: From the drop-down list, select subaccount of: **6040 Selling Expense**.

Step 7: From the drop-down list for Tax Line, select **SchC: Advertising**.

Step 8: Click **Next**. Using the instructions above, add the next subaccount: **6042 Promotion Expense**.

Step 9: ⊟ **Print** the revised chart of accounts. (Hint: From the *Chart of Accounts* window, click the **Reports** button, then click **Account Listing**.

- Remember to use Portrait orientation and Fit to 1 page(s) wide.

- To use the Memorized Report for the Chart of Accounts that you created earlier, select **Reports** from the menu, select **Memorized Reports**, then **Chart of Accounts**.

TASK 4: SAVE EXERCISE 2.2

Save Exercise 2.2 as a portable QuickBooks file to the location specified by your instructor.

Step 1: If necessary, insert a removable disk.

Step 2: From the menu bar, click **File | Portable Company File | Create File**.

Step 3: When the *Close and Reopen* window appears, click **OK**.

Step 4: When the following *Create Portable Company File* window appears, enter the filename: **[your name] Exercise 2.2** and the appropriate location. Then click **Save**.

Step 5: Click **OK** after the portable file has been created successfully.

Step 6: Close the company file by clicking **File** (Menu), **Close Company**.

You have now saved the portable company file Exercise 2.2.QBM.

EXERCISE 2.3: WEB QUEST

When setting up a chart of accounts for a business, it is often helpful to review the tax form that the business will use. Then accounts can be used to track information needed for the business tax return.

The tax form used by the type of organization is listed below.

Type of Organization	Tax Form
Sole Proprietorship	Schedule C (Form 1040)
Partnership	Form 1065 & Schedule K-1
Corporation	Form 1120
S Corporation	Form 1120S

In this Exercise, you will download a tax form from the Internal Revenue Service web site.

Step 1: Go to the Internal Revenue Service web page: www.irs.gov

Step 2: As shown above, a sole proprietorship files tax form Schedule C that is attached to the individual's Form 1040 tax form. 🖨 **Print** the tax form Schedule C: Profit or Loss From Business (Sole Proprietorship).

Step 3: ✎ **Circle** Advertising Expense on the Schedule C.

CHAPTER 2 PRINTOUT CHECKLIST
NAME: _____ DATE:_____

INSTRUCTIONS:
1. *CHECK OFF THE PRINTOUTS YOU HAVE COMPLETED.*
2. *STAPLE THIS PAGE TO YOUR PRINTOUTS.*

☑ *PRINTOUT CHECKLIST – CHAPTER 2*
☐ Chart of Accounts (Accounting Listing)

☑ *PRINTOUT CHECKLIST – EXERCISE 2.1*
☐ Task 3: Statement of Cash Flows
☐ Task 4: To Do List

☑ *PRINTOUT CHECKLIST – EXERCISE 2.2*
☐ Task 3: Revised Chart of Accounts (Account Listing)

☑ *PRINTOUT CHECKLIST – EXERCISE 2.3*
☐ Schedule C Tax Form

CHAPTER 3
BANKING

SCENARIO

The next morning as you pass the open door of Mr. Castle's office, you notice he is looking at the financial statements you prepared. You try to slip past his door unnoticed, but you take only a few steps when you hear him curtly call your name.

You turn to see Mr. Castle charging toward you with documents in hand.

"I need you to keep an eye on the bank accounts. Cash is the lifeblood of a business. A business can't survive if it doesn't have enough cash flowing through its veins to pay its bills. So it's very important that someone keep an eye on the cash in our bank accounts—the cash inflows into the accounts and the cash outflows from the accounts. That is your job now."

Handing you more documents, Mr. Castle continues, *"We fell behind on our bank reconciliations. Here is last month's bank statement that needs to be reconciled."*

CHAPTER 3
LEARNING OBJECTIVES

In Chapter 3, you will perform the following QuickBooks activities:

INTRODUCTION

In Chapter 3, you will learn about using QuickBooks to perform banking tasks, such as making deposits, writing checks, and reconciling bank statements. Online banking is covered in Appendix B: QuickBooks Online Features.

To begin Chapter 3, start QuickBooks software and then open the portable QuickBooks file.

Step 1: Start QuickBooks by clicking on the **QuickBooks** desktop icon or click **Start**, **Programs**, **QuickBooks**, **QuickBooks Pro 2006**.

Step 2: To open the portable company file (.QBM) file and convert the portable file to a regular company file with a .QBW extension, from the menu bar, click **File | Portable Company File | Open File**.

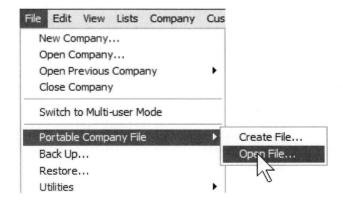

Step 3: Identify the filename and location for the portable company file:

- Click the **Browse** button to find the location of the portable company file on the hard drive or removable media. In the example below, the portable file was saved to the hard drive. If you saved the portable company file to removable media such as USB, floppy disk, or CD, you would specify the location of the removable media.

- Select the file: **[your name] Exercise 2.2**. The .QBM may appear automatically based upon your Windows settings, but if it does not appear automatically, do **not** type it.

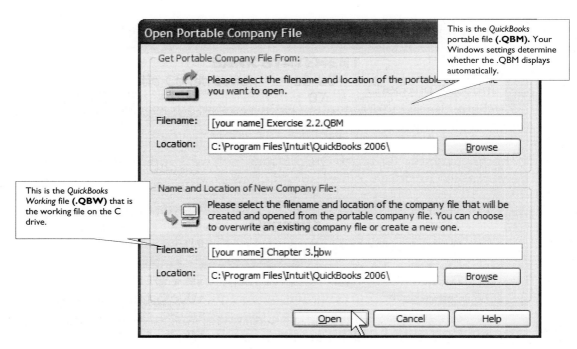

Step 4: Identify the name and location of the new company file (.QBW) file to use for Chapter 3:

- Filename: **[your name] Chapter 3**. The **.QBW** extension should appear automatically based upon your Windows settings. The .QBW identifies this as a QuickBooks working file.

- Location: **C:\Program Files\Intuit\QuickBooks 2006**. This is the location of the .QBW file on the hard drive of your computer. You can click the Browse button to specify another location.

Step 5: Click **Open** to open the portable company file.

Step 6: Click **Cancel** when the following *Create a Backup* window appears.

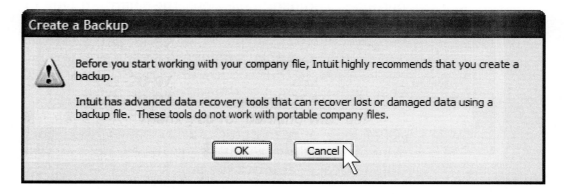

Step 7: If prompted, enter your User ID and password.

Step 8: Click **OK** when the following window appears.

Recall that the filename is the .QBW or .QBM filename that is changed when you save the file. The company name is the name that appears on reports and is changed through the Company Information window.

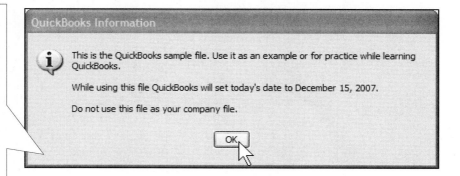

Step 9: Change the company name to: **[your name] Chapter 3 Rock Castle Construction**. (For step-by-step instructions, see Part 3: Quick Reference Guide.)

To change the company name, click **Company** (menu), **Company Information**.

If necessary, change the Checking account title to include your name.

The portable company file (.QBM) should now be converted to a regular company file (Chapter 3.QBW) that can be used to complete the assignments for Chapter 3.

After opening the portable company file for Rock Castle Construction, click the Home page icon in the Navigation Bar.

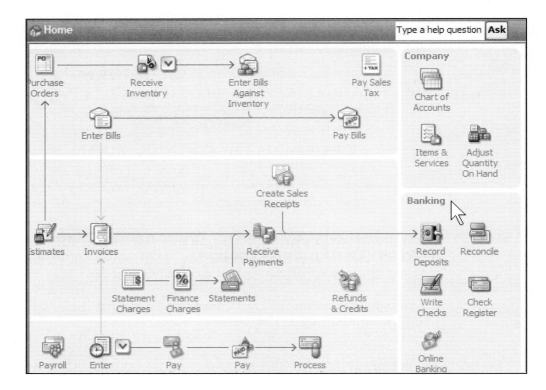

From the Banking section of the Home page, you can record:

- Deposits (cash flowing into the Checking account).
- Checks (cash going out of the Checking account).
- Bank reconciliations.
- Check register transactions.
- Online banking.

A business should establish a *business* checking account completely separate from the owner's *personal* checking account. The company's checking account should be used *only* for business transactions, such as business insurance and mortgage payments for the company's office building. Owners should maintain a completely separate checking account for personal transactions, such as mortgage payments for the owner's home.

VIEW AND PRINT CHECK REGISTER

The check register is a record of all transactions affecting the Checking account. QuickBooks' onscreen check register looks similar to a checkbook register used to manually record deposits and checks.

To view the QuickBooks check register:

Step 1: Click the **Check Register** icon in the Banking section of the Home page.

Step 2: The following window will appear asking you to specify a bank account. Select **[your name] Checking**, then click **OK**.

Step 3: The following *Check Register* window should appear on your screen. Notice there are separate columns for:

- Payments (checks)
- Deposits
- Balance of the checking account

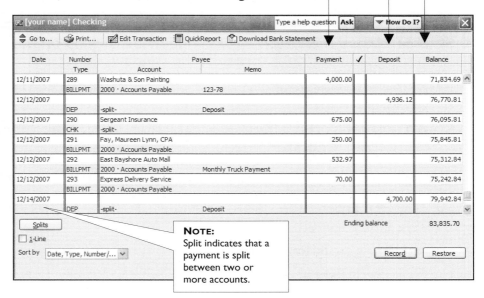

Step 4: To view the source documents for the transaction with Sergeant Insurance, double-click on the **Sergeant Insurance** entry on **12-12-2007** in the check register.

If necessary, scroll up or down to locate the Sergeant Insurance entry.

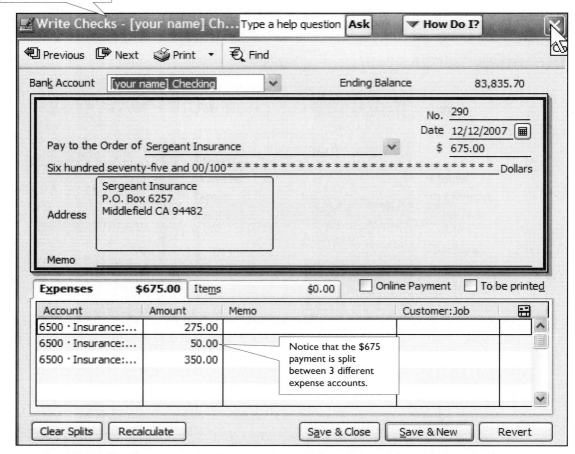

Step 5: **Close** the *Write Checks* window by clicking on the ⊠ in the upper right corner of the window.

To print the Check Register:

Step 1: Display the check register, then click **File** (menu), **Print Register**.

Step 2: When the *Print Register* window appears:

- Enter the Date Range: From: **12/01/2007** Through: **12/15/2007**.

- Check **Print split detail**.

- Click **OK**.

Step 3: ▣ Select the appropriate print options, then click **Print**.

> ✓ *The check register printout for Rock Castle should list a deposit on 12/14/2007 for $4,700.00 and the Checking Account balance on 12/14/2007 is $79,942.84.*

Step 4: **Close** the *Check Register* window by clicking the ⊠ in the upper right corner of the *Check Register* window.

You can either record deposits and checks directly in the check register or use the *Make Deposits* window and the *Write Checks* window.

MAKE DEPOSITS

Deposits are additions to the Checking account. Any cash coming into a business should be recorded as a deposit to one of the company's accounts.

QuickBooks classifies deposits into two types:

1. Payments from customers.

2. Nonsales receipts (deposits other than customer payments) such as:

   - Cash received from loans.

   - Investments from owners.

   - Interest earned.

   - Other income, such as rental income.

Payments from customers are entered using the Customer section of the Home page. For more information about recording payments from customers, see Chapter 4: Customers and Sales.

Deposits other than customer payments are recorded using the Banking section of the Home page.

Mr. Castle wants to invest an additional $72,000 in the business by depositing his $72,000 check in Rock Castle Construction's Checking account.

To record nonsales receipts (a deposit other than a customer payment):

Step 1: From the Banking section of the Home page, click the **Record Deposits** icon. The following *Payments to Deposit* window will appear.

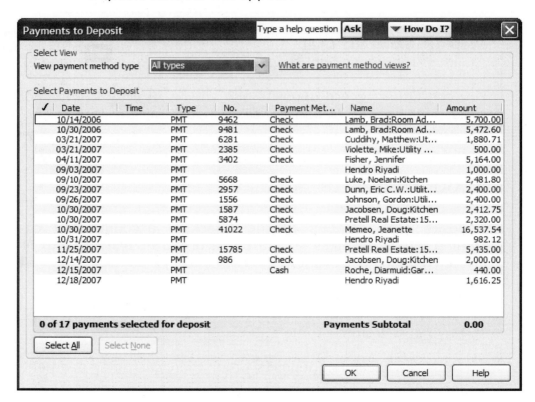

Step 2: QuickBooks uses a two-step process to record customer payments:

> (1) Record the customer's payment received but not yet deposited (undeposited funds) and
>
> (2) Record the deposit.

The payments listed above are undeposited funds that have been recorded as received but not yet deposited in the bank.

Since these amounts will be deposited at a later time, confirm that none of the payments are selected for deposit, then click **OK**.

Step 3: When the following *Make Deposits* window appears, record Mr. Castle's $72,000 deposit as follows:

> ■ Select Deposit To: **[your name] Checking.**

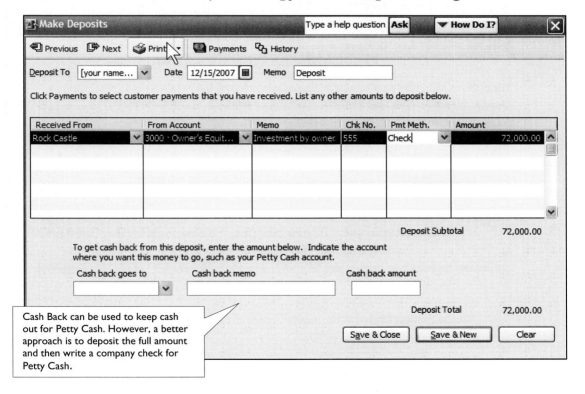

- Click in the Received From column and type: **Rock Castle**. Press the **Tab** key. When prompted, select **Quick Add** to add the name to the Name List.

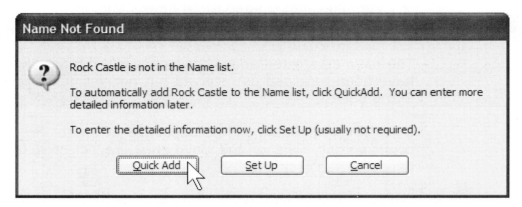

- Select Name Type: **Other**, then click **OK**.

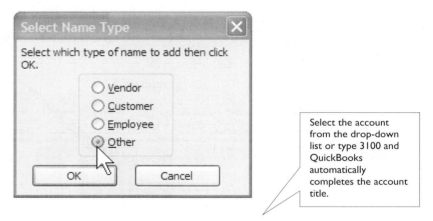

Select the account from the drop-down list or type 3100 and QuickBooks automatically completes the account title.

- Click in the *From Account* column. From the drop-down list of accounts, select **3100 Owner's Contribution Equity**. Press **Tab**.

- Enter Memo: **Investment by owner**.

- Enter Check No.: **555** (the number of Mr. Castle's check).

- From the Payment Method drop-down list, select **Check**.

- Enter Amount: **72000**. (QuickBooks will automatically enter the comma in the amount.)

Step 4: Next, you will print a deposit summary. QuickBooks permits you to print a deposit slip (you must use a QuickBooks preprinted form) and a deposit summary.

To 🖨 **print** a summary of the deposit you just recorded:

- Click the **Print** button at the top of the *Make Deposits* window.

- Select **Deposit summary only**. Then click **OK**.

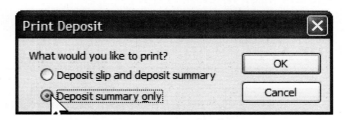

- Select the appropriate printer, then click **Print**. The deposit summary should list the $72,000 check from Mr. Castle.

Mr. Castle's $72,000 investment in the company has now been recorded as a deposit in Rock Castle Construction's Checking account.

Step 5: Close the *Make Deposits* window by clicking **Save & Close**.

WRITE CHECKS

A business needs to track all cash paid out of the company's checking account. Examples of payments include purchases of inventory, office supplies, employee salaries, rent payments, insurance payments, and more.

Supporting documents (source documents) for payments include canceled checks, receipts, and paid invoices. These source documents provide proof that the transaction occurred; therefore, source documents should be kept on file for tax purposes.

QuickBooks provides two ways to pay bills:

One-step approach to bill paying:

❶ Record and pay the bill at the same time. When using this approach, the bill is paid when it is received.

Two-step approach to bill paying:

❶ Record the bill when it is received.

❷ Pay the bill later when it is due.

ONE-STEP APPROACH TO BILL PAYING

❶ **Pay Bills When Received:** Record bill and print check to pay bill.

> Covered in Chapter 3: Banking.

QuickBooks:
1.   Reduces the Checking account (credit).
2.   Records the Expense (debit).

> Covered in Chapter 5: Vendors, Purchases, and Inventory.

TWO-STEP APPROACH TO BILL PAYING

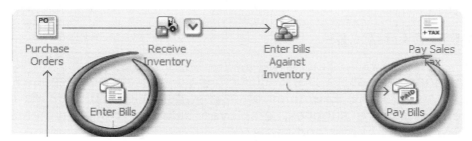

❶ **Enter Bills:** Record bills for services, such as utilities.

QuickBooks:
1.   Records an Expense (debit).
2.   Records an obligation (liability) to pay later (credit).

❷ **Pay Bills:** Select bills to pay, then print checks.

When the bill is paid and the obligation fulfilled, QuickBooks:
1.   Reduces the liability account (debit).
2.   Reduces Checking account (credit).

The *Write Checks* window (One-Step Approach) should ***not*** be used to pay:

1. Paychecks to pay employees' wages and salaries. (Use the Employee Navigator, *Pay Employees* window instead).

2. Payroll taxes and liabilities (Use the Employee Navigator, *Pay Liabilities* window instead).

3. Sales taxes (Use the Vendor Navigator, *Pay Sales Taxes* window instead).

4. Bills already entered in the *Enter Bills* window (Use the Vendor Navigator, *Pay Bills* window instead).

The *Write Checks* window (One-Step Approach) can be used to pay:

1. Expenses, such as rent, utilities, and insurance.

2. Non-inventory items, such as office supplies.

3. Services, such as accounting or legal services.

In this chapter, you will use the *Write Checks* window (One-Step Approach) to pay a computer repair service bill for Rock Castle Construction.

> You can also open the *Write Checks* window by clicking **Write Checks** on the Icon Bar or the Shortcut List.

To use the *Write Checks* window to pay bills:

Step 1: From the Banking section of the Home page, click the **Write Checks** icon and the following onscreen check will appear.

Step 2: If a warning message appears that you have outstanding bills or open item receipts, click **OK**.

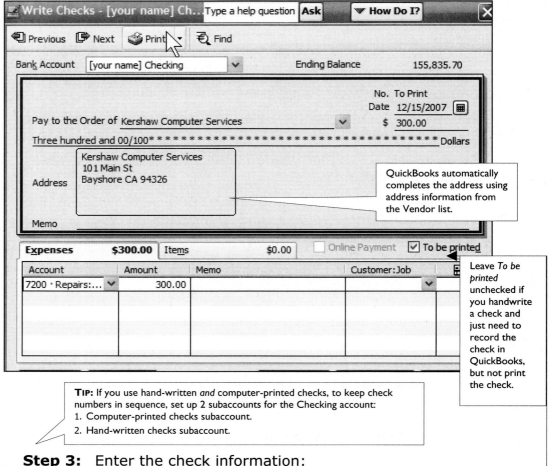

TIP: If you use hand-written *and* computer-printed checks, to keep check numbers in sequence, set up 2 subaccounts for the Checking account:
1. Computer-printed checks subaccount.
2. Hand-written checks subaccount.

Step 3: Enter the check information:

- Select Bank Account: **[your name] Checking**.

- Select Date: **12/15/2007**.

- For the *Pay to the Order of* field, select: **Kershaw Computer Services**. (Select Kershaw from the drop-down list or type the first few letters of the name. If a *Warning* window appears telling you that you have outstanding bills with this vendor, click **OK**.)

TIP: If you use more than one Checking account, change the Checking account color:
1. Edit menu.
2. Change Account Color.

- Enter the check amount: **300**.

- Click the checkbox preceding **To be printed** so that a check mark appears. This tells QuickBooks to both record and print the check. The Check No. field will now display: To Print.

Step 4: Next, record the payment in the correct account using the lower portion of the *Write Checks* window:

- Click the **Expenses** tab.

To record an Inventory item, use the Items tab.

> Instead of printing one check at a time, you can record all your checks and then print them all at once:
> 1. **File**
> 2. **Print Forms**
> 3. **Checks**

- Select Account: **7220 Repairs: Computer Repairs**. The $300 should automatically appear in the expense Amount column.

- Notice that if the payment was related to a specific customer or job, you could enter that information now.

Step 5: 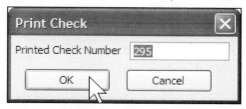 **Print** the check:

- Click the **Print** button located at the top of the *Write Checks* window.

- Enter Check No.: **295**, then click **OK**.

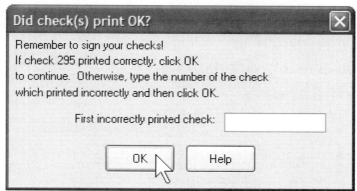

- If you are using the preprinted check forms, insert check forms in the printer now.

- Select Check Style: **Standard**.

- Select: **Print company name and address**.

- Select the appropriate printer.

- Click **Print**.

- Click **OK** if your check printed correctly. If not, enter the first incorrectly printed check.

Step 6: Click **Save & Close** to close the *Write Checks* window. QuickBooks automatically records the check in the Check Register.

PRINT JOURNAL

QuickBooks uses two different ways to enter information:

1. Onscreen forms, such as the onscreen check you just completed.

2. An onscreen journal that uses debits and credits.

When you enter information into an onscreen form, QuickBooks automatically converts that information into a journal entry with debits and credits. If you will not be using the journal, you may skip this section.

To view the journal entry for the check that you just recorded:

Step 1: Click the **Report Center** icon in the Navigation Bar to open the *Report Center* window.

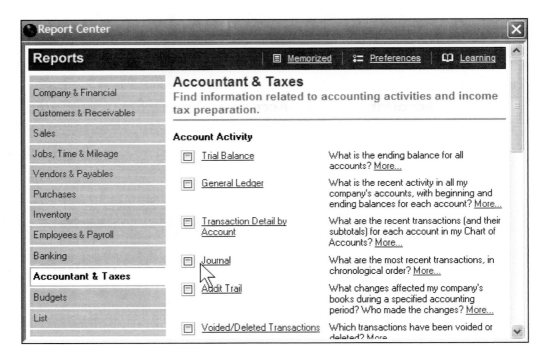

Step 2: Select: **Accountant & Taxes**.

Step 3: Select: **Journal**.

Step 4: Set Dates: **Today** From: **12/15/2007** To: **12/15/2007**.

Step 5: Your *Journal* window should appear as shown below.

Trans #	Type	Date	Num	Name	Memo	Account	Debit	Credit
						6000 · Automobile	10.60	
							10.60	10.60
1257	Deposit	12/15/2007			Deposit	[your name] Check...	72,000.00	
				Rock Castle	Investment b...	3100 · Owner's Co...		72,000.00
							72,000.00	72,000.00
1258	Check	12/15/2007	295	Kershaw Compute...		[your name] Check...		300.00
				Kershaw Compute...		7220 · Computer R...	300.00	
							300.00	300.00
TOTAL							143,920.94	143,920.94

[your name] Chapter 3 Rock Castle Construction
Journal
December 15, 2007

Step 6: The journal entry to record the deposit of Mr. Castle's $72,000 check includes a debit to the Checking account and a credit to Account 3100 Owner's Contributions.

The following tables summarize information about debits and credits and their effects on account balances.

Account	Account Type[a]	Debit/ Credit	Effect on Balance[b]
Checking	Asset	Debit	Increase
Owner's Contributions	Equity	Credit	Increase

[a]Listed below are the five different types of accounts.

[b]Listed below are the effects that debits and credits have on the different types of accounts.

Account Type[a]	Debit/Credit	Effect on Balance[b]
Asset	Debit	Increase
Liability	Credit	Increase
Owner's Equity	Credit	Increase
Revenues (Income)	Credit	Increase
Expenses	Debit	Increase

Step 7: Notice the entry on 12/15/2007 to record the check written to Kershaw Computers for computer repair services. This entry debits (increases) the Computer Repair Expense balance and credits (decreases) the Checking account balance.

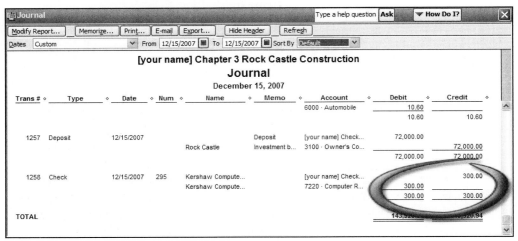

Step 8: Double-click on a journal entry, to *drill down* to the related source document. If you double-click on the journal entry that records the computer repair, the *Write Checks* window appears, displaying the onscreen check that you just prepared. **Close** the *Write Checks* window.

Step 9: 🖨 **Print** the Journal report.

Step 10: ✎ **Circle** the journal entry on your printout that corresponds to the check written to Kershaw Computer Services.

Step 11: Close the *Journal* window and the *Report Center* window.

RECONCILE BANK STATEMENTS

Typically once a month, the bank sends a checking account bank statement to you. The bank statement lists each deposit check, and withdrawal from the account during the month.

A bank reconciliation is the process of comparing, or reconciling, the bank statement with your accounting records for the Checking account. The bank reconciliation has two objectives: (1) to detect errors and (2) to update your accounting records for unrecorded items listed on the bank statement (such as service charges).

Differences between the balance the bank reports on the bank statement and the balance the company shows in its accounting records usually arise for two reasons:

1. **Errors** (either the bank's errors or the company's errors).

2. **Timing differences.** This occurs when the company records an amount before the bank does or the bank records an amount before the company does. For example, the company may record a deposit in its accounting records, but the bank does not record the deposit before the company's bank statement is prepared and mailed.

    Timing differences include:

    Items the bank has not recorded yet, such as:

    ▪ **Deposits in transit:** deposits the company has recorded but the bank has not.

    ▪ **Outstanding checks:** checks the company has written and recorded but the bank has not recorded yet.

    Items the company has not recorded yet, such as:

    ▪ **Unrecorded charges:** charges that the bank has recorded on the bank statement but the company has not recorded in its accounting records yet. Unrecorded charges include service charges, loan payments, automatic withdrawals, and ATM withdrawals.

    ▪ **Interest earned on the account:** interest the bank has recorded as earned but the company has not recorded yet.

The following bank statement lists the deposits and checks for Rock Castle Construction according to the bank's records as of November 20, 2007.

BANK STATEMENT

Rock Castle Construction Company		11-20-07
1735 County Road		Checking
Bayshore, CA 94326		

Previous Balance	10-20-07	$219,914.70
+ Deposits	1	5,000.00
- Checks	5	5,661.15
- Service Charge		10.00
+ Interest Paid		0.00
Ending Balance	11-20-07	$219,243.55

Deposits

Date	Amount
11-05-07	5,000.00

Checks Paid

Date	No.	Amount
11-14-07	242	3,200.00
11-14-07	243	850.00
11-15-07	245	675.00
11-15-07	246	711.15
11-19-07	249	225.00

Thank you for banking with us!

To reconcile this bank statement with Rock Castle's QuickBooks records, complete the following steps:

Step 1: From the Banking section of the Home page, click the **Reconcile** icon to display the *Begin Reconciliation* window shown below.

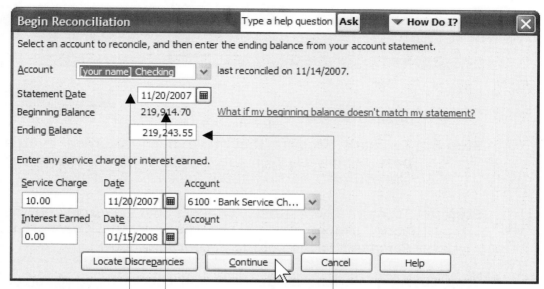

Step 2: Select Account to Reconcile: **[your name] Checking**.

Step 3: Enter date shown on the bank statement: **11/20/2007**.

Step 4: Compare the amount shown in the *Beginning Balance* field with the beginning (previous) balance of **$219.914.70** on the bank statement.

Step 5: In the *Ending Balance* field, enter the ending balance shown on the bank statement: **$219,243.55**.

Step 6: In *Service Charge* field, enter the bank's service charge: **$10.00**. Then change the date to **11/20/07** and select the Account: **Bank Service Charges**.

Step 7: Click **Continue**.

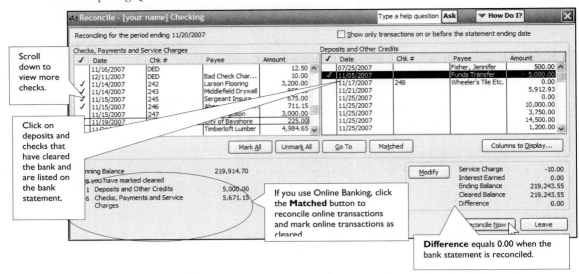

Step 8: To mark deposits that have been recorded by the bank, simply click on the deposit in the *Deposits and Other Credits* section of the *Reconcile* window.

Step 9: To mark checks and payments that have cleared the bank, simply click on the check in the *Checks and Payments* section of the *Reconcile* window.

Step 10: After marking all deposits and checks that appear on the bank statement, compare the Ending Balance and the Cleared Balance at the bottom of the *Reconcile* window.

> ✓ **The Difference amount in the lower right corner of the Reconcile window should equal $0.00.**

After you click **Reconcile Now**, you can view the Bank Reconciliation by selecting **Report** menu, **Banking**, **Previous Reconciliation**.
If you need to make changes to the bank reconciliation:
1. To return to the reconciliation screen to make changes, from the *Begin Reconciliation* window, click **Locate Discrepancies | Undo Last Reconciliation**, or
2. Another way to change the status of a cleared item: Display the Checking Register, then click the Cleared Status column until the appropriate status (cleared or uncleared) appears.

If the difference is $0.00, click **Reconcile Now**. (NOTE: If you are not finished and plan to return to this bank reconciliation later, click **Leave.**)

If there is a difference between the Ending balance and the Cleared balance, then try to locate the error or have QuickBooks make a balance adjustment.

Step 11: 🖳 When the *Select Reconciliation Report* window appears, select type of Reconciliation Report: **Both**. Click **Print**.

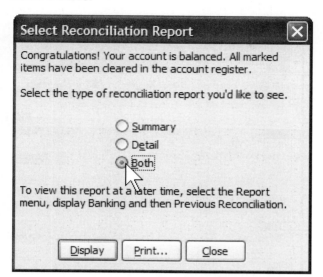

You have now completed the November bank reconciliation for Rock Castle Construction.

If you have access to online banking services, see Appendix B: QuickBooks Online Features.

↗ ONLINE BANKING

QuickBooks offers an Online Banking feature so that you can conduct banking transactions online using the Internet. To use Online Banking with QuickBooks, see Appendix B: QuickBooks Online Features.

SAVE CHAPTER 3

Save Chapter 3 as a portable QuickBooks file to the location specified by your instructor.

Step 1: If necessary, insert a removable disk.

Step 2: From the menu bar, click **File | Portable Company File | Create File**.

Step 3: When the *Close and Reopen* window appears, click **OK**.

Step 4: When the following *Create Portable Company File* window appears, enter the filename: **[your name] Chapter 3** and the appropriate location. Then click **Save**.

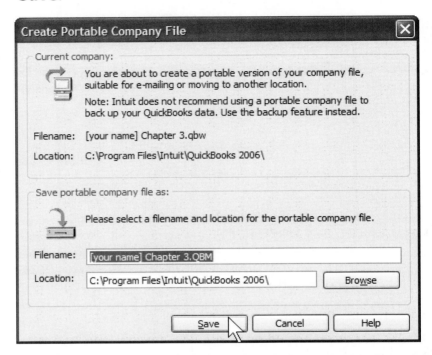

Step 5: Click **OK** after the portable file has been created successfully.

Step 6: Close the company file by clicking **File** (Menu), **Close Company**.

NOTE: In this text, you will save a portable company file with a .QBM extension at the end of each chapter, exercise, or project.

If you are continuing your computer session, proceed to Exercise 3.1.

If you are ending your computer session now, see the Quick Reference Guide in Part 3 for instructions to (1) close the company file and (2) exit QuickBooks.

ASSIGNMENTS

> **NOTE: See the Quick Reference Guide in Part 3 for step-by-step instructions to frequently used tasks.**

EXERCISE 3.1: MAKE DEPOSIT, VOID CHECK, AND WRITE CHECK

SCENARIO

As you glance up from your work, you notice Mr. Castle charging past your cubicle with more documents in hand. He tosses a hefty stack of papers into your creaking inbox. *"Here is another deposit to record. Also, Washuta called to say they did not receive the check we sent them. You will need to void that check—I believe it was check no. 263. I have already called the bank and stopped payment. Also, here are more bills to pay."*

TASK 1: OPEN PORTABLE COMPANY FILE

To open the portable company file (.QBM) file, convert the portable file to a regular company file with a .QBW extension as follows:

Step 1: From the menu bar, click **File | Portable Company File | Open File**.

Step 2: Identify the filename and location for the portable company file:

- Click the **Browse** button to find the location of the portable company file on the hard drive or removable media. In the example below, the portable file was saved to the hard drive. If you saved the portable company file to removable media such as USB, floppy disk, or CD, you would specify the location of the removable media.

- Select the file: **[your name] Chapter 3**. The .QBM may appear automatically based upon your Windows settings.

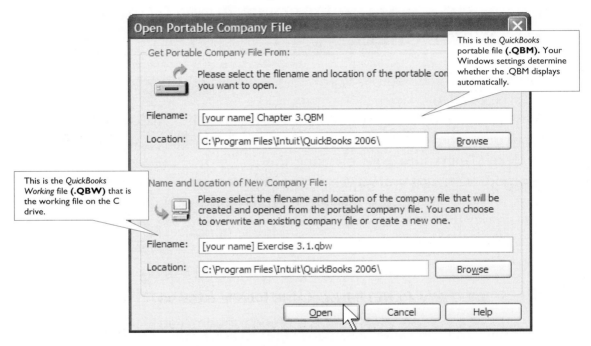

This is the *QuickBooks* portable file **(.QBM).** Your Windows settings determine whether the .QBM displays automatically.

This is the *QuickBooks Working* file **(.QBW)** that is the working file on the C drive.

Step 3: Identify the name and location of the new company file (.QBW) file to use for completing Exercise 3.1:

- Filename: **[your name] Exercise 3.1**. The **.QBW** extension should appear automatically based upon your Windows settings. The .QBW identifies this as a QuickBooks working file.

- Location: **C:\Program Files\Intuit\QuickBooks 2006**. This is the location of the .QBW file on the hard drive of your computer. You can click the Browse button to specify another location.

Step 4: Click **Open** to open the portable company file.

Step 5: Click **Cancel** when the *Create a Backup* window appears.

Step 6: If prompted, enter your **User Name** and **Password**, then click **OK**.

Step 7: Click **OK** when the QuickBooks sample company message appears.

Step 8: Change the company name to: **[your name] Exercise 3.1 Rock Castle Construction**. (If you need instructions to change the company name, see Part 3: Quick Reference Guide.)

TASK 2: MAKE DEPOSIT

Step 1: Record the deposit for Mr. Castle's $1,000 check (No. 556). Record the deposit in Account 3100 Owner's Contributions with a deposit date of 12/15/2007.

Step 2: 🖨 **Print** the deposit summary.

TASK 3: FIND CHECK

Find Check No. 263 made out to Washuta & Son in the QuickBooks Check Register by completing the following steps.

Step 1: View the Check Register. (Click **Check Register** icon in the Banking section of the Home page.)

Step 2: Next, search the Check Register for Check No. 263 using the Go To feature. Click the **Go To** button in the upper left corner of the *Check Register* window.

Step 3: In the *Go To* window:

- Select Which Field: **Number/Ref**.
- Enter Search For: **263**.

Step 4: Click the **Next** button. If asked if you want to search from the beginning, click **Yes**.

Step 5: Check No. 263 on 11/28/2007 to Washuta & Son Painting should appear in the *Check Register* window.

Step 6: **Close** the *Go To* window.

Step 7: To view Check No. 263, double-click on the Check Register entry for Washuta & Son Painting to drill down to the check. After viewing the check, **close** the *Check* window.

TASK 4: VOID CHECK

The next task is to void Check No. 263. There are two ways to remove a check amount from the check register:

1. Delete the check: This removes all record of the transaction.

2. Void the check: QuickBooks changes the amount deducted in the check register to zero, but the voided check still appears in the check register, thus leaving a record of the transaction. Should questions arise later about the transaction, a voided check provides a better record then a deleted check.

For Check No. 263, you want to maintain a record of the transaction; therefore, you want to void the check rather than delete it.

Void Check No. 263 by completing the following steps:

Step 1: Select Check No. 263 in the check register, then click **Edit *on the menu bar***. (**Note:** There is an Edit Transaction button in the *Checking* window and an Edit button on the menu bar. Use the *Edit button on the menu bar*.)

Step 2: Select **Void Bill Pmt - Check**. VOID should now appear next to Check No. 263 in the Check Register.

Step 3: Click the **Record** button in the lower right corner of the *Check Register* window.

Step 4: When asked if you are sure you want to record the voided check, click **Yes**.

Step 5: 🖨 **Print** the Check Register for 11/28/2007. Verify that Check No. 263 has been voided and shows a check amount of $0.00.

Step 6: **Close** the *Check Register* window.

TASK 5: WRITE CHECK

Step 1: Enter checks to pay the following bills and save.

Check No.	Select: To be printed
Date	12/15/2007
Vendor	Express Delivery Service
Amount	$45.00
Expense Account	6400 Freight & Delivery

Check No.	Select: To be printed
Date	12/15/2007
Vendor	Davis Business Associates
Amount	$200.00
Expense Account	6041 Advertising Expense

Step 2: 🖨 **Print** checks in a batch as follows:

- Click the down arrow by the **Print** button in the *Write Checks* window. Select **Print Batch**.

- When the *Select Checks to Print* window appears, **select only the above two checks that you entered**. Note that there are other checks that Rock Castle has not printed. Your total for checks to print should be $245.00

- First Check Number is **302**.

- Click **OK**.

- Select **Standard** check style.

- Select **Print company name and address**.
- Click **Print.**

TASK 6: SAVE EXERCISE 3.1

Save Exercise 3.1 as a portable QuickBooks file to the location specified by your instructor.

Step 1: If necessary, insert a removable disk.

Step 2: From the menu bar, click **File | Portable Company File | Create File**.

Step 3: When the *Close and Reopen* window appears, click **OK**.

Step 4: When the *Create Portable Company File* window appears, enter the filename: **[your name] Exercise 3.1** and the appropriate location. Then click **Save**.

Step 5: Click **OK** after the portable file has been created successfully.

Step 6: Close the company file by clicking **File** (Menu), **Close Company**.

EXERCISE 3.2: BANK RECONCILIATION

When you arrive at work the next morning, Rock Castle Construction's December bank statement is on your desk with the following note from Mr. Castle attached.

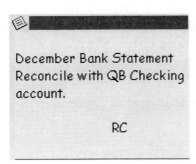

December Bank Statement
Reconcile with QB Checking account.

RC

TASK 1: OPEN PORTABLE COMPANY FILE

To open the portable company file (.QBM) file, convert the portable file to a regular company file with a .QBW extension as follows:

Step 1: From the menu bar, click **File | Portable Company File | Open File**.

Step 2: Identify the filename and location for the portable company file:

- Click the **Browse** button to find the location of the portable company file on the hard drive or removable media.

- Select the file: **[your name] Exercise 3.1**. The .QBM may appear automatically based upon your Windows settings.

Step 3: Identify the name and location of the new company file (.QBW) file to use for completing Exercise 3.2:

- Filename: **[your name] Exercise 3.2**. The **.QBW** extension should appear automatically based upon your Windows settings. The .QBW identifies this as a QuickBooks working file.

- Location: **C:\Program Files\Intuit\QuickBooks 2006**. This is the location of the .QBW file on the hard drive of your computer.

Step 4: Click **Open** to open the portable company file.

Step 5: Click **Cancel** when the *Create a Backup* window appears.

Step 6: If prompted, enter your **User Name** and **Password**, then click **OK**.

Step 7: Click **OK** when the QuickBooks sample company message appears.

Step 8: Change the company name to: **[your name] Exercise 3.2 Rock Castle Construction**. (If you need instructions to change the company name, see Part 3: Quick Reference Guide.)

TASK 2: PRINT PREVIOUS BANK STATEMENT

🖶 **Print** the previous bank reconciliation as follows:

Step 1: Click the **Report Center** icon on the Navigation Bar to open the *Report Center* window.

Step 2: Click **Banking.**

Step 3: Click **Previous Reconciliation.**

Step 4: Select Type of Report: **Both**.

Step 5: Select: **Transactions cleared plus any changes made to those transactions since the reconciliation**.

Step 6: Click **Display**.

Step 7: 🖶 **Print** the Reconciliation Summary report.

Step 8: 🖶 **Print** the Reconciliation Detail report.

TASK 3: RECONCILE BANK STATEMENT

Reconcile Rock Castle's December bank statement that appears on the following page.

NOTE: Remember to change the Service Charge Date to **12/20/2007**.

> **WARNING!** If the difference between the Ending Balance and the Cleared Balance is not zero, and you want to return to the bank reconciliation later, do NOT click *Reconcile Now*. Instead, click **Leave**.

✓ *In the Reconcile window (lower left corner) "Items you have marked cleared" should agree with the December bank statement:*

13 Deposits and Other Credits	**$76,302.87**
13 Checks, Payments, and Service Charges	**$20,496.66**
Ending Balance	**$275,049.76**
Cleared Balance	**$275,049.76**
Difference	**$ 0.00**

After you click **Reconcile Now**, you can return to this Bank Reconciliation by selecting **Report** menu, **Banking, Previous Reconciliation**.

Another way to change the status of a cleared item:
1. Display the Checking Register.
2. Click the Cleared Status column until the appropriate status (cleared or uncleared) appears.

TASK 4: PRINT BANK RECONCILIATION REPORT

🖨 **Print** a Summary Reconciliation report.

BANK STATEMENT		
Rock Castle Construction Company	12-20-07	Checking Account
Previous Balance	11-20-07	$219,243.55
+ Deposits	13	76,302.87
- Checks	12	20,486.66
- Service Charge	1	10.00
+ Interest Paid		0.00
Current Balance	12-20-07	$275,049.76

Deposits	
Date	**Amount**
11-21-07	5,912.93
11-25-07	10,000.00
11-25-07	3,750.00
11-25-07	14,500.00
11-25-07	1,200.00
11-25-07	4,264.78
11-25-07	4,225.41
11-29-07	446.25
11-30-07	4,135.50
12-02-07	1,668.00
12-03-07	1,200.00
12-05-07	25,000.00

Checks Paid		
Date	**No.**	**Amount**
11-15-07	247	3,000.00
11-21-07	250	4,984.65
11-25-07	251	37.85
11-25-07	252	97.53
11-25-07	253	72.18
11-28-07	257	300.00
11-28-07	258	500.00
11-28-07	259	600.00
11-28-07	260	800.00
11-28-07	261	6,790.00
11-28-07	262	2,000.00
11-30-07	264	1,304.45

Thank you for banking with us!

TASK 5: SAVE EXERCISE 3.2

Save Exercise 3.2 as a portable QuickBooks file to the location specified by your instructor.

Step 1: If necessary, insert a removable disk.

Step 2: From the menu bar, click **File | Portable Company File | Create File**.

Step 3: When the *Close and Reopen* window appears, click **OK**.

Step 4: When the *Create Portable Company File* window appears, enter the filename: **[your name] Exercise 3.2** and the appropriate location. Then click **Save**.

Step 5: Click **OK** after the portable file has been created successfully.

Step 6: Close the company file by clicking **File** (Menu), **Close Company**.

EXERCISE 3.3: WEB QUEST

Various preprinted check forms and deposit slips are available from Intuit. These preprinted forms can be used with your printer to create checks and deposit slips.

> **THE WEB INFORMATION LISTED IS SUBJECT TO CHANGE.**

Step 1: Go to www.quickbooks.com.

Step 2: ▣ Locate and **print** information about preprinted checks and deposits slips.

Step 3: ▤ Using word processing software or email software, prepare and ▣ **print** a short e-mail to Mr. Castle recommending which check forms and deposit slips Rock Castle Construction should purchase for use with QuickBooks.

CHAPTER 3 PRINTOUT CHECKLIST
NAME:_____DATE:_____

INSTRUCTIONS:
1. *CHECK OFF THE PRINTOUTS YOU HAVE COMPLETED.*
2. *STAPLE THIS PAGE TO YOUR PRINTOUTS.*

☑ *PRINTOUT CHECKLIST – CHAPTER 3*
☐ Check Register
☐ Deposit Summary
☐ Check
☐ Journal
☐ Bank Reconciliation Report

☑ *PRINTOUT CHECKLIST – EXERCISE 3.1*
☐ Task 2: Deposit Summary
☐ Task 4: Check Register
☐ Task 5: Checks

☑ *PRINTOUT CHECKLIST – EXERCISE 3.2*
☐ Task 2: Previous Bank Statement Report
☐ Task 4: Bank Reconciliation Report

☑ *PRINTOUT CHECKLIST – EXERCISE 3.3*
☐ QuickBooks Preprinted Forms Printouts

CHAPTER 4
CUSTOMERS AND SALES

SCENARIO

Just as you are finishing the last bank reconciliation, Mr. Castle reappears. He always seems to know just when you are about to finish a task.

"While cash flow is crucial to our survival," he says, *"we also need to keep an eye on profits. We are in the business of selling products and services to our customers. We have to be certain that we charge customers enough to cover our costs and make a profit."*

Mr. Castle pulls out a pen and begins scribbling on a sheet of paper on your desk:

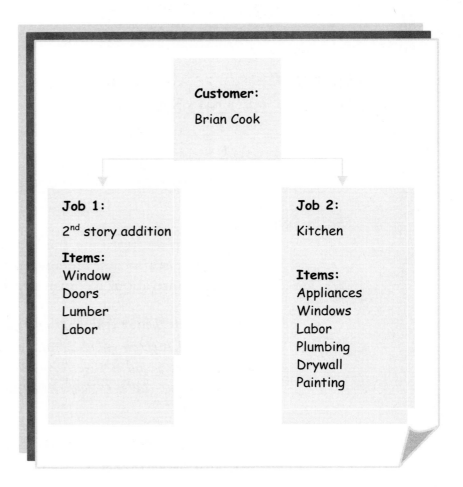

"We track the costs of each job we work on. A job is a project for a specific customer. For example, we are working on two jobs for Brian Cook: Job 1 is a 2nd story addition and Job 2 is remodeling his kitchen.

"In QuickBooks we use items to track the products and services we use on each project. On the 2nd story addition job we used four different items."

Pushing a stack of papers toward you, Mr. Castle says, "Here are some customer transactions that need to be recorded in QuickBooks."

CHAPTER 4
LEARNING OBJECTIVES

In Chapter 4, you will learn the following QuickBooks features:

INTRODUCTION

In Chapter 4, you will learn how to use QuickBooks software to record customer transactions, including sales to customers and collection of customer payments. Furthermore, you will learn about financial reports that will help you manage your sales.

To begin Chapter 4, first start QuickBooks software and then open the portable QuickBooks file.

Step 1: Start QuickBooks by clicking on the **QuickBooks** desktop icon or click **Start**, **Programs**, **QuickBooks**, **QuickBooks Pro 2006**.

Step 2: To open the portable company file (.QBM) file and convert the portable file to a regular company file with a .QBW extension, from the menu bar, click **File | Portable Company File | Open File**.

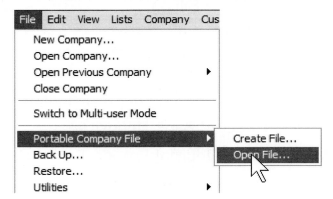

Step 3: Identify the filename and location for the portable company file:

- Click the **Browse** button to find the location of the portable company file on the hard drive or removable media. In the example below, the portable file was saved to the hard drive. If you saved the portable company file to removable media such as USB, floppy disk, or CD, you would specify the location of the removable media.

- Select the file: **[your name] Exercise 3.2**. The .QBM may appear automatically based upon your Windows settings, but if it does not appear automatically, do **not** type it.

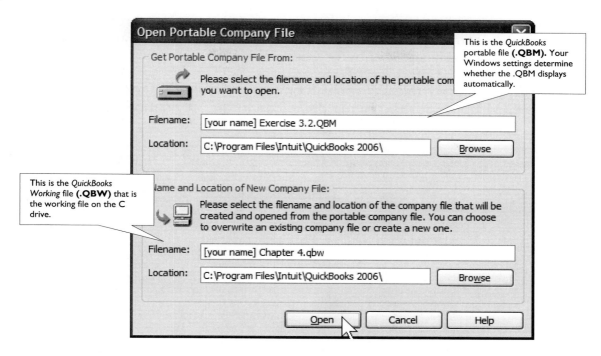

Step 4: Identify the name and location of the new company file (.QBW) file to use for Chapter 4:

- Filename: **[your name] Chapter 4**. The **.QBW** extension should appear automatically based upon your Windows settings. The .QBW identifies this as a QuickBooks working file.

- Location: **C:\Program Files\Intuit\QuickBooks 2006**. This is the location of the .QBW file on the hard drive of your computer.

Step 5: Click **Open** to open the portable company file.

Step 6: Click **Cancel** when the *Create a Backup* window appears.

Step 7: If prompted, enter your **User ID** and **Password**.

Step 8: Click **OK** when the sample company window appears.

Step 9: Change the company name to: **[your name] Chapter 4 Rock Castle Construction**. If necessary, change the Checking account title to include your name.

To change the company name, click **Company** (menu), **Company Information**.

The portable company file (.QBM) should now be converted to a regular company file (Chapter 4.QBW) that can be used to complete the assignments for Chapter 4.

After opening the portable company file for Rock Castle Construction, click the Home page icon in the Navigation Bar.

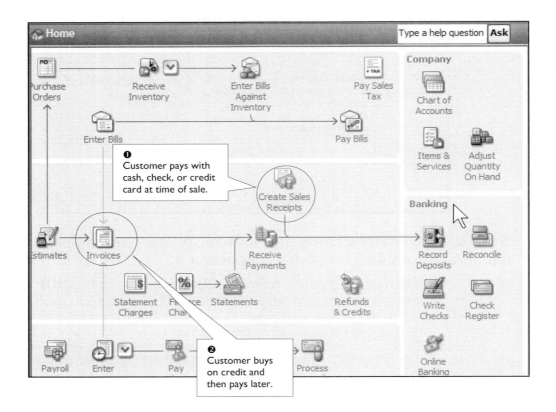

The Customer section of the Home page is a flowchart of customer transactions. As the flowchart indicates, Rock Castle Construction can record a customer sale in two different ways:

❶ Sales Receipts: Customer pays when Rock Castle Construction provides the good or service to the customer. The customer pays with cash, check, or credit card at the time of sale. The sale is recorded on a Sales Receipt.

❷ Invoice/Receive Payment: The sale is recorded on an Invoice when the good or service is provided to the customer. The customer promises to pay later. These customer promises are called accounts *receivable* — amounts that Rock Castle Construction expects to *receive* in the future. The customer may pay its account with cash, check, credit card or online payment.

Other QuickBooks features available from the Customer section include:

- **Finance Charges**: Add finance charges to customer bills whenever bills are not paid by the due date.

- **Refunds and Credits**: Record refunds and credits for returned or damaged merchandise.

- **Statements**: Prepare billing statements to send to customers.

The first step in working with customer transactions is to enter customer information in the Customer List.

CUSTOMER LIST

The Customer List contains customer information such as address, telephone number, and credit terms. Once customer information is entered in the Customer List, QuickBooks automatically transfers the customer information to the appropriate forms, such as Sales Invoices and Sales Returns. This feature enables you to enter customer information only once instead of entering the customer information each time a form is prepared.

The Customer List in QuickBooks also tracks projects (jobs) for each customer. For example, Rock Castle Construction is working on two projects for Brian Cook:

Job 1: 2nd Story Addition

Job 2: Kitchen

VIEW CUSTOMER LIST

To view the Customer List for Rock Castle Construction:

Step 1: Click the **Customer Center** icon in the Navigation Bar.

Step 2: The following *Customer Center and Customer List* appears, listing customers and jobs. Notice the two jobs listed for Brian Cook: (1) 2nd story addition and (2) Kitchen.

The Customer & Jobs List displays:

- The customer name
- The job name
- The balance for each job

To view additional information about a customer, click the customer or job name. The Customer/Job Information section displays:

- Customer address and contact information.
- Transaction information for the customer.
- Estimate information (if an estimate for the job was prepared).
- Notes about the job.

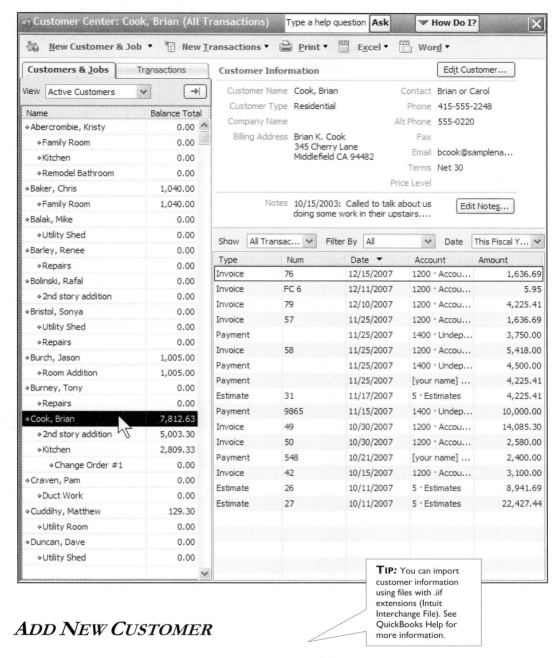

TIP: You can import customer information using files with .iif extensions (Intuit Interchange File). See QuickBooks Help for more information.

ADD NEW CUSTOMER

Rock Castle Construction needs to add a new customer, Tom Whalen, to the Customer List.

To add a new customer to the Customer List:

Step 1: Click the **New Customer & Job** button at the top of the Customer Center.

Step 2: Click **New Customer** on the drop-down menu.

Step 3: A blank *New Customer* window should appear. Enter the information shown below in the *New Customer | Address Info* window.

Customer	Whalen, Tom
First Name	Tom
M.I.	M
Last Name	Whalen
Contact	Tom
Phone	415-555-1234
Alt. Ph.	415-555-5678
Addresses Bill To:	Tom M Whalen 100 Sunset Drive Bayshore, CA 94326

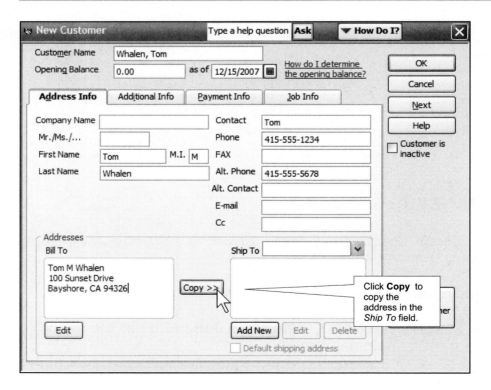

Step 4: Click the **Additional Info** tab to display another customer information window. Enter the information shown below into the *Additional Info* fields.

Type	Residential
Terms	Net 30
Tax Item	San Tomas
Tax Code	Tax

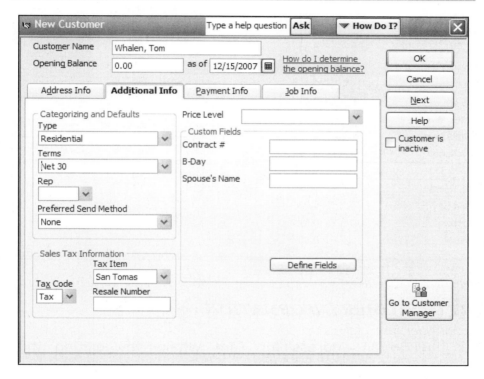

Step 5: To enter payment information for the customer, click the **Payment Info** tab.

Step 6: Enter the following information in the *Payment Info* fields:

Account	7890
Credit Limit	50,000
Preferred Payment	Check

Step 7: Click **OK** to add the new customer to Rock Castle Construction's Customer List.

Step 8: Click the **Name bar** to alphabetize the customer list.

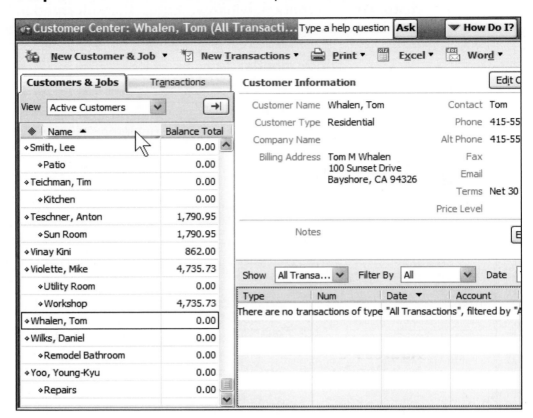

EDIT CUSTOMER INFORMATION

Enter the E-mail address for Tom Whalen by editing the customer information as follows:

Step 1: Select **Tom Whalen** in the Customer List.

Step 2: Click the **Edit Customer...** button in the Customer Information window.

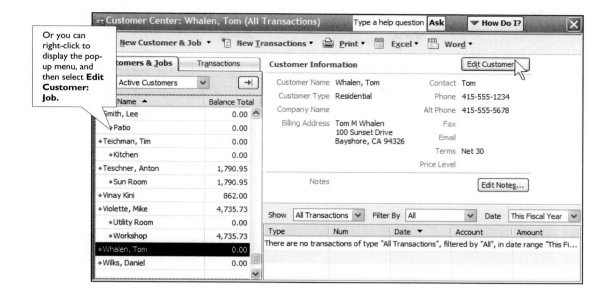

Or you can right-click to display the pop-up menu, and then select **Edit Customer: Job.**

Step 3: When the *Edit Customer* window appears, enter the new information or revise the current customer or job information as needed. In this instance, click the **Address Info** tab. Then enter the E-mail address: **twhalen@www.com**.

Step 4: Click **OK** to record the new information and close the *Edit Customer* window.

ADD A JOB

To add the Screen Porch Job for Tom Whalen, complete the following steps:

Step 1: Click on the customer, **Tom Whalen**, in the *Customer & Jobs* window.

Step 2: Click the **New Customer & Job** button at the top of the Customer Center window. Select **Add Job** from the drop-down menu.

Or right-click to display the pop-up menu, and then select **Add Job.**

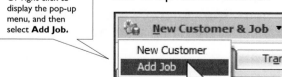

Step 3: In the *New Job* window, enter the Job Name: **Screen Porch**. Then enter the Beginning Balance: **0.00**.

Step 4: Click the **Job Info** tab.

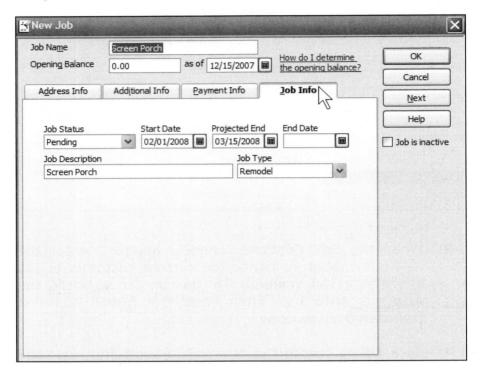

Step 5: Enter the following information in the *Job Info* fields:

Job Status	Pending
Start Date	02/01/2008
Projected End	03/15/2008
Job Description	Screen Porch
Job Type	Remodel

Tom Whalen tells Rock Castle Construction that he will hire them to do the screen porch job on one condition—he needs Rock Castle Construction as soon as possible to replace a damaged exterior door that will not close. Rock Castle sends a workman out to begin work on replacing the door right away.

To add the Exterior Door job:

Step 1: From the Screen Porch job window, click **Next** to add another job.

Step 2: In the Job Name field at the top of the *New Job* window, enter: **Exterior Door**. Enter Opening Balance: **0.00**.

Step 3: Click the **Job Info** tab, then enter the following information.

Job Status	Awarded
Start Date	12/15/2007
Projected End	12/18/2007
Job Description	Replace Exterior Door
Job Type	Repairs

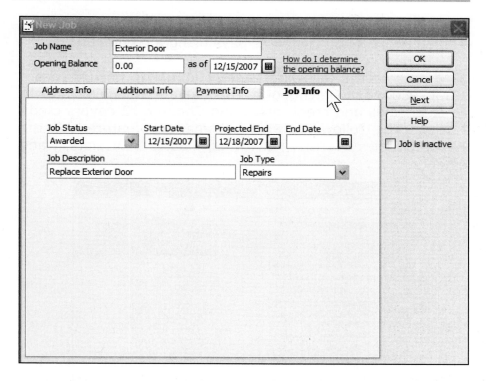

Step 4: Click **OK** to record the new job and close the *New Job* window.

Step 5: As shown below, Rock Castle Construction's Customer List should now list two jobs for Tom Whalen: Exterior Door and Screen Porch. **Close** the *Customer Center* window.

⬦Whalen, Tom	0.00
⬦Exterior Door	0.00
⬦Screen Porch	0.00

RECORDING SALES IN QUICKBOOKS

How you record a sale in QuickBooks depends upon how the customer pays for the goods or services. There are three possible ways for a customer to pay for goods and services:

- Cash sale: Customer pays cash (or check) at the time of sale.

- Credit sale: Customer promises to pay later.

- Credit card sale: Customer pays using a credit card.

The diagrams on the following pages summarize how to record sales transactions in QuickBooks. This chapter will cover how to record cash sales and credit sales and Chapter 12 covers credit card sales. The following table summarizes features of the QuickBooks sales forms: Invoices, Sales Receipts, and Statements.

Choosing the Right Sales Form

This list shows the form(s) you should use for each business task.

In my business, I...	Invoice Learn More Display Form	Sales Receipt Learn More Display Form	Statement Learn More Display Form
Track how much my customers owe me	√		√
Receive payments in advance	√		√
Track sales tax that I owe	√	√	
Apply discounts or markups to item prices	√	√	
Write detailed, multiple-line descriptions of services/products	√	√	
Prepare estimates, then bill online	√		
Track what I sell	√	√	
Collect payment in full at time of service or sale of product		√	
Create a summary of sales income and sales tax owed		√	
Accumulate charges before requesting payment			√
Show customers a history of their account activity			√
Assess finance charges	√		√
E-mail my sales form to customers	√		√
Get paid online	√		√

CASH SALES

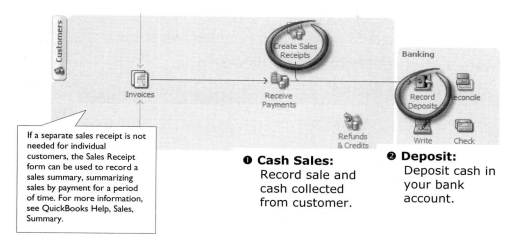

If a separate sales receipt is not needed for individual customers, the Sales Receipt form can be used to record a sales summary, summarizing sales by payment for a period of time. For more information, see QuickBooks Help, Sales, Summary.

❶ **Cash Sales:** Record sale and cash collected from customer.

❷ **Deposit:** Deposit cash in your bank account.

CREDIT SALES

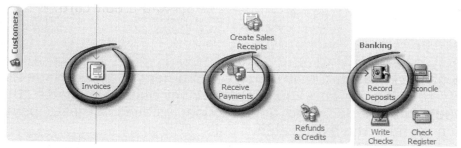

❶ **Invoices:** Prepare sale and cash collected from customer.

❷ **Receive Payments:** Record payments received from customers (undeposited funds).

❸ **Deposit:** Record deposit in bank

CASH SALES

When a customer pays for goods or services at the time the good or service is provided, it is typically called a cash sale.

Recording a cash sale in QuickBooks requires two steps:

> Use Sales Receipts if you create a daily or weekly summary of sales income and sales tax owed, instead of on a "per sale" basis.

❶ Create a sales receipt to record the cash sale.

❷ Record the bank deposit.

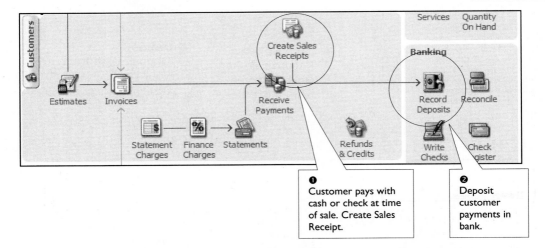

❶ Customer pays with cash or check at time of sale. Create Sales Receipt.

❷ Deposit customer payments in bank.

One of Rock Castle Construction's customers, Ernesto Natiello, wants to purchase an extra set of cabinet pulls that match the cabinets that Rock Castle Construction installed. Ernesto pays $10 in cash for the extra cabinet pulls.

To record the cash sale in QuickBooks:

Step 1: From the Customer section of the Home page, click **Create Sales Receipts** to display the *Enter Sales Receipts* window.

Step 2: Enter the following information in the *Enter Sales Receipts* window:

- Enter Customer name: **Natiello, Ernesto**.
- Select Date: **12/15/2007**.

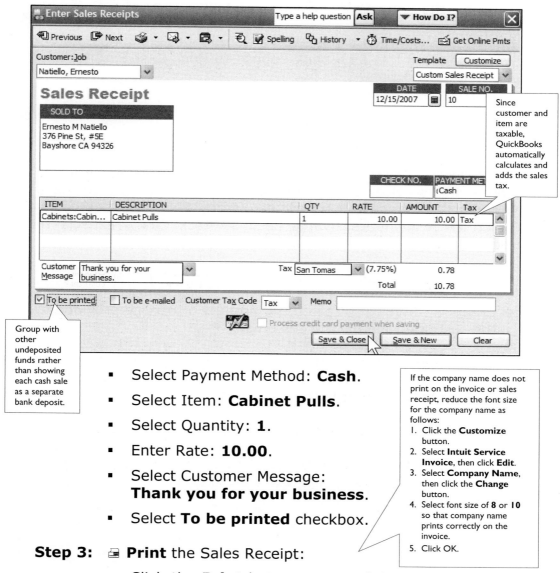

- Select Payment Method: **Cash**.
- Select Item: **Cabinet Pulls**.
- Select Quantity: **1**.
- Enter Rate: **10.00**.
- Select Customer Message: **Thank you for your business**.
- Select **To be printed** checkbox.

Step 3: 🖨 **Print** the Sales Receipt:

- Click the **Print** button at top of the *Sales Receipts* window.
- Select Print on: **Blank paper**.

If the company name does not print on the invoice or sales receipt, reduce the font size for the company name as follows:
1. Click the **Customize** button.
2. Select **Intuit Service Invoice**, then click **Edit**.
3. Select **Company Name**, then click the **Change** button.
4. Select font size of **8** or **10** so that company name prints correctly on the invoice.
5. Click OK.

- If necessary, uncheck: **Do not print lines around each field**.
- Click **Print**.

Step 4: Click **Save & Close** to record the cash sale and close the *Enter Sales Receipts* window.

QuickBooks will record the $10.78 as undeposited funds. Later, you will record this as a bank deposit to Rock Castle's Checking Account.

CREDIT SALES

Credit sales occur when Rock Castle Construction provides goods and services to customers and in exchange receives a promise that the customers will pay later. This promise to pay is called an Account Receivable because Rock Castle expects to *receive* the account balance in the future.

Recording a credit sale in QuickBooks requires three steps:

❶ Create an Invoice to record the product or service provided to the customer and bill the customer.

❷ Receive payment from the customer.

❸ Deposit the payment in the bank.

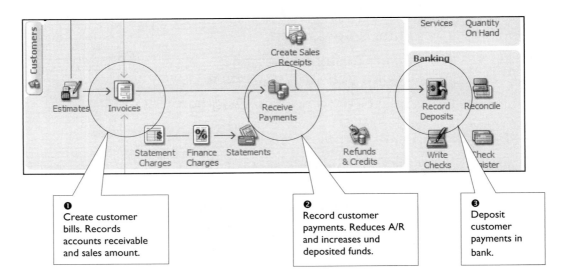

❶ Create customer bills. Records accounts receivable and sales amount.

❷ Record customer payments. Reduces A/R and increases und deposited funds.

❸ Deposit customer payments in bank.

CREDIT SALES: CREATE INVOICES

An Invoice is used to record sales on credit when the customer will pay later. An Invoice is a bill that contains detailed information about the items (products and services) provided to a customer.

For more information about time tracking, see Chapter 6.

A **Progress Invoice** is used if the customer is billed as the work progresses rather than when the work is fully completed.

If QuickBooks' time tracking feature (tracking time worked on each job) is *not* used, then time worked on a job is entered directly on the Invoice. In this chapter, assume that time tracking is not used and that time worked on a job is entered on the Invoice form.

Next, you will create an Invoice for Rock Castle Construction. Rock Castle sent a workman to the Whalen Residence immediately after receiving the phone call from Tom Whalen requesting an exterior door replacement as soon as possible. The workman spent one hour at the site the first day.

Click the **Estimates** icon on the Customers Navigator to create a customer estimate using QuickBooks.

In this instance, Rock Castle Construction was not asked to provide an estimate before starting the work. Charges for products and labor used on the Whalen door replacement job will be recorded on an Invoice.

To create an Invoice to record charges:

Step 1: In the Customers section of the Home page, click the **Invoices** icon to display the *Create Invoices* window.

Step 2: Select the invoice template: **Time & Expense Invoice**.

The Invoice templates can be customized.

Step 3: Enter the Customer:Job by selecting **Whalen, Tom: Exterior Door** from the drop-down Customer & Job list. Make certain that you select the customer name and the correct job: Exterior Door.

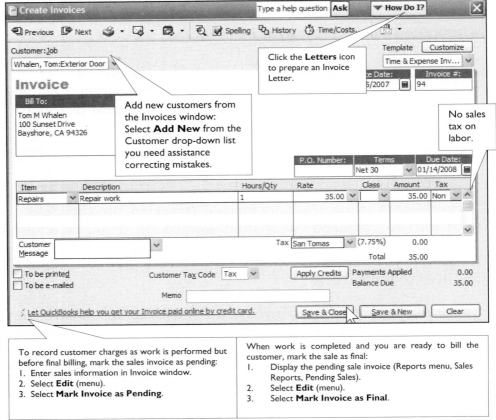

Step 4: Enter charges for the service provided the customer:

- Select Item: **Repairs.** Press **Tab.**

- Description should automatically display: Repair work.

> See **Correcting Errors** in the **Quick Reference Guide** if you would like assistance correcting mistakes.

- Enter Hours/Qty: **1** (hour).

- The Rate should automatically display $35.00.

- The Amount should automatically display $35.00.

- From the drop-down list, select Tax: **LBR Non-Taxable Labor**.

Step 5: You will wait until the job is complete to print the Invoice. In the meantime, you will mark the invoice as pending:

- **Right-click** to display the pop-up menu.

- Select: **Mark Invoice As Pending**.

Step 6: If you wanted to enter another Invoice, you would click Next. Instead, click **Save & Close** to close the *Invoice* window.

The next day, December 16, 2007, Rock Castle Construction finished installing a new exterior door at the Whalen residence. The following products and services were used:

Exterior wood door	1 @ $120	Taxable Sales
Repair Labor	4 hours	Non-Taxable Labor

Step 1: To display the invoice for the Exterior Door Repair job again:

- Click the **Invoices** icon.

- When the *Invoice* window appears, click **Edit** (menu) **Find Invoices**.

- Enter Invoice No.: **94**.

- Click **Find**.

Step 2: Record the exterior door and repair labor provided on December 16 on Invoice No. 94 for the Whalen Exterior Door job.

Step 3: Mark the invoice as final as follows:

- **Right-click** to display the pop-up menu.

- Select: **Mark Invoice as Final.**

Step 4: With Invoice No. 94 displayed, print the invoice as follows:

> To print envelopes for invoices and shipping labels, click the down arrow by the Print icon.

- Select the **Print** icon.

- Select Print on: **Blank paper**.

- If necessary, uncheck: **Do not print lines around each field**.

- ▣ Click **Print**.

Step 5: Click **Save & Close** to close the *Invoice* window. If asked if you want to record your changes, select **Yes**.

> ✓ *The invoice total is $304.30. Notice that the Exterior Door is a taxable item and QuickBooks automatically calculates and adds sales tax of $9.30 for the door.*

QuickBooks will record the sale and record an account receivable for the amount to be received from the customer in the future.

ONLINE BILLING

QuickBooks has the capability to E-mail invoices to customers. Customer E-mail numbers are filled in automatically from the Customer List information. You can E-mail single invoices or send a batch of invoices.

To email Invoice No. 94 which you just prepared:

Step 1: Open Invoice No. 94 on your screen. (Click the **Invoices** icon, then click **Previous** until the invoice appears or Click the **Find** button and enter Invoice No. **94**.)

Step 2: Click the **arrow** beside the **E-mail** icon at the top of the *Invoices* window.

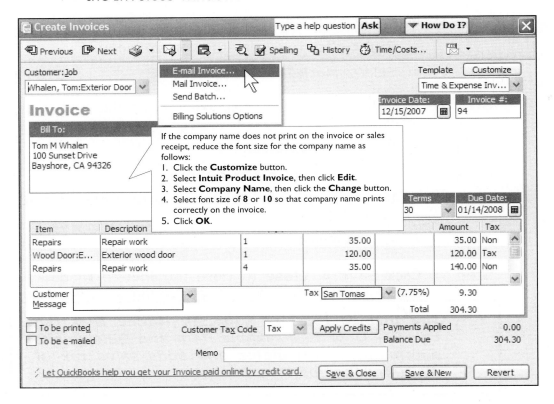

Step 3: Select **E-Mail Invoice**.

Step 4: When the following *Send Invoice* window appears, notice that both Rock Castle Construction's E-mail address and the customer's E-mail address are automatically completed from the E-mail information contained in the Customer List.

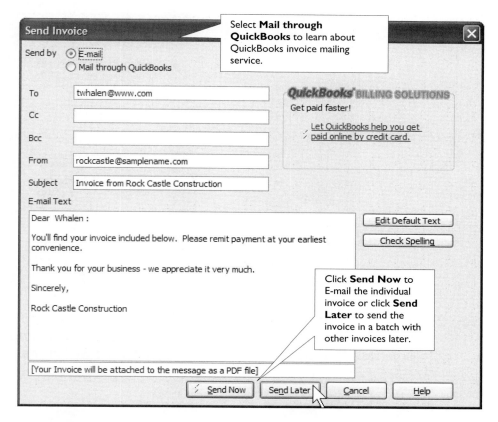

Step 5: Modify the E-mail text to read: **Dear Mr. Whalen:**.

Step 6: Click **Send Later** to send the E-mail later in a batch. Then click **Save & Close** to close the *Invoice* window.

After additional invoices are prepared, a batch of invoices can be sent at the same time using E-mail (Click Send Forms from the File menu.)

If your company signs up for Online Bill Paying services, after receiving your E-mail invoices, customers can pay you online.

To learn more about online billing and merchant services:

Step 1: In the Customize section on the right side of the Home page, click **Add Services to QuickBooks**.

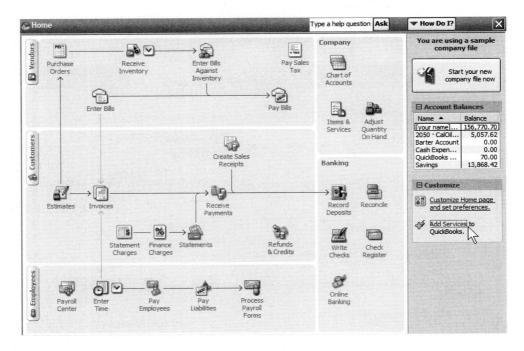

Step 2: When the *Pro and Premier Add-Ons 2006* window appears, if necessary scroll down to view the following Business Solutions section. Click **Merchant Services**.

Step 3: To learn more about merchant services through QuickBooks, click **View Tour**. **Close** the window to return to the Home page.

CREDIT SALES: CREATE REMINDER STATEMENTS

Reminder statements are sent to remind customers to pay their bill. A reminder statement summarizes invoice charges and provides an account history for the customer. It does not provide the detailed information that an invoice provides.

If a company wants to provide a customer with detailed information about charges, a copy of the invoice should be sent instead of a reminder statement.

Reminder statements summarize:

- The customer's previous account balance.
- Charges for sales during the period.
- Payments received from the customer.
- The customer's ending account balance.

To print a QuickBooks reminder statement for the Whalen Exterior Door job:

Step 1: Click the **Statements** icon in the Customer section of the Home page to display the *Create Statements* window.

Step 2: Select Template: **Intuit Standard Statement**.

Step 3: Select Statement Date: **12/16/2007**.

Step 4: Select Statement Period From : **11/17/2007** To: **12/16/2007**.

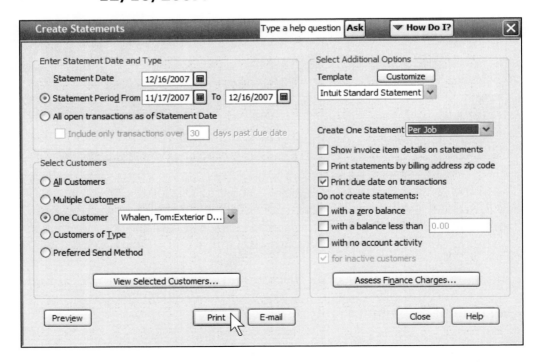

Step 5: In the *Select Customers* section, select **One Customer**. From the drop-down list, select: **Whalen, Tom: Exterior Door**.

Step 6: Select Print One Statement: **Per Job.**

Step 7: Check **Print due date on transactions**.

Step 8: ▣ Click **Print** to print the reminder statement, then click **Close**.

CREDIT SALES: RECORD CUSTOMER PAYMENTS

Recall that when recording credit sales in QuickBooks, you first create an Invoice and then record the customer's payment. When a credit sale is recorded on an Invoice, QuickBooks records (debits) an account receivable—an amount to be received from the customer in the future. When the customer's payment is received, the account receivable is reduced (credited).

Customers may pay in the following ways:

1. **Credit Card** using Visa, Master Card, American Express or Diners Club to pay over the phone, in-person, or by mail. Using QuickBooks' Merchant Account Service, you can obtain online authorization and then download payments directly into QuickBooks.

2. **Online** using a credit card or bank account transfer. (See previous section regarding Online Billing.)

3. **Customer Check** received either in person or by mail.

To record the customer's payment by check for the Exterior Door job, complete the following steps:

Step 1: Click the **Receive Payments** icon in the Customer section of the Home page to display the *Receive Payments* window.

Step 2: Select Date: **12/17/2007**.

Step 3: Select Received From: **Whalen, Tom: Exterior Door**.

Invoice No. 94 for $304.30 should appear as an outstanding invoice.

Step 4: Enter Amount: **$304.30**.

QuickBooks will automatically apply this payment to the outstanding invoice. A check mark should appear before the outstanding invoice of $304.30.

Step 5: Select: Pmt. Method: **Check**. Enter Check No. **1005**.

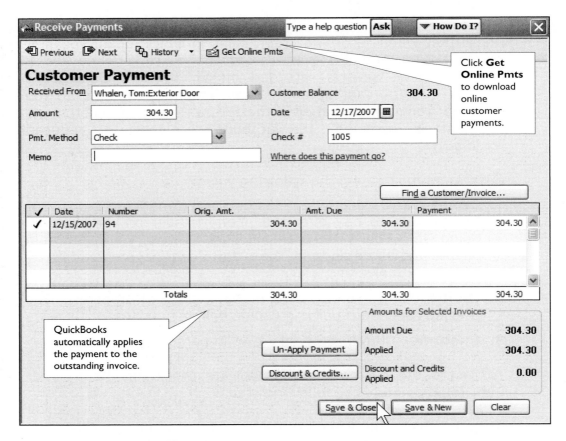

Step 6: Click **Save & Close** to record the payment and close the *Receive Payments* window.

QuickBooks will increase (debit) cash and decrease (credit) the customer's account receivable.

RECORD BANK DEPOSITS

After recording a customer's payment in the *Receive Payments* window, the next step is to indicate which payments to deposit in which bank accounts.

To select customer payments to deposit:

Step 1: Click the **Deposits** icon in the Banking section of the Home page to display the *Payments to Deposit* window. The *Payments to Deposit* window lists undeposited funds that have been received but not yet deposited in the bank.

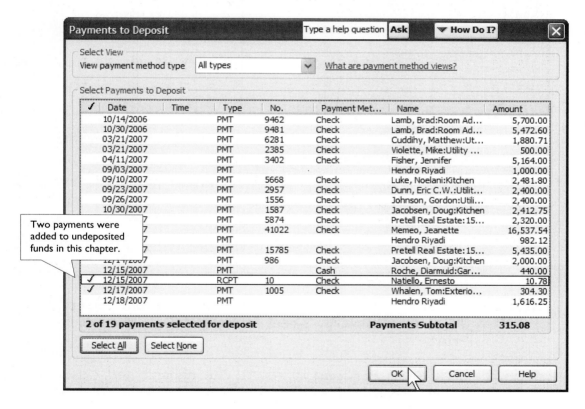

Step 2: **Select** the above two payments that were added to undeposited funds in this chapter.

- $10.78 cash receipt from Ernesto Natiello on 12/15/2007

- $304.30 cash payment from Tom Whalen on 12/17/2007

Step 3:   Click **OK** to display the following *Make Deposits* window.

Step 4:   Select Deposit To: **[your name] Checking**. Select Date: **12/17/2007**.

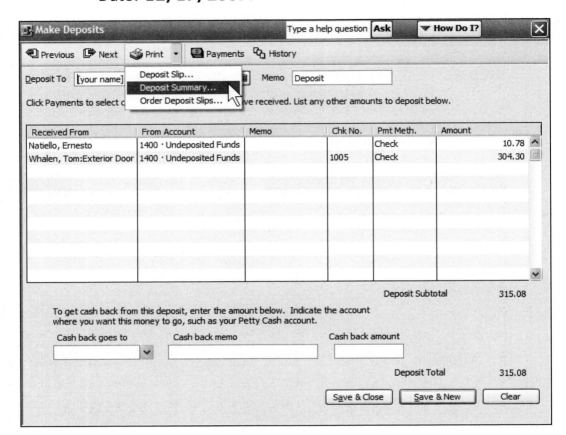

Step 5:   Click the arrow on the **Print** button. Select **Deposit summary**. Select printer settings, then click **Print**.

Step 6:   Click **Save & Close** to record the deposit and close the *Make Deposits* window.

> ✓ ***Deposit Total is $315.08.***

PRINT JOURNAL ENTRIES

As you entered transaction information into QuickBooks' onscreen forms, QuickBooks automatically converted the transaction information into journal entries.

To print the journal entries for the transactions you entered:

Step 1: Click **Report** Center icon in the Navigation Bar, to display the *Report Center* window.

Step 2: Select: **Accountant & Taxes.**

Step 3: Select: **Journal**.

Step 4: Select Dates From: **12/15/2007** To: **12/16/2007**.

Step 5: To filter for Invoice transactions only:

- Click the **Modify Report** button, then click the **Filters** tab.
- Select Filter: **Transaction Type**.
- Select Transaction Type: **Invoice**, then click **OK**.

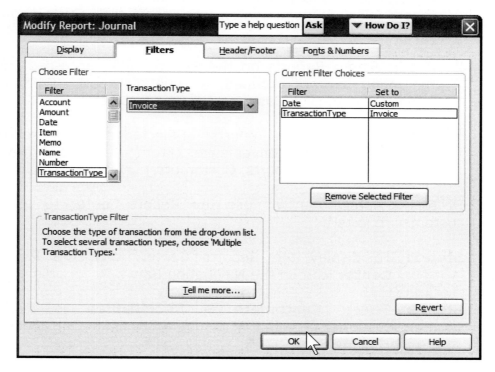

Step 6: 🖨 **Print** the Journal.

Step 7: ✎ **Circle** the journal entry that corresponds to Invoice No. 94. Notice that the journal entry records an increase (debit) to Accounts Receivable for $304.30, the net amount of the invoice.

CUSTOMER REPORTS

There are many different customer reports that a business may find useful. QuickBooks creates reports to answer the following questions:

- Which customers owe us money?

- Which customers have overdue balances?

- Which customers are profitable?

- Which jobs are profitable?

Customer reports can be accessed in QuickBooks in several different ways:

1. Report Center: permits you to locate reports by type of report (Click Report Center icon, then click Customers & Receivables.)

2. Report Menu: Reports on the Report menu accessed from the menu bar are grouped by type of report. (From the Reports menu, click Customers & Receivables.)

3. Memorized Customer Reports: Selected customer reports are memorized for convenience. (From the Reports menu, select Memorized Reports, Customers.)

In this chapter, you will use the Report Center to access customer reports.

Step 1: To display the Reports Center, click the **Report Center** icon on the Navigation Bar.

Step 2: Select: **Customers & Receivables** to display customer reports that can be accessed in QuickBooks.

Step 3:   The customer reports are divided into 3 categories:

- Accounts Receivable Aging reports
- Customer Balance reports
- Customer List reports

ACCOUNTS RECEIVABLE REPORTS: WHICH CUSTOMERS OWE US MONEY?

Accounts Receivable reports provide information about which customers owe your business money. When Rock Castle Construction makes a credit sale, the company provides goods and services to a customer in exchange for a promise that the customer will pay later. Sometimes the customer breaks the promise and does not pay. Therefore, a business should have a credit policy to ensure that credit is extended only to customers who are likely to keep their promise and pay their bills.

After credit has been extended, a business needs to track accounts receivable to determine if accounts are being collected in a timely manner. The following reports provide information useful in tracking accounts receivable.

1. Accounts Receivable Aging Summary (the age of amounts due you by customers)
2. Accounts Receivable Detail report
3. Customers with Open Invoices (invoices that have not yet been paid)
4. Collections Report (which customer accounts are overdue with their contact information)

ACCOUNTS RECEIVABLE AGING SUMMARY REPORT

The Accounts Receivable Aging Summary report provides information about the age of customer accounts. This report lists the age of accounts receivable balances. In general, the older an account, the less likely the customer will pay the bill. Therefore, it is important to monitor the age of accounts receivable and take action to collect old accounts.

To print the Accounts Receivable Aging Summary:

Step 1: From the Report Center, select **Customer & Receivables**.

Step 2: Select **A/R Aging Summary Report**.

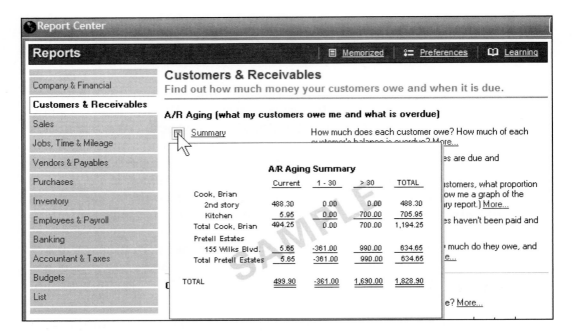

Step 3: Select Date: **Today**.

Step 4: If necessary, adjust the column widths by clicking and dragging.

Step 5: **Export** the report to Excel. (Click the Export button, a new Excel workbook, Export).

Step 6: **Print** the report from Excel.

Step 7: **Save** the Excel report. (From the Excel file menu, click Save As, specify the Excel filename: Aging Report.) **Close** Excel.

Step 8: **Close** the *A/R Aging Summary* window.

CUSTOMERS WITH OPEN INVOICES REPORT

Customers with open invoices are customer invoices with an unbilled or unpaid balance.

It is important to track the status of open accounts to determine:

- Are these amounts unbilled? The sooner the balances are billed, the sooner your company receives cash to pay your bills.

- Are these amounts billed but not yet due?

- Are these amounts billed and overdue? These accounts should be monitored closely with an action plan for collecting the accounts.

The Open Invoices report lists all customers with open balances and can be printed as follows:

Step 1: From the Customer and Receivables section of the Report Center, click **Open Invoices**.

Step 2: Select Date: **Today**.

Step 3: 🖨 **Print** the Open Invoices report using **Landscape** orientation.

Step 4: Notice the *Aging* column in the report. This column indicates the age of overdue accounts. **Circle** all overdue customer accounts.

Step 5: **Close** the *Open Invoices* window.

COLLECTIONS REPORT: CUSTOMERS WITH OVERDUE BALANCES

When reviewing the age of accounts receivable, a business should monitor overdue accounts closely and maintain ongoing collection efforts to collect its overdue accounts.

The Collections Report lists customers with overdue account balances. In addition, the collection report includes a contact phone number for convenience in contacting the customer.

To print the Collections Report summarizing information for all customers with overdue balances:

Step 1: From the Customers & Receivables section of the Report Center, select: **Collections**.

Step 2: Select: **Today**.

Step 3: Eleven customers have overdue balances. To obtain more information about a specific invoice, simply double-click on the invoice.

Step 4: 🖨 **Print** the Collections Report.

Step 5: **Close** the *Collections Report* window.

The Collections Report provides the information necessary to monitor and contact overdue accounts and should be prepared on a regular basis.

PROFIT AND LOSS REPORTS: WHICH CUSTOMERS AND JOBS ARE PROFITABLE?

To improve profitability in the future, a business should evaluate which customers and jobs have been profitable in the past. This information permits a business to improve profitability by:

- Increasing business in profitable areas.

- Improving performance in unprofitable areas.

- Discontinuing unprofitable areas.

The following QuickBooks reports provide information about customer and job profitability:

1. Income by Customer Summary Report

2. Income by Customer Detail report

3. Job Profitability Summary Report

4. Job Profitability Detail Report

INCOME BY CUSTOMER SUMMARY REPORT

To determine which customers are generating the most profit for your business, it is necessary to look at both the sales for the customer and the associated costs. To print the Income by Customer Summary report:

Step 1: From the Report Center, click **Company & Financial.**

Step 2: Select: **Income by Customer Summary**.

Step 3: Select: **This Fiscal Year-to-date**.

Step 4: 🖨 **Print** the report.

Step 5: ✏ **Circle** Rock Castle Construction's most profitable customer.

Step 6: **Close** the *Income by Customer Summary* Report window.

JOB PROFITABILITY SUMMARY REPORT

To print the Job Profitability Summary Report:

Step 1: From the Report Center, click **Jobs, Time & Mileage**.

Step 2: Select **Job Profitability Summary.**

Step 3: Select Date: **This Fiscal Year**.

Step 4: 🖨 **Print** the report using **Landscape** orientation.

Step 5: ✏ **Circle** the job that generated the most profit for Rock Castle Construction.

Step 6: **Close** the *Job Profitability Summary* window.

QuickBooks offers other additional reports about customers that provide information useful to a business. These reports can be accessed from the Report Center.

SAVE CHAPTER 4

Save Chapter 4 as a portable QuickBooks file to the location specified by your instructor.

Step 1: If necessary, insert a removable disk.

Step 2: From the menu bar, click **File | Portable Company File | Create File**.

Step 3: When the *Close and Reopen* window appears, click **OK**.

Step 4: When the following *Create Portable Company File* window appears, enter the filename: **[your name] Chapter 4** and the appropriate location. Then click **Save**.

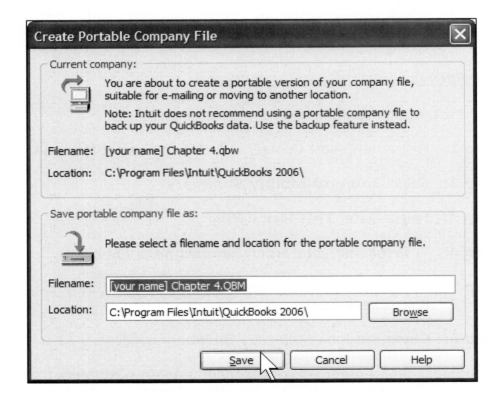

Step 5: Click **OK** after the portable file has been created successfully.

Step 6: Close the company file by clicking **File** (Menu), **Close Company**.

If you are continuing your computer session, proceed to Exercise 4.1.

If you are ending your computer session now, see the Quick Reference Guide in Part 3 for instructions to (1) close the company file and (2) exit QuickBooks.

ASSIGNMENTS

> **NOTE: See the Quick Reference Guide in Part 3 for step-by-step instructions to frequently used tasks.**

EXERCISE 4.1: BILL CUSTOMER

SCENARIO

"I just finished the Beneficio job, Mr. Castle." A workman tosses a job ticket over your cubicle wall into your inbox as he walks past. *"Mrs. Beneficio's pet dog, Wrecks, really did a number on that door. No wonder she wanted it replaced before her party tonight. Looks better than ever now!"*

You hear Mr. Castle reply, *"We want to keep Mrs. Beneficio happy. She will be a good customer."*

TASK 1: OPEN PORTABLE COMPANY FILE

To open the portable company file (.QBM) file, convert the portable file to a regular company file with a .QBW extension as follows:

Step 1: From the menu bar, click **File | Portable Company File | Open File**.

Step 2: Identify the filename and location for the portable company file:

- Click the **Browse** button to find the location of the portable company file on the hard drive or removable media.

- Select the file: **[your name] Chapter 4.QBM**.

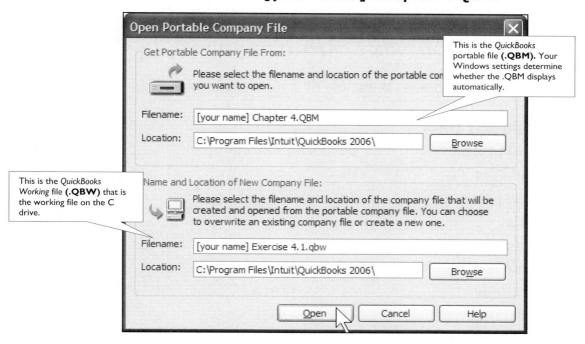

Step 3: Identify the name and location of the new company file (.QBW) file to use for completing Exercise 4.1:

- Filename: **[your name] Exercise 4.1**. The **.QBW** extension should appear automatically based upon your Windows settings.

- Location: **C:\Program Files\Intuit\QuickBooks 2006**. This is the location of the .QBW file on the hard drive of your computer. Click the Browse button to specify another location.

Step 4: Click **Open** to open the portable company file.

Step 5: Click **Cancel** when the *Create a Backup* window appears.

Step 6: If prompted, enter your **User Name** and **Password**, then click **OK**.

Step 7: Click **OK** when the QuickBooks sample company message appears.

Step 8: Change the company name to: **[your name] Exercise 4.1 Rock Castle Construction**. (If you need instructions to change the company name, see Part 3: Quick Reference Guide.)

> You can add a new customer from the *Customer Center* or open the *Invoices* window and from the Customer: Job drop-down list, select **Add New**.

TASK 2: ADD NEW CUSTOMER & JOB

Step 1: Add Mrs. Beneficio as a new customer.

Address Info:	
Customer	Beneficio, Katrina
Mr./Ms./...	Mrs.
First Name	Katrina
M.I.	L
Last Name	Beneficio
Contact	Katrina
Phone	415-555-1818
Alt. Ph.	415-555-3636
Addresses: Bill To	10 Pico Blvd Bayshore, CA 94326

Additional Info:	
Type	Residential
Terms	Net 30
Tax Code	Tax
Tax Item	San Tomas

Payment Info:	
Account No.	12736
Credit Limit	10,000
Preferred Payment Method	VISA

Step 2: **Close** the *New Customer* window.

Step 3: Add a new job for Katrina Beneficio.

Job Name: Door Replacement	
Job Status	Closed
Start Date	12/17/2007
Projected End	12/17/2007
End Date	12/17/2007
Job Description	Interior Door Replacement
Job Type	Repairs

TASK 3: CREATE INVOICE

Step 1: Create an invoice for an interior door replacement using the following information:

Customer: Job	Beneficio, Katrina: Door Replacement
Customer Template	Time & Expense Invoice
Date	12/17/2007
Invoice No.	95
Items	1 Wood Door: Interior @ $72.00 1 Hardware: Standard Doorknob @ 30.00 Installation Labor: 3 hours

Step 2: 🖨 **Print** the invoice.

✓ **The Invoice Total is $214.91.**

TASK 4: SAVE EXERCISE 4.1

Save Exercise 4.1 as a portable company file to the location specified by your instructor.

Step 1: If necessary, insert a removable disk.

Step 2: From the menu bar, click **File | Portable Company File | Create File**.

Step 3: When the *Close and Reopen* window appears, click **OK**.

Step 4: When the *Create Portable Company File* window appears, enter the filename: **[your name] Exercise 4.1** and the appropriate location. Click **Save**.

Step 5: Click **OK** after the portable file has been created successfully.

Step 6: Close the company file by clicking **File** (Menu), **Close Company**.

EXERCISE 4.2: RECORD CUSTOMER PAYMENT AND CUSTOMER CREDIT

SCENARIO

"It's time you learned how to record a credit to a customer's account." Mr. Castle groans, then rubbing his temples, he continues, *"Mrs. Beneficio called earlier today to tell us she was very pleased with her new bathroom door. However, she ordered locking hardware for the door, and standard hardware with no lock was installed instead. Although she appreciates our prompt service, she would like a lock on her bathroom door. We sent a workman over to her house, and when the hardware was replaced, she paid the bill.*

"We need to record a credit to her account for the standard hardware and then record a charge for the locking hardware set. And we won't charge her for the labor to change the hardware."

TASK 1: OPEN PORTABLE COMPANY FILE

To open the portable company file (.QBM) file, convert the portable file to a regular company file with a .QBW extension as follows:

Step 1: From the menu bar, click **File | Portable Company File | Open File**.

Step 2: Identify the filename and location for the portable company file:

- Click the **Browse** button to find the location of the portable company file on the hard drive or removable media.

- Select the file: **[your name] Exercise 4.1.QBM**.

Step 3: Identify the name and location of the new company file (.QBW) file to use for completing Exercise 4.2:

- Filename: **[your name] Exercise 4.2**. The **.QBW** extension should appear automatically based upon your Windows settings.

- Location: **C:\Program Files\Intuit\QuickBooks 2006**. This is the location of the .QBW file on the hard drive of your computer.

Step 4: Click **Open** to open the portable company file.

Step 5: Click **Cancel** when the *Create a Backup* window appears.

Step 6: If prompted, enter your **User Name** and **Password**, then click **OK**.

Step 7: Click **OK** when the QuickBooks sample company message appears.

Step 8: Change the company name to: **[your name] Exercise 4.2 Rock Castle Construction**. (If you need instructions to change the company name, see Part 3: Quick Reference Guide.)

TASK 2: RECORD CUSTOMER CREDIT

Record a credit to Mrs. Beneficio's account for the $30.00 she was previously charged for standard door hardware by completing the following steps:

Step 1: Click the **Refunds and Credits** icon in the Customer section of the Home page.

Step 2: Select Customer & Job: **Beneficio, Katrina: Door Replacement.**

Step 3: Select Template: **Custom Credit Memo.**

Step 4: Select Date: **12/20/2007**.

Step 5: Select Item: **Hardware Standard Doorknobs**.

Step 6: Enter Quantity: **1**.

Step 7: 🖨 **Print** the Credit Memo.

Step 8: Click **Save & Close.**

Step 9: When the following *Available Credit* window appears, click **Apply to an invoice**. Click **OK**.

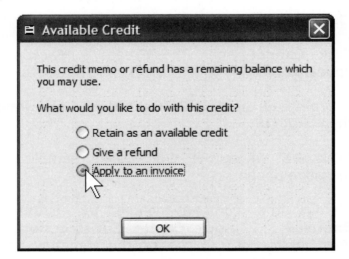

Step 10: When the following *Apply Credit to Invoices* window appears, select **Invoice No. 95**. Click **Done**.

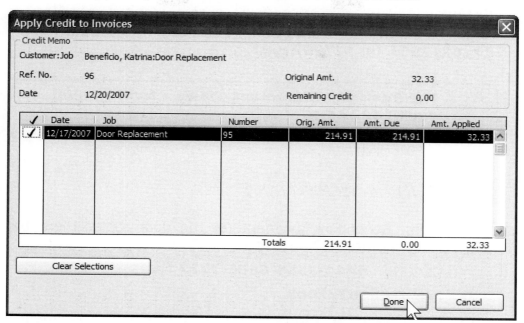

Step 11: If necessary, click **Save & Close** to close the *Create Credit Memos/Refunds* window.

> ✓   ***The Credit Memo No. 96 totals $-32.33 ($30.00 plus $2.33 tax).***

TASK 3: CREATE INVOICE

Step 1: Create a new invoice (Invoice No. 97) for Katrina Beneficio: Door Replacement on 12/20/2007 to record the charges for the interior door locking hardware.

Step 2: 🖨 **Print** the invoice.

> ✓   ***Invoice No. 97 totals $40.95.***

TASK 4: PRINT REMINDER STATEMENT

🖨 **Print** a reminder statement for the Beneficio Door Replacement Job for 12/20/2007. Use Statement Period From: **12/02/2007** To: **12/20/2007**.

> ✓ **The Reminder Statement shows a total amount due of $223.53.**

TASK 5: RECEIVE PAYMENT

Record Mrs. Beneficio's payment for the door replacement by VISA credit card for $223.53 on 12/20/2007.

- Card No.: **4444-5555-6666-7777**
- Exp. Date: **07/2008**
- Click **Save & Close** to close the *Receive Payments* window.

TASK 6: RECORD BANK DEPOSIT

Step 1: Record the deposit for $223.53 on 12/20/2007.

Step 2: 🖨 **Print** a deposit summary using Portrait orientation.

TASK 7: SAVE EXERCISE 4.2

Save Exercise 4.2 as a portable company file to the location specified by your instructor.

Step 1: If necessary, insert a removable disk.

Step 2: From the menu bar, click **File | Portable Company File | Create File**.

Step 3: When the *Close and Reopen* window appears, click **OK**.

Step 4: When the *Create Portable Company File* window appears, enter the filename: **[your name] Exercise 4.2** and the appropriate location. Then click **Save**.

Step 5: Click **OK** after the portable file has been created successfully.

Step 6: Close the company file by clicking **File** (Menu), **Close Company**.

EXERCISE 4.3: CUSTOMER REPORTS & COLLECTION LETTERS

In this Exercise, you will create additional customer reports that a business might find useful.

TASK 1: OPEN PORTABLE COMPANY FILE

To open the portable company file (.QBM) file, convert the portable file to a regular company file with a .QBW extension as follows:

Step 1: From the menu bar, click **File | Portable Company File | Open File**.

Step 2: Identify the filename and location for the portable company file:

- Click the **Browse** button to find the location of the portable company file on the hard drive or removable media.
- Select the file: **[your name] Exercise 4.2.QBM**.

Step 3: Identify the name and location of the new company file (.QBW) file to use for completing Exercise 4.3:

- Filename: **[your name] Exercise 4.3**. The **.QBW** extension should appear automatically based upon your Windows settings.
- Location: **C:\Program Files\Intuit\QuickBooks 2006**. This is the location of the .QBW file on the hard drive of your computer.

Step 4: Click **Open** to open the portable company file.

Step 5: Click **Cancel** when the *Create a Backup* window appears.

Step 6: If prompted, enter your **User Name** and **Password**, then click **OK**.

Step 7: Click **OK** when the QuickBooks sample company message appears.

Step 8: Change the company name to: **[your name] Exercise 4.3 Rock Castle Construction**.

TASK 2: EDIT CUSTOMER LIST

Edit Ecker Designs' E-mail address in the Customer List.

Step 1: Open the Customer Center.

Step 2: Select customer: **Ecker Designs**.

Step 3: Click **Edit Customer** to display the *Edit Customer* window for Ecker Designs.

Step 4: Edit the E-mail address for Ecker Designs: **decker@www.com**.

Step 5: Click **OK** to save the customer information and **close** the *Edit Customer* window.

TASK 3: PRINT CUSTOMER REPORT

Print the transactions for Ecker Designs as follows.

Step 1: From the Customer List, select **Ecker Designs.**

Step 2: In the Customer Information section, transactions for Ecker Designs should appear. With your cursor over the customer transaction section of the *Customer Center* window, **right-click** to display the following pop-up menu. Select **View as a Report**.

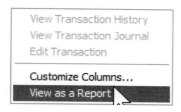

Step 3: Select Dates From: **11/01/2007** To: **12/31/2007**.

Step 4: 🖶 **Print** the report for Ecker Designs.

> ✓ ***The last amount charged to Ecker Design's account was Invoice No. 78 for $1,468.30 on December 15, 2007.***

Step 5: **Close** the *Report* window and the *Customer Center* window.

TASK 4: ACCOUNTS RECEIVABLE AGING DETAIL REPORT

🖶 **Print** the Accounts Receivable Aging Detail report for Rock Castle Construction as follows.

Step 1: From the Report Center, select **Customers & Receivables**.

Step 2: Select **A/R Aging Detail** report. Select Date: **12/15/2007**.

Step 3: 🖶 **Print** the A/R Aging Detail report.

Step 4: ✎ **Circle** the accounts that are over 90 days past due.

TASK 5: COLLECTION LETTER

Next, prepare a collection letter to the customer with an account over 90 days past due:

Step 1: From the Customer Center, select the customer: **Jennifer Fisher**.

Step 2: Click on the **Word** icon at the top of the Customer Center.

Step 3: Select: **Prepare Collection Letters**.

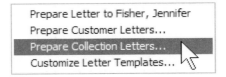

Step 4: When the following window appears, make the selections as shown. Click **Next**.

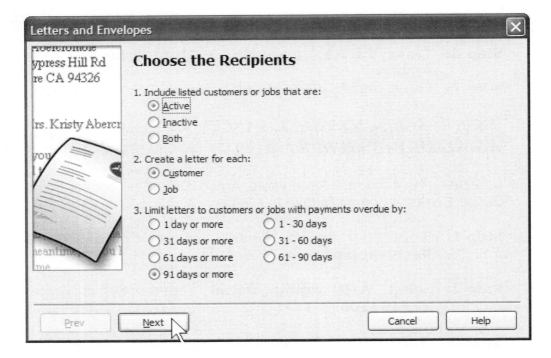

Step 5: Select **Jennifer Fisher**. Click **Next**.

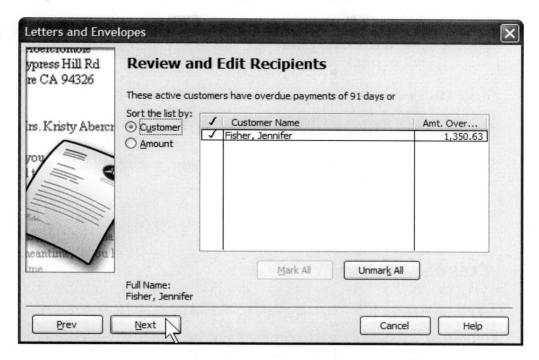

Step 6: Select: **Formal Collection Letter**. Click **Next**.

Step 7: Enter Name: **Rock Castle**. Enter Title: **President**. Click **Next**.

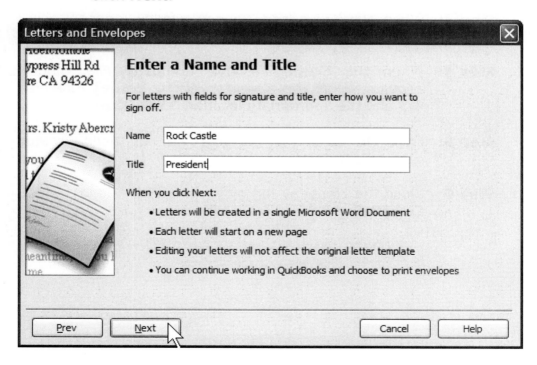

Step 8: If a missing information message appears, click **OK**.

Step 9: QuickBooks will automatically open Word and prepare the collection letter for Jennifer Fisher. 🖨 **Print** the letter from Word.

Step 10: Save the Word document by clicking **File, Save As**. Name the document: **[your name] Exercise 4.3 Collection Letter**.

Step 11: Click **Cancel** when asked if you would like to print envelopes.

Step 12: **Close** the Customer Center.

TASK 6: SAVE EXERCISE 4.3

Save Exercise 4.3 as a portable company file to the location specified by your instructor.

Step 1: If necessary, insert a removable disk.

Step 2: From the menu bar, click **File | Portable Company File | Create File**.

Step 3: When the *Close and Reopen* window appears, click **OK**.

Step 4: When the *Create Portable Company File* window appears, enter the filename: **[your name] Exercise 4.3** and the appropriate location. Click **Save**.

Step 5: Click **OK** after the portable file has been created successfully.

Step 6: Close the company file by clicking **File** (Menu), **Close Company**.

EXERCISE 4.4: TRIAL BALANCE

In this Exercise, you will print a trial balance to double check that your accounting system is in balance and that your account balances are correct.

TASK 1: OPEN PORTABLE COMPANY FILE

To open the portable company file (.QBM) file, convert the portable file to a regular company file with a .QBW extension as follows:

Step 1: From the menu bar, click **File | Portable Company File | Open File**.

Step 2: Identify the filename and location for the portable company file:

- Click the **Browse** button to find the location of the portable company file on the hard drive or removable media.

- Select the file: **[your name] Exercise 4.3.QBM**.

Step 3: Identify the name and location of the new company file (.QBW) file to use for completing Exercise 4.4:

- Filename: **[your name] Exercise 4.4**. The **.QBW** extension should appear automatically based upon your Windows settings.

- Location: **C:\Program Files\Intuit\QuickBooks 2006**. This is the location of the .QBW file on the hard drive of your computer.

Step 4: Click **Open** to open the portable company file.

Step 5: Click **Cancel** when the *Create a Backup* window appears.

Step 6: If prompted, enter your **User Name** and **Password**, then click **OK**.

Step 7: Click **OK** when the QuickBooks sample company message appears.

Step 8: Change the company name to: **[your name] Exercise 4.4 Rock Castle Construction**.

TASK 2: PRINT TRIAL BALANCE

🖷 **Print** the trial balance as follows.

Step 1: From the Report Center, select **Accountant and Taxes**.

Step 2: Select **Trial Balance**.

Step 3: Select Date From: **12/20/2007** To: **12/20/2007**.

Step 4: 🖷 **Print** the trial balance.

Step 5: Compare your printout totals and account balances to the following printout. Correct any errors you find.

| Dates | Custom | ✔ | From | 12/20/2007 ▦ | To | 12/20/2007 ▦ | Sort By | Default | ✔ |

[your name] Exercise 4.4 Rock Castle Construction
Trial Balance

Accrual Basis   As of December 20, 2007

	Dec 20, 07	
	Debit	Credit
[your name] Checking	149,676.03	
Savings	13,868.42	
Barter Account	0.00	
1200 · Accounts Receivable	80,453.98	
Tools & Equipment	5,000.00	
Employee Loans	62.00	
1120 · Inventory Asset	23,043.90	
1350 · Retainage	2,461.80	
1400 · Undeposited Funds	58,742.77	
Land	90,000.00	
Buildings	325,000.00	
1500 · Trucks	78,352.91	
1500 · Trucks:1520 · Depreciation	0.00	
Computers	28,501.00	
Furniture	7,325.00	
Accumulated Depreciation		121,887.78
Pre-paid Insurance	1,041.85	
2000 · Accounts Payable		54,280.04
QuickBooks Credit Card		70.00
2050 · CalOil Card		5,057.62
2101 · Payroll Liabilities		7,082.68
2200 · Sales Tax Payable		5,541.08
Bank of Anycity Loan		19,932.65
Equipment Loan		3,911.32
2250 · Note Payable		3,440.83
2300 · Truck Loan		50,162.38
3500 · Opening Bal Equity		593,019.25
3000 · Owner's Equity:3100 · Owner's Contribution		98,000.00
3000 · Owner's Equity:3200 · Owner's Draw	6,000.00	
3300 · Retained Earnings	129,916.38	
4000 · Construction:4100 · Labor		37,874.25
4000 · Construction:4200 · Materials		69,531.51
4000 · Construction:4400 · Miscellaneous		4,735.55
4000 · Construction:4300 · Subcontractors		57,207.01
5000 · Cost of Goods Sold	8,716.51	
6000 · Automobile	10.60	
6000 · Automobile:Insurance	712.56	
6000 · Automobile:6020 · Fuel	231.10	
6040 · Selling Expense:6041 · Advertising Expense	200.00	
6100 · Bank Service Charges	67.50	
6400 · Freight & Delivery	184.60	
6500 · Insurance	297.66	
6500 · Insurance:6510 · Disability Insurance	300.00	
6500 · Insurance:6520 · Liability Insurance	2,100.00	
6500 · Insurance:6530 · Work Comp	1,650.00	
6600 · Interest Expense	651.77	
6600 · Interest Expense:6620 · Loan Interest	288.05	
7400 · Job Expenses:7410 · Equipment Rental	1,000.00	
7400 · Job Expenses:7420 · Job Materials	38,059.07	
7400 · Job Expenses:7430 · Permits and Licenses	700.00	
7400 · Job Expenses:7440 · Subcontractors	44,166.00	
6560 · Payroll Expenses	29,513.77	
7000 · Professional Fees:7010 · Accounting	250.00	
7100 · Rent	1,200.00	
7200 · Repairs:7210 · Building Repairs	175.00	
7200 · Repairs:7220 · Computer Repairs	345.00	
7200 · Repairs:7230 · Equipment Repairs	0.00	
7500 · Tools and Machinery	1,160.00	
7600 · Utilities:7610 · Gas and Electric	277.08	
7600 · Utilities:7620 · Telephone	100.71	
7600 · Utilities:7630 · Water	61.85	
8000 · Interest Income		93.42
8100 · Other Income		37.50
TOTAL	**1,131,864.87**	**1,131,864.87**

Step 6: **Close** the trial balance and the Report Center.

TASK 3: SAVE EXERCISE 4.4

Save Exercise 4.4 as a portable company file to the location specified by your instructor.

Step 1: If necessary, insert a removable disk.

Step 2: From the menu bar, click **File** | **Portable Company File** | **Create File**.

Step 3: When the *Close and Reopen* window appears, click **OK**.

Step 4: When the *Create Portable Company File* window appears, enter the filename: **[your name] Exercise 4.4** and the appropriate location. Click **Save**.

Step 5: Click **OK** after the portable file has been created successfully.

Step 6: Close the company file by clicking **File** (Menu), **Close Company**.

EXERCISE 4.5: WEB QUEST

Rock Castle has heard that QuickBooks now offers a Point of Sale product to go with QuickBooks. He wants to know more about the product and whether it is a good choice for Rock Castle Construction.

Step 1: Using an Internet search engine, such as Google, research QuickBooks Point of Sale products.

Step 2: ✉ Prepare an email to Rock Castle summarizing the main features of the Point of Sale product. Include your recommendation whether this is a worthwhile product for Rock Castle to use.

CHAPTER 4 PRINTOUT CHECKLIST
NAME: _____ DATE:_____

INSTRUCTIONS:
1. **CHECK OFF THE PRINTOUTS YOU HAVE COMPLETED.**
2. **STAPLE THIS PAGE TO YOUR PRINTOUTS.**

☑ **PRINTOUT CHECKLIST – CHAPTER 4**
☐ Cash Sales Receipt
☐ Invoice No. 94
☐ Reminder Statement
☐ Deposit Summary
☐ Journal
☐ Accounts Receivable Aging Summary Report
☐ Open Invoices Report
☐ Collections Report
☐ Income by Customer Summary Report
☐ Job Profitability Summary Report

☑ **PRINTOUT CHECKLIST – EXERCISE 4.1**
☐ Task 3: Invoice No. 95

☑ **PRINTOUT CHECKLIST – EXERCISE 4.2**
☐ Task 2: Credit Memo No. 96
☐ Task 3: Invoice No. 97
☐ Task 4: Statement
☐ Task 6: Deposit Summary

☑ **PRINTOUT CHECKLIST – EXERCISE 4.3**
☐ Task 3: Customer Report
☐ Task 4: Accounts Receivable Aging Detail Report
☐ Task 5: Customer Collection Letter

☑ **PRINTOUT CHECKLIST – EXERCISE 4.4**
☐ Task 2: Trial Balance

☑ **PRINTOUT CHECKLIST – EXERCISE 4.5**
☐ QuickBooks Point of Sale Information

NOTES:

CHAPTER 5
VENDORS, PURCHASES, AND INVENTORY

SCENARIO

As you work your way through stacks of paper in your inbox, you hear Mr. Castle's rapid footsteps coming in your direction. He whips around the corner of your cubicle with another stack of papers in hand.

In his usual rapid-fire delivery, Mr. Castle begins, *"This is the way we do business."* He quickly sketches the following:

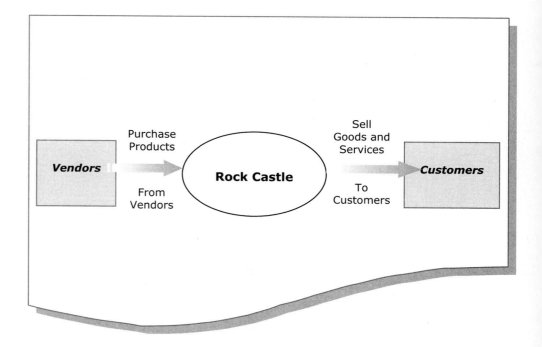

"We purchase products from our vendors and suppliers, and then we sell those products and provide services to our customers. We use QuickBooks to track the quantity and cost of items we purchase and sell."

Mr. Castle tosses the papers into your inbox. *"Here are vendor and purchase transactions that need to be recorded."*

CHAPTER 5
LEARNING OBJECTIVES

In Chapter 5, you will learn the following QuickBooks features:

INTRODUCTION

In Chapter 5 you will focus on recording vendor transactions, including placing orders, receiving goods, and paying bills.

QuickBooks considers a vendor to be any individual or organization that provides products or services to your company.

QuickBooks considers all of the following to be vendors:

- Suppliers from whom you buy inventory or supplies.

- Service companies that provide services to your company, such as cleaning services or landscaping services.

- Financial institutions, such as banks, that provide financial services including checking accounts and loans.

- Tax agencies such as the IRS. The IRS is considered a vendor because you pay taxes to the IRS.

- Utility and telephone companies.

If your company is a merchandising business that buys and resells goods, then you must maintain inventory records to account for the items you purchase from vendors and resell to customers.

The following diagram summarizes vendor and customer transactions.

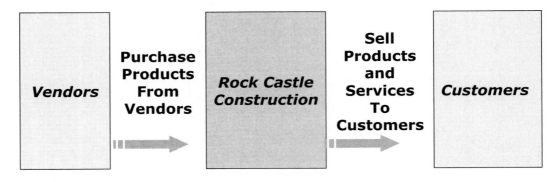

Vendor Transactions	Customer Transactions
1. Enter vendor information	7. Enter customer information
2. Set up inventory	8. Sell goods and bill customers
3. Order goods	9. Receive customer payments
4. Receive goods	
5. Receive bill	10. Deposit customer payment
6. Pay for goods	

The following table summarizes how to record Rock Castle Construction's business operations using QuickBooks.

	Activity	Record Using...
1.	Record vendor information.	*Vendor List*
2.	Record inventory information: Set up inventory records to track the quantity and cost of items purchased.	*Items List*
3.	Order goods: Forms called Purchase Orders (PO's) are used to order goods from vendors.	*Purchase Order*
4.	Receive goods: Goods are received and recorded as inventory.	*Receive Items*
5.	Receive bill: Record an obligation to pay a bill later (Accounts Payable).	*Enter Bill*
6.	Pay for goods: Bills for the goods are paid.	*Pay Bills*
7.	Record customer information.	*Customer List*
8.	Sell goods and bill customers: Record customer's promise to pay later (Account Receivable).	*Invoice*
9.	Receive customer payment: Record cash collected and customer's Account Receivable is decreased.	*Receive Payments*
10.	Deposit customers' payments in bank account.	*Deposit*

Vendor Transactions (items 1–6)

Customer Transactions (items 7–10)

To begin Chapter 5, first start QuickBooks software and then open the portable QuickBooks file.

Step 1: Start QuickBooks by clicking on the **QuickBooks** desktop icon or click **Start**, **Programs**, **QuickBooks**, **QuickBooks Pro 2006**.

Step 2: To open the portable company file (.QBM) file and convert the portable file to a regular company file with a .QBW extension, from the menu bar, click **File | Portable Company File | Open File**.

Step 3: Identify the filename and location for the portable company file:

- Click the **Browse** button to find the location of the portable company file on the hard drive or removable media.

- Select the file: **[your name] Exercise 4.4**. The .QBM may appear automatically based upon your Windows settings, but if it does not appear automatically, do **not** type it.

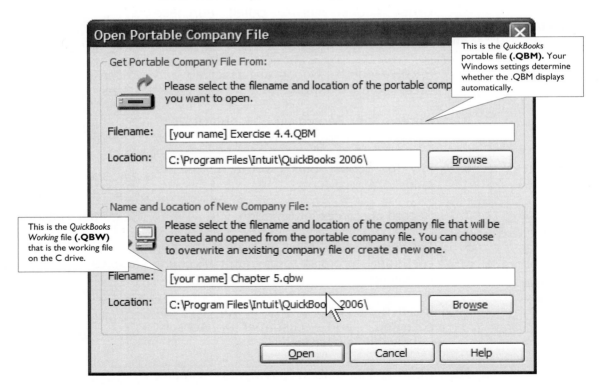

Step 4: Identify the name and location of the new company file (.QBW) file to use for Chapter 5:

- Filename: **[your name] Chapter 5**. The **.QBW** extension should appear automatically based upon your Windows settings. The .QBW identifies this as a QuickBooks working file.

- Location: **C:\Program Files\Intuit\QuickBooks 2006**. This is the location of the .QBW file on the hard drive of your computer.

Step 5: Click **Open** to open the portable company file.

Step 6: Click **Cancel** when the *Create a Backup* window appears.

Step 7: If prompted, enter your **User ID** and **Password**.

Step 8: Click **OK** when the sample company window appears.

Step 9: Change the company name to: **[your name] Chapter 5 Rock Castle Construction**. If necessary, change the Checking account title to include your name.

The portable company file (.QBM) should now be converted to a regular company file (Chapter 5.QBW) that can be used to complete the assignments for Chapter 5.

After opening the portable company file for Rock Castle Construction, click the Home page icon in the Navigation Bar.

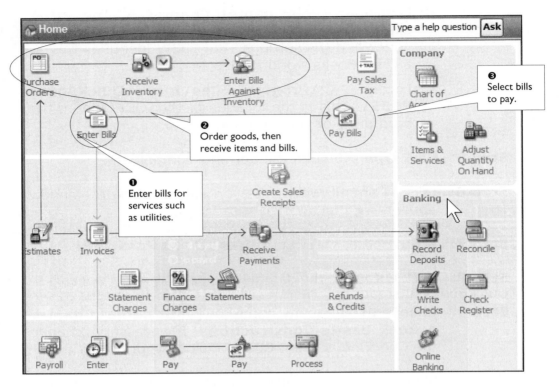

The Vendor section of the Home page is a flowchart of vendor transactions. As the flowchart indicates, Rock Castle Construction can record bills in QuickBooks as follows.

❶ **Record services received:** Use the *Enter Bills* window to record bills for services received. Examples include rent, utilities expense, insurance expense, accounting and professional services. QuickBooks will record an obligation (Accounts Payable liability) to pay the bill later.

❷ **Record goods purchased:** Use the *Purchase Orders* window to record an order to purchase goods. Use the *Receive Items* window to record goods received. When the bill is received, use the *Receive Bill* window to record the bill. Again, when the bill is entered, QuickBooks records Accounts Payable to reflect the obligation to pay the bill later.

❸ **Select bills to pay.** Use the *Pay Bills* window to select the bills that are due and you are ready to pay.

Another QuickBooks feature available from the Vendor Section of the Home page includes:

Pay Sales Tax: Sales taxes are charged on retail sales to customers. The sales tax collected from customers must be paid to the appropriate state agency.

VENDOR LIST

The first step in working with vendor transactions is to enter vendor information in the Vendor List.

The Vendor List contains information for each vendor, such as address, telephone number, and credit terms. Vendor information is entered in the Vendor List and then QuickBooks automatically transfers the vendor information to the appropriate forms, such as purchase orders and checks. This feature enables you to enter vendor information only once in QuickBooks instead of entering the vendor information each time a form is prepared.

VIEW VENDOR LIST

To view the Vendor List for Rock Castle Construction:

Step 1: Click on the **Vendor Center** icon in the Navigation Bar.

Step 2: The following Vendor List appears listing vendors with whom Rock Castle Construction does business. The Vendor List also displays the balance currently owed each vendor.

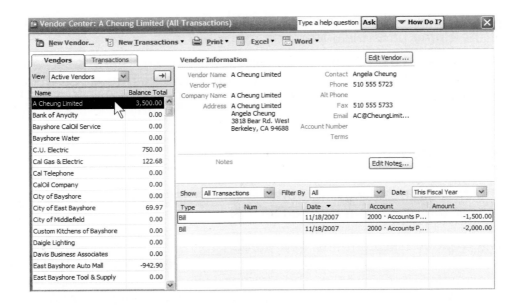

Step 3: To view additional information about a vendor, click the vendor's name and the Vendor Information will appear on the right side of the Vendor Center.

ADD NEW VENDOR

Rock Castle Construction needs to add a new vendor, Nic's Window & Door, to the Vendor List.

To add a new vendor to the Vendor List:

Step 1: Click the **New Vendor** button at the top of the Vendor Center.

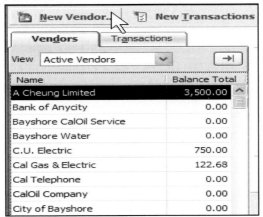

Step 2: A blank *New Vendor* window should appear. Enter the information shown below into the *New Vendor | Address Info* window.

Vendor	Nic's Window & Door
Address	10 Big Bend Blvd Bayshore, CA 94326
Contact	Melissa
Phone	415-555-3000
Alt. Contact	Debbie
E-mail	Nic@windowdoor.com
Print on check as	Nic's Window & Door

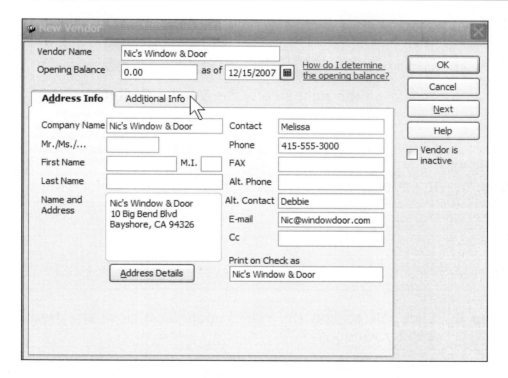

Step 3: Click the **Additional Info** tab to display another vendor information window. Enter the information shown below into the *Additional Info* fields.

Account	78789
Type	Materials
Terms	Net 30
Vendor eligible for 1099	Yes
Tax ID	37-1890123

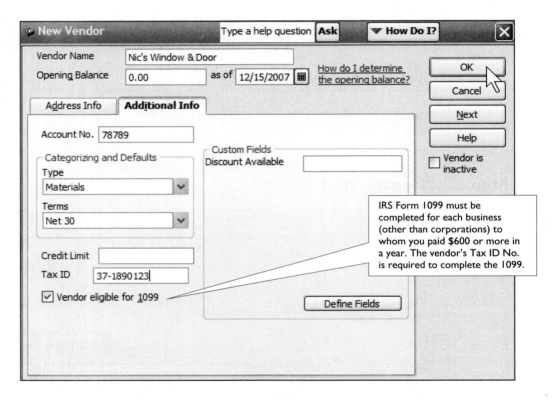

Step 4: Click **OK** to add the new vendor and close the *New Vendor* window.

To edit vendor information, simply click the vendor's name in the *Vendor List* window. The vendor information will appear on the right side of the Vendor Center. Click the Edit Vendor button, make the necessary changes in the *Edit Vendor* window that appears, and then click OK to close the *Edit Vendor* window.

PRINT VENDOR LIST

🖨 **Print** the Vendor List as follows:

Step 1: Click the **Print** button at the top of the Vendor Center.

Step 2: Select **Vendor List** from the drop-down menu.

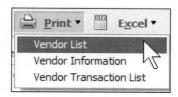

Step 3: When the *Print Reports* window appears, select **Portrait** and **Fit report to 1 page wide**.

Step 4: Click **Print**.

Step 5: **Close** the Vendor Center.

The Items and Services List, discussed next, is used to record information about goods and services purchased from vendors.

> Items provide supporting detail for accounts.

ITEMS: INVENTORY ITEMS, NON-INVENTORY ITEMS, AND SERVICES

QuickBooks defines an item as anything that your company buys, sells, or resells including products, shipping charges, and sales taxes. QuickBooks classifies goods and services purchased and sold into three different categories of items:

1. **Service Items:** Service items can be services that are purchased *or* sold. For example, service items include:

   ▪ Services you *buy* from vendors, such as cleaning services.

   ▪ Services you *sell* to customers, such as installation labor.

2. **Inventory Items:** Inventory items are goods that a business purchases, holds as inventory, and then resells to customers. QuickBooks traces the quantity and cost of inventory items in stock.

> *IMPORTANT!* QuickBooks tracks inventory costs using the weighted-average method. QuickBooks does not use FIFO (First-in, First-out) or LIFO (Last-in, First-out) inventory costing. The average cost of an inventory item is displayed in the *Edit Item* window.

For consistency, the *same* inventory item is used when recording *sales* and *purchases*. QuickBooks has the capability to track both the cost and the sales price for inventory items. For example, in Chapter 4, you recorded the *sale* of an inventory item, an interior door. When the interior door was recorded on a sales invoice, QuickBooks automatically updated your inventory records by reducing the quantity of doors on hand. If you *purchased* an interior door, then you would record the door on the purchase order using the same inventory item number that you used on the invoice, except the purchase order uses the door cost while the invoice uses the door selling price.

> QuickBooks does *not* track the **quantity** of non-inventory items. If it is important for your business to know the quantity of an item on hand, record the item as an inventory item.

3. **Non-Inventory Items:** QuickBooks does not track the quantity on hand for non-inventory items. Non-inventory items include:

- Items purchased for a specific customer job, such as a custom counter top.

- Items purchased and used by your company instead of resold to customers, such as office supplies or carpentry tools.

- Items purchased and resold (if the quantity on hand does not need to be tracked).

ITEMS AND SERVICES LIST

The Items and Services List (Item List) summarizes information about items (inventory items, non-inventory items, and service items) that a company purchases or sells.

To view the Item List in QuickBooks:

Step 1: Click the **Items and Services** icon in the Company section of the Home page.

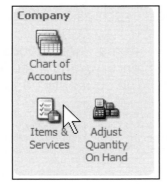

Step 2: The following *Item List* window will appear.

Name	Description	Type	Account	On Hand	Price
◆Metal Wrk	Metal Work	Service	4000 · Construction:4...		0.00
◆Painting	Painting	Service	4000 · Construction:4...		0.00
◆Plumbing	Plumbing	Service	4000 · Construction:4...		0.00
◆Roofing	Roofing	Service	4000 · Construction:4...		0.00
◆Tile &Counter	Install tile or counter	Service	4000 · Construction:4...		0.00
◆Cabinets	Cabinets	Inventory...	4000 · Construction:4...	-2	0.00
◆Cabinet Pulls	Cabinet Pulls	Inventory...	4000 · Construction:4...	103	0.00
◆Light Pine	Light pine kitchen cabinet wall unit	Inventory...	4000 · Construction:4...	8	1,799.00
◆Door Frame	standard interior door frame	Inventory...	4000 · Construction:4...	2	0.00
◆Hardware		Inventory...	4000 · Construction:4...	0	0.00
◆Brass hinges	standard interior brass hinge	Inventory...	4000 · Construction:4...	460	0.00
◆Doorknobs Std	Standard Doorknobs	Inventory...	4000 · Construction:4...	103	30.00
◆Lk Doorknobs	Locking interior doorknobs	Inventory...	4000 · Construction:4...	109	38.00
◆Wood Door	Doors	Inventory...	4000 · Construction:4...	0	0.00
◆Exterior	Exterior wood door	Inventory...	4000 · Construction:4...	2	120.00
◆Interior	Interior wood door	Inventory...	4000 · Construction:4...	31	72.00
◆Interior Door kit	complete Interior door	Inventory...	4000 · Construction:4...	4	0.00
◆Appliance		Non-inven...	4000 · Construction:4...		0.00
◆Cabinets - Custom	Custom counters	Non-inven...	4000 · Construction:4...		0.00
◆Counter	Custom made counter top	Non-inven...	4000 · Construction:4...		1,899.98
◆Flooring		Non-inven...	4000 · Construction:4...		0.00
◆Fluorescent Ceiling...	Fluorescent Lights	Non-inven...	4000 · Construction:4...		0.00

Notice that the Item List contains the following information:

- Item name

- Item description

- Item type (service, inventory, non-inventory, other charge, discount, sales tax item)

- Account used

- Quantity on hand

- Price of the item

Scroll down through the list to view the inventory and non-inventory items for Rock Castle Construction.

ADD NEW ITEM TO ITEM LIST

Rock Castle Construction needs to add two new items to the Item List: bifold doors and bifold door hardware. Because Rock Castle Construction wants to track the quantity of each item, both will be inventory items.

To add an inventory item to the Item List:

Step 1: From the *Item List* window, right-click to display the following pop-up menu. Select **New**.

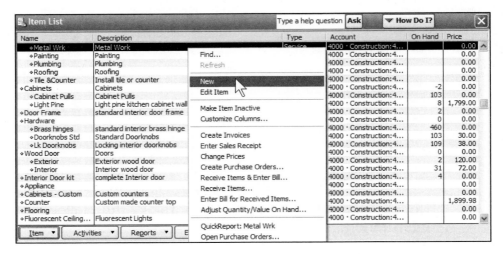

Step 2: In the *New Item* window that appears, you will enter information about the bifold door inventory item. From the Type drop-down list, select **Inventory Part**.

> Use **Group** if the same group of items are bought or sold as a package.

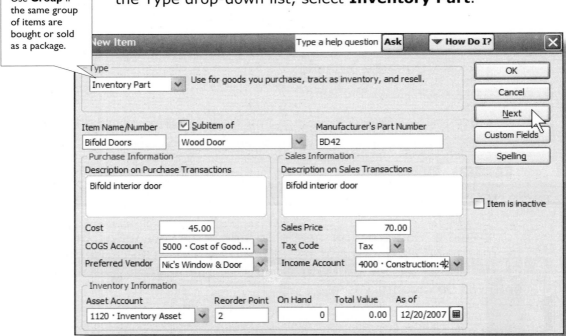

Step 3: Enter the following information in the *New Item* window.

Item Name/Number	Bifold Doors
Subitem of	Wood Door
Manufacturer's Part Number	BD42
Description on Purchase Transactions	Bifold interior door
Description on Sales Transactions	Bifold interior door
Cost	45.00
COGS Account	5000 – Cost of Goods Sold
Preferred Vendor	Nic's Window & Door
Sales Price	70.00
Tax Code	Tax
Income Account	4000 – Construction: 4200 Materials
Asset Account	1120 – Inventory Asset
Reorder Point	2
Qty on Hand	0
Total Value	0.00
As of	12/20/2007

If spell checker starts, click **Close**.

Step 4: Click **Next** to record this inventory item and clear the fields to record another inventory item.

Step 5: Enter bifold door knobs as an inventory item in the Item List using the following information:

Item Name/Number	Bifold Knobs
Subitem of	Hardware
Manufacturer's Part Number	BK36
Description on Purchase Transactions	Bifold door hardware
Description on Sales Transactions	Bifold door hardware
Cost	6.00
Sales Price	10.00
Tax Code	Tax
COGS Account	5000 – Cost of Goods Sold
Preferred Vendor	Patton Hardware Supplies
Income Account	4000 – Construction: 4200 Materials
Asset Account	1120 – Inventory Asset
Reorder Point	2
Qty on Hand	0
Total Value	0.00
As of	12/20/2007

Step 6: Click **OK** to record the item and close the *New Item* window.

PRINT THE ITEM LIST

🖨 **Print** the Item List as follows:

Step 1: Click the **Reports** button in the lower left corner of the *Item List* window.

Step 2: Select **Item Listing**.

Step 3: Click the **Print** button.

Step 4: Select the **Landscape** print settings, then click **Print**.

Step 5: **Close** the *Item List* window.

VENDOR TRANSACTIONS

After creating a Vendor List and an Item List, you are ready to enter vendor transactions.

There are two basic ways to enter vendor transactions using QuickBooks.

1. Enter Bills. This is used to record services, such as utilities or accounting services. After the bill is entered, it is paid when it is due.

2. Enter Purchase Order, Receive Inventory, Enter Bill. This is used to record the purchase of inventory items where it is necessary to keep a record of the order placed. The purchase order provides this record.

The diagrams on the following page summarizes how to use QuickBooks to record the different vendor transactions.

ENTER BILLS FOR SERVICES RECEIVED

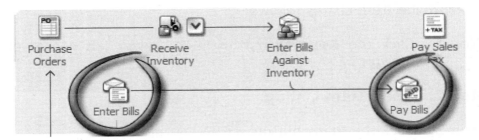

❶ **Enter Bills:** Record bills for services, such as utilities.

❷ **Pay Bills:** Select bills to pay, then print checks.

ORDER GOODS, RECEIVE INVENTORY, RECEIVE BILL

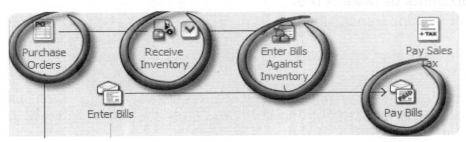

❶ **Purchase Order**: Prepare an order to purchase items from vendors.

❷ **Receive Inventory:** Record inventory items received.

❸ **Enter Bill for Inventory:** Record bill received as accounts payable.

❹ **Pay Bills:** Select bills to pay, then print checks.

ORDER GOODS, RECEIVE INVENTORY, RECEIVE BILL

Display the Home page to view the flowchart of vendor transactions. Recording the purchase of goods using QuickBooks involves the following steps:

❶ Create a Purchase Order to order items from vendors.

❷ Receive item and record as an inventory or non-inventory part.

❸ Receive bill and record an obligation to pay the vendor later (accounts payable).

❹ Pay bill by selecting bills to pay.

❺ Print checks to vendors. Since the obligation is fulfilled, accounts payable is reduced.

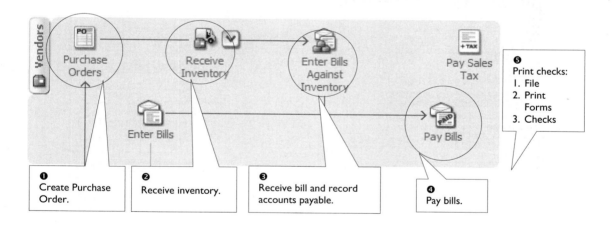

CREATE PURCHASE ORDERS

A Purchase Order is a record of an order to purchase inventory from a vendor.

Rock Castle Construction wants to order 6 bifold interior doors and 6 sets of bifold door hardware to stock in inventory.

To create a Purchase Order:

Step 1: Click the **Purchase Orders** icon in the Vendor section of the Home page.

Step 2: From the drop-down vendor list, select the vendor name: **Nic's Window & Door**.

Step 3: Select Form Template: **Custom Purchase Order**.

Step 4: Enter the purchase order date: **12/20/2007**.

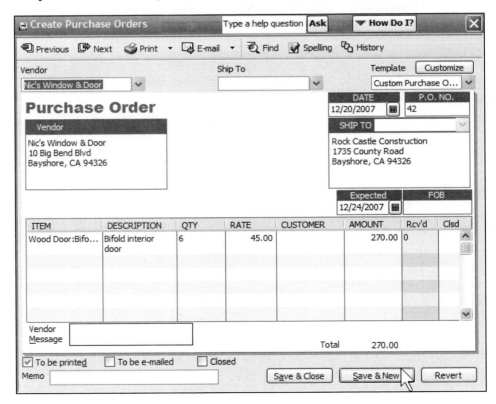

Step 5: Enter the Expected Date: **12/24/2007**.

Step 6: Select item ordered: **Wood Doors: Bifold Doors**. ($45.00 now appears in the Rate column.)

Step 7: Enter Quantity: **6**. ($270.00 should now appear in the Amount column.)

Step 8: Print the Purchase Order as follows:

- Click **Print**.

- Select Print on: **Blank paper**.

- If necessary, uncheck **Do not print lines around each field**.

- Click **Print**.

Step 9: Click **Save & New** (or **Next**) to record the Purchase Order and clear the fields in the *Purchase Order* window.

Step 10: Create and print a purchase order for bifold door hardware using the following information.

Vendor	Patton Hardware Supplies
Custom Template	Custom Purchase Order
Date	12/20/2007
Expected Date	12/24/2007
Item	Hardware: Bifold knobs
QTY	6

> ✓ **The Purchase Order total for bifold door hardware is $36.**

Step 11: Click **Save & Close** to record the purchase order and close the *Purchase Order* window.

RECEIVE INVENTORY

To record inventory items received on 12/22/2007 that were ordered from the vendor, Nic's Window & Door, complete the following steps:

Step 1: Click the **Receive Inventory** icon in Vendor section of the Home page.

Step 2: Select: **Receive Inventory without Bill.**

Step 3: In the *Create Item Receipts* window, select vendor: **Nic's Window & Door**.

Step 4: If a purchase order for the item exists, QuickBooks will display the following *Open PO's Exist* window.

- Click **Yes**.

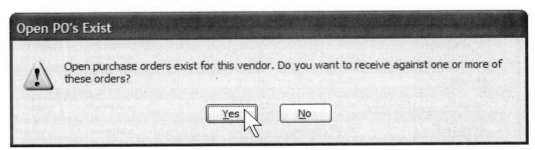

- When the following *Open Purchase Orders* window appears, select the Purchase Order for the items received, and then click **OK**.

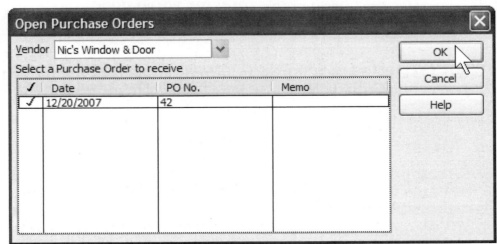

Step 5: The *Create Item Receipts* window will appear with a total of $270. If necessary, change the Date to: **12/22/2007**.

Although Rock Castle Construction ordered 6 bifold doors, only 5 were received. Change the quantity from 6 to **5**.

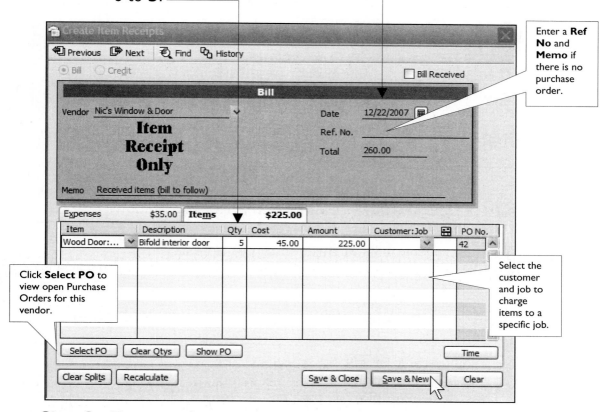

Enter a **Ref No** and **Memo** if there is no purchase order.

Click **Select PO** to view open Purchase Orders for this vendor.

Select the customer and job to charge items to a specific job.

Step 6: To record expenses associated with the items received, such as freight charges:

- Click the **Expenses** tab in the *Create Item Receipts* window.

- To record $35.00 in freight charges on the bifold doors received, select Account: **6400 Freight & Delivery**.

- Enter Amount: $**35.00**.

- Click the **Recalculate** button.

✓ ***The Total on the Create Item Receipts window is now $260.00.***

Step 7: Click **Save & New** (or **Next**) to record the bifold doors received and clear the window.

Step 8: Record the receipt of the bifold door hardware using the following information:

Vendor	Patton Hardware Supplies
Date	12/22/2007
PO No.	43
Item	Bifold door hardware
Qty	6

Step 9: Click **Save & Close** to record the items received and close the *Create Item Receipts* window.

RECEIVE BILLS

You may receive bills at three different times:

	Receive Bill...	Record Using...
1.	You receive a bill for services and no inventory items will be received, as for example, if the bill is for janitorial services.	*Enter Bills*
2.	You receive a bill at the same time you receive inventory items.	*Receive Inventory with Bill*
3.	You receive inventory without a bill, and you receive a bill later after you receive the inventory items.	*a. Receive Inventory without a Bill* *b. Enter Bills Against Inventory*

Later, you will learn how to record bills for situation 1 and 2 above. Next, you will record the bill received for the bifold doors ordered from Nic's Window & Door (situation 3 above).

ENTER BILLS AGAINST INVENTORY

To enter a bill received after inventory items are received:

Step 1: Click the **Enter Bills Against Inventory** icon on the Vendor section of the Home page.

Step 2: When the *Select Item Receipt* window appears:

- Select Vendor: **Nic's Window & Door**. If necessary, press **Tab**.

- Select the Item Receipt that corresponds to the bill.

- Click **OK**.

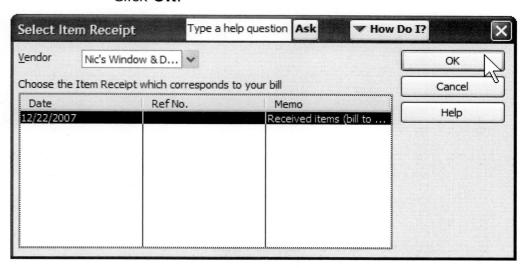

Step 3: The following *Enter Bills* window will appear. Notice that the *Enter Bills* window is the same as the *Create Item Receipts* window except:

(1) *Item Receipt Only* stamp does not appear, and

(2) Bill Received in the upper right corner is checked.

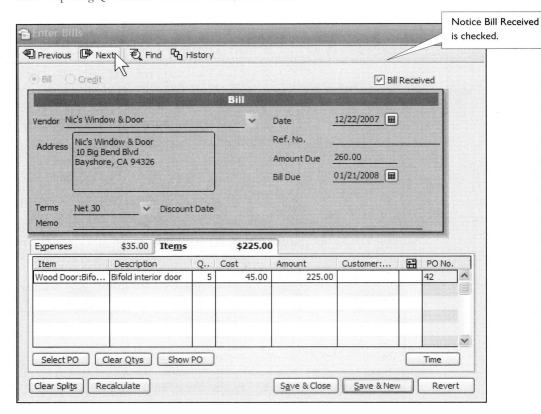

Step 4: At this point, you can make any changes necessary, such as:

- Change the date if the bill is received on a date different from the date the item was received. In this instance, the item and bill are both received on **12/22/2007**.

- Terms

- Ref No.

- Memo

- Expenses, such as freight charges

Step 5: The Amount Due of $260.00 should agree with the amount shown on the vendor's bill.

Step 6: Click **Next** to advance to the Item Receipt for the bifold door hardware purchased from Patton Hardware Supplies.

Step 7: To record the bill received for the bifold door hardware from Patton Hardware Supplies, check **Bill Received** in the upper right corner of the window. Notice that the Item Receipt Only stamp is no longer displayed and the window name changed from *Create Item Receipts* to *Enter Bills*.

Step 8: Use the following information to record the bill for the bifold door hardware.

Vendor	Patton Hardware Supplies
Date Bill Received	12/22/2007
PO No.	43
Terms	Net 30
Item	Bifold door hardware
Qty	6

Step 9: Click **Save & Close** to record the bill and close the *Enter Bills* window. If asked if you want to change the terms, click **Yes**.

When you enter a bill, QuickBooks automatically adds the bill amount to your Accounts Payable account balance.

PAY BILLS

After receiving the items and entering the bill, the next step is to pay the bill.

To select the bills to pay:

Step 1: Click the **Pay Bills** icon in the Vendor section of the Home page.

Step 2: Select Show Bills: **Show all bills**.

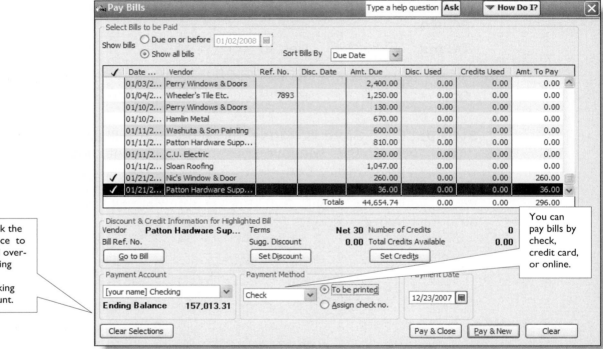

Step 3: Select the bills you want to pay. Typically, you would select the bills that are due first. In this case, however, select **bills that you just recorded for:**

- **Nic's Window and Door for $260.00**

- **Patton Hardware for $36.00**

If necessary, scroll down to view the above bills.

Step 4: In the *Payment Method* section, select: **Check**. Then select: **To be printed**.

Step 5: Select Payment Date: **12/23/2007**.

Step 6: Click **Pay & Close** to close the *Pay Bills* window.

> ✓ *Bills selected for payment total $296.00*

To print checks complete the following steps:

Step 1: From the **File** menu, select **Print forms | Checks**.

Step 2: When the *Select Checks to Print* window appears, select Bank Account: **[your name] Checking**.

Step 3: Select First Check Number: **304**.

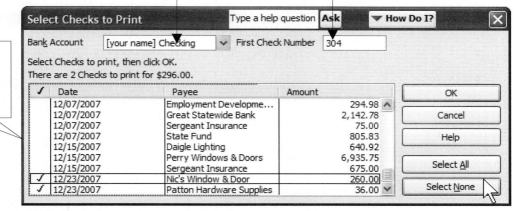

QuickBooks prints one check for each vendor, combining all amounts due to the same vendor.

Step 4: Click **Select None**.

Step 5: Scroll down and select the two checks checked above:

- **12/23/2007 Nic's Window & Door for $260.00**
- **12/23/2007 Patton Hardware for $36.00**

Step 6: Click **OK**.

Step 7: Select Check Style: **Standard**. Select: **Print company name and address**.

Step 8: If you use Intuit's preprinted check forms, you would now insert the check forms in your printer. Then click **Print**.

ENTER BILLS WITH INVENTORY

If you receive the inventory item and the bill at the same time (situation 2 mentioned earlier), record both the items and the related bill by completing the following steps:

Step 1: Click the **Receive Inventory** icon in the Vendor section of the Home page.

Step 2: Select: **Receive Inventory with Bill**.

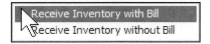

Step 3: In the following *Enter Bills* window:

- Enter Vendor: **Wheeler Tile, Inc.**

- Select the open purchase order that corresponds to the bill received: **PO No. 4**.

- Click **OK**.

- Make any necessary changes to date, quantity or cost. In this case, if necessary change the date to: **12/23/2007**.

> Notice that this *Enter Bills* window is the same window that appeared when you clicked the *Enter Bills Against Inventory* icon.

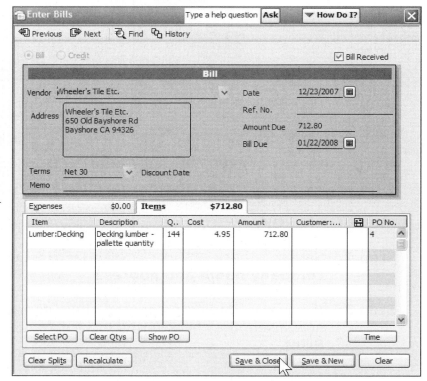

Step 4: Click **Save & Close** to close the *Enter Bills* window.

ENTER BILLS

When you received inventory items from vendors, you recorded those items using either the *Receive Inventory with Bill* option or *Receive Inventory without Bill* option, entering the bill later.

To record services instead of inventory received, use the Enter Bills icon. Expenses that can be recorded using the *Enter Bills* window include utilities, insurance, and rent.

To enter bills for expenses:

Step 1: Click the **Enter Bills** icon in the Vendor section of the Home page.

Step 2: The following *Enter Bills* window will appear. Click the **Expenses** tab.

> Notice that the *Enter Bills* window is the same window that appeared when you clicked the *Receive Inventory* or *Enter Bills Against Inventory* icon.

> You can record a bill as an Expense or an Item (inventory or non-inventory).

Step 3:   Enter the following information for Rock Castle's water bill in the *Enter Bills* window.

Vendor	Bayshore Water
Date	12/24/2007
Amount Due	$36.00
Terms	Net 30
Account	7630: Water

Step 4:   Click **Save & Close** to close the *Enter Bills* window.

Step 5:   The next time you pay bills in QuickBooks, the water bill will appear on the list of bills to pay.

PAY SALES TAX

QuickBooks tracks the sales tax that you collect from customers and must remit to governmental agencies. When you set up a new company in QuickBooks, you identify which items and customers are subject to sales tax. In addition, you must specify the appropriate sales tax rate. Then whenever you prepare sales invoices, QuickBooks automatically calculates and adds sales tax to the invoices.

Rock Castle Construction is required to collect sales tax from customers on certain items sold. Rock Castle then must pay the sales tax collected to the appropriate governmental tax agency.

QuickBooks uses a two-step process to remit sales tax:

1. The *Pay Sales Tax* window lists the sales taxes owed and allows you to select the individual sales tax items you want to pay.

2. Print the check to pay the sales tax.

To select the sales tax to pay:

Step 1: Click the **Pay Sales Tax** icon in the Vendor section of the Home page.

Step 2: When the following *Pay Sales Tax* window appears:

- Select Pay From Account: **[your name] Checking**
- Select Check Date: **12/31/2007**.
- Show sales tax due through: **12/31/2007**.
- Check **To be printed**.

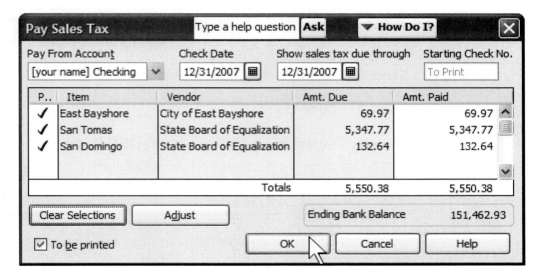

Step 3: Select: **Pay All Tax**.

Step 4: Click **OK**.

To print the check to pay sales tax to a governmental agency:

Step 1: Click **File** (Menu).

Step 2: Select **Print Forms**.

Step 3: Select **Checks**.

Step 4: When the following *Select Checks to Print* window appears, select **City of East Bayshore** and **State Board of Equalization**.

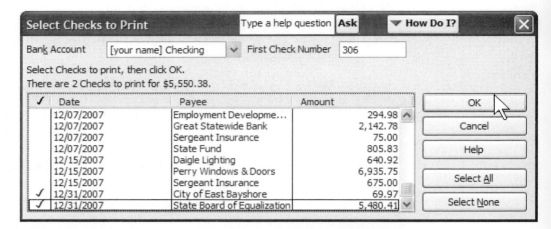

Step 5: Select Bank Account: **[your name] Checking**.

Step 6: Select First Check Number: **306**.

Step 7: Click **OK**.

Step 8: Select print settings, then click **Print**.

VENDOR REPORTS

QuickBooks provides vendor reports to answer the following questions:

- How much do we owe? (Accounts Payable reports)
- How much have we purchased? (Purchase reports)
- How much inventory do we have? (Inventory reports)

QuickBooks offers several different ways to access vendor reports:

1. **Vendor Center:** Summarizes vendor information in one location (Access the Vendor Center by clicking the Vendor Center icon on the Navigation Bar.)

2. **Report Center:** Permits you to locate reports by type of report (Click the Report Center icon in the Navigation Bar, then, see Vendors & Payables, Purchases, and Inventory reports).

3. Report Menu: Reports are grouped by type of report (See Vendors & Payables, Purchases, and Inventory reports).

VENDOR CENTER

The Vendor Center summarizes vendor information in one convenient location. Display the Vendor Center as follows:

Step 1: From the Navigation Bar, select **Vendor Center**.

Step 2: Select Vendor: **Nic's Window & Door**.

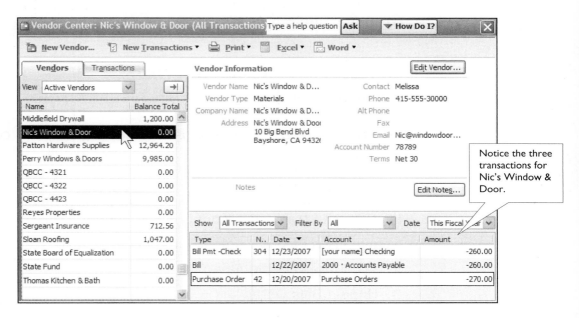

The Vendor Information section summarizes information about the vendor selected, including listing the transactions for the specific vendor. In this case, you recorded three transactions for Nic's Window & Door:

- Purchase Order on 12/20/2007
- Bill Received on 12/22/2007
- Bill Paid on 12/23/2007

Step 3: **Double-click** the **Bill Payment transaction on 12/23/2007** to drill-down and view the check to pay Nic's Window & Door. After viewing, close the window.

Step 4: With the cursor over the vendor transaction section of the window, **right-click** to display the following pop-up menu. Select **View as a Report**.

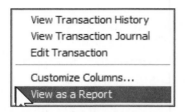

Step 5: 🖶 **Print** the report of all transactions for Nic's Window & Door for this fiscal year.

Step 6: **Close** the report window.

ACCOUNTS PAYABLE REPORTS: HOW MUCH DO WE OWE?

Accounts Payable consists of amounts that your company is obligated to pay in the future. Accounts Payable reports tell you how much you owe vendors and when amounts are due.

The following Accounts Payable reports provide information useful when tracking amounts owed vendors:

1. Accounts Payable Aging Summary
2. Accounts Payable Aging Detail
3. Unpaid Bills Detail

ACCOUNTS PAYABLE AGING SUMMARY

The Accounts Payable Aging Summary summarizes accounts payable balances by the age of the account. This report helps to track any past due bills as well as provides information about bills that will be due shortly.

Although you can access the vendor reports in several different ways, we will access this report from the Report Center.

To print the A/P Aging Summary report:

Step 1: From the **Report Center**, select: **Vendors & Payables**.

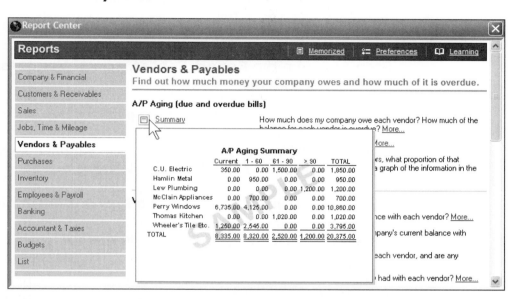

> Double-click an entry to drill down to display transaction detail. Double-click again to view the bill.

Step 2: Select: **A/P Aging Summary**.

Step 3: Select Date: **12/22/2007**. Click **Refresh**.

Step 4: 🖨 **Print** the report using the **Portrait** orientation.

Step 5: ✏ **Circle** the vendors and amounts of any account payable that is 31-60 days past due.

Step 6: **Close** the *A/P Aging Summary* window.

✓   ***$4,837.56 is 31-60 days past due.***

ACCOUNTS PAYABLE AGING DETAIL

The Accounts Payable Aging Detail report lists the specific bills that make up the account payable balances.

To print the A/P Aging Detail report:

Step 1: From the **Report Center**, select: **Vendors & Payables**.

Step 2: Select: **A/P Aging Detail**.

> Double-click on an entry to drill down to the related bill.

Step 3: When the *A/P Aging Detail* window appears, select Date: **12/22/2007**. Click **Refresh**.

Step 4: 🖨 **Print** the report using **Portrait** orientation.

Step 5: **Close** the *A/P Aging Detail* window.

UNPAID BILLS DETAIL

QuickBooks permits you to view all of your unpaid bills or unpaid bills for a specific vendor.

To view all of your unpaid bills, use the Unpaid Bills Detail report:

Step 1: From the **Report Center**, select: **Vendors & Payables.**

Step 2: Select: **Unpaid Bills Detail**.

Step 3: When the *Unpaid Bills Detail* window appears, select Date: **12/22/2007**. Click **Refresh**. All of the unpaid bills will appear.

Step 4: 🖨 **Print** the Unpaid Bills Detail report.

Step 5: ✎ **Circle** any bills past due.

Step 6: **Close** the *Unpaid Bills Detail* window.

PURCHASE REPORTS:
HOW MUCH HAVE WE PURCHASED?

Purchase reports provide information about purchases by item, by vendor, or by open purchase orders. Purchase reports include:

1. Open Purchase Orders Report (Outstanding Purchase Orders)

2. Purchases by Vendor Summary

3. Purchases by Item Summary

OPEN PURCHASE ORDERS REPORT

Open purchase orders are purchase orders for items ordered but not yet received. QuickBooks permits you to view open purchase orders for a specific vendor or to view all open purchase orders.

To print the Open Purchase Orders Report that lists all open purchase orders:

Step 1: From the **Report Center**, select: **Purchases**.

Step 2: Select: **Open Purchase Orders**.

Step 3: Select Dates: **All**. Click **Refresh**.

Step 4: 🖨 **Print** the report using **Portrait** orientation.

Step 5: **Close** the *Open Purchase Orders* window.

> ✓ **Open purchase orders equal $62,031.25.**

INVENTORY REPORTS:
HOW MUCH INVENTORY DO WE HAVE?

Inventory reports list the amount and status of inventory. Inventory reports include:

1. Inventory Stock Status By Item
2. Physical Inventory Worksheet

INVENTORY STOCK STATUS BY ITEM

This report lists quantity of inventory items on hand and on order. This information is useful for planning when and how many units to order.

To print the Inventory Stock Status By Item report:

Step 1: From the **Report Center**, select: **Inventory**.

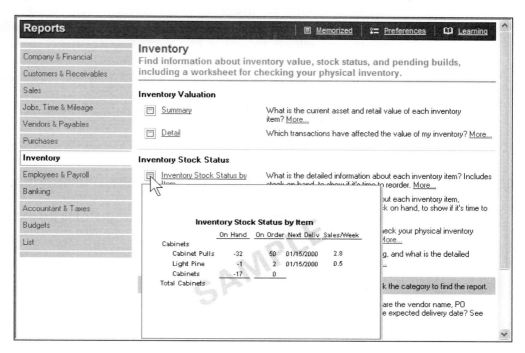

Step 2: Select: **Inventory Stock Status By Item**.

Step 3: Enter Date: From: **12/22/2007** To: **12/22/2007**. Click **Refresh**.

Step 4: 🖨 **Print** the report using **Landscape** orientation.

Step 5: **Close** the *Stock Status By Item* window.

> ✓ ***On 12/22/2007, 5 bifold wood doors are on hand and 1 more is on order.***

PHYSICAL INVENTORY WORKSHEET

The Physical Inventory Worksheet is used when taking a physical count of inventory on hand. The worksheet lists the quantity of inventory items on hand and provides a blank column in which to enter the quantity counted during a physical inventory count. This worksheet permits you to compare your physical inventory count with your QuickBooks records.

To print the Physical Inventory Worksheet:

Step 1: From the **Report Center**, select: **Inventory**.

Step 2: Select: **Physical Inventory Worksheet**.

Step 3: 🖨 **Print** the worksheet using **Portrait** orientation. Use the Fit to Page feature as needed.

Step 4: **Close** the *Physical Inventory Worksheet* window.

QuickBooks offers other additional vendor reports that provide useful information to a business. These reports can also be accessed from the Reports menu or from the Report Center.

SAVE CHAPTER 5

Save Chapter 5 as a portable QuickBooks file to the location specified by your instructor.

Step 1: If necessary, insert a removable disk.

Step 2: From the menu bar, click **File | Portable Company File | Create File**.

Step 3: When the *Close and Reopen* window appears, click **OK**.

Step 4: When the following *Create Portable Company File* window appears, enter the filename: **[your name] Chapter 5** and the appropriate location. Then click **Save**.

Step 5: Click **OK** after the portable file has been created successfully.

Step 6: Close the company file by clicking **File** (Menu), **Close Company**.

> *If you are continuing your computer session, proceed to Exercise 5.1.*
>
> *If you are ending your computer session now, see the Quick Reference Guide in Part 3 for instructions to (1) close the company file and (2) exit QuickBooks.*

ASSIGNMENTS

> **NOTE: See the Quick Reference Guide in Part 3 for step-by-step instructions to frequently used tasks.**

EXERCISE 5.1: PURCHASE INVENTORY

SCENARIO

Mr. Castle tosses you a document as he charges past your cubicle, shouting over his shoulder, *"That's info about our new supplier. From now on, Rock Castle will install closet shelving instead of waiting on unreliable subcontractors. We do a better job and we get it done on time!"*

Vendor:	Rishe's Racks
Contact:	Patrick Rishe
Address:	9 Big Bend Blvd
	Bayshore, CA 94326
Phone:	415-555-0414
Email:	prishe@racks.com
Alt Contact	Jonathan
Account:	78790
Type:	Materials
Terms:	Net 30
Vendor 1099:	No

New Inventory Item: Closet Materials

New Subitems:

6' Closet Shelving	Cost: $11.00	Sales Price: $15.00
12' Closet Shelving	Cost: $18.00	Sales Price: $25.00
Closet Installation Kit	Cost: $ 5.00	Sales Price: $ 8.00

Reorder Point: 2 each item

TASK 1: OPEN PORTABLE COMPANY FILE

To open the portable company file (.QBM) file, convert the portable file to a regular company file with a .QBW extension as follows:

Step 1: From the menu bar, click **File | Portable Company File | Open File**.

Step 2: Identify the filename and location for the portable company file:

- Click the **Browse** button to find the location of the portable company file on the hard drive or removable media.

- Select the file: **[your name] Chapter 5.QBM**.

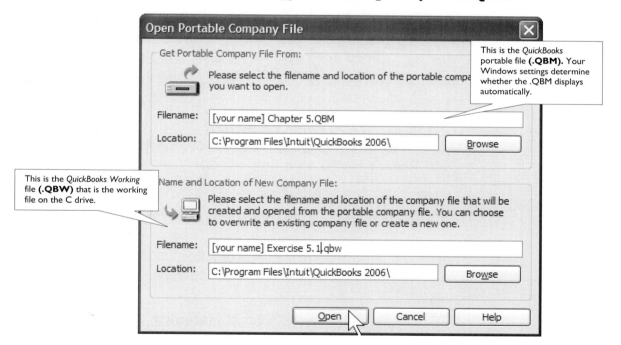

Step 3: Identify the name and location of the new company file (.QBW) file to use for completing Exercise 5.1:

- Filename: **[your name] Exercise 5.1**. The **.QBW** extension should appear automatically based upon your Windows settings.

- Location: **C:\Program Files\Intuit\QuickBooks 2006**. This is the location of the .QBW file on the hard drive of your computer. Click the Browse button to specify another location.

Step 4: Click **Open** to open the portable company file.

Step 5: Click **Cancel** when the *Create a Backup* window appears.

Step 6: If prompted, enter your **User Name** and **Password**, then click **OK**.

Step 7: Click **OK** when the QuickBooks sample company message appears.

Step 8: Change the company name to: **[your name] Exercise 5.1 Rock Castle Construction**. (If you need instructions to change the company name, see Part 3: Quick Reference Guide.)

> See the Scenario information on previous pages for information to complete Tasks 2, 3, and 4.

TASK 2: ADD NEW VENDOR

Add Rishe's Racks as a new vendor.

TASK 3: ADD NEW INVENTORY ITEM

Step 1: Add the new inventory item, Closets, to the Items List for Rock Castle Construction.

Item Name/Number	Closet Materials
Item Type	Inventory Part
Item Description	Closet Materials
COGS Account	5000 – Cost of Goods Sold
Income Account	4200 – Materials
Asset Account	1120 – Inventory Asset
Tax Code	Tax

Step 2: Add the following three new inventory parts as subitems to Closet Materials. Use **Rishe's Racks** as the preferred vendor.

Item Name	6' Closet Shelving
Item Description	6' Closet Shelving
Cost	$11.00
Sales Price	$15.00

Item Name	12' Closet Shelving
Item Description	12' Closet Shelving
Cost	$18.00
Sales Price	$25.00

Item Name	Closet Install Kit
Item Description	Closet Installation Kit
Cost	$5.00
Sales Price	$8.00

TASK 4: CREATE PURCHASE ORDER

Step 1: Create a Purchase Order to order **6** each of the new inventory items from **Rishe's Racks** on **12/23/2007**. Expected delivery date: **12/24/2007**.

Step 2: ▭ **Print** the Purchase Order.

✓ **The total amount of the purchase order is $204.00.**

TASK 5: RECEIVE INVENTORY

On **12/24/2007**, record the receipt of the closet inventory items ordered on **12/23/2007**. There are no freight charges.

TASK 6: RECEIVE BILL

Record the receipt of the bill for the closet items on **12/27/2007**. Use the **Enter Bills Against Inventory** icon in the Vendor section of the Home page.

TASK 7: PAY BILLS

Pay the bill for the closet materials ordered from Rishe's Racks on **12/28/ 2007** with Check No. **308**. ▤ **Print** the check.

TASK 8: SAVE EXERCISE 5.1

Save Exercise 5.1 as a portable company file to the location specified by your instructor.

Step 1: If necessary, insert a removable disk.

Step 2: From the menu bar, click **File | Portable Company File | Create File**.

Step 3: When the *Close and Reopen* window appears, click **OK**.

Step 4: When the *Create Portable Company File* window appears, enter the filename: **[your name] Exercise 5.1** and the appropriate location. Click **Save**.

Step 5: Click **OK** after the portable file has been created successfully.

Step 6: Close the company file by clicking **File** (Menu), **Close Company**.

EXERCISE 5.2:
RECORD SALE (CHAPTER 4 REVIEW)

SCENARIO

"I told you replacing Mrs. Beneficio's door hardware would pay off. She is going to become one of our best customers. Just wait and see." Mr. Castle appears to be in a much better mood today. *"Katrina Beneficio just had us install new closet shelving in her huge walk-in closet. She said she wanted us to do it because we stand by our work."*

TASK 1: OPEN PORTABLE COMPANY FILE

To open the portable company file (.QBM) file, convert the portable file to a regular company file with a .QBW extension as follows:

Step 1: From the menu bar, click **File | Portable Company File | Open File**.

Step 2: Identify the filename and location for the portable company file:

- Click the **Browse** button to find the location of the portable company file on the hard drive or removable media.

- Select the file: **[your name] Exercise 5.1.QBM**.

Step 3: Identify the name and location of the new company file (.QBW) file to use for completing Exercise 5.2:

- Filename: **[your name] Exercise 5.2**. The **.QBW** extension should appear automatically based upon your Windows settings.

- Location: **C:\Program Files\Intuit\QuickBooks 2006**. This is the location of the .QBW file on the hard drive of your computer. Click the Browse button to specify another location.

Step 4:   Click **Open** to open the portable company file.

Step 5:   Click **Cancel** when the *Create a Backup* window appears.

Step 6:   If prompted, enter your **User Name** and **Password**, then click **OK**.

Step 7:   Click **OK** when the QuickBooks sample company message appears.

Step 8:   Change the company name to: **[your name] Exercise 5.2 Rock Castle Construction**. (If you need instructions to change the company name, see Part 3: Quick Reference Guide.)

NOTE: Use the Customer icons on the Home page to record Tasks 2 – 5.

TASK 2: ADD CUSTOMER JOB

Add the Closet Shelving job for Katrina Beneficio to the Customer & Job List. (Hint: From the Customer Center, select Beneficio, then right-click to display menu, select Add Job.)

Job Name	Closet Shelving
Job Status	Closed
Start Date	12/27/2007
Projected End	12/27/2007
End Date	12/27/2007
Job Description	Replace Closet Shelving
Job Type	Repairs

TASK 3: CREATE INVOICE

Step 1: Create an invoice for the Beneficio closet shelving job using the following information.

Customer: Job	Beneficio, Katrina: Closet Shelving
Custom Template	Time & Expense Invoice
Date	12/27/2007
Invoice No.	98
Items	(2) 12' Closet Shelves $25.00 each
	(1) 6' Closet Shelves $15.00 each
	(1) Closet Installation Kit $ 8.00 each
	Installation Labor 3 hours

Step 2: 🖨 **Print** the invoice.

> ✓ **The invoice for the Closet Shelving job totals $183.66.**

TASK 4: RECEIVE CUSTOMER PAYMENT

Record Katrina Beneficio's payment for the Closet Job (Check No. 625) for the full amount on **12/29/2007**.

TASK 5: RECORD BANK DEPOSIT

Step 1: Record the bank deposit for Katrina Beneficio's payment.

Step 2: 🖨 **Print** a deposit summary.

TASK 6: SAVE EXERCISE 5.2

Save Exercise 5.2 as a portable company file to the location specified by your instructor.

Step 1: If necessary, insert a removable disk.

Step 2: From the menu bar, click **File | Portable Company File | Create File**.

Step 3: When the *Close and Reopen* window appears, click **OK**.

Step 4: When the *Create Portable Company File* window appears, enter the filename: **[your name] Exercise 5.2** and the appropriate location. Click **Save**.

Step 5: Click **OK** after the portable file has been created successfully.

Step 6: Close the company file by clicking **File** (Menu), **Close Company**.

EXERCISE 5.3: ENTER BILLS

SCENARIO

When you arrive at work, you decide to sort through the papers stacked in the corner of your cubicle. You discover two unpaid utility bills amid the clutter.

TASK 1: OPEN PORTABLE COMPANY FILE

To open the portable company file (.QBM) file, convert the portable file to a regular company file with a .QBW extension as follows:

Step 1: From the menu bar, click **File | Portable Company File | Open File**.

Step 2: Identify the filename and location for the portable company file:

- Click the **Browse** button to find the location of the portable company file on the hard drive or removable media.

- Select the file: **[your name] Exercise 5.2.QBM**.

Step 3: Identify the name and location of the new company file (.QBW) file to use for completing Exercise 5.3:

- Filename: **[your name] Exercise 5.3**. The **.QBW** extension should appear automatically based upon your Windows settings.

- Location: **C:\Program Files\Intuit\QuickBooks 2006**. This is the location of the .QBW file on the hard drive of your computer. Click the Browse button to specify another location.

Step 4: Click **Open** to open the portable company file.

Step 5: Click **Cancel** when the *Create a Backup* window appears.

Step 6: If prompted, enter your **User Name** and **Password**, then click **OK**.

Step 7: Click **OK** when the QuickBooks sample company message appears.

Step 8: Change the company name to: **[your name] Exercise 5.3 Rock Castle Construction**. (If you need instructions to change the company name, see Part 3: Quick Reference Guide.)

TASK 2: ENTER BILLS

Using the **Enter Bills** icon in the Vendor section of the Home page, enter the following two utility bills for Rock Castle Construction.

Vendor	Cal Gas & Electric
Date	12/24/2007
Amount	$87.00
Account	7610: Gas and Electric

Vendor	Cal Telephone
Date	12/24/2007
Amount	$54.00
Account	7620: Telephone

TASK 3: PAY BILLS

On **12/28/2007**, pay the two utility bills that you entered in Task 2. (Hint: Select **Show all bills**.) 🖶 **Print** the checks.

> ✓ **The Amt. To Pay on the Pay Bills window totals $141.00.**

TASK 4: SAVE EXERCISE 5.3

Save Exercise 5.3 as a portable company file to the location specified by your instructor.

Step 1: If necessary, insert a removable disk.

Step 2: From the menu bar, click **File | Portable Company File | Create File**.

Step 3: When the *Close and Reopen* window appears, click **OK**.

Step 4: When the *Create Portable Company File* window appears, enter the filename: **[your name] Exercise 5.3** and the appropriate location. Click **Save**.

Step 5: Click **OK** after the portable file has been created successfully.

Step 6: Close the company file by clicking **File** (Menu), **Close Company**.

EXERCISE 5.4: VENDOR REPORT

In this Exercise, you will print a stock status report for the closet materials inventory and a trial balance to verify that your account balances are correct.

TASK 1: OPEN PORTABLE COMPANY FILE

To open the portable company file (.QBM) file, convert the portable file to a regular company file with a .QBW extension as follows:

Step 1: From the menu bar, click **File | Portable Company File | Open File**.

Step 2: Identify the filename and location for the portable company file:

- Click the **Browse** button to find the location of the portable company file on the hard drive or removable media.

- Select the file: **[your name] Exercise 5.3.QBM**.

Step 3: Identify the name and location of the new company file (.QBW) file to use for completing Exercise 5.4:

- Filename: **[your name] Exercise 5.4**. The **.QBW** extension should appear automatically based upon your Windows settings.

- Location: **C:\Program Files\Intuit\QuickBooks 2006**. This is the location of the .QBW file on the hard drive of your computer. Click the Browse button to specify another location.

Step 4: Click **Open** to open the portable company file.

Step 5: Click **Cancel** when the *Create a Backup* window appears.

Step 6: If prompted, enter your **User Name** and **Password**, then click **OK**.

Step 7: Click **OK** when the QuickBooks sample company message appears.

Step 8: Change the company name to: **[your name] Exercise 5.4 Rock Castle Construction**. (If you need instructions to change the company name, see Part 3: Quick Reference Guide.)

TASK 2: PRINT STOCK STATUS REPORT

Print the stock status report for closet materials inventory.

Step 1: **Print** an Inventory Stock Status By Item report to check the status of the closet inventory items as of **12/31/2007**.

Step 2: **Circle** the closet inventory items on the Inventory Stock Status printout.

Step 3: **Close** the report window.

TASK 3: PRINT TRIAL BALANCE

Next, print a trial balance to double check that your accounting system is in balance and that your account balances are correct.

Print the trial balance as follows.

Step 1: From the Report Center, select **Accountant and Taxes**.

Step 2: Select **Trial Balance**.

Step 3: Select Date From: **12/31/2007** To: **12/31/2007**.

Step 4: **Print** the trial balance.

Step 5: Compare your printout totals and account balances to the following printout. Correct any errors you find.

Modify Report...	Memorize...	Print...	E-mail	Export...	Hide Header	Collapse	Refresh

Dates Custom ▾ From 12/31/2007 📅 To 12/31/2007 📅 Sort By Default ▾

[your name] Exercise 5.4 Rock Castle Construction
Trial Balance
As of December 31, 2007

Accrual Basis

	Dec 31, 07 Debit	Dec 31, 07 Credit
[your name] Checking	151,301.59	
Savings	13,868.42	
Barter Account	0.00	
1200 · Accounts Receivable	77,472.00	
Tools & Equipment	5,000.00	
Employee Loans	62.00	
1120 · Inventory Asset	23,340.40	
1350 · Retainage	2,461.80	
1400 · Undeposited Funds	58,742.77	
Land	90,000.00	
Buildings	325,000.00	
1500 · Trucks	78,352.91	
1500 · Trucks:1520 · Depreciation	0.00	
Computers	28,501.00	
Furniture	7,325.00	
Accumulated Depreciation		121,887.78
Pre-paid Insurance	1,041.85	
2000 · Accounts Payable		55,028.84
QuickBooks Credit Card		70.00
2050 · CalOil Card		5,057.62
2101 · Payroll Liabilities		7,082.68
2200 · Sales Tax Payable		5.66
Bank of Anycity Loan		19,932.65
Equipment Loan		3,911.32
2250 · Note Payable		3,440.83
2300 · Truck Loan		50,162.38
3500 · Opening Bal Equity		593,019.25
3000 · Owner's Equity:3100 · Owner's Contribution		98,000.00
3000 · Owner's Equity:3200 · Owner's Draw	6,000.00	
3300 · Retained Earnings	129,916.38	
4000 · Construction:4100 · Labor		40,397.25
4000 · Construction:4200 · Materials		69,604.51
4000 · Construction:4400 · Miscellaneous		5,155.55
4000 · Construction:4300 · Subcontractors		59,011.01
5000 · Cost of Goods Sold	8,885.01	
6000 · Automobile	10.60	
6000 · Automobile:Insurance	712.56	
6000 · Automobile:6020 · Fuel	231.10	
6040 · Selling Expense:6041 · Advertising Expense	200.00	
6100 · Bank Service Charges	67.50	
6400 · Freight & Delivery	219.60	
6500 · Insurance	297.66	
6500 · Insurance:6510 · Disability Insurance	300.00	
6500 · Insurance:6520 · Liability Insurance	2,100.00	
6500 · Insurance:6530 · Work Comp	1,650.00	
6600 · Interest Expense	651.77	
6600 · Interest Expense:6620 · Loan Interest	288.05	
7400 · Job Expenses:7410 · Equipment Rental	1,000.00	
7400 · Job Expenses:7420 · Job Materials	38,771.87	
7400 · Job Expenses:7430 · Permits and Licenses	700.00	
7400 · Job Expenses:7440 · Subcontractors	44,166.00	
6560 · Payroll Expenses	29,513.77	
7000 · Professional Fees:7010 · Accounting	250.00	
7100 · Rent	1,200.00	
7200 · Repairs:7210 · Building Repairs	175.00	
7200 · Repairs:7220 · Computer Repairs	345.00	
7200 · Repairs:7230 · Equipment Repairs	0.00	
7500 · Tools and Machinery	1,160.00	
7600 · Utilities:7610 · Gas and Electric	364.08	
7600 · Utilities:7620 · Telephone	154.71	
7600 · Utilities:7630 · Water	97.85	
8000 · Interest Income		93.42
8100 · Other Income		37.50
TOTAL	**1,131,898.25**	**1,131,898.25**

Step 6: **Close** the *Trial Balance report* window and the *Report Center* window.

TASK 3: SAVE EXERCISE 5.4

Save Exercise 5.4 as a portable company file to the location specified by your instructor.

Step 1: If necessary, insert a removable disk.

Step 2: From the menu bar, click **File | Portable Company File | Create File**.

Step 3: When the *Close and Reopen* window appears, click **OK**.

Step 4: When the *Create Portable Company File* window appears, enter the filename: **[your name] Exercise 5.4** and the appropriate location. Click **Save**.

Step 5: Click **OK** after the portable file has been created successfully.

EXERCISE 5.5: WEB QUEST

Online bill paying services can be used by small businesses to pay their bills using the Internet.

Step 1: On the right side of the Home page in the Customize section, click **Add Services to QuickBooks**.

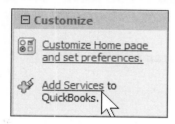

Step 2: When the web page opens, scroll down to **What's Your Need? We've Got a Business Solution**.

Step 3: Under Financial Services, click on **QuickBooks Bill Pay Service**.

Step 4: Read about online bill paying.

Step 5: ✍ Using word processing or E-mail software, prepare and print an e-mail to Mr. Castle summarizing the advantages and disadvantages of online bill paying. Include your recommendations regarding whether Rock Castle Construction should use online bill paying and why.

CHAPTER 5 PRINTOUT CHECKLIST
NAME:_____DATE:_____

INSTRUCTIONS:
1. **CHECK OFF THE PRINTOUTS YOU HAVE COMPLETED.**
2. **STAPLE THIS PAGE TO YOUR PRINTOUTS.**

- ☑ **PRINTOUT CHECKLIST – CHAPTER 5**
- ☐ Vendor List
- ☐ Item List
- ☐ Purchase Order No. 42 & 43
- ☐ Checks No. 304 – 305
- ☐ Check No. 306 – 307 for sales tax
- ☐ Vendor Transaction Report
- ☐ A/P Aging Summary Report
- ☐ A/P Aging Detail Report
- ☐ Unpaid Bills Detail Report
- ☐ Open Purchase Orders Report
- ☐ Inventory Stock Status By Item Report
- ☐ Physical Inventory Worksheet

- ☑ **PRINTOUT CHECKLIST – EXERCISE 5.1**
- ☐ Task 4: Purchase Order 44
- ☐ Task 7: Check No. 308

- ☑ **PRINTOUT CHECKLIST – EXERCISE 5.2**
- ☐ Task 3: Customer Invoice No. 98
- ☐ Task 5: Bank Deposit Summary

- ☑ **PRINTOUT CHECKLIST – EXERCISE 5.3**
- ☐ Task 3: Checks No. 309 – 310

- ☑ **PRINTOUT CHECKLIST – EXERCISE 5.4**
- ☐ Inventory Stock Status By Item Report
- ☐ Trial Balance

- ☑ **PRINTOUT CHECKLIST – EXERCISE 5.5**
- ☐ E-mail Summarizing Online Bill Paying Recommendation

CHAPTER 6
EMPLOYEES AND PAYROLL

SCENARIO

The next morning on your way to your cubicle, two employees ask you if their paychecks are ready yet. Apparently, Rock Castle employees expect their paychecks today?!

Deciding that you do not want all the employees upset with you if paychecks are not ready on time, you take the initiative and ask Mr. Castle about the paychecks.

His reply: *"Oops! I was so busy I almost forgot about paychecks."* He hands you another stack of documents. *"Here—you will need these. I'm sure you won't have any trouble using QuickBooks to print the paychecks. And don't forget to pay yourself!"* he adds with a chuckle as he rushes out the door.

CHAPTER 6

LEARNING OBJECTIVES

In Chapter 6, you will learn the following QuickBooks features:

INTRODUCTION

In Chapter 6 you will focus on recording employee and payroll transactions. Payroll involves preparing employee paychecks, withholding the appropriate amount in taxes, and paying the company's share of payroll taxes.

To assist in processing payroll, QuickBooks offers a time tracking feature that permits you to track the amount of time worked. QuickBooks uses time tracked to:

1. Calculate employee paychecks.

2. Transfer time to sales invoices to bill customers for work performed.

Although this chapter focuses on time worked by employees, work can be performed by employees, subcontractors, or owners. The time tracking feature can be used to track time worked by any of the three. How you record the payment, however, depends upon who performs the work: employee, subcontractor, or business owner.

	Status	Pay using QB Window....	Navigator
Employees complete Form W-4 when hired. Form W-2 summarizes annual wages and tax withholdings.	**Employee**	*Pay Employees* Window	Employee Navigator
No tax withholdings if independent contractor status. Tax Form 1099-MISC summarizes payments.	**Subcontractor (Vendor)**	*Enter Bills* Window *Pay Bills* Window	Vendor Navigator
If owner is also an employee, wages are recorded as payroll. If not wages, then payment to owner is a withdrawal (sole proprietorship) or dividends (corporation).	**Owner**	*Write Checks* Window	Banking Navigator

It is important that you determine the status of the individual performing work. The status determines whether you record payments to the individual as an employee paycheck, vendor payment, or owner withdrawal.

To begin Chapter 6, first start QuickBooks software and then open the portable QuickBooks file.

Step 1: Start QuickBooks by clicking on the **QuickBooks** desktop icon or click **Start, Programs, QuickBooks, QuickBooks Pro 2006**.

Step 2: To open the portable company file (.QBM) file and convert the portable file to a regular company file with a .QBW extension, from the menu bar, click **File | Portable Company File | Open File**.

Step 3: Identify the filename and location for the portable company file:

- Click the **Browse** button to find the location of the portable company file on the hard drive or removable media.

- Select the file: **[your name] Exercise 5.4**. The .QBM may appear automatically based upon your Windows settings, but if it does not appear automatically, do *not* type it.

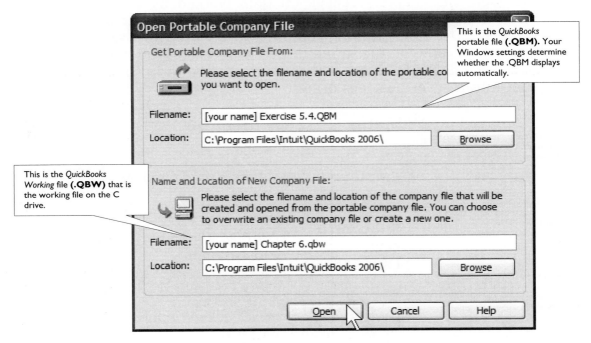

Step 4: Identify the name and location of the new company file (.QBW) file to use for Chapter 6:

- Filename: **[your name] Chapter 6**. The **.QBW** extension should appear automatically based upon your Windows settings. The .QBW identifies this as a QuickBooks working file.

- Location: **C:\Program Files\Intuit\QuickBooks 2006**. This is the location of the .QBW file on the hard drive of your computer.

Step 5: Click **Open** to open the portable company file.

Step 6: Click **Cancel** when the *Create a Backup* window appears.

Step 7: If prompted, enter your **User ID** and **Password**.

Step 8: Click **OK** when the sample company window appears.

Step 9: Change the company name to: **[your name] Chapter 6 Rock Castle Construction**. If necessary, change the Checking account title to include your name.

The portable company file (.QBM) should now be converted to a regular company file (Chapter 6.QBW) that can be used to complete the assignments for Chapter 6.

PAYROLL SETUP

Payroll setup in QuickBooks is accessed from the Employees menu. (From the Employees menu, click Payroll Setup).

The following table that summarizes the steps to set up QuickBooks payroll and time tracking:

Payroll for Rock Castle Construction has already been set up. In Chapter 6, you will focus on recording the employee and payroll transactions. Chapter 11 covers how to setup QuickBooks payroll.

The following table summarizes the steps to set preferences and complete information necessary for using the payroll feature of QuickBooks.

QuickBooks Time Tracking and Payroll Roadmap

Action	Using QuickBooks...
1. Set up payroll.	Employees menu, Payroll Setup
2. Turn on time tracking.	Preferences, Time Tracking
3. Turn on payroll, enter Payroll and Employee Preferences.	Preferences, Payroll & Employees
4. Enter customer and jobs on which time will be worked.	Customer & Job List
5. Record labor as a service item.	Item List
6. Enter employees and nonemployees whose time will be tracked: ▸ Employee information ▸ Subcontractors ▸ Owners	 Employee List Vendor List Other List

QuickBooks automatically creates a chart of accounts with payroll liability and payroll expense accounts. QuickBooks also uses Payroll Items to track supporting detail for the payroll accounts.

Payroll accounts for Rock Castle Construction have already been established. To learn more about payroll setup, see Chapter 11.

To track time and process payroll in QuickBooks you will use the Employee section of the Home page. If necessary, click Home page to view the Employees section.

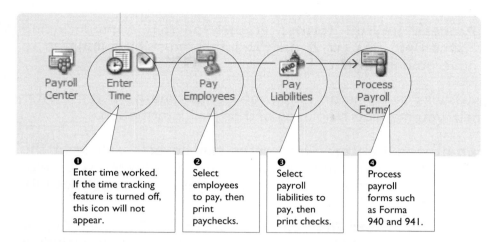

The Employee section of the Home page is a flowchart of payroll transactions. As the flowchart indicates, there are four main steps to processing payroll using QuickBooks:

❶ **Track time**: QuickBooks Pro and QuickBooks Premier permit you to track employee time in the following ways:

- **Stopwatch**: Use the Stopwatch to time an activity and enter the time data. QuickBooks automatically records the time on the employee's weekly timesheet.

- **Timesheet**: Use the weekly Timesheet to enter time worked by each employee on various jobs during the week.

- **QuickBooks Timer**: QuickBooks Timer is a separate computer program. Employees and subcontractors can track time with the Timer program without access to QuickBooks software or your QuickBooks company data file. Then you can import Timer files (*.iif files) into QuickBooks to process payroll.

❷ **Pay Employees**: Select employees to pay and create their paychecks.

❸ **Pay payroll liabilities**: Pay payroll tax liabilities due governmental agencies such as the IRS. Payroll tax liabilities include federal income taxes withheld, state income taxes withheld, FICA (Social Security and Medicare), and unemployment taxes.

❹ **Process payroll forms**: Process payroll forms including Forms 940, 941, W-2, and W-3 that must be submitted to governmental agencies.

QuickBooks also has an Employee Center and a Payroll Center to help you manage employee and payroll information.

- **Employee Center**: This center can be accessed from the Navigation Bar and contains the Employee List with employee information, such as address and social security number.

- **Payroll Center**: This center is part of the Employee Center and is used to manage payroll and tax information, including information about wages, benefits, and withholding. The Payroll Center can be accessed by clicking the Payroll Center icon in the Employee section of the Home page.

Next, you will set QuickBooks preferences for time tracking and payroll.

TIME TRACKING AND PAYROLL PREFERENCES

Use QuickBooks Preferences to customize time tracking and payroll to suit your company's specific needs. There are two types of preferences that affect payroll:

1. Time Tracking Preferences.
2. Payroll and Employees Preferences.

TIME TRACKING PREFERENCES

To turn on the QuickBooks time tracking feature, complete the following steps:

Step 1: From the Customize section of the Home page, click **Customize Home page and set preferences**.

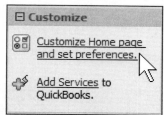

Step 2: When the *Preferences* window appears, select **Time Tracking** from the left scrollbar.

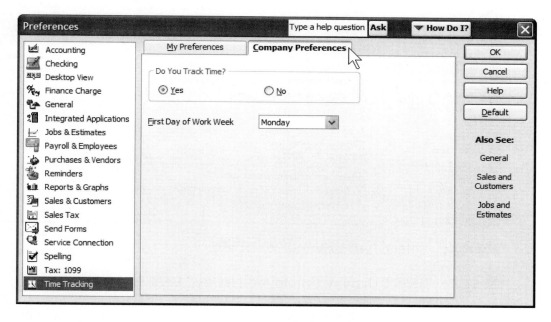

Step 3: If necessary, select the **Company Preferences** tab.

Step 4: Select Do You Track Time: **Yes**. Select First Day of Work Week: **Monday**.

Step 5: Leave the *Preferences* window open.

PAYROLL AND EMPLOYEES PREFERENCES

Next, select QuickBooks Payroll and Employees Preferences for your company.

With the *Preferences* window open:

Step 1: From the left scrollbar of the *Preferences* window, click on the **Payroll & Employees** icon.

Step 2: Select the **Company Preferences** tab.

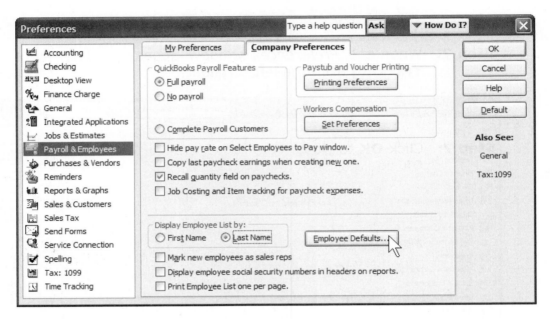

Step 3: Select **Full payroll features**.

Step 4: Select Display Employee List by: **Last Name**.

Step 5: Click the **Employee Defaults** button to select payroll defaults.

Step 6: Select the checkbox: **Use time data to create paychecks**. Now QuickBooks will automatically use tracked time to calculate payroll.

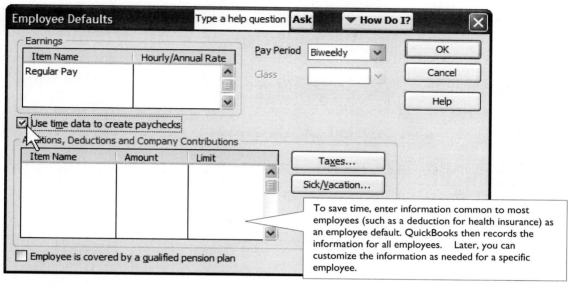

Step 7: Click **OK** to close the *Employee Defaults* window. Click **OK** again to close the *Preferences* window.

Step 8: When the following warning message appears, click **OK**.

Now that the time tracking and payroll preferences are set, you will edit and print the Employee List.

EMPLOYEE LIST

The Employee List contains employee information such as address, telephone, salary or wage rate, and social security number.

To view the Employee List for Rock Castle Construction:

Step 1: Click the **Employee Center** icon on the Navigation Bar.

Step 2: Click the **Employees** tab to display a list of employees.

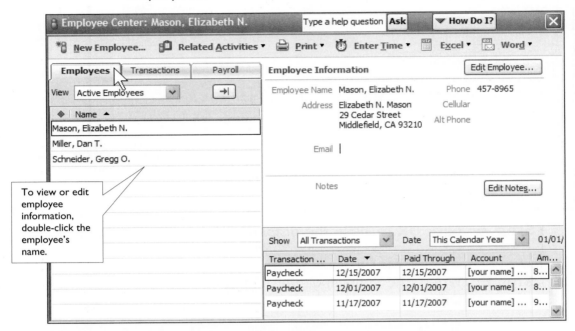

ADD NEW EMPLOYEE

To enter your name as a new employee in the Employee List:

Step 1: Click the **New Employee** button at the top of the Employee Center.

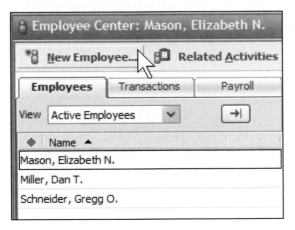

Step 2: When the following blank *New Employee* window appears, select **Personal Info** in the Change tabs field.

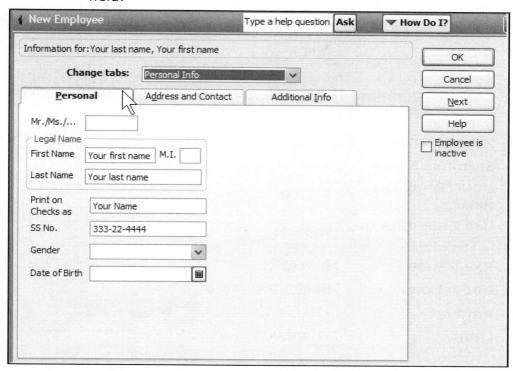

- Enter the following information in the **Personal** tab.

Personal:	
First Name	[enter your first name]
Last Name	[enter your last name]
SS No.	333-22-4444
Gender	[enter gender]
Date of birth	[enter date of birth]

- Click the **Address and Contact** tab, then enter the following information.

Address and Contact:	
Address	555 Lakeview Lane Bayshore, CA 94326
Phone	415-555-6677
E-mail	[enter your email address]

- Click the **Additional Information** tab, then enter the following information.

Additional Info:	
Employee ID No.	333-22-4444
B-Day	[enter your birth date]

Step 3: In the *Change Tabs* field, select: **Payroll and Compensation Info**, then enter the following payroll information.

Payroll Info:	
Earnings Name	Regular Pay
Hour/Annual Rate	$10.00
Use time data to create paychecks	Yes
Pay Period	Biweekly
Deductions	Health Insurance
Amount	-25.00
Limit	-1200.00

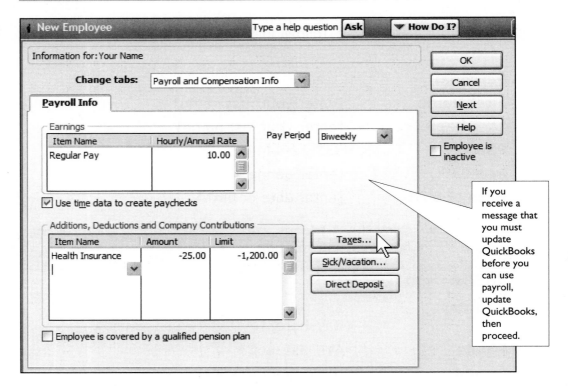

Step 4: Click the **Taxes** button to view federal, state, and other tax information related to your employment, such as filing status and allowances. Enter the following:

> New employees complete Form W-4 to indicate filing status and allowances.

- Filing Status: **Single**
- Allowances for **Federal** and **State**: **1**
- Click **OK** to close the *Taxes* window.

Step 5: Click **OK** again to add your name to Rock Castle Construction's Employee List.

Step 6: When asked if you want to set up payroll information for sick leave and vacation, click **Leave As Is** to use the employee default information for these items.

Step 7: Leave the *Employee Center* window open.

> If you start using QuickBooks midyear, enter year-to-date amounts for payroll *before* you start using QuickBooks to process paychecks.

PRINT EMPLOYEE LIST

🖨 **Print** the Employee List as follows:

Step 1: Click the **Name** bar to sort employee names in alphabetical order.

Step 2: Click the **Print** button at the top of the Employee Center.

Step 3: Select **Employee List**.

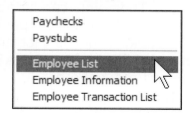

Step 4: 🖨 **Print** the report using Portrait orientation.

Step 5: ✏ **Circle** your information on the Employee List printout.

Step 6: **Close** the *Employee Center* window.

For more information about payroll setup, see Chapter 11. The remainder of this chapter will cover time tracking, payroll processing and payroll reports.

TIME TRACKING

QuickBooks Pro and QuickBooks Premier permit you to track time worked on various jobs. As mentioned earlier, time can be tracked for employees, subcontractors, or owners.

When employees use time tracking, the employee records the time worked on each job. The time data is then used to:

1. Prepare paychecks.
2. Bill customers for time worked on specific jobs.

QuickBooks Pro and QuickBooks Premier provide three different ways to track time.

1. **Single Activity/Stopwatch**: Use the Stopwatch to time an activity and enter the time data. QuickBooks automatically records the time on the employee's weekly timesheet.

2. **Weekly Timesheet**: Use the weekly Timesheet to enter time worked by each employee on various jobs during the week.

3. **QuickBooks Timer**: QuickBooks Timer is a separate computer program. Employees and subcontractors can track time with the Timer program. Then you can import Timer files (*.iif files) into QuickBooks to process payroll. The advantage to using the QuickBooks Timer is that employees and subcontractors do not need access to QuickBooks or your company data file to enter time worked.

STOPWATCH

You will use the QuickBooks Stopwatch feature to time how long it takes you to complete payroll activities in this chapter.

To start the Stopwatch:

Step 1: From the Employee section of the Home page, click the **Enter Time** icon.

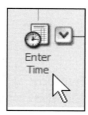

Step 2: From the pop-up menu, select: **Time/Enter Single Activity**.

Step 3: When the following window appears:

> You can only use the Stopwatch to time activities for today's date. However, for this activity, use the programmed date for the sample company: 12/15/2007.

- Select Date: **12/15/2007**.

- Select Name: **Your Name**.

- If the work was for a particular job or customer, you would enter the job or customer name and the service item, then click Billable. In this case, your time is not billable to a particular customer's job, so **uncheck Billable**.

- Select Payroll Item: **Regular Pay**.

- Enter Notes: **Process payroll**.

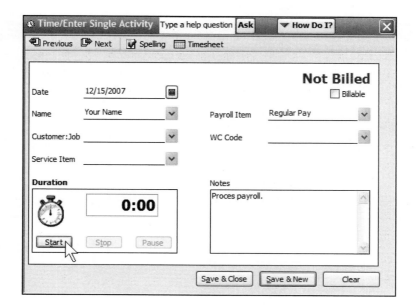

Step 4:   Click the **Start** button to start the stopwatch.

Step 5:   Leave the window open while you complete the following payroll activities.

TIMESHEET

Rock Castle Construction pays employees biweekly. Checks are issued on Wednesday for the pay period ending that day.

Use the timesheet to enter the hours you worked for Rock Castle Construction during the last pay period.

To use QuickBooks timesheet feature:

Step 1:   Click the **Home** icon on the Navigation bar.

Step 2:   In the Employee section of the Home page, click **Enter Time.**

Step 3:   Select: **Use Weekly Timesheet.**

Step 4:   If necessary, click the **Next** button to change the date to the Week Of: **Dec 17 to Dec 23, 2007**.

Step 5:   Select Name: **[Your Name]**.

Step 6:   From the Payroll Item drop-down list, select **Regular Pay**.

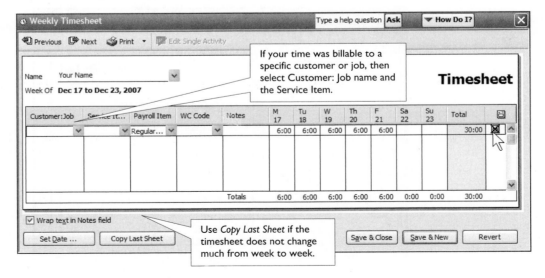

Step 7: Because your time is not billable to a specific customer or job, click the white **Invoice** icon in the last column to indicate these charges will not be transferred to an invoice. A red ☒ should appear over the Invoice icon.

Step 8: Enter **6** hours for each of the following dates for a total of 30 hours for the week:

- **Monday (December 17th)**
- **Tuesday (December 18th)**
- **Wednesday (December 19th)**
- **Thursday (December 20th)**
- **Friday (December 21st)**

Step 9: Click the **Next** button in the upper left corner of the *Weekly Timesheet* window to advance to the timesheet for the week of **Dec 24 to Dec 30, 2007**.

Step 10: Enter **6** hours for each of the following dates for a total of 18 hours:

- **Wednesday (December 26th)**
- **Thursday (December 27th)**
- **Friday (December 28th)**

> Remember to enter **Regular Pay** and click the **Invoice icon** to mark your hours as nonbillable.

Step 11: Click **Save & New** to record your hours and display a new timesheet.

If time is billable to a specific customer or job, this is indicated on the weekly timesheet. For example, Elizabeth Mason, a Rock Castle Construction employee, worked on the Teschner sunroom; therefore, her hours are billable to the Teschner sunroom job.

To enter billable hours on Elizabeth Mason's weekly timesheet:

Step 1: On the new timesheet, select Name: **Elizabeth N. Mason**.

Step 2: Click the **Previous** button in the upper left corner of the *Timesheet* window to change the timesheet dates to **Dec 17 to Dec 23, 2007**.

Step 3:   To record time billable to a specific customer:

- Select Customer: Job: **Teschner, Anton: Sunroom**.

- Select Service Item: **Framing**.

Step 4:   Enter the following hours into the weekly timesheet to record time Elizabeth worked framing the sunroom:

Monday, December 17	8 hours
Tuesday, December 18	8 hours
Wednesday, December 19	8 hours
Thursday, December 20	6 hours

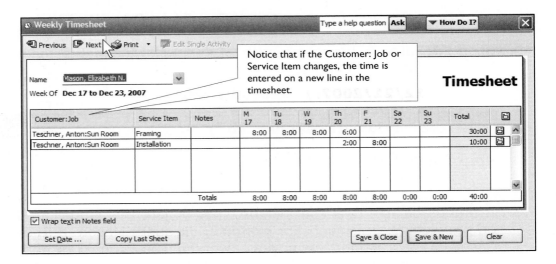

Step 5:   Move to the next line in the timesheet to enter the installation work that Elizabeth performed on the Teschner sunroom.

- Select Customer: Job: **Teschner, Anton: Sunroom**.

- Select Service Item: **Installation**.

- Enter hours worked:

Thursday, December 20	2 hours
Friday, December 21	8 hours

Step 6: Click the **Next** button to record Elizabeth's hours and display a new timesheet.

Step 7: Record **8** hours for each of the following dates that Elizabeth worked on installing the Teschner sunroom:

- **Wednesday (December 26th)**
- **Thursday (December 27th)**
- **Friday (December 28th)**

Step 8: Leave the *Weekly Timesheets* window open.

To print the weekly timesheets for yourself and Elizabeth Mason, complete the following steps:

Step 1: From the *Weekly Timesheet* window, click the **Print** button.

Step 2: When the following *Select Timesheets to Print* window appears, select Dated: **12/17/2007** thru **12/21/2007**. If necessary, press **Tab**.

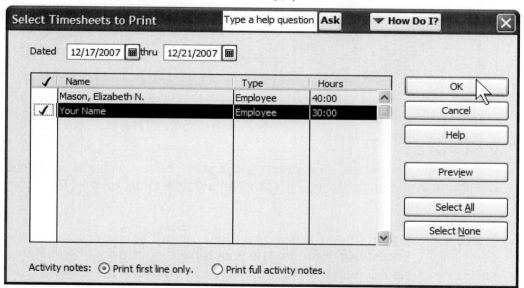

Step 3: Select **Your Name**. Click **OK**.

Step 4: 🖨 **Print** the timesheet.

Step 5: ✐ **Sign** the timesheet by Mr. Rock Castle.

Step 6: Click **Save & Close** to close the *Weekly Timesheet* window.

TRANSFER TIME TO SALES INVOICES

Billable time can be transferred to a specific customer's invoice. This is shown in the Home page flowchart with the arrow going from the Enter Time icon to the Invoices icon.

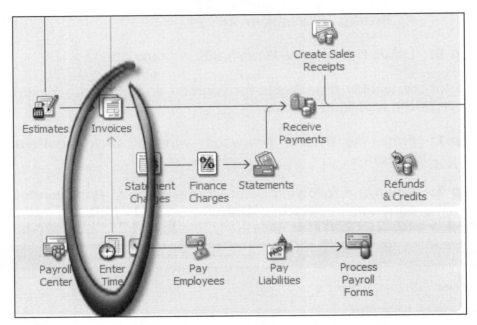

First, you must enter time worked, then open the *Create Invoices* window for the customer, and select the time billable to that specific customer.

For the Teschner sunroom job, you have already entered Elizabeth Mason's time. To transfer billable time to the Teschner sales invoice:

Step 1: Open the *Create Invoices* window by clicking the **Invoices** icon in the Customer section of the Home page.

Step 2: From the *Create Invoices* window, select the customer job to be billed. In this instance, select Customer: Job: **Teschner, Anton: Sunroom**.

Step 3: If the following *Billable Time/Costs* window appears, click **OK**.

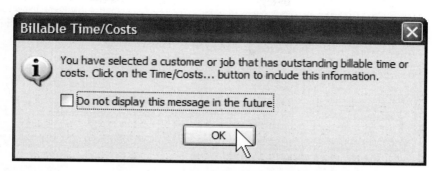

Step 4: Select Template: **Time & Expense Invoice**.

Step 5: Select Date: **12/28/2007**.

Step 6: Click the **Time/Costs** button on the upper right of the *Create Invoices* window.

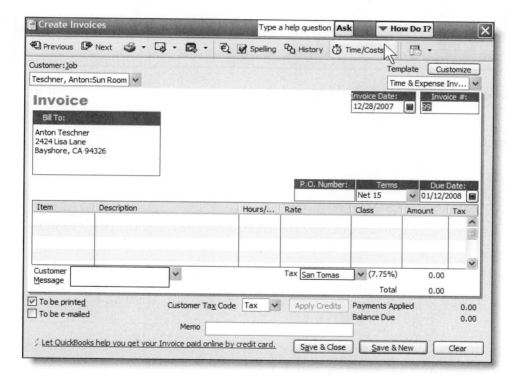

Step 7:   When the *Choose Billable Time and Costs* window appears, click the **Time** tab.

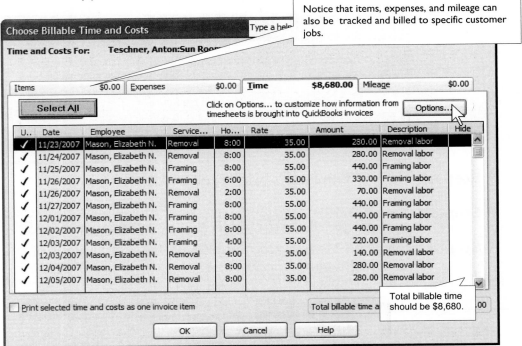

Notice that items, expenses, and mileage can also be tracked and billed to specific customer jobs.

Total billable time should be $8,680.

Step 8:   Click the **Select All** button to select all the billable times listed for the Teschner Sunroom job.

Step 9:   You can transfer time to an invoice in three different ways:

(1) Combine all the selected times and costs into *one* entry on the invoice.

(2) List a *subtotal* for each *service* item on the invoice, or

(3) List a separate invoice line item for each *activity* you check.

In this instance, you will list a separate invoice line item for each activity you check, so:

- *Uncheck* **Print selected time and costs as one invoice item** in the lower left corner of the *Billable Time and Costs* window, *and*

- Click the **Options** button, then select **Enter a separate line on the invoice for each activity** on the *Options for Transferring Billable Time* window.

- Select **Transfer item descriptions**.

To create a report detailing time spent on a specific job:
1. Report Center
2. Jobs & Time
3. Time by Job Detail
4. Filter for Customer & Job

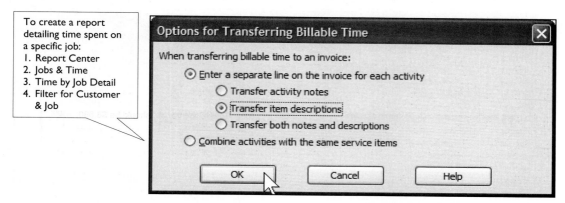

- Click **OK** to close the *Options for Transferring Billable Time* window.

Step 10: Click **OK** to close the *Billable Time and Costs* window and add the labor cost to the Teschner sales invoice.

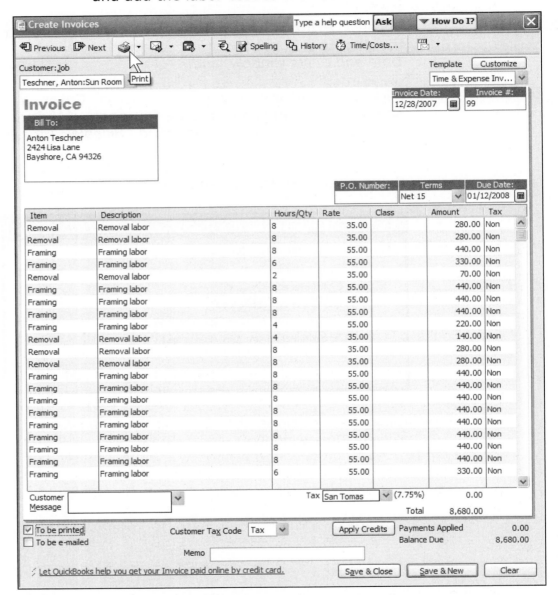

Step 11: 🖨 **Print** the invoice. Select **blank paper** and **print lines around fields**.

Step 12: Click **Save & Close** to record the invoice and close the *Create Invoices* window.

> ⏱ ***Stop the Stopwatch now, by clicking the Stop button and then clicking Clear. Close the Stopwatch window.***

PAYROLL SERVICES

After entering time worked, the next step is to create employee paychecks.

There are two ways that a company can perform payroll calculations.

1. Use QuickBooks Payroll Services:

   - QuickBooks Standard/Enhanced Payroll

   - QuickBooks Assisted Payroll

   - Intuit Complete Payroll

2. Manually calculate payroll taxes.

> Intuit provided tax tables with QuickBooks 99; however, to receive tax table updates with later QuickBooks versions, you must subscribe to one of the payroll tax services.

QUICKBOOKS PAYROLL SERVICES

QuickBooks offers three levels of payroll services: QuickBooks Standard/Enhanced Payroll, QuickBooks Assisted Payroll, and Complete Payroll. When you subscribe to a payroll service, QuickBooks automatically calculates tax deductions, requiring an Internet connection. QuickBooks Standard/Enhanced Payroll provides automatic payroll tax updates and automatically calculates the payroll deductions. The QuickBooks Assisted Payroll offers the additional feature of preparing federal and state payroll forms and electronically paying federal and state payroll taxes. Complete Payroll offers a full-service payroll service.

> If you receive a message about updating QuickBooks before using payroll, update QuickBooks and then proceed. If you are not able to use QB payroll tax tables, then enter amounts shown on the following pages manually in the *Create Paychecks* window.

For more information about QuickBooks Payroll Services, from the Home page, click **Add Services to QuickBooks**, select **QuickBooks Payroll**.

CALCULATE PAYROLL TAXES MANUALLY

If you do not use a QuickBooks payroll tax service, you must calculate tax withholdings and payroll taxes manually using IRS Circular E. Then enter the amounts in QuickBooks to process payroll. To use the QuickBooks manual payroll option, see Chapter 11.

PRINT PAYCHECKS

The QuickBooks Payroll Subscription is active for the sample company file, Rock Castle Construction.

To create paychecks for Rock Castle Construction using the QuickBooks payroll service:

Step 1: From the Employee section of the Home page, click the **Pay Employees** icon to display the *Select Employees to Pay* window.

Step 2: Select Check Date: **12/24/2007**. This date will print on each check.

Step 3: Select Pay Period Ends: **12/22/2007**. This is the last day of this pay period.

Step 4: When the following *Select Employees to Pay* window appears, select Employees: **Elizabeth N. Mason** and **Your Name**.

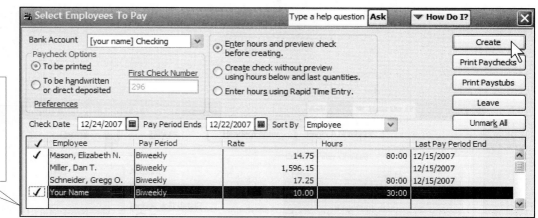

If you use a QuickBooks payroll service, payroll taxes and deductions would automatically be calculated and appear in the *Preview Paycheck* window.

Step 5: Select **To be printed**. This indicates that you will print the checks. Uncheck this box if you want to record the paychecks but not print them.

Step 6: Select Bank Account: **[your name] Checking**.

Step 7: Select **Enter hours and preview check before creating**. This permits you to preview the check and make any necessary changes.

Step 8: Click **Create**.

Step 9: When the *Preview Paycheck* window appears, the Regular pay amount will appear automatically. If you are using a QuickBooks payroll service, the tax withholding amounts will appear automatically. If you are calculating payroll taxes manually, you must calculate tax withholding amounts and enter them in this window.

Step 10: Click **Create** to create Elizabeth Mason's paycheck.

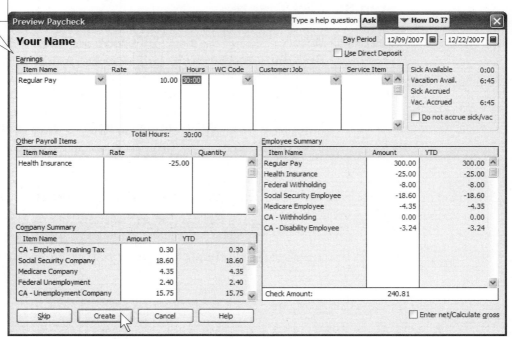

Step 11: If the message appears that the withholding amount is $0.00, click **OK**.

Payroll deductions may vary based upon which payroll update you are using.

Step 12: The *Preview Paycheck* window should now display your paycheck information. Click **Create**.

To print your paycheck and Mason's paycheck:

Step 1: Click the **Print Paychecks** button on the right side of the *Select Employees to Pay* window.

Step 2: In the *Select Paychecks to Print* window shown above, select:

- **Elizabeth Mason (12/24/2007)**
- **[your name] (12/24/2007)**

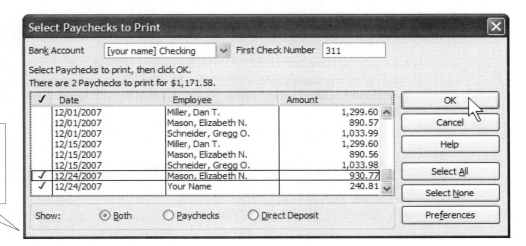

Some businesses use a separate Payroll Checking account instead of using the regular Checking account.

If you use standard checks, to print paystubs, select **Print Paystubs** under Related Activities on the Employee Navigator.

Step 3: Select Bank Account: **[your name] Checking**, then click **OK**.

Step 4: Select Check Style: **Voucher**. Check **Print company name and address**.

Step 5: 🖨 Click **Print**.

Step 6: Click **Leave** to close the *Select Employees to Pay* window.

> ✓ *Mason's net pay is $930.77 your net pay is $240.81. (Note: These amounts may vary depending upon your payroll update.)*

PAY PAYROLL LIABILITIES

Payroll liabilities include amounts for:

- Federal income taxes withheld from employee paychecks.

- State income taxes withheld from employee paychecks.

- FICA (Social Security and Medicare, including both the employee and the employer portions).

- Unemployment taxes.

Federal income taxes, state income taxes, and the employee portion of FICA are withheld from the employee, and the company has an obligation (liability) to remit these amounts to the appropriate tax agency. The employer share of FICA and unemployment taxes are payroll taxes the employer owes.

TIP: To help you keep track of filing dates, see the IRS Tax Calendar at www.irs.gov, Tax Info for Business, Tax Calendar.

To pay the payroll tax liability:

Step 1: Click the **Pay Liabilities** icon in the Employee section of the Home page.

Step 2: If the payroll liabilities were due, you would select dates and amounts to pay, then click Create. At this time, Rock Castle Construction is not paying payroll liabilities, so click **Cancel**.

PAYROLL REPORTS

QuickBooks provides payroll reports that answer the following questions:

- How much did we pay our employees and pay in payroll taxes? (Payroll reports)
- How much time did we spend classified by employee and job? (Project reports)

Payroll reports can be accessed in the following ways:

1. Reports menu (select **Employees & Payroll** from the Reports menu).

2. Report Center (click **Report Center** icon on the Navigation Bar, select Employees & Payroll.)

3. Employee Center (click **Employee Center** icon on the Navigation Bar, see right of *Employee Center* window for payroll reports for employees.)

PAYROLL REPORTS: HOW MUCH DID WE PAY FOR PAYROLL?

The payroll reports list the amounts paid to employees and the amounts paid in payroll taxes.

To print the Payroll Summary report:

Step 1: From the *Report Center* window, click **Employees & Payroll**.

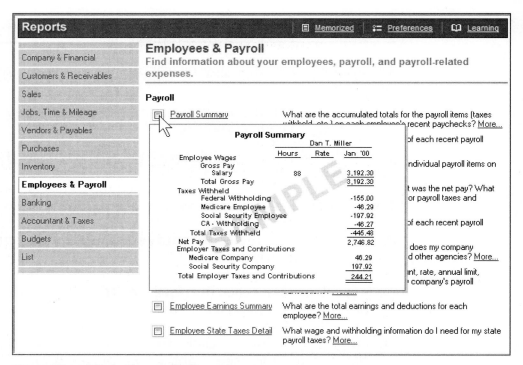

Step 2: Click **Payroll Summary**.

Step 3: Select Dates: **This Month** From: **12/01/2007** To: **12/31/2007**.

Step 4: Select **Landscape** orientation, then click **Print**.

> ✓ **Net pay for Dan Miller for December was $2,599.20.**

PROJECT REPORTS: HOW MUCH TIME DID WE USE?

Four different projects reports are available in QuickBooks:

1. Time by Job Summary: Lists time spent on each job.

2. Time by Job Detail: Lists time by category spent on each job.

3. Time by Name Report: Lists the amount of time worked by each employee.

4. Time by Job Detail Report: Lists the time worked on a particular job by service.

Project reports are accessed from the *Employee List* window as follows:

Step 1: From the Report Center, select: **Jobs, Time & Mileage**.

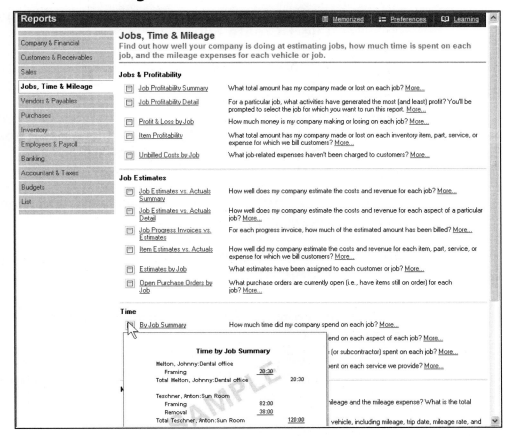

Step 2: Select **Time by Job Summary**.

Step 3: ▣ **Print** the Time by Job Summary report for **This Month** from **12/01/2007** To: **12/31/2007**. Select **Portrait** orientation.

SAVE CHAPTER 6

Save Chapter 6 as a portable QuickBooks file to the location specified by your instructor.

Step 1:   If necessary, insert a removable disk.

Step 2:   From the menu bar, click **File | Portable Company File | Create File**.

Step 3:   When the *Close and Reopen* window appears, click **OK**.

Step 4:   When the following *Create Portable Company File* window appears, enter the filename: **[your name] Chapter 6** and the appropriate location. Then click **Save**.

Step 5:   Click **OK** after the portable file has been created successfully.

Step 6:   Close the company file by clicking **File** (Menu), **Close Company**.

If you are continuing your computer session, proceed to Exercise 6.1.

If you are ending your computer session now, see the Quick Reference Guide in Part 3 for instructions to (1) close the company file and (2) exit QuickBooks.

ASSIGNMENTS

> **NOTE:** *See the Quick Reference Guide in Part 3 for step-by-step instructions to frequently used tasks.*

EXERCISE 6.1:
TRACK TIME AND PRINT PAYCHECKS

SCENARIO

When sorting through the payroll documents that Mr. Castle gave you, you find the following timesheets for Dan Miller and Greg Schneider.

Timesheet						
Dan Miller	**Salary**	**Dec 17**	**Dec 18**	**Dec 19**	**Dec 20**	**Dec 21**
Cook: 2ⁿᵈ Story	Installation	8	8	2		4
Pretell: 75 Sunset	Framing			6	7	4

Timesheet						
Dan Miller	**Salary**	**Dec 24**	**Dec 25**	**Dec 26**	**Dec 27**	**Dec 28**
Pretell: 75 Sunset	Framing			8	8	3
Pretell: 75 Sunset	Installation					5

Timesheet						
Gregg Schneider	**Regular Pay**	**Dec 17**	**Dec 18**	**Dec 19**	**Dec 20**	**Dec 21**
Jacobsen: Kitchen	Installation	8	8	8	2	
Pretell: 75 Sunset	Framing				6	8

Timesheet						
Gregg Schneider	**Regular Pay**	**Dec 24**	**Dec 25**	**Dec 26**	**Dec 27**	**Dec 28**
Pretell: 75 Sunset	Framing			8	8	
Pretell: 75 Sunset	Installation					8

TASK 1: OPEN PORTABLE COMPANY FILE

To open the portable company file (.QBM) file, convert the portable file to a regular company file with a .QBW extension as follows:

Step 1: From the menu bar, click **File | Portable Company File | Open File**.

Step 2: Identify the filename and location for the portable company file:

- Click the **Browse** button to find the location of the portable company file on the hard drive or removable media.

- Select the file: **[your name] Chapter 6.QBM**.

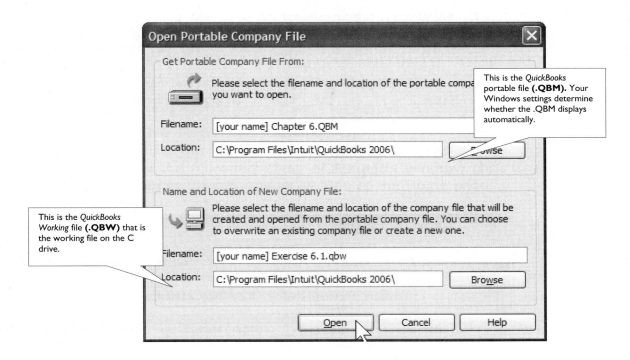

Step 3: Identify the name and location of the new company file (.QBW) file to use for completing Exercise 6.1:

- Filename: **[your name] Exercise 6.1**. The **.QBW** extension should appear automatically based upon your Windows settings.

- Location: **C:\Program Files\Intuit\QuickBooks 2006**. This is the location of the .QBW file on the hard drive of your computer. Click the Browse button to specify another location.

Step 4: Click **Open** to open the portable company file.

Step 5: Click **Cancel** when the *Create a Backup* window appears.

Step 6: If prompted, enter your **User Name** and **Password**, then click **OK**.

Step 7: Click **OK** when the QuickBooks sample company message appears.

Step 8: Change the company name to: **[your name] Exercise 6.1 Rock Castle Construction**.

See the Scenario information on previous pages for information to complete Tasks 2 and 3.

TASK 2: TIMESHEET

Step 1: Enter the hours **Dan Miller** worked using QuickBooks weekly timesheet.

Step 2: Enter the hours **Gregg Schneider** worked using QuickBooks weekly timesheet.

Step 3: ▱ **Print** timesheets for Dan Miller and Gregg Schneider.

TASK 3: PRINT PAYCHECKS

Step 1: Create paychecks for **Dan Miller** and **Gregg Schneider**. Select Check Date: **12/24/2007**. Select Pay Period Ends: **12/22/2007**.

Step 2: Print paychecks using voucher checks for **Dan Miller** and **Gregg Schneider** dated: **12/24/2007**.

TASK 4: SAVE EXERCISE 6.1

Save Exercise 6.1 as a portable company file to the location specified by your instructor.

Step 1: If necessary, insert a removable disk.

Step 2: From the menu bar, click **File | Portable Company File | Create File**.

Step 3: When the *Close and Reopen* window appears, click **OK**.

Step 4: When the *Create Portable Company File* window appears, enter the filename: **[your name] Exercise 6.1** and the appropriate location. Click **Save**.

Step 5: Click **OK** after the portable file has been created successfully.

Step 6: Close the company file by clicking **File** (Menu), **Close Company**.

EXERCISE 6.2:
TRANSFER TIME TO SALES INVOICE

SCENARIO

"By the way, did I mention that I need a current sales invoice for the Jacobsen Kitchen job? Make sure all labor charges have been posted to the invoice," Mr. Castle shouts over the top of your cubicle as he rushes past.

TASK 1: OPEN COMPANY FILE

To open the portable company file (.QBM) file, convert the portable file to a regular company file with a .QBW extension as follows:

Step 1: From the menu bar, click **File | Portable Company File | Open File**.

Step 2: Identify the filename and location for the portable company file:

- Click the **Browse** button to find the location of the portable company file on the hard drive or removable media.

- Select the file: **[your name] Exercise 6.1.QBM**.

Step 3: Identify the name and location of the new company file (.QBW) file to use for completing Exercise 6.2:

- Filename: **[your name] Exercise 6.2**. The **.QBW** extension should appear automatically based upon your Windows settings.

- Location: **C:\Program Files\Intuit\QuickBooks 2006**. This is the location of the .QBW file on the hard drive of your computer. Click the Browse button to specify another location.

Step 4: Click **Open** to open the portable company file.

Step 5: Click **Cancel** when the *Create a Backup* window appears.

Step 6: If prompted, enter your **User Name** and **Password**, then click **OK**.

Step 7: Click **OK** when the QuickBooks sample company message appears.

Step 8: Change the company name to: **[your name] Exercise 6.2 Rock Castle Construction**.

TASK 2: TRANSFER TIME TO SALES INVOICE

Step 1: From the Customer section of the Home page, click the **Invoices** icon.

Recall that subcontractors are considered vendors, not employees. Subcontractor payments are entered using the *Enter Bills* window.

Step 2: Click the **Time/Costs** button to transfer time data to a sales invoice dated **12/24/2007** for the Jacobsen Kitchen job.

Step 3: From the *Choose Billable Time & Costs* window, click the **Items** tab. Click the **Select All** button to transfer subcontractors work to the invoice.

Step 4: From the *Choose Billable Time & Costs* window, click the **Time** tab, then click the **Select All** button to transfer employee time worked to the invoice.

✓ *Items total $1,900. Time totals $2,380.*

Step 5: 🖨 **Print** the invoice.

✓ *Invoice No. 100 totals $4,280.*

TASK 3: BACK UP EXERCISE 6.2

Save Exercise 6.2 as a portable company file to the location specified by your instructor.

Step 1: If necessary, insert a removable disk.

Step 2: From the menu bar, click **File | Portable Company File | Create File**.

Step 3: When the *Close and Reopen* window appears, click **OK**.

Step 4: When the *Create Portable Company File* window appears, enter the filename: **[your name] Exercise 6.2** and the appropriate location. Click **Save**.

Step 5: Click **OK** after the portable file has been created successfully.

Step 6: Close the company file by clicking **File** (Menu), **Close Company**.

EXERCISE 6.3:
QUICKBOOKS PAYROLL SERVICES

To learn more about the payroll services offered by QuickBooks:

Step 1: From the Home page, select **Add Services to QuickBooks**. Read about QuickBooks payroll options. Print information summarizing the differences between the QuickBooks Standard/Enhanced Payroll, QuickBooks Assisted Payroll, and QuickBooks Complete Payroll.

Step 2: ✒ Using word processing or email software, prepare and print a short e-mail to Mr. Castle with your recommendation regarding which payroll service Rock Castle Construction should use.

EXERCISE 6.4: WEB QUEST

The IRS prepares a publication, the Employer's Tax Guide that summarizes information about payroll taxes.

To obtain a copy of the Employer's Tax Guide:

Step 1: Go to the www.irs.gov web site.

Step 2: Search the IRS site to find information about Form 940 and Form 941.

Step 3: 🖨 **Print** the instructions for Forms 940 and 941.

EXERCISE 6.5: WEB QUEST

When hiring individuals to perform work for a business, it is important to identify the status of the individual as either an employee or independent contractor. For an employee, your business must withhold taxes and provide a W-2. For an independent contractor, your business does not have to withhold taxes. Instead of a W-2, you provide a contractor with a Form 1099-MISC. To learn more about whether a worker is classified for tax purposes as an employee or independent contractor, visit the IRS web site.

Step 1: Go to the www.irs.gov web site. Search for requirements that determine employee status and contractor status. 🖨 **Print** your search results.

Step 2: To learn more about employee versus contractor status, in QuickBooks click **Company** (menu bar) | **Planning & Budgeting** | **Decision Tools** | **Employee, Contractor, or Temp?**.

CHAPTER 6 PRINTOUT CHECKLIST
NAME:_____DATE:_____

INSTRUCTIONS:
1. *CHECK OFF THE PRINTOUTS YOU HAVE COMPLETED.*
2. *STAPLE THIS PAGE TO YOUR PRINTOUTS.*

☑ *PRINTOUT CHECKLIST – CHAPTER 6*
☐ Employee List
☐ Timesheets
☐ Invoice No. 99
☐ Paychecks (voucher checks) No. 311 & 312
☐ Payroll Summary Report
☐ Time by Job Summary Report

☑ *PRINTOUT CHECKLIST – EXERCISE 6.1*
☐ Task 2: Timesheets
☐ Task 3: Paychecks (voucher checks)

☑ *PRINTOUT CHECKLIST – EXERCISE 6.2*
☐ Task 2: Customer Invoice No. 100

☑ *PRINTOUT CHECKLIST – EXERCISE 6.3*
☐ QuickBooks Payroll Service Printouts
☐ E-mail Summarizing QuickBooks Payroll Service Recommendation

☑ *PRINTOUT CHECKLIST – EXERCISE 6.4*
☐ IRS Employer's Tax Guide, Forms 940 and 941

☑ *PRINTOUT CHECKLIST – EXERCISE 6.5*
☐ IRS Printouts for Employee Status and Independent Contractor

NOTES:

Chapter 7
Reports and Graphs

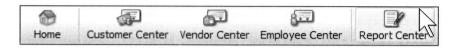

Scenario

"I need an income tax summary report ASAP—" Mr. Castle barks as he races past your cubicle. In a few seconds he charges past your cubicle again. *"Don't forget to adjust the accounts first. You'll need to use those confounded debits and credits!*

"Also, I need a P&L, balance sheet, and cash flow statement for my meeting with the bankers this afternoon. Throw in a graph or two if it'll make us look good."

CHAPTER 7
LEARNING OBJECTIVES

In Chapter 7, you will learn the following QuickBooks features:

THE ACCOUNTING CYCLE

The accounting cycle is a series of activities that a business performs each accounting period.

Financial reports are the end result of the accounting cycle. The accounting cycle usually consists of the following steps:

Chart of Accounts

The chart of accounts is a list of all accounts used to accumulate information about assets, liabilities, owners' equity, revenues, and expenses. Create a chart of accounts when the business is established and modify the chart of accounts as needed over time.

Record Transactions

During the accounting period, record transactions with customers, vendors, employees and owners.

An accounting period can be one month, one quarter, or one year.

Trial Balance

A trial balance lists each account and the account balance at the end of the accounting period. Prepare a trial balance to verify that the accounting system is in balance—total debits should equal total credits. An *unadjusted* trial balance is a trial balance prepared *before* adjustments.

Adjustments

At the end of the accounting period before preparing financial statements, make any adjustments necessary to bring the accounts up to date. Adjustments are entered in the Journal using debits and credits.

Adjusted Trial Balance

Prepare an *adjusted* trial balance (a trial balance *after* adjustments) to verify that the accounting system still balances. If additional account detail is required, print the General Ledger (the collection of all the accounts listing the transactions that affected the accounts).

Financial Statements and Reports

Prepare financial statements for external users (profit & loss, balance sheet, and statement of cash flows). Prepare income tax summary reports and reports for managers.

Three types of reports that a business prepares are:

> The objective of financial reporting is to provide information to external users for decision making. The rules followed when preparing financial statements are called GAAP (Generally Accepted Accounting Principles.)

1. **Financial Statements**: Financial reports used by investors, owners, and creditors to make decisions. A banker might use the financial statements to decide whether to make a loan to a company. A prospective investor might use the financial statements to decide whether to invest in a company.

> Financial statements can be prepared monthly, quarterly, or annually. Always make adjustments *before* preparing financial statements.

The three financial statements most frequently used by external users are:

- Profit & loss (also called the income statement): lists income and expenses.
- Balance sheet: lists assets, liabilities, and owners' equity.
- Statement of cash flows: lists cash flows from operating, investing, and financing activities.

2. **Tax Forms**: The objective of the tax form is to provide information to the Internal Revenue Service and state tax authorities. When preparing tax returns, a company uses different rules from those used to prepare financial statements. When preparing a federal tax return, use the Internal Revenue Code.

Tax forms include the following:
- IRS Income Tax Return
- State Tax Return
- Forms 940, 941, W-2, W-3, 1099

3. **Management Reports**: Financial reports used by internal users (managers) to make decisions regarding company operations. These reports do not have to follow a particular set of rules and can be created to satisfy a manager's information needs.

Examples of reports that managers use include:
- Cash forecast
- Cash budget
- Accounts Receivable Aging Summary
- Accounts Payable Aging Summary

In this chapter, you will prepare some of these reports for Rock Castle Construction. First, you will prepare a trial balance and adjustments.

OPEN PORTABLE COMPANY FILE

To begin Chapter 7, first start QuickBooks software and then open the portable QuickBooks file.

Step 1: Start QuickBooks by clicking on the **QuickBooks** desktop icon or click **Start**, **Programs**, **QuickBooks**, **QuickBooks Pro 2006**.

Step 2: To open the portable company file (.QBM) file and convert the portable file to a regular company file with a .QBW extension, from the menu bar, click **File | Portable Company File | Open File**.

Step 3: Identify the filename and location for the portable company file:

- Click the **Browse** button to find the location of the portable company file on the hard drive or removable media.

- Select the file: **[your name] Exercise 6.2**. The .QBM may appear automatically based upon your Windows settings, but if it does not appear automatically, do **not** type it.

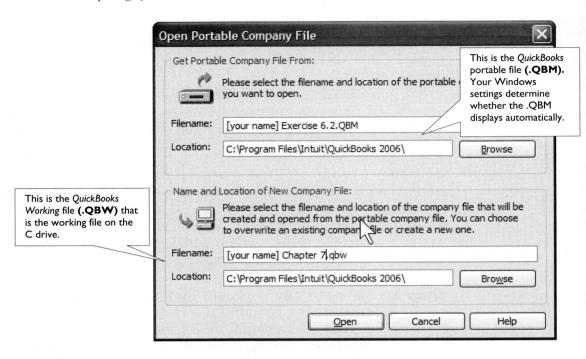

Step 4: Identify the name and location of the new company file (.QBW) file to use for Chapter 7:

- Filename: **[your name] Chapter 7**. The **.QBW** extension should appear automatically based upon your Windows settings. The .QBW identifies this as a QuickBooks working file.

- Location: **C:\Program Files\Intuit\QuickBooks 2006**. This is the location of the .QBW file on the hard drive of your computer.

Step 5: Click **Open** to open the portable company file.

Step 6: Click **Cancel** when the *Create a Backup* window appears.

Step 7: If prompted, enter your **User ID** and **Password**.

Step 8: Click **OK** when the sample company window appears.

Step 9: Change the company name to: **[your name] Chapter 7 Rock Castle Construction**. If necessary, change the Checking account title to include your name.

TRIAL BALANCE

A trial balance is a listing of all of a company's accounts and the ending account balances. A trial balance is often printed both before and after making adjustments. The purpose of the trial balance is to verify that the accounting system balances.

On a trial balance, all debit ending account balances are listed in the debit column and credit ending balances are listed in the credit column. If the accounting system balances, total debits equal total credits.

To print the trial balance for Rock Castle Construction:

Step 1: Click the **Report Center** icon on the Navigation Bar.

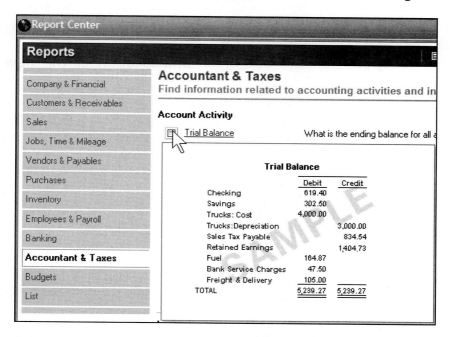

Step 2: Select: **Accountant & Taxes**.

Step 3: Select Report: **Trial Balance**.

Step 4: Select Date Range: **This Fiscal Quarter** From: **10/01/2007** To: **12/31/2007**.

Step 5: 🖶 **Print** the report using a **Portrait** print setting.

Modify Report...	Memorize...	Print...	E-mail	Export...	Hide Header	Collapse	Refresh

Dates [This Fiscal Quarter] From [10/01/2007] To [12/31/2007] Sort By [Default]

[your name] Chapter 7 Rock Castle Construction
Trial Balance
As of December 31, 2007

Accrual Basis

	Dec 31, 07	
	Debit	Credit
[your name] Checking	147,726.76	
Savings	13,868.42	
Barter Account	0.00	
1200 · Accounts Receivable	90,432.00	
Tools & Equipment	5,000.00	
Employee Loans	62.00	
1120 · Inventory Asset	23,340.40	
1350 · Retainage	2,461.80	
1400 · Undeposited Funds	58,742.77	
Land	90,000.00	
Buildings	325,000.00	
1500 · Trucks	78,352.91	
1500 · Trucks:1520 · Depreciation	0.00	
Computers	28,501.00	
Furniture	7,325.00	
Accumulated Depreciation		121,887.78
Pre-paid Insurance	1,041.85	
2000 · Accounts Payable		55,028.84
QuickBooks Credit Card		70.00
2050 · CalOil Card		5,057.62
2101 · Payroll Liabilities		8,723.75
2200 · Sales Tax Payable		5.66
Bank of Anycity Loan		19,932.65
Equipment Loan		3,911.32
2250 · Note Payable		3,440.83
2300 · Truck Loan		50,162.38
3500 · Opening Bal Equity		593,019.25
3000 · Owner's Equity:3100 · Owner's Contribution		98,000.00
3000 · Owner's Equity:3200 · Owner's Draw	6,000.00	
3300 · Retained Earnings	129,916.38	
4000 · Construction:4100 · Labor		51,457.25
4000 · Construction:4200 · Materials		69,604.51
4000 · Construction:4400 · Miscellaneous		5,155.55
4000 · Construction:4300 · Subcontractors		60,911.01
5000 · Cost of Goods Sold	8,885.01	
6000 · Automobile	10.60	
6000 · Automobile:Insurance	712.56	
6000 · Automobile:6020 · Fuel	231.10	
6040 · Selling Expense:6041 · Advertising Expense	200.00	
6100 · Bank Service Charges	67.50	
6400 · Freight & Delivery	219.60	
6500 · Insurance	297.66	
6500 · Insurance:6510 · Disability Insurance	300.00	
6500 · Insurance:6520 · Liability Insurance	2,100.00	
6500 · Insurance:6530 · Work Comp	1,650.00	
6600 · Interest Expense	651.77	
6600 · Interest Expense:6620 · Loan Interest	288.05	
7400 · Job Expenses:7410 · Equipment Rental	1,000.00	
7400 · Job Expenses:7420 · Job Materials	38,771.87	
7400 · Job Expenses:7430 · Permits and Licenses	700.00	
7400 · Job Expenses:7440 · Subcontractors	44,166.00	
6560 · Payroll Expenses	34,729.67	
7000 · Professional Fees:7010 · Accounting	250.00	
7100 · Rent	1,200.00	
7200 · Repairs:7210 · Building Repairs	175.00	
7200 · Repairs:7220 · Computer Repairs	345.00	
7200 · Repairs:7230 · Equipment Repairs	0.00	
7500 · Tools and Machinery	1,160.00	
7600 · Utilities:7610 · Gas and Electric	364.08	
7600 · Utilities:7620 · Telephone	154.71	
7600 · Utilities:7630 · Water	97.85	
8000 · Interest Income		93.42
8100 · Other Income		37.50
TOTAL	1,146,499.32	1,146,499.32

Step 6: Compare your answers to the above trial balance printout. Correct any errors.

Step 7: To memorize the report, click the **Memorize** button. In the name field, enter: **Trial Balance**, then click **OK**.

Step 8: **Close** the *Trial Balance* window.

ADJUSTING ENTRIES

In QuickBooks, the journal is used to record adjustments (and corrections). Adjustments are often necessary to bring the accounts up to date at the end of the accounting period.

If you are using the accrual basis to measure profit, the following five types of adjusting entries may be necessary.

> Financial statements for external users use straight-line depreciation. For tax forms, MACRS (Modified Accelerated Cost Recovery System) is usually used. See your accountant for more information about calculating depreciation or see IRS Publication 946.

1. **Depreciation**: Depreciation has several different definitions. When conversing with an accountant it is important to know which definition of depreciation is used. See the table on the following page for more information about depreciation.

> To view the fixed assets that need to be depreciated, click **Lists** (menu), **Fixed Asset Item List**.

2. **Prepaid Items**: Items that are prepaid, such as prepaid insurance or prepaid rent. An adjustment may be needed to record the amount of the prepaid item that has not expired at the end of the accounting period. For example, an adjustment may be needed to record the amount of insurance that has not expired as Prepaid Insurance (an asset with future benefit).

3. **Unearned Revenue**: If a customer pays in advance of receiving a service, such as when a customer makes a deposit, your business has an obligation (liability) to either provide the service in the future or return the customer's money. An adjustment may be necessary to bring the revenue account and unearned revenue (liability) account up to date.

> A small business may want to hire an outside accountant to prepare adjusting entries at year-end. You can create a copy of your company data file for your accountant to use when making adjustments. For more information about creating an Accountant's Review Copy, see Chapter 12.

4. **Accrued Expenses**: Expenses that are incurred but not yet paid or recorded. Examples of accrued expenses include accrued interest expense (interest expense that you have incurred but have not yet paid).

5. **Accrued Revenues**: Revenues that have been earned but not yet collected or recorded. Examples of accrued revenues include interest revenue that has been earned but not yet collected or recorded.

Depreciation

The accounting definitions of depreciation differ from the popular definition of depreciation as a decline in value.

Depreciation is listed on….	Report Objective	Reporting Rules	Definition of Depreciation	Depreciation Calculation
Financial statements Profit & Loss, Balance Sheet, Statement of Cash Flows	Provide information to external users (bankers and investors)	GAAP (Generally Accepted Accounting Principles)	*Financial Accounting Definition:* Allocation of asset's cost to periods used.	Straight-line depreciation = (Cost – Salvage)/ Useful life
Income tax returns	Provide information to the Internal Revenue Service	Internal Revenue Code	*Tax Definition:* Recovery of asset's cost through depreciation deductions on return	MACRS (See IRS Publication 946 on depreciation)

RECORD ADJUSTING JOURNAL ENTRIES

In a traditional accounting system, transactions are recorded using journal entries with debits and credits. QuickBooks uses onscreen forms to record transactions, and the journal is used to record adjustments and corrections. QuickBooks also permits you to record adjustments directly in the accounts.

Some small business owners, instead of preparing the adjusting entries themselves, have their accountants prepare the adjusting entries. If you are using QuickBooks: Premier Accountant Edition 2006, you can use the Fixed Asset Manager to record fixed assets and record entries for depreciation.

Rock Castle Construction needs to make an adjustment to record $3,000 of depreciation expense on its truck.

To make the adjusting journal entry in QuickBooks:

Step 1: From the **Company** menu, select **Make General Journal Entries**.

You can also access the journal from the Banking Navigator.

Step 2: When the following *General Journal Entry* window appears, select Date: **12/31/2007**.

Adjusting entries are dated the last day of the accounting period.

Type the Account No. **6200** and QuickBooks will automatically complete the account title.

Step 3: Enter Entry No: **ADJ 1**.

Step 4: Select Account to debit: **6200 Depreciation Expense**.

TIP: Memorize the journal entry to reuse each accounting period:
1. With the Journal Entry displayed, click **Edit** (menu).
2. Select **Memorize General Journal**.
To use the memorized transaction, select Memorized Transactions from the Lists menu.

Step 5: Enter Debit amount: **3000.00**.

Step 6: Select Account to credit: **1520 Depreciation**. (If a message appears asking if you want to use an inactive account, click **Make It Active**.)

Step 7: If it does not appear automatically, enter Credit amount: **3000.00**.

Step 8: Click **Save & Close** to record the journal entry and close the *Make General Journal Entries* window.

PRINT JOURNAL ENTRIES

To view the journal entry you just recorded, display the journal. The journal also contains journal entries for all transactions recorded using onscreen forms, such as sales invoices. QuickBooks automatically converts transactions recorded in onscreen forms into journal entries with debits and credits.

To display and print the General Journal:

Step 1: Click the **Report Center** icon in the Navigation Bar.

Step 2: Select: **Accountant & Taxes**.

Step 3: Select Report: **Journal**.

Step 4: Select Dates From: **12/24/2007** To: **12/31/2007**.

Notice that the sales invoice you recorded on 12/24/2007 for the Jacobsen Kitchen job has now been converted to a journal entry.

Notice the adjusting entry for depreciation.

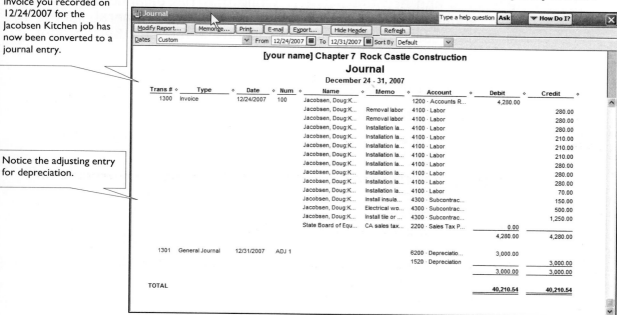

Step 5: 🖨 **Print** the journal using **Portrait** orientation.

Step 6: **Close** the *Journal* window.

ADJUSTED TRIAL BALANCE

The adjusted trial balance is prepared to verify that the accounting system still balances after adjusting entries are made.

Step 1: 🖨 **Print** an adjusted **trial balance** as of **December 31, 2007**, using the **Portrait** orientation.

Step 2: ✏ **Circle** the account balances that are different from the trial balance amounts.

> ✓ **Total debits and total credits equal $1,149,499.32.**

GENERAL LEDGER

The General Ledger is a collection of all of the company's accounts and account activity. While the trial balance lists only the ending balance for each account, the general ledger provides detail about all transactions affecting the account during a given period.

Each account in the General Ledger lists:

- Beginning balance.

- Transactions that affected the account for the selected period.

- Ending balance.

Normally, the General Ledger is not provided to external users, such as bankers. However, the General Ledger can provide managers with supporting detail needed to answer questions bankers might ask about the financial statements.

To print the General Ledger:

Step 1: If the Report Center is not open, click the **Report Center** icon on the Navigation Bar.

Step 2: Select: **Accountant & Taxes**.

Step 3: Select Report: **General Ledger**.

Step 4: Select Date Range: **This Fiscal Quarter**.

Step 5: The General Ledger report lists each account and all the transactions affecting the account. **Double-click on a transaction listed in the Checking account** to drill down to the original source document, such as a check or an invoice. **Close** the source document window.

Step 6: Use a filter to view only selected accounts in the General Ledger. For example, to view only the bank accounts, complete the following steps:

- Click the **Modify Report** button at the top of the *General Ledger* window. Then click the **Filters** tab.

- Select Filter: **Account**.

- Select Account: **All bank accounts**.

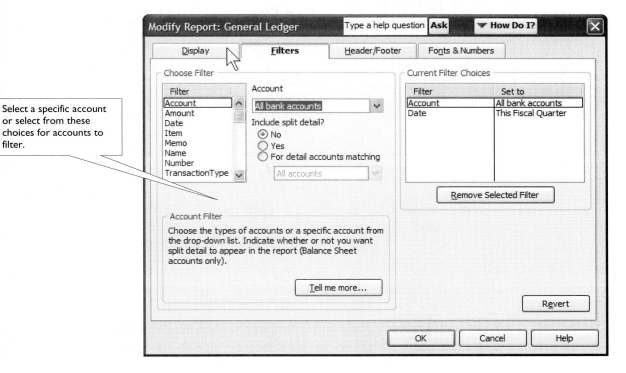

Select a specific account or select from these choices for accounts to filter.

Step 7: To omit accounts with zero balances in the General Ledger report, from the *Modify Report* window:

- Click the **Display** tab, and then click the **Advanced** button.

- Select Include: **In Use**.

- Click **OK**.

Step 8: Click **OK** to close the *Modify Report* window.

Step 9: 🖬 **Print** the selected General Ledger account using **Portrait** orientation. Select **Fit to 1 page(s) wide**.

Step 10: **Close** the *General Ledger* window.

FINANCIAL STATEMENTS

Financial statements are standardized financial reports given to bankers and investors. The three main financial statements are the profit and loss, balance sheet, and statement of cash flows. The statements are prepared following Generally Accepted Accounting Principles (GAAP).

> The profit & loss statement is also called P&L or income statement.

PROFIT AND LOSS

The profit and loss statement lists sales (sometimes called revenues) and expenses for a specified accounting period. Profit, or net income, can be measured two different ways:

1. **Cash basis**: A sale is recorded when cash is collected from the customer. Expenses are recorded when cash is paid.

> GAAP requires the accrual basis for the profit and loss statement because it provides a better matching of income and expenses.

2. **Accrual basis**: Sales are recorded when the good or service is provided regardless of whether the cash is collected from the customer. Expenses are recorded when the cost is incurred or expires, even if the expense has not been paid .

QuickBooks permits you to prepare the profit and loss statement using either the accrual or the cash basis. QuickBooks also permits you to prepare profit and loss statements monthly, quarterly, or annually.

To prepare a quarterly profit and loss statement for Rock Castle Construction using the accrual basis:

Step 1: Display the **Report Center**.

Step 2: Select: **Company & Financial**.

Step 3: Select Report: **Profit & Loss Standard**.

Step 4: Select Dates: **This Fiscal Quarter**.

Step 5: Click the **Modify Report** button. Click the **Display** tab, and then select Report Basis: **Accrual**. Click **OK**.

Step 6: 🖶 **Print** the profit and loss statement using **Portrait** orientation.

Step 7: **Close** the *Profit and Loss* window.

INCOME AND EXPENSE GRAPH

QuickBooks provides you with the ability to easily graph profit and loss information. A graph is simply another means to communicate financial information.

To create an income and expense graph for Rock Castle Construction:

Step 1: From the **Report Center**, select: **Company & Financial**.

Step 2: Select Report: **Income and Expense Graph**.

Step 3: Select Dates: **This Quarter** to display the following *QuickInsight: Income and Expense Graph* window.

Step 4: Click the **By Account** button. The income and expense graph depicts a bar chart of income and expense for the three months in the fiscal quarter. The pie chart in the lower section of the window displays the relative proportion of each expense as a percentage of total expenses.

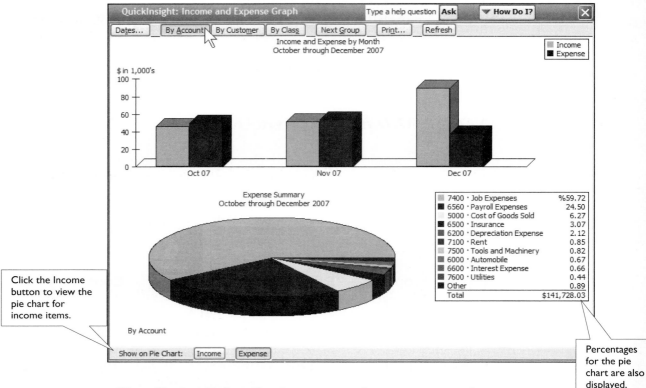

Click the Income button to view the pie chart for income items.

Percentages for the pie chart are also displayed.

Step 5: 🖨 **Print** the income and expense graph.

Step 6: **Close** the *QuickInsight: Income and Expense Graph* window.

BALANCE SHEET

The balance sheet presents a company's financial position on a particular date. The balance sheet can be prepared at the end of a month, quarter, or year. The balance sheet lists:

1. **Assets**: What a company owns. On the balance sheet, assets are recorded at their historical cost, the amount you paid for the asset when you purchased it. Note that

historical cost can be different from the market value of the asset, which is the amount the asset is worth now.

2. **Liabilities**: What a company owes. Liabilities are obligations which include amounts owed vendors (accounts payable) and bank loans (notes payable).

3. **Owner's equity**: The residual that is left after liabilities are satisfied. This is also called net worth. Owner's equity is increased by the owner's contributions and net income. Owner's equity is decreased by the owner's withdrawals (or dividends) and net losses.

To prepare a balance sheet for Rock Castle Construction at 12/31/2007:

Step 1: From the **Report Center,** select: **Company & Financial**.

Step 2: Select Report: **Balance Sheet Standard**.

Step 3: Select Dates: **This Fiscal Quarter**.

Step 4: 🖶 **Print** the balance sheet using the **Portrait** orientation.

Step 5: **Close** the *Balance Sheet* window.

Step 6: ✎ **Circle** the single largest asset listed on the balance sheet.

STATEMENT OF CASH FLOWS

The Statement of Cash Flows summarizes cash inflows and cash outflows for a business over a period of time. Cash flows are grouped into three categories:

1. **Cash flows from Operating Activities**: Cash inflows and outflows related to the company's primary business, such as cash flows from sales and operating expenses.

2. **Cash flows from Investing Activities**: Cash inflows and outflows related to acquisition and disposal of long-term assets.

3. **Cash flows from Financing Activities**: Cash inflows and outflows to and from investors and creditors (except for interest payments). Examples include: loan principal repayment and investments by owners.

To print the statement of cash flows for Rock Castle Construction:

Step 1: From the Report Center, select: **Company & Financial**.

Step 2: Select Report: **Statement of Cash Flows**.

Step 3: Select Date: **This Fiscal Quarter**.

Step 4: ⊟ **Print** the Statement of Cash Flows using the **Portrait** orientation.

Step 5: **Close** the *Statement of Cash Flows* window.

TAX REPORTS

QuickBooks provides two different approaches that you can use when preparing your tax return.

(1) Print QuickBooks income tax reports and then manually enter the tax information in your income tax return.

(2) Export your QuickBooks accounting data to tax software, such as TurboTax software, and then use TurboTax to complete your income tax return.

Three different income tax reports are provided by QuickBooks:

1. **Income Tax Preparation Report**: lists the assigned tax line for each account.

2. **Income Tax Summary Report**: summarizes income and expenses that should be listed on a business income tax return.

3. **Income Tax Detail Report**: provides more detailed information about the income or expense amount appearing on each tax line of the income tax summary.

INCOME TAX PREPARATION REPORT

Before printing the Income Tax Summary report, check your QuickBooks accounts to see that the correct Tax Line is selected for each account. An easy way to check the Tax Line specified for each account is to print the Income Tax Preparation report as follows.

Step 1: From the Report Center, select: **Accountant & Taxes**.

Step 2: Select Report: **Income Tax Preparation**.

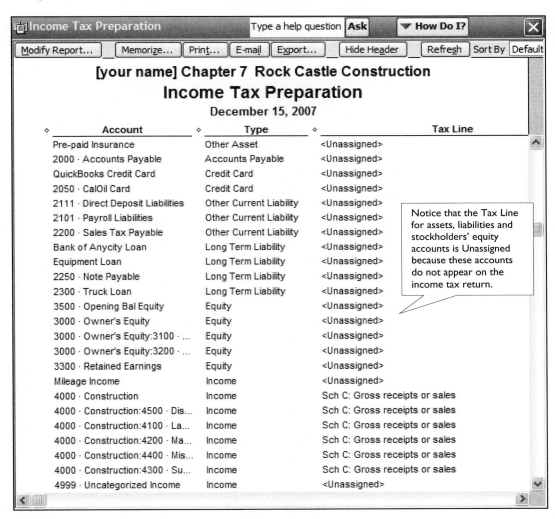

Step 3: 🖶 **Print** the Income Tax Preparation Report.

Step 4: **Close** the *Income Tax Preparation* window.

To determine if the correct tax line has been entered for each account, compare the tax lines listed on the Income Tax Preparation report with your business income tax return.

If you need to change the Tax Line for an account:

Step 1: Open the *Chart of Accounts* window. (From the Company section of the Home page, click the Chart of Accounts icon.)

Step 2: Select the account, then right-click to display a popup menu. Select **Edit Account** on the popup menu to edit the account.

Step 3: When the following *Edit Account* window appears, change the Tax Line as needed.

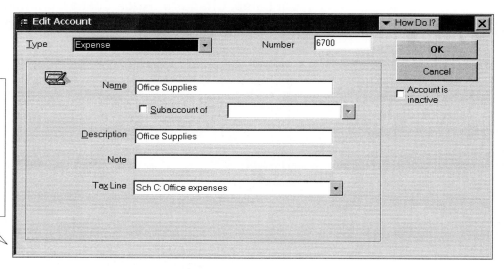

Recall that when you create a new account, you specify a Tax Line for the account. The Tax Line determines the tax line of the Income Tax Summary that the account balance will appear. See Chapter 2 for more information about account Tax Lines.

Step 4: To save the changes, you would click OK. In this activity, click **Cancel** to close the *Edit Account* window.

INCOME TAX SUMMARY REPORT

A sole proprietorship files Schedule C (attached to the owner's personal 1040 tax return). A corporation files Form 1120; a subchapter S corporation files Form 1120S.

After you have confirmed that the Tax Line for each account is correct, you are ready to print an Income Tax Summary Report. The Income Tax Summary report lists sales and expenses that should appear on the business federal tax return filed with the IRS.

To print the Income Tax Summary report:

Step 1: From the Report Center, select: **Accountant & Taxes**.

Step 2: Select Report: **Income Tax Summary**.

Step 3: Select Date: **This Tax Year** From: **01/01/2007** To: **12/31/2007**.

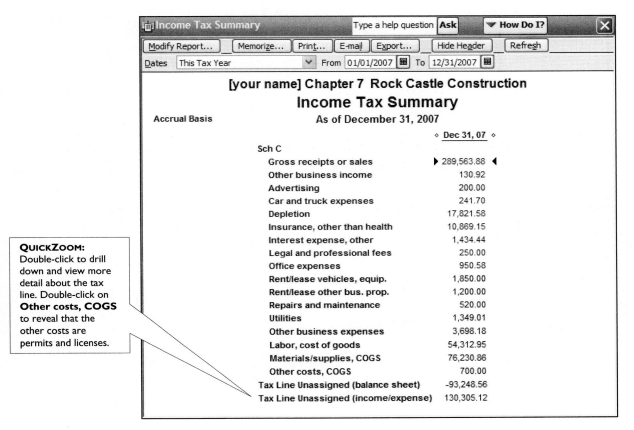

QUICKZOOM:
Double-click to drill down and view more detail about the tax line. Double-click on **Other costs, COGS** to reveal that the other costs are permits and licenses.

Step 4: 🖶 **Print** the Income Tax Summary report.

Step 5: **Close** the *Income Tax Summary* window.

A business can use the information on the Income Tax Summary report to manually complete its income tax return.

INCOME TAX DETAIL REPORT

If you want to view detail for the line items shown on the Income Tax Summary report, display the Income Tax Detail report as follows:

Step 1: From the Report Center, select: **Accountant & Taxes**.

Step 2: Select Report: **Income Tax Detail**.

Step 3: Select Dates: **This Tax Year**. Detailed information is then listed for each line item in the *Income Tax Detail* window.

Step 4: **Close** the *Income Tax Detail* window.

EXPORT TO TURBOTAX

> TurboTax for Home and Business is used for a sole proprietorship Schedule C. TurboTax for Business is for corporations, S corporations, and partnerships.

Another approach to preparing a tax return is to export the account information from QuickBooks into TurboTax software.

To import your QuickBooks tax data into TurboTax software:

Step 1: Make a copy of your QuickBooks company data file.

Step 2: Start TurboTax software.

Step 3: Import your QuickBooks company file into TurboTax. In TurboTax, go to the File menu, and click Import.

MANAGEMENT REPORTS

Reports used by management do not have to follow a specified set of rules such as GAAP or the Internal Revenue Code. Instead, management reports are prepared as needed to provide management with information for making operating and business decisions.

Management reports include:

1. Cash flow forecast.

2. Budgets (See Chapter 12).

3. Accounts Receivable Aging (See Chapter 4).

4. Accounts Payable Aging (See Chapter 5).

5. Inventory Reports (See Chapter 5).

CASH FLOW FORECAST

QuickBooks permits you to forecast cash flows. This enables you to project whether you will have enough cash to pay bills when they are due. If it appears that you will need additional cash, then you can arrange for a loan or line of credit to pay your bills.

To print a Cash Flow Forecast report for Rock Castle Construction:

Step 1: From the Report Center, select: **Company & Financial**.

Step 2: Select Report: **Cash Flow Forecast**.

Step 3: Select Dates: **Next 4 Weeks** to display the *Cash Flow Forecast* window.

This report lists projected cash inflows and cash outflows.

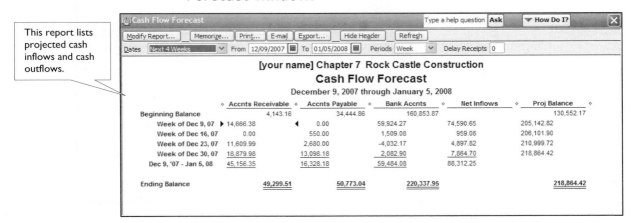

Step 4: 🖨 **Print** the Cash Flow Forecast using **Portrait** orientation.

Step 5: Leave the *Cash Flow Forecast* window open.

EXPORT REPORTS TO MICROSOFT® EXCEL®

To export to an existing Excel spreadsheet, select: **Send report to an existing Excel spreadsheet**. Click **Browse** to select the file.

QuickBooks permits you to export a report to Microsoft Excel spreadsheet software. In order to use this feature of QuickBooks, you must have Microsoft Excel software installed on your computer.

To export the Cash Flow Forecast report to Excel:

Step 1: With the *Cash Flow Forecast* window still open, click the **Export** button at the top of the window.

Step 2: When the following *Export Report* window appears, select Export QuickBooks report to: **a new Excel workbook**.

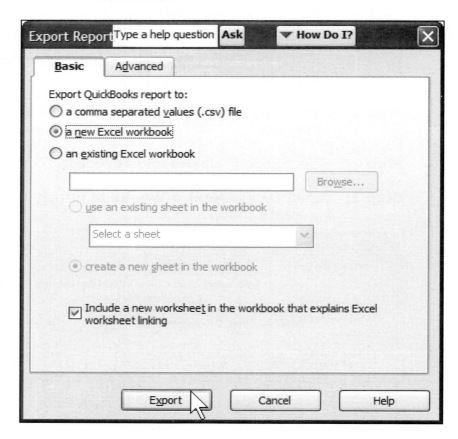

Step 3: Then click **Export** to export the QuickBooks report to Excel.

Step 4: Excel will automatically open. When the spreadsheet appears on your screen, **click on the cell that contains the Ending Balance of Accounts Receivable**. Notice that Excel has already entered a formula into the cell.

Step 5: To save the Excel file:

- In Excel, click **File** on the menu bar.
- Select **Save As**.
- Select the drive to which you are saving (A drive, C drive, USB drive, or CD drive).
- Enter Filename: **Cash Forecast**.
- Click **Save**.

Step 6: 🖨 **Print** the Excel spreadsheet.

Step 7: **Close** the Cash Forecast Excel workbook, then **close** Excel software by clicking the ⊠ in the upper right corner of the Excel window.

SAVE REPORTS TO DISK

QuickBooks also permits you to save a report to a file instead of printing the report. You can select from the following file formats:

- ASCII text file: After saving as a text file, the file can be used with word processing software.
- Comma delimited file: Comma delimited files can be imported into word processing, spreadsheet, or database software. Commas identify where columns begin and end.
- Tab delimited file: Tab delimited files can be used with word processing or database software. Tabs identify where columns begin and end.

SAVE CHAPTER 7

Save Chapter 7 as a portable QuickBooks file to the location specified by your instructor.

Step 1: If necessary, insert a removable disk.

Step 2: From the menu bar, click **File | Portable Company File | Create File**.

Step 3: When the *Close and Reopen* window appears, click **OK**.

Step 4: When the following *Create Portable Company File* window appears, enter the filename: **[your name] Chapter 7** and the appropriate location. Then click **Save**.

Step 5: Click **OK** after the portable file has been created successfully.

Step 6: Close the company file by clicking **File** (Menu), **Close Company**.

If you are continuing your computer session, proceed to Exercise 7.1.

If you are ending your computer session now, see the Quick Reference Guide in Part 3 for instructions to (1) close the company file and (2) exit QuickBooks.

ASSIGNMENTS

> **NOTE: See the Quick Reference Guide in Part 3 for step-by-step instructions to frequently used tasks.**

EXERCISE 7.1: PROFIT & LOSS: VERTICAL ANALYSIS

SCENARIO

You vaguely recall from your college accounting course that performing financial statement analysis can reveal additional useful information. Since Mr. Castle asked for whatever additional information he might need, you decide to print a vertical analysis of the income statement using QuickBooks.

TASK 1: OPEN PORTABLE COMPANY FILE

To open the portable company file (.QBM) file, convert the portable file to a regular company file with a .QBW extension as follows:

Step 1: From the menu bar, click **File | Portable Company File | Open File**.

Step 2: Identify the filename and location for the portable company file:

- Click the **Browse** button to find the location of the portable company file on the hard drive or removable media.

- Select the file: **[your name] Chapter 7.QBM**.

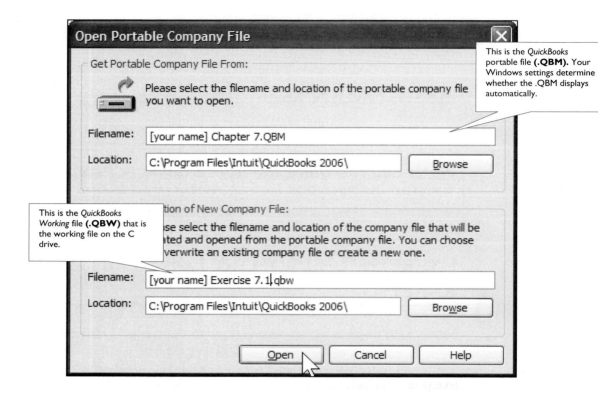

Step 3: Identify the name and location of the new company file (.QBW) file to use for completing Exercise 7.1:

- Filename: **[your name] Exercise 7.1**. The **.QBW** extension should appear automatically based upon your Windows settings.

- Location: **C:\Program Files\Intuit\QuickBooks 2006**. This is the location of the .QBW file on the hard drive of your computer. Click the Browse button to specify another location.

Step 4: Click **Open** to open the portable company file.

Step 5: Click **Cancel** when the *Create a Backup* window appears.

Step 6: If prompted, enter your **User Name** and **Password**, then click **OK**.

Step 7: Click **OK** when the QuickBooks sample company message appears.

Step 8: Change the company name to: **[your name] Exercise 7.1 Rock Castle Construction**.

TASK 2: PROFIT & LOSS: VERTICAL ANALYSIS

Prepare a customized profit and loss statement that shows each item on the statement as a percentage of sales (income):

Step 1: Open the Report Center (click the **Report Center** icon in the Navigation Bar).

Step 2: Select: **Company & Financial**.

Step 3: Select Report: **Profit & Loss Standard**.

Step 4: Select Dates: **This Fiscal Quarter**.

Step 5: To customize the report, click the **Modify Report** button.

Step 6: When the following *Modify Report* window appears, select: **% of Income**. Click **OK**.

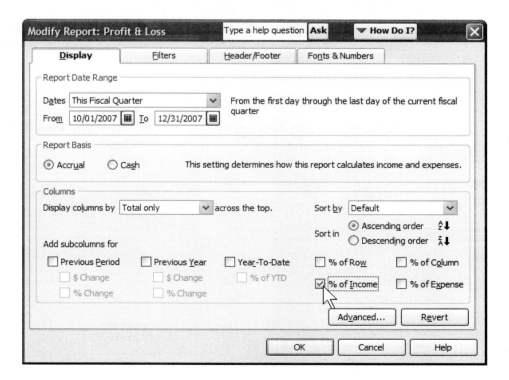

Step 7: ▣ Click the **Print** button to print the report using the **Portrait** orientation.

Step 8: ✐ On the printout, **circle** or highlight the single largest expense as a percentage of income.

Step 9: ✐ On the printout, **circle** or highlight the profit margin (income as a percentage of sales).

TASK 3: SAVE EXERCISE 7.1

Save Exercise 7.1 as a portable company file to the location specified by your instructor.

Step 1: If necessary, insert a removable disk.

Step 2: From the menu bar, click **File | Portable Company File | Create File**.

Step 3: When the *Close and Reopen* window appears, click **OK**.

Step 4: When the *Create Portable Company File* window appears, enter the filename: **[your name] Exercise 7.1** and the appropriate location. Click **Save**.

Step 5: Click **OK** after the portable file has been created successfully.

Step 6: Close the company file by clicking **File** (Menu), **Close Company**.

EXERCISE 7.2:
BALANCE SHEET: VERTICAL ANALYSIS

SCENARIO

You decide to also prepare a customized balance sheet that displays each account on the balance sheet as a percentage of total assets. This vertical analysis indicates the proportion of total assets that each asset represents. For example, inventory might be 30 percent of total assets. Vertical analysis also helps to assess the percentage of assets financed by debt versus owner's equity.

TASK 1: OPEN PORTABLE COMPANY FILE

To open the portable company file (.QBM) file, convert the portable file to a regular company file with a .QBW extension as follows:

Step 1: From the menu bar, click **File | Portable Company File | Open File**.

Step 2: Identify the filename and location for the portable company file:

- Click the **Browse** button to find the location of the portable company file on the hard drive or removable media.

- Select the file: **[your name] Exercise 7.1.QBM**.

Step 3: Identify the name and location of the new company file (.QBW) file to use for completing Exercise 7.1:

- Filename: **[your name] Exercise 7.2**. The **.QBW** extension should appear automatically based upon your Windows settings.

- Location: **C:\Program Files\Intuit\QuickBooks 2006**. This is the location of the .QBW file on the hard drive of your computer. Click the Browse button to specify another location.

Step 4:   Click **Open** to open the portable company file.

Step 5:   Click **Cancel** when the *Create a Backup* window appears.

Step 6:   If prompted, enter your **User Name** and **Password**, then click **OK**.

Step 7:   Click **OK** when the QuickBooks sample company message appears.

Step 8:   Change the company name to: **[your name] Exercise 7.2 Rock Castle Construction**.

TASK 2: BALANCE SHEET: VERTICAL ANALYSIS, EXPORT TO EXCEL

Prepare a customized balance sheet that shows each account as a percentage of total assets.

Step 1:   From the Report Center, select: **Company & Financial**.

Step 2:   Select Report: **Balance Sheet Standard**.

Step 3:   Select Dates: **This Fiscal Quarter**.

Step 4:   Click the **Modify Report** button and select: **% of Column**.

Step 5:   🖨 **Print** the customized balance sheet using the **Portrait** orientation.

Step 6:   ✏ On the printout, **circle** or highlight the asset that represents the largest percentage of assets.

Step 7:   ✏ On the printout, **circle** or highlight the percentage of assets financed with debt. (Hint: What is the percentage of total liabilities?)

Step 8:   Export the customized balance sheet to Excel by clicking the **Excel** button in the *Balance Sheet* window. 🖨 **Print** the Excel spreadsheet and compare it to your QuickBooks printout.

TASK 3: SAVE EXERCISE 7.2

Save Exercise 7.2 as a portable company file to the location specified by your instructor.

Step 1: If necessary, insert a removable disk.

Step 2: From the menu bar, click **File** | **Portable Company File** | **Create File**.

Step 3: When the *Close and Reopen* window appears, click **OK**.

Step 4: When the *Create Portable Company File* window appears, enter the filename: **[your name] Exercise 7.2** and the appropriate location. Click **Save**.

Step 5: Click **OK** after the portable file has been created successfully.

Step 6: Close the company file by clicking **File** (Menu), **Close Company**.

EXERCISE 7.3: DEPRECIATION DECISION TOOL

To learn more about depreciation, see the QuickBooks Decision Tools.

Step 1: Select **Company** on the menu bar, and then click **Planning & Budgeting**.

Step 2: Click **Decision Tools**.

Step 3: Select: **Depreciate Your Assets**. Then read about depreciation basics.

Step 4: ✍ Using word processing or E-mail software, prepare and print a short E-mail to Mr. Castle that summarizes depreciation basics and answers the following questions:

- What set of accounting rules are followed when preparing financial statements for bankers?

- What set of rules are followed when preparing federal income tax forms?

- What is the popular definition of depreciation?

- What is the financial accounting definition of depreciation?

- What is the tax definition of depreciation?

EXERCISE 7.4: YEAR-END GUIDE PRINTOUT

QuickBooks provides a Year-End Guide to assist in organizing the tasks that a business must complete at the end of its accounting period.

🖨 **Print** the Year-End Guide as follows:

Step 1: From the **Help** menu, select **Year-End Guide**.

Step 2: 🖨 **Print** the Year-End Guide by clicking the **Print** icon at the top of the window.

EXERCISE 7.5: WEB QUEST

To learn more information about TurboTax software, visit Intuit's TurboTax web site.

Step 1: Go to www.turbotax.com web site.

Step 2: ✍ Prepare a short e-mail to Mr. Castle summarizing the difference between TurboTax Basic, Deluxe, Premier and TurboTax for Business. Which TurboTax would you recommend for Rock Castle Construction?

EXERCISE 7.6: WEB QUEST

Publicly traded companies (companies that sell stock to the public) are required to provide an annual report to stockholders. The annual report contains financial statements including an income statement, balance sheet, and statement of cash flows. Many publicly traded companies now post their financial statements on their websites. Print financial statements for Intuit, the company that sells QuickBooks software.

Step 1: Go to www.intuit.com web site. Click **About Intuit.**

Step 2: Click **Investor Relations**. Click **Annual Reports**. Select **Fiscal 2003 Annual Report**.

Step 3: From the drop-down menu, select **Annual Report to Stockholders**.

Step 4: Click **Consolidated Financial Statements**. Click **Consolidated Statement of Operations**.

Step 5: **Print** Intuit's Consolidated Statement of Operations which shows results for three years.

Step 6: **Circle** net income for the year Intuit was most profitable.

CHAPTER 7 PRINTOUT CHECKLIST
NAME:_____DATE:_____

INSTRUCTIONS:
1. ***CHECK OFF THE PRINTOUTS YOU HAVE COMPLETED.***
2. ***STAPLE THIS PAGE TO YOUR PRINTOUTS.***

☑ ***PRINTOUT CHECKLIST – CHAPTER 7***
- ☐ Trial Balance
- ☐ Journal
- ☐ Adjusted Trial Balance
- ☐ General Ledger
- ☐ Profit & Loss
- ☐ Income and Expense Graph
- ☐ Balance Sheet
- ☐ Statement of Cash Flows
- ☐ Income Tax Preparation Report
- ☐ Income Tax Summary
- ☐ Cash Flow Forecast
- ☐ Excel Spreadsheet Cash Flow Forecast

☑ ***PRINTOUT CHECKLIST – EXERCISE 7.1***
- ☐ Task 2: Profit & Loss: Vertical Analysis

☑ ***PRINTOUT CHECKLIST – EXERCISE 7.2***
- ☐ Task 2: Balance Sheet: Vertical Analysis & Excel Spreadsheet

☑ ***PRINTOUT CHECKLIST – EXERCISE 7.3***
- ☐ Depreciation Basics E-mail

☑ ***PRINTOUT CHECKLIST – EXERCISE 7.4***
- ☐ Year-End Guide Printout

☑ ***PRINTOUT CHECKLIST – EXERCISE 7.5***
- ☐ TurboTax Recommendation E-mail

☑ ***PRINTOUT CHECKLIST – EXERCISE 7.6***
☐ Statement of Operations for Intuit, Inc.

NOTES:

Part 2
Small Business Accounting with QuickBooks Pro 2006

CHAPTER 8
CREATING A SERVICE COMPANY IN QUICKBOOKS

SCENARIO

Lately, you've considered starting your own business and becoming an entrepreneur. You have been looking for a business opportunity that would use your talents to make money.

While working at Rock Castle Construction, you have overheard conversations that some of the customers have been dissatisfied with the quality of the paint jobs. In addition, you believe there is a demand for custom painting. You know that Rock Castle Construction lost more than one job because it could not find a subcontractor to do custom painting.

One morning when you arrive at work, you hear Mr. Castle's voice booming throughout the office. *"That's the second time this month!"* he roars into the telephone. *"How are we supposed to finish our jobs on time when the painting subcontractor doesn't show up?!"* Mr. Castle slams down the phone.

That morning you begin to seriously consider the advantages and disadvantages of starting your own painting service business. Perhaps you could pick up some work from Rock Castle Construction. You could do interior and exterior painting for homes and businesses, including custom-painted murals while continuing to work part-time for Rock Castle Construction maintaining its accounting records. Now that you have learned QuickBooks, you can quickly enter transactions and create the reports Mr. Castle needs, leaving you time to operate your own painting service business.

When you return from lunch, you notice Katrina Beneficio in Mr. Castle's office. Then you overhear Mr. Castle telling her, *"We would like to help you, Mrs. Beneficio, but we don't have anyone who can do a custom-painted landscape on your dining room wall. If I hear of anyone who does that type of work, I will call you."*

You watch as the two of them shake hands and Mrs. Beneficio walks out the front door. Sensing a window of opportunity, you pursue Mrs. Beneficio into the parking lot. *"Mrs. Beneficio—"*

She stops and turns to look at you. *"Mrs. Beneficio—I understand that you are looking for someone to paint a landscape mural in your home. I would like to bid on the job."*

With a sparkle in her eye, Mrs. Beneficio asks, *"How soon can you start?"*

"As soon as I get off work this afternoon!" you reply as the two of you shake hands. *"Would you like a bid on the job?"*

Without hesitation, Mrs. Beneficio replies, *"I trust you will be fair to your first customer."*

When you reenter the office building, Mr. Castle is waiting for you. You can feel Mr. Castle's gaze as you debate how best to tell him about your business plans.

Finally, Mr. Castle speaks. *"Give Tom Whalen a call. He would like you to do marble faux painting in his home's foyer."*

"Thanks, Mr. Castle. I'll do that right away," you reply as you head toward your cubicle, wondering how Mr. Castle knew about your business plans.

Walking back to your cubicle, you quickly make three start-up decisions:
1. To use the sole proprietorship form of business.
2. To name your business Fearless Painting Service.
3. To invest in a computer so that you can use QuickBooks to maintain the accounting records for your business.

Now you will have two sources of income:
- Wages from Rock Castle Construction reported on your W-2 and attached to your 1040 tax return.
- Income from your painting business reported on a Schedule C attached to your 1040 tax return.

CHAPTER 8
LEARNING OBJECTIVES

In Chapter 8, you will learn the following QuickBooks activities:

INTRODUCTION

In this chapter, you will set up a new service company in QuickBooks by completing the following steps:

1. EasyStep Interview

Use the EasyStep Interview to enter information and preferences for the new company. Based on the information entered, QuickBooks automatically creates a chart of accounts.

2. Customize the Chart of Accounts

Modify the chart of accounts to customize it for your business.

3. Customer List

In the Customer List, enter information about customers to whom you sell products and services.

4. Vendor List

In the Vendor List, enter information about vendors from whom you buy products, supplies, and services.

5. Item List

In the Item List, enter information about (1) products and services you *sell to customers* and (2) products and services you *buy from vendors*.

If you hired employees, you would also enter information into the Employee List. In this case, Fearless Painting Service has no employees.

To begin Chapter 8, start QuickBooks software by clicking on the **QuickBooks** desktop icon or click **Start**, **Programs**, **QuickBooks**, **QuickBooks Pro 2006**.

SET UP A NEW COMPANY

To create a new company data file in QuickBooks, use the EasyStep Interview. The EasyStep Interview asks you a series of questions about your business. Then QuickBooks uses the information to customize QuickBooks to fit your business needs.

Open the EasyStep Interview as follows:

Step 1: Select the **File** menu.

Step 2: Select **New Company**. The following *EasyStep Interview* window will appear.

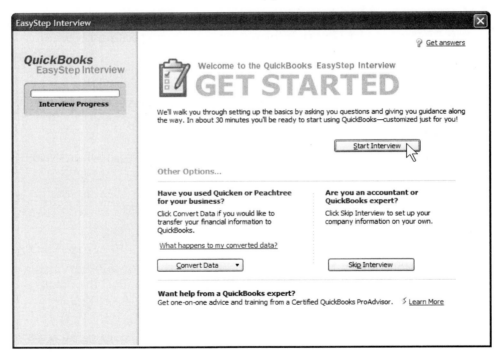

Step 3: Click **Start Interview**.

Step 4: When the following Enter *Your Company Information* window appears:

This is your DBA (Doing Business As) name. This name is used to identify your company for sales, advertising, and marketing.

- Enter Company Name: **[your name] Fearless Painting Service**.

- Press the **Tab** key and QuickBooks will automatically enter the Company Name in the *Legal Name* field. Since your company will do business under its legal name, the *Company Name* and *Legal Name* fields are the same.

- Enter the following information, then click **Next**.

Your company's Legal Name is used on all legal documents, such as contracts, tax returns, licenses, and patents.

Tax ID	333-22-4444
Address	1230 Olive Boulevard
City	Bayshore
State	CA
Zip	94326
Phone #	800-555-3344
Email	<Enter your own email address>

Since your company is a sole proprietorship, the business income is reported on Schedule C which is attached to your 1040 tax return. Accordingly, you use your social security number for the business federal tax ID number.

For a Federal Tax ID number:
1. A sole proprietorship uses the owner's social security number.
2. A corporation uses an EIN (Employer Identification Number).

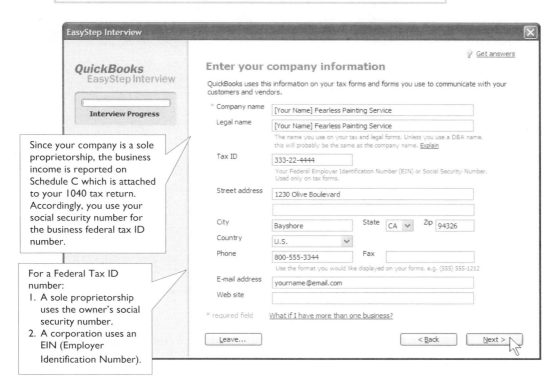

Step 5: In the *Set Up Your Administrator Password* window:

- Enter your Administrator password.
- Retype the password.
- Click **Next.**

Step 6: When the *Create Your Company File* window appears, click **Next** to choose a file name and location to save your company file.

Step 7: When the Filename for New Company window appears:

- Enter File name: **[Your Name] Chapter 8.**
- Click **Save**.

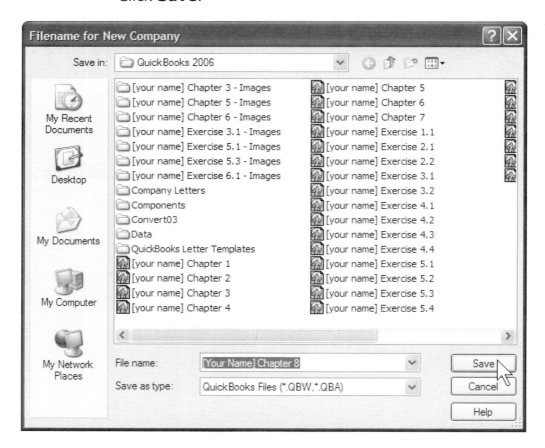

Step 8: Click **Next** when the *Customizing QuickBooks For Your Business* window appears.

Step 9: When the *Select Your Industry* window appears:

- Select: **Miscellaneous Services**.
- Click **Next**.

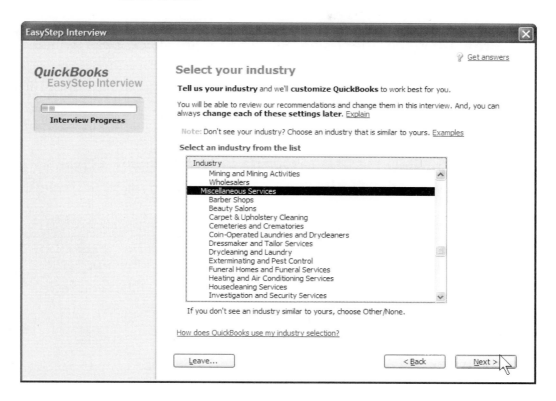

Step 10: When the *What Do You Sell* window appears:

- Select: **Services only**.
- Click **Next**.

Step 11: When asked "Do you charge sales tax?"

- Select: **No**.
- Click **Next**.

Step 12: When the *Estimates* window appears:

- "Do you want to create in QuickBooks?" Select **Yes**.
- Click **Next**.

Step 13: When the *Sales Receipts* window appears:

- "Do you want to use sales receipts in QuickBooks?" Select **Yes**.
- Click **Next**.

Step 14: When the *Using Statements in QuickBooks* window appears:

- "Do you want to use billing statements in QuickBooks?" select: **Yes**.
- Click **Next**.

Step 15: When the *Using Progress Invoicing* window appears:

- "Do you want to use progress invoicing?", select: **No**.
- Click **Next**.

Step 16: When the *Managing Bills You Owe* window appears:

- "Do you want to keep track of bills you owe?", select: **Yes**.
- Click **Next**.

Step 17: When the *Credit Card* window appears:

- "Do you accept credit cards?", select: **I don't currently accept credit cards, but I would like to**.
- Click **Next**.

Step 18: When the *Tracking Time in QuickBooks* window appears:

- "Do you want to track time in QuickBooks?", select: **Yes**.
- Click **Next**.

> **NOTE:** You are not considered an employee because you are the owner.

Step 19: When the *Employee* window appears:

- "Do you have employees?", select: **No**.
- Click **Next**.

Step 20: Read the *Using Accounts in QuickBooks* window. Click **Next**.

Step 21: When the *Enter Your Start Date* window appears:

- Enter Start Date: **01/01/2008**.
- Click **Next**.

Step 22: When *the Add Your Bank Account* window appears:

- "Would you like to add an existing bank account?" select: **Yes**.
- Click **Next**.

Step 23: When the *Tell Us About Your Bank Account* window appears:

- Enter Bank Account Name: **[your name] Checking**.
- "When did you open this bank account?" select: **On or after 01/01/2008**.
- Click **Next**.

Step 24: Read the *About Your Account Balance* window. Click **Next**.

Step 25: When the *Review Bank Accounts* window appears:

- Select **No** when asked if you want to add another bank account.
- Click **Next**.

Step 26: When the *Review Expense Accounts* window appears:

- "Do you want to use these expense accounts?" select: **Yes**.
- Click **Next**.

Step 27: When the *Review Income Accounts* window appears:

- "Do you want to use these income accounts?" select: **Yes**.
- Click **Next**.

Step 28: When the following *Congratulations!* window appears, click **Finish**.

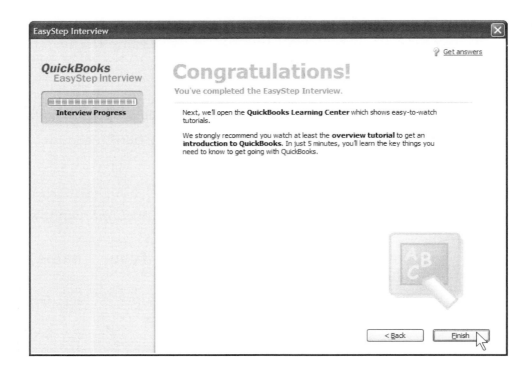

Step 29: If the *QuickBooks Learning Center* window appears on your screen, review the information, then click **Begin Using QuickBooks.**

Step 30: If *Reminder* windows appear, select: **Remind Me Again**.

HOME PAGE

Notice that the Home page for Fearless Painting Service differs from the Home page for Rock Castle Construction.

The Vendor section of the Home page for Fearless Painting Service does not include Purchase Order, Receive Inventory, and Enter Bills Against Inventory icons because during the company setup, you indicated that Fearless Painting Service was a service company. Since you will not be selling a product, you will not be tracking inventory for resale.

Also notice that the Employee section does not include the Pay Employees and Pay Liabilities icons. During the company setup, you indicated that there were no employees so these icons are not needed for Fearless Painting Service.

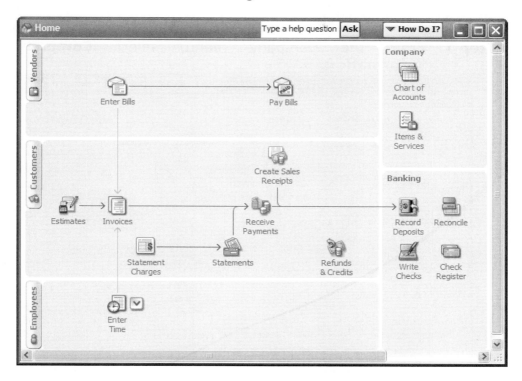

COMPLETE COMPANY SETUP

After the EasyStep Interview is finished, use the following checklist to complete the company setup:

- Complete the company information
- Edit the chart of accounts
- Add customers
- Add vendors
- Add products and services as items

ENTER COMPANY INFORMATION

To enter additional company information:

Step 1: From the Company menu, select **Company Information**.

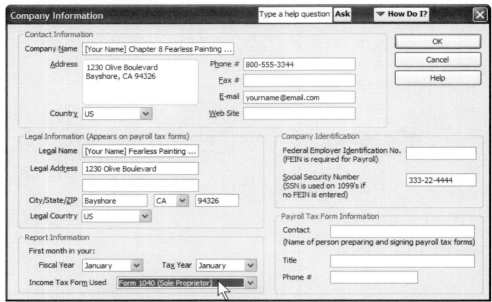

Business tax returns:
1. A sole proprietorship files Schedule C which is attached to the owner's Form 1040 tax return.
2. A corporation files a Form 1120.
3. An S corporation files Form 1120S.
4. A partnership files Form 1065.

Step 2: Select Income Tax Form Used: **Form 1040 (Sole Proprietor)**.

Step 3: Change the Company Name: **[Your Name] Chapter 8 Fearless Painting Service**.

Step 4: Click **OK** to close the *Company Information* window.

EDIT CHART OF ACCOUNTS

The Chart of Accounts is a list of all the accounts Fearless Painting Service will use when maintaining its accounting records. The chart of accounts is like a table of contents for accounting records.

In the EasyStep Interview, when you selected Miscellaneous Service Company as the type of business, QuickBooks automatically created a chart of accounts for Fearless Painting. QuickBooks permits you to customize the chart of accounts to fit your accounting needs.

DISPLAY CHART OF ACCOUNTS

To display the following *Chart of Accounts* window, click **Chart of Accounts** in the Company section of the Home page.

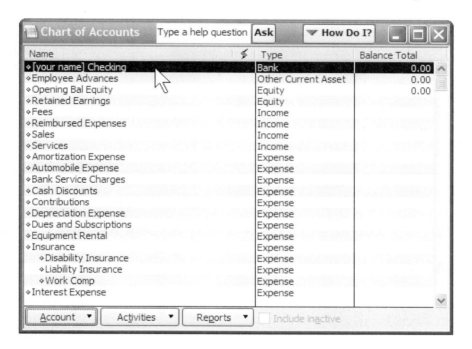

DISPLAY ACCOUNT NUMBERS

Notice that the Chart of Accounts does not list the account numbers. Display account numbers in the Chart of Accounts by completing the following steps:

Step 1: From the Home page, select **Customize Home page and set preferences**.

Step 2: When the following *Preferences* window appears:

- Click the **Accounting** icon on the left scrollbar.
- Click the **Company Preferences** tab.
- Select **Use account numbers**.

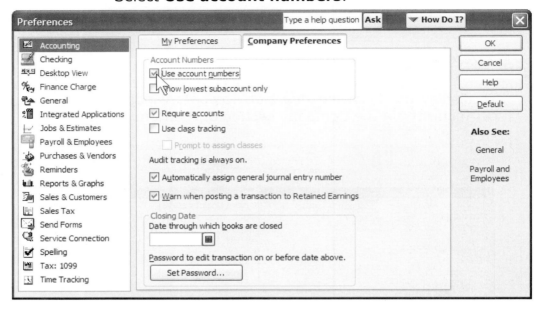

Step 3: Click **OK** to close the *Preferences* window.

The Chart of Accounts should now display account numbers.

ADD NEW ACCOUNTS

Fearless Painting needs to add the following accounts to its Chart of Accounts:

> New in QuickBooks Pro 2004 is the Fixed Asset List. If your business has a large number of fixed asset accounts, you can use the Fixed Asset Manager (see Chapter 7) to enter and track fixed assets. If you are using QuickBooks: Premier Accountant Edition 2006, you can use the Fixed Asset Manager to calculate depreciation for fixed assets.

Account	Computer
Subaccount	Computer Cost
Subaccount	Accumulated Depreciation Computer

The Computer Cost account contains the original cost of the computer. Accumulated Depreciation for the computer accumulates all depreciation recorded for the computer over its useful life.

To add new accounts to the Chart of Accounts for Fearless Painting:

Step 1: From the following *Chart of Accounts* window:

- **Right-click** to display the popup menu.
- Select **New**.

The chart of accounts now lists account numbers.

Step 2: When the following *New Account* window appears:

- Select Account Type: **Fixed Asset**.

- Enter Account Number: **1410**.

- Enter Name: **Computer**.

- Enter Description: **Computer**.

- Select Tax Line: **<Unassigned>**.

- Enter Opening Balance: **0** as of **01/01/2008**.

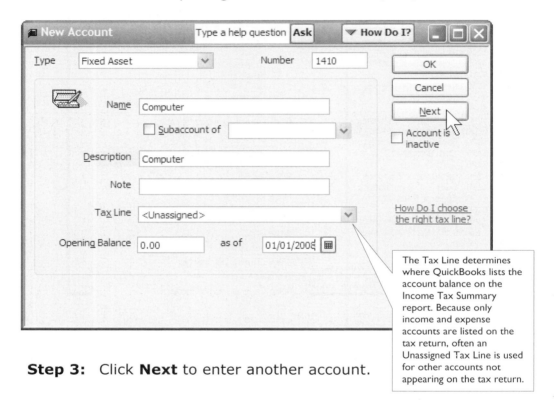

Step 3: Click **Next** to enter another account.

To enter new subaccounts, complete the following steps.

Step 1: Add the Computer Cost subaccount by entering the following information when a blank *New Account* window appears:

- Select Account Type: **Fixed Asset**.
- Enter Account Number: **1420**.
- Enter Name: **Computer Cost**.
- Check ✓ Subaccount of: **1410 – Computer**.
- Enter Description: **Computer Cost**.
- Select Tax Line: **<Unassigned>**.
- Enter Opening Balance: **0.00** as of **01/01/2008**.

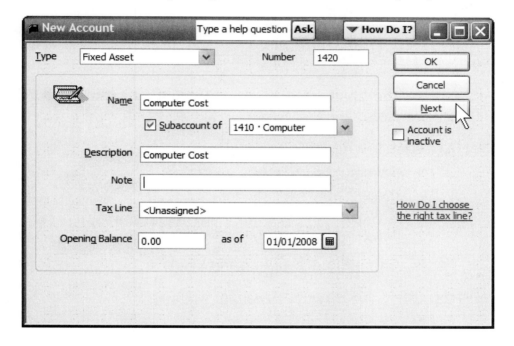

Step 2: Click **Next** to add another subaccount.

Step 3: Add the Accumulated Depreciation Computer subaccount by entering the following information in the *New Account* window:

Account No.	1430
Account Type	Fixed Asset
Account Name	Accumulated Depr Computer
Subaccount of	1410 Computer
Account Description	Accumulated Depr Computer
Tax Line	Unassigned
Opening Balance	0 as of 01/01/2008

Step 4: Click **OK** to close the *New Account* window.

PRINT THE CHART OF ACCOUNTS

To 🖨 **print** the chart of accounts (Accounting Listing report) complete the following steps:

Step 1: From the *Report Center:*

- Select: **Accountant & Taxes**.

- Select: **Account Listing**.

- 🖨 Click **Print**. Select **Portrait** orientation and **Fit report to 1 page(s) wide**. Click **Print** again.

- **Close** the *Account Listing* window.

Step 2: **Close** the *Chart of Accounts* window.

CREATE A CUSTOMER LIST

As you learned in Chapter 4, the Customer List contains information about the customers to whom you sell services. In addition, the Customer List also contains information about jobs or projects for each customer.

Fearless Painting has two customers:

1. Katrina Beneficio, who wants a custom landscape mural painted on her dining room wall.

2. Tom Whalen, who wants marbled faux painting in his home's foyer.

To add a new customer to Fearless Painting's Customer List:

> **TIP:** You can import list information using Excel and files with .iif extensions (Intuit Interchange File). See QuickBooks Help for more information.

Step 1: Click the **Customer Center** icon on the Navigator Bar.

Step 2: To add a new customer, click the **New Customer & Job** button.

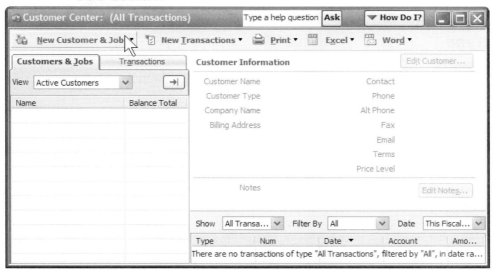

Step 3: Click **New Customer** to add a new Customer.

Step 4: When the *New Customer* window appears, enter the following information about your first customer, Katrina Beneficio.

Customer	Beneficio, Katrina
Opening Balance	0.00
As of	01/01/2008
Address Info:	
Mr./Ms./...	Mrs.
First Name	Katrina
Last Name	Beneficio
Contact	Katrina Beneficio
Phone	415-555-1078
Alt. Ph.	415-555-3434
Address	10 Pico Blvd Bayshore, CA 94326

Additional Info:	
Type	Residential
Terms	Net 30

Select **Add New**.

Payment Info:	
Account	1001
Preferred Payment Method	Check

Step 5: Click **OK** to close the *New Customer* window.

Step 6: To add a new job, select Katrina Beneficio in the Customer List, **right-click** to display popup menu. Select **Add Job**.

Job Info:	
Job Name	Dining Room
Opening Balance	0.00
As of	01/01/2008
Job Status	Awarded
Start Date	01/03/2008
Job Description	Dining Room Landscape Mural
Job Type	Mural

Select **Add New**.

Step 7: 🖨 **Print** the Customer List.

- Click the **Print** button at the top of the Customer Center.

- Click **Customer & Job List**.

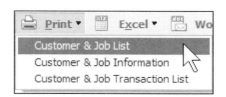

- Select **Portrait** Orientation.
- Click **Print**.

Step 8: **Close** the Customer Center.

CREATE A VENDOR LIST

As you learned in Chapter 5, the Vendor List contains information about vendors from whom you buy products and services.

To add vendors to the Vendor List for Fearless Painting:

Step 1: Click the **Vendor Center** icon on the Navigation Bar.

Step 2: To add a new vendor, click the **New Vendor** button.

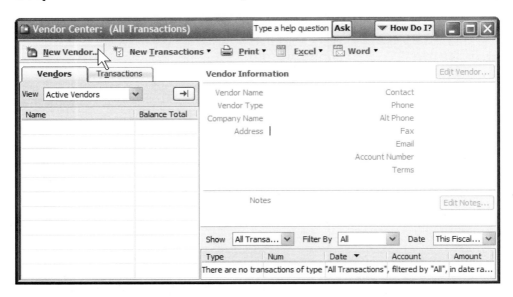

Step 3: When the *New Vendor* window appears, enter the following information about Hinson Paint Supplies.

Vendor Name	Hinson Paint Supplies
Opening Balance	0.00
As of	01/01/2008
Address Info:	
Company Name	Hinson Paint Supplies
Address	200 Garden Street Bayshore, CA 94326
Contact	Steve Hinson
Phone	415-555-6070
Print on Check as	Hinson Paint Supplies

Additional Info:	
Account	2008
Type	Supplies
Terms	Net 30
Credit Limit	3000.00
Tax ID	37-7832541

Step 4: Click **OK** to close the *New Vendor* window.

Step 5: 🖨 **Print** the Vendor List.

Step 6: **Close** the Vendor Center.

CREATE AN ITEM LIST

As you learned in Chapter 5, the Item List contains information about service items, inventory items, and non-inventory items sold to customers. Fearless Painting plans to sell four different service items to customers:

1. Labor: mural painting

2. Labor: faux painting

3. Labor: interior painting

4. Labor: exterior painting

To add a service item to the Item List:

Step 1: Click the **Items & Services** icon in the Company section of the Home page.

Step 2: When the *Item List* window appears, click the **Item** button.

Step 3: Click **New** to add new items to the Items List.

Step 4: When the following *New Item* window appears:

- Enter Type: **Service**
- Enter Item Name: **Labor**
- Enter Description: **Painting Labor**
- Select Account: **4070 - Services**

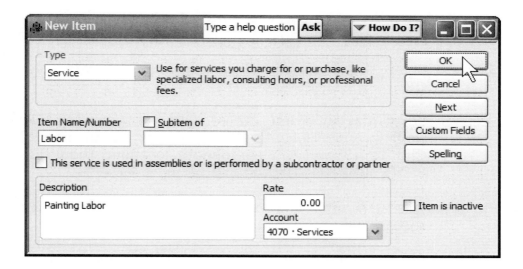

Step 5: Click **OK** to close the *New Item* window.

Step 6: 🖶 **Print** the Item List at **January 1, 2008**. (Hint: Click the **Reports** button, then click **Item Listing**.)

Step 7: **Close** the *Item List* window.

SAVE CHAPTER 8

Save Chapter 8 as a portable QuickBooks file to the location specified by your instructor.

Step 1: If necessary, insert a removable disk.

Step 2: From the menu bar, click **File | Portable Company File | Create File**.

Step 3: When the *Close and Reopen* window appears, click **OK**.

Step 4: When the following *Create Portable Company File* window appears, enter the filename: **[your name] Chapter 8** and the appropriate location. Then click **Save**.

Step 5: Click **OK** after the portable file has been created successfully.

Step 6: Close the company file by clicking **File** (Menu), **Close Company**.

ASSIGNMENTS

> **NOTE: See the Quick Reference Guide in Part 3 for step-by-step instructions to frequently used tasks.**

EXERCISE 8.1: CHART OF ACCOUNTS, CUSTOMER LIST, VENDOR LIST, AND ITEM LIST

In this Exercise, you will add new accounts and subaccounts to Fearless Painting's chart of accounts and add new customers and vendors.

TASK 1: OPEN PORTABLE COMPANY FILE

To open the portable company file (.QBM) file, convert the portable file to a regular company file with a .QBW extension as follows:

Step 1: From the menu bar, click **File | Portable Company File | Open File**.

Step 2: Identify the filename and location for the portable company file:

- Click the **Browse** button to find the location of the portable company file on the hard drive or removable media.

- Select the file: **[your name] Chapter 8.QBM**.

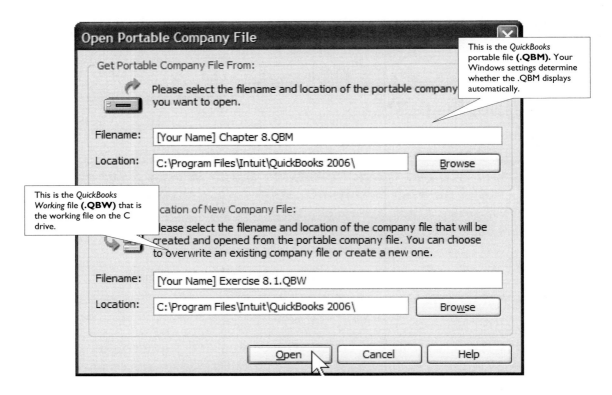

Step 3: Identify the name and location of the new company file (.QBW) file to use for completing Exercise 8.1:

- Filename: **[your name] Exercise 8.1**. The **.QBW** extension should appear automatically based upon your Windows settings.

- Location: **C:\Program Files\Intuit\QuickBooks 2006**. This is the location of the .QBW file on the hard drive of your computer. Click the Browse button to specify another location.

Step 4: Click **Open** to open the portable company file.

Step 5: Click **Cancel** when the *Create a Backup* window appears.

Step 6: If prompted, enter your **User Name** and **Password**, then click **OK**.

Step 7: Click **OK** when the QuickBooks sample company message appears.

Step 8: Change the company name to: **[your name] Exercise 8.1 Fearless Painting Service**.

TASK 2: ADD ACCOUNTS

Step 1: Add the following new accounts and subaccounts to the chart of accounts for Fearless Painting Service. Click **Next** after entering each account.

Account No.	1100
Account Type	Accounts Receivable
Account Name	Accounts Receivable
Account Description	Accounts Receivable
Tax Line	Unassigned

Account No.	1310
Account Type	Other Current Asset
Account Name	Paint Supplies
Account Description	Paint Supplies
Tax Line	Unassigned

Account No.	1440
Account Type	Fixed Asset
Account Name	Equipment
Account Description	Equipment
Tax Line	Unassigned

Account No.	1450
Account Type	Fixed Asset
Account Name	Equipment Cost
Account Description	Equipment Cost
Subaccount of	1440 Equipment
Tax Line	Unassigned

Account No.	1460
Account Type	Fixed Asset
Account Name	Accum Depr-Equipment
Account Description	Accum Depr-Equipment
Subaccount of	1440 Equipment
Tax Line	Unassigned

Account No.	2110
Account Type	Accounts Payable
Account Name	Accounts Payable
Account Description	Accounts Payable
Tax Line	Unassigned

Account No.	6430
Account Type	Expense
Account Name	Depr Expense-Computer
Account Description	Depr Expense-Computer
Tax Line	Unassigned

Account No.	6460
Account Type	Expense
Account Name	Depr Expense-Equipment
Account Description	Depr Expense-Equipment
Tax Line	Unassigned

Account No.	6551
Account Type	Expense
Account Name	Paint Supplies Expense
Account Description	Paint Supplies Expense
Tax Line	Sch C: Supplies (not from COGS)

Step 2: 🖨 **Print** the chart of accounts (Click **Reports** button, **Account Listing**).

TASK 3: ADD CUSTOMER

Step 1: Add Tom Whalen to Fearless Painting's Customer List.

Customer	Whalen, Tom
Opening Balance	0.00
As of	01/01/2008
Address Info:	
Mr./Ms./...	Mr.
First Name	Tom
Last Name	Whalen
Contact	Tom Whalen
Phone	415-555-1234
Alt. Ph.	415-555-5678
Alt. Contact	Work phone
Address	100 Sunset Drive Bayshore, CA 94326

Additional Info:	
Type	Residential
Terms	Net 30

Payment Info:	
Account	1002
Preferred Payment	Check

Step 2: Click **OK** to close the *New Customer* window.

TASK 4: ADD JOB

Step 1: To add a new job, select: **Tom Whalen**.

Step 2: **Right-click** to display popup menu. Select **Add Job**.

Step 3: After entering the following job information, **close** the *New Job* window.

Job Info:	
Job Name	Foyer
Opening balance	0.00
As of	01/01/2008
Job Status	Pending
Job Description	Foyer Marbled Faux Painting
Job Type	Faux Painting

Select **Add New**.

Step 4: 🖨 **Print** the Customer List.

- Click the **Print** button at the top of the Customer Center.

- Click **Customer & Job List**.

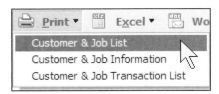

- Select **Portrait** Orientation.

- Click **Print**.

Step 5: **Close** the Customer Center.

TASK 5: ADD VENDORS

Step 1: Add the following vendors to the Vendor List for Fearless Painting.

Vendor	Cornell Computers
Opening balance	0.00
As of	01/01/2008
Address Info:	
Company Name	Cornell Computers
Address	72 Business Parkway Bayshore, CA 94326
Contact	Becky Cornell
Phone	415-555-7507
Additional Info:	
Account	2002
Type	Supplies
Terms	Net 30
Credit Limit	3000.00
Tax ID	37-4356712

Step 2: Click **Next** to add another vendor.

Vendor	Hartz Leasing
Opening balance	0.00
As of	01/01/2008
Address Info:	
Company Name	Hartz Leasing
Address	13 Appleton Drive Bayshore, CA 94326
Contact	Joe Hartz
Phone	415-555-0412
Additional Info:	

Account	2003
Type	Leasing
Terms	Net 30
Tax ID	37-1726354

Select **Add New**.

Step 3: 🖶 **Print** the Vendor List.

TASK 6: ADD ITEMS

Step 1: Add the following items to Fearless Painting's Item List. Click **Next** after entering each item.

Item Type	Service
Item Name	Labor Mural
Subitem of	Labor
Description	Labor: Mural Painting
Rate	40.00
Account	4070 – Services

Item Type	Service
Item Name	Labor Faux
Subitem of	Labor
Description	Labor: Faux Painting
Rate	40.00
Account	4070 – Services

Item Type	Service
Item Name	Labor Interior
Subitem of	Labor
Description	Labor: Interior Painting
Rate	20.00
Account	4070 – Services

Item Type	Service
Item Name	Labor Exterior
Subitem of	Labor
Description	Labor: Exterior Painting
Rate	30.00
Account	4070 - Services

Step 2: 🖨 **Print** the Item List.

TASK 8: SAVE EXERCISE 8.1

Save Exercise 8.1 as a portable company file to the location specified by your instructor.

Step 1: If necessary, insert a removable disk.

Step 2: From the menu bar, click **File | Portable Company File | Create File**.

Step 3: When the *Close and Reopen* window appears, click **OK**.

Step 4: When the *Create Portable Company File* window appears, enter the filename: **[your name] Exercise 8.1** and the appropriate location. Click **Save**.

Step 5: Click **OK** after the portable file has been created successfully.

Step 6: Close the company file by clicking **File** (Menu), **Close Company**.

EXERCISE 8.2: NEW COMPANY SETUP

SCENARIO

Villa Floor & Carpet, a start-up business, provides custom hardwood floor cleaning and refinishing. In addition, his business provides specialized cleaning of fine oriental rugs.

First, set up a new QuickBooks Company for Villa Floor & Carpet using the EasyStep Interview. Then create the Customer List, Vendor List, and the Item List for the new company.

TASK 1: NEW COMPANY SETUP

Step 1: Create a new company in QuickBooks for Villa Floor & Carpet. Use the following information.

Company name	[your name] Exercise 8.2 Villa Floor & Carpet
Legal name	[your name] Exercise 8.2 Villa Floor & Carpet
Tax ID	130-13-3636
Address	2300 Kansas Boulevard
City	Bayshore
State	CA
Zip	94326
Phone	415-555-1313
E-mail	[enter your own email address]
Save in	C:/Program Files/Intuit/QuickBooks 2006
Filename	[your name] Exercise 8.2
Industry	Carpet & Upholstery Cleaning
What do you sell?	Services only
Sales tax	No

Estimates	No
Sales receipts	Yes
Billing statements	No
Invoices	Yes
Progress billing	No
Track bills you owe	Yes
Accept credit cards	I don't currently accept credit cards and I don't plan to.
Track time	Yes
Employees	No
Start date	01/01/2008
Add a bank account?	Yes
Bank account name	[your name] Checking
Bank account opened	On or after 01/01/2008
Use recommended expense accounts?	Yes
Use recommended Income accounts?	Yes

Step 2: Click **Finish** to exit the EasyStep Interview.

Step 3: To select the income tax form used, from the Company menu, select **Company Information**.

Step 4: Select Income Tax Form Used: **Form 1040 (Sole Proprietor)**.

Step 5: Click **OK** to close the *Company Information* window.

TASK 2: ADD ACCOUNTS

Step 1: Display account numbers.

Step 2: Add the following new accounts and subaccounts to the chart of accounts for Villa Floor & Carpet. Click **Next** after entering each account.

Account No.	1310
Account Type	Other Current Asset
Account Name	Cleaning Supplies
Account Description	Cleaning Supplies
Tax Line	Unassigned

Account No.	1440
Account Type	Fixed Asset
Account Name	Cleaning Equipment
Account Description	Cleaning Equipment
Tax Line	Unassigned

Account No.	1450
Account Type	Fixed Asset
Account Name	Cleaning Equipment Cost
Account Description	Cleaning Equipment Cost
Subaccount of	1440 Cleaning Equipment
Tax Line	Unassigned

Account No.	1460
Account Type	Fixed Asset
Account Name	Accum Depr-Cleaning Equipment
Account Description	Accum Depr-Cleaning Equipment
Subaccount of	1440 Cleaning Equipment
Tax Line	Unassigned

Account No.	2110
Account Type	Accounts Payable
Account Name	Accounts Payable
Account Description	Accounts Payable
Tax Line	Unassigned

Account No.	6551
Account Type	Expense
Account Name	Supplies Expense
Account Description	Supplies Expense
Tax Line	Sch C: Supplies (not from COGS)

Step 3: 🖨 **Print** the chart of accounts.

TASK 3: ADD CUSTOMER & JOB

Step 1: Add David Allison to Villa Floor & Carpet Customer List.

Customer	Allison, David
Address Info:	
First Name	David
Last Name	Allison
Contact	David Allison
Phone	415-555-4242
Address	36 KayCee Drive Bayshore, CA 94326

Additional Info:	
Type	Residential
Terms	Net 15

Payment Info:	
Account	1005
Preferred Payment	Check

Step 2: Click **OK** to close the *New Customer* window.

Step 3: To add a new job, select David Allison in the Customer List, **right-click** to display popup menu. Select **Add Job**.

Job Info:	
Job Name	Oriental Rugs
Job Status	Pending
Job Description	Oriental rug cleaning
Job Type	Residential

Select **Add New**.

Step 4: 🖨 **Print** the Customer List.

- Click the **Print** button at the top of the Customer Center.

- Click **Customer & Job List**.

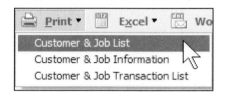

- Select **Portrait** Orientation.

- Click **Print**.

Step 5: **Close** the Customer Center.

TASK 4: ADD VENDORS

Step 1: Add the following vendors to the Vendor List for Villa Floor & Carpet.

Vendor	Griffin Cleaning Supplies
Opening balance	0
As of	01/01/2008
Address Info:	
Company Name	Griffin Cleaning Supplies
Address	72 Chief Parkway Bayshore, CA 94326
Contact	Griffin
Phone	415-555-7272

Additional Info:	
Account	2004
Type	Supplies
Terms	Net 30
Tax ID	37-6543219

Step 2: 🖨 **Print** the Vendor List.

TASK 5: ADD ITEMS

Step 1: Add the following items to Villa Floor & Carpet. Click **Next** after entering each item.

Item Type	Service
Item Name	Rug Cleaning
Description	Oriental Rug Cleaning
Account	4070 – Services

Item Type	Service
Item Name	3x5 Rug Cleaning
Subitem of	Rug Cleaning
Description	3x5 Oriental Rug Cleaning
Rate	50.00
Account	4070 – Services

Item Type	Service
Item Name	5x7 Rug Cleaning
Subitem of	Rug Cleaning
Description	5x7 Oriental Rug Cleaning
Rate	100.00
Account	4070 – Services

Item Type	Service
Item Name	8x10 Rug Cleaning
Subitem of	Rug Cleaning
Description	8x10 Oriental Rug Cleaning
Rate	150.00
Account	4070 - Services

Step 2: 🖨 **Print** the Item List.

TASK 6: SAVE EXERCISE 8.2

Save Exercise 8.2 as a portable company file to the location specified by your instructor.

Step 1: If necessary, insert a removable disk.

Step 2: From the menu bar, click **File | Portable Company File | Create File**.

Step 3: When the *Close and Reopen* window appears, click **OK**.

Step 4: When the *Create Portable Company File* window appears, enter the filename: **[your name] Exercise 8.2** and the appropriate location. Click **Save**.

Step 5: Click **OK** after the portable file has been created successfully.

Step 6: Close the company file by clicking **File** (Menu), **Close Company**.

EXERCISE 8.3: WEB QUEST

The Small Business Administration (SBA) summarizes government resources to assist the small business owner. When starting a new business, an entrepreneur is faced with numerous decisions. As a result, planning becomes crucial for business success. The SBA web site provides information about how to write a successful business plan.

Step 1: Go to www.sba.gov web site.

Step 2: At the top of the Small Business Administration web site, click **Starting**.

Step 3: Under Planning Topics, click and then read **Business Plan Basics**. ▣ **Print** the page and then briefly answer the four core startup questions with respect to Fearless Painting Service.

Step 4: Click and then read **Writing the Plan**. ▣ **Print** the page.

✎ Place a ✓ by the business plan Financial Data Items that QuickBooks could help you prepare.

Step 5: Click **Using the Plan**. Click **Sample Business Plans**. Select a sample business plan, read and ▣ **print** the following sections from the sample business plan you selected:

- Executive Summary
- Financial Plan

✎ Place a ✓ by the items in the Financial Plan section that QuickBooks could help you prepare.

CHAPTER 8 PRINTOUT CHECKLIST

NAME:_____ DATE:_____

INSTRUCTIONS:
1. CHECK OFF THE PRINTOUTS YOU HAVE COMPLETED.
2. STAPLE THIS PAGE TO YOUR PRINTOUTS.

☑ **PRINTOUT CHECKLIST – CHAPTER 8**
☐ Chart of Accounts (Account Listing)
☐ Customer List
☐ Vendor List
☐ Item List

☑ **PRINTOUT CHECKLIST – EXERCISE 8.1**
☐ Task 2: Chart of Accounts
☐ Task 4: Customer List
☐ Task 5: Vendor List
☐ Task 6: Item List

☑ **PRINTOUT CHECKLIST – EXERCISE 8.2**
☐ Task 2: Chart of Accounts
☐ Task 3: Customer List
☐ Task 4: Vendor List
☐ Task 5: Item List

☑ **PRINTOUT CHECKLIST – EXERCISE 8.3**
☐ Business Plan Printouts

CHAPTER 9
ACCOUNTING FOR A SERVICE COMPANY

SCENARIO

Preferring to use your savings rather than take out a bank loan, you invest $6,000 of your savings to launch Fearless Painting Service.

You prepare the following list of items your business will need.

Computer & Printer	$1,500
Paint equipment (ladders, drop cloths, etc.)	$ 500
Paint supplies (paint brushes, rollers, et.c)	$ 300
Van lease	$ 200/month

CHAPTER 9
LEARNING OBJECTIVES

In Chapter 9, you will learn the following QuickBooks activities:

INTRODUCTION

In this chapter, you will enter business transactions for Fearless Painting's first year of operations. These include transactions with the owner, customers, and vendors.

To begin Chapter 9, first start QuickBooks software and then open the portable QuickBooks file.

Step 1: Start QuickBooks by clicking on the **QuickBooks** desktop icon or click **Start**, **Programs**, **QuickBooks**, **QuickBooks Pro 2006**.

Step 2: To open the portable company file (.QBM) file and convert the portable file to a regular company file with a .QBW extension, from the menu bar, click **File | Portable Company File | Open File**.

Step 3: Identify the filename and location for the portable company file:

- Click the **Browse** button to find the location of the portable company file on the hard drive or removable media.

- Select the file: **[your name] Exercise 8.1**. The .QBM may appear automatically based upon your Windows settings, but if it does not appear automatically, do *not* type it.

Step 4: Identify the name and location of the new company file (.QBW) file to use for Chapter 9:

- Filename: **[your name] Chapter 9**. The **.QBW** extension should appear automatically based upon your Windows settings. The .QBW identifies this as a QuickBooks working file.

- Location: **C:\Program Files\Intuit\QuickBooks 2006**. This is the location of the .QBW file on the hard drive of your computer.

Step 5: Click **Open** to open the portable company file.

Step 6: Click **Cancel** when the *Create a Backup* window appears.

Step 7:   If prompted, enter your **User ID** and **Password**.

Step 8:   Click **OK** when the sample company window appears.

Step 9:   Change the company name to: **[your name] Chapter 9 Fearless Painting Service**.

The portable company file (.QBM) has been converted to a regular company file (Chapter 9.QBW) for use in completing Chapter 9 assignments.

RECORD OWNER'S INVESTMENT

To launch your new business, you invest $6,000 in Fearless Painting. In order to keep business records and your personal records separate, you open a business checking account at the local bank for Fearless Painting. You then deposit your personal check for $6,000 in the business checking account.

In Chapters 3 and 4 you recorded deposits using the Deposits icon in the Banking section of the Home page. You can also record deposits directly in the Check Register. QuickBooks then transfers the information to the *Make Deposits* window.

To record the deposit to Fearless Painting's checking account using the *Make Deposits* window, complete the following steps:

Step 1:   Click the **Record Deposits** icon in the Banking section of the Home page.

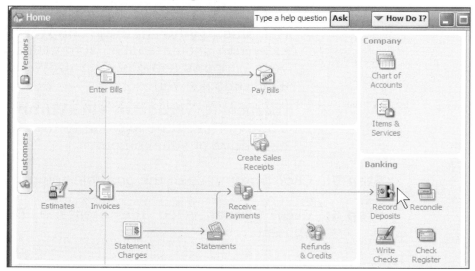

Step 2:   Enter the following information in the *Make Deposit* window:

- Date: **01/01/2008**.

- On the *Receive From* drop-down list, select **<Add New>**. Select **Other**, then click **OK**. Enter Name: **[Your Name]**. Click **OK**.

- Account: **3000: Opening Balance Equity**. Press the **Tab** key.

- Memo: **Invested $6,000 in the business**.

- Check No.: **1001**.

- Payment Method: **Check**.

- Amount: **6000.00**.

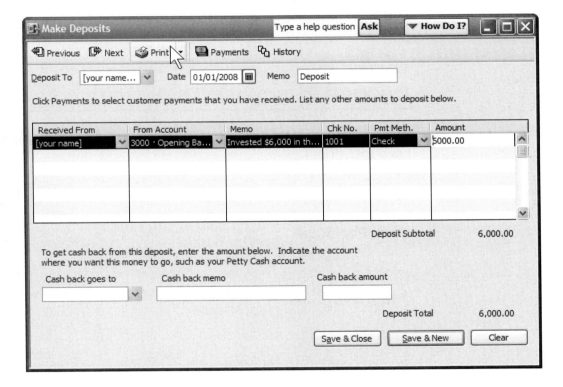

Step 3: 🖨 To **print** the deposit slip:

- Click the **Print** button at the top of the *Make Deposits* window.
- Select **Deposit Summary Only**.

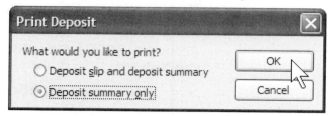

- Click **OK**.
- Select **Portrait** printer setting, then click **Print**.

Step 4: Click **Save & Close** to close the *Make Deposits* window.

RECORD PURCHASE TRANSACTIONS

Purchases can be either cash purchases or credit purchases on account.

Transaction	Description	Record Using...
Cash Purchase	Pay cash at the time of purchase	*Write Checks* window
Credit Purchase	Pay for purchase at a later time	1. *Enter Bills* window 2. *Pay Bills* window 3. Print checks

Fearless Painting purchased a computer, painting equipment, and paint supplies. To record these purchases, complete the following steps.

RECORD CASH PURCHASES
USING THE WRITE CHECKS WINDOW

Fearless Painting first purchased a computer and printer for $1,500 cash. Because Fearless Painting paid cash for the purchase, you can use the *Write Checks* window to record the purchase.

To record the computer and printer purchase using the *Write Checks* window:

Step 1: Click the **Write Checks** icon in the Banking section of the Home page.

> To save time entering dates, change the Windows system date to the current date as follows:
> 1. Double-click on the time displayed in the lower right corner of your Windows taskbar.
> 2. Select Date: January 1, 2008.
> 3. Click OK to save.
> 4. Exit QuickBooks software.
> 5. Restart QuickBooks. Now when opening the *Write Checks* window, the date displayed should be 01/01/2008.
> 6. Remember to reset to the current system date when finished with your QuickBooks assignments.

Step 2: Enter the following information in the *Write Checks* window:

- Date: **01/01/2008**.

- Pay to the Order of: **Cornell Computers**.

- Amount: **1500.00**.

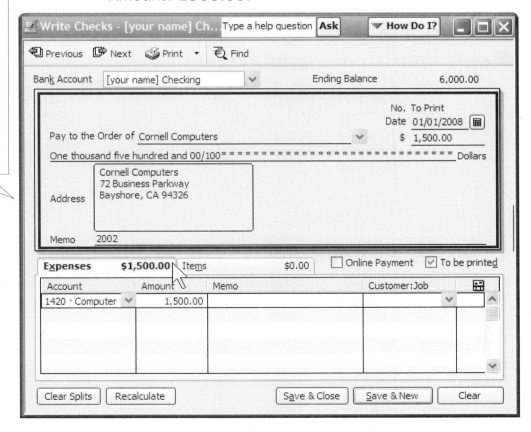

- Check: **To be printed**.
- Select Account: **1420 Computer Cost**.
- When the *Tracking Fixed Assets* window appears, click **Yes** to create a fixed asset item.

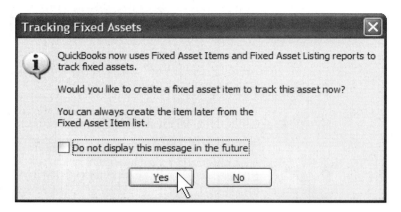

- Enter the following information about the computer into the *New Item* window. Click **OK**.

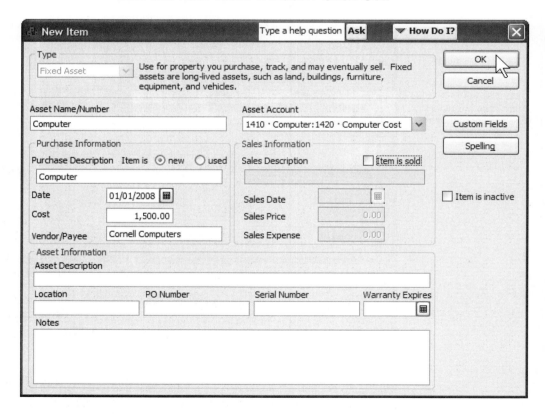

Step 3: 🖶 **Print** the check as follows:

- Click the **Print** button.
- When the *Print Check* window appears, enter Check No. **501**, then click **OK**.

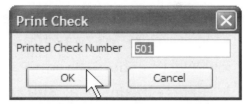

- Select **Print company name and address**.
- Select Check Style: **Standard**
- Click **Print**.
- When asked if the check(s) printed OK, select **OK**.

Step 4: Click **Save & Close** to record Check No. 501 and close the *Write Checks* window.

RECORD CREDIT PURCHASES USING THE ENTER BILLS WINDOW

When items are purchased on credit, a two-step process is used to record the purchase in QuickBooks.

	Action	Record Using...	Result
1	**Enter bill when received**	*Enter Bills* Window	QuickBooks records an expense (or asset) and records an obligation to pay the bill later (Accounts Payable).
2	**Pay bill when due**	1. *Pay Bills* Window 2. Print Checks	QuickBooks reduces cash and reduces Accounts Payable.

Next, you will enter bills for items Fearless Painting purchased on credit. The first bill is for paint and supplies that Fearless Painting purchased for the Beneficio job.

Step 1: Click the **Enter Bills** icon in the Vendor section of the Home page.

Step 2: Enter the following information in the *Enter Bills* window:

- Select **Bill**.
- Enter Date: **01/03/2008**.
- Select Vendor: **Hinson Paint Supplies**.
- Enter Amount Due: **300.00**.
- Select Terms: **Net 30**.

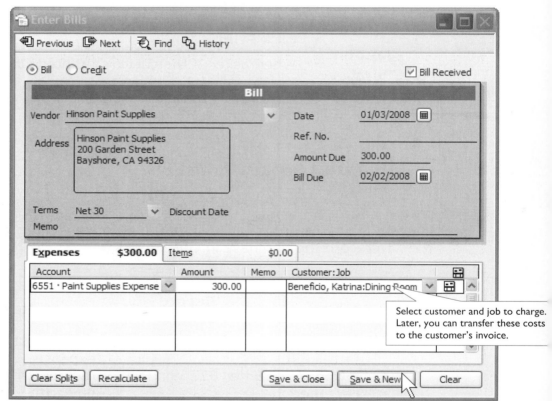

- Click the **Expenses** tab.
- Select Account: **6551 Paint Supplies Expense**.
- Select Customer & Job: **Beneficio, Katrina: Dining Room**.

Step 3: Click **Save & New** to enter another bill.

Step 4: Fearless Painting made a credit purchase of painting equipment including ladders, drop cloths, etc. The painting equipment is recorded as an asset because it will benefit more than one accounting period. The painting equipment will be depreciated over the useful life of the equipment.

Enter the following bill for paint equipment purchased on account and add the Paint Equipment to the Fixed Asset List.

> To add an item to the Fixed Asset List:
> 1. Click Lists | Fixed Asset Item List.
> 2. Click Item | New.

Date	01/04/2008
Vendor	Hinson Paint Supplies
Amount Due	500.00
Terms	Net 30
Account	1450 Equipment Cost
Purchase Description	Paint equipment, ladders, drop cloths
Memo	Purchased paint equipment

Step 5: Click **Save & Close** to record the bill and close the *Enter Bills* window.

QuickBooks records these bills as accounts payable, indicating that Fearless Painting has an obligation to pay these amounts to vendors. QuickBooks increases liabilities (accounts payable) on the company's balance sheet.

▤ **Print** the Fixed Asset Listing as follows:

Step 1: From the Report Center, select: **Accountant & Taxes**. Select **Fixed Asset Listing**.

Step 2: ▤ **Print** Fixed Asset Listing report, and then **close** the *Fixed Asset Listing* window.

Step 3: **Close** the *Report Navigator* window.

✓   ***Total fixed assets equal $2,000 (consisting of the Computer account of $1,500 and the Equipment account of $500).***

RECORD A MEMORIZED TRANSACTION

Often a transaction is recurring, such as monthly rent or utility payments. QuickBooks' memorized transaction feature permits you to memorize recurring transactions.

Fearless Painting Service leases a van for a monthly lease payment of $200. You will use a memorized transaction to reuse each month to record the lease payment.

To create a memorized transaction:

Step 1: First, enter the transaction in QuickBooks. You will enter the bill for the van lease payment for Fearless Painting.

- Click the **Enter Bills** icon in the Vendor section of the Home page.

- Enter the following information about the van lease bill.

Date	01/04/2008
Vendor	Hartz Leasing
Amount Due	200.00
Terms	Net 30
Account	6170 Equipment Rental
Memo	Van lease

Step 2: With the *Enter Bills* window still open, click **Edit** on the menu bar.

Step 3: Click **Memorize Bill** on the *Edit* menu.

Step 4:   When the following *Memorize Transaction* window appears:

- Select **Remind Me**.

- Select How Often: **Monthly**.

- Enter Next Date: **02/01/2008**.

- Click **OK** to record the memorized transaction.

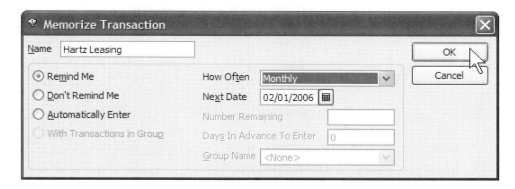

Step 5:   Click **Save & Close** to close the *Enter Bills* window and record the van lease.

To use the memorized transaction at a later time:

Step 1:   Click **Lists** on the menu bar.

Step 2:   Click **Memorized Transaction List** from the *Lists* menu.

Step 3:   When the following *Memorized Transactions List* window appears, double-click the memorized transaction you want to use.

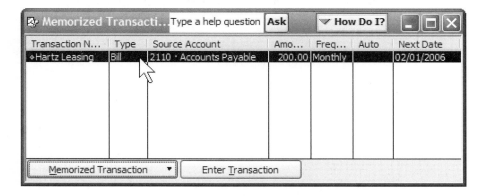

Step 4: QuickBooks displays the *Enter Bills* window with the memorized transaction data already entered. You can make any necessary changes on the form (such as changing the date). To record the bill in QuickBooks, you would click Save & Close.

At this time, **close the *Enter Bills* window without saving**. Then **close** the *Memorized Transaction List* window. Later, you will use the memorized transaction in **Exercise 9.1** at the end of the chapter.

PAY BILLS

To pay bills already entered:

Step 1: Click the **Pay Bills** icon in the Vendor section of the Home page.

Step 2: When the following *Pay Bills* window appears:

- Select Show Bills: **Due on or before 02/04/2008**, then press the **Tab** key.

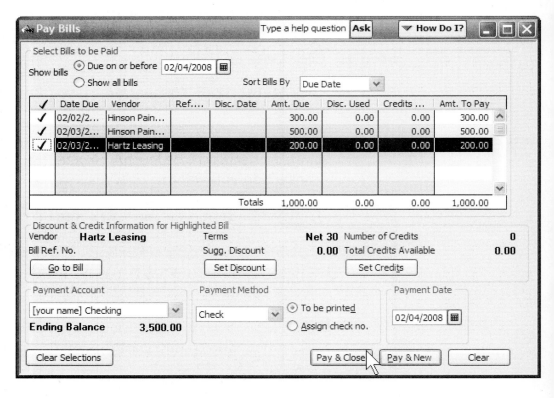

- Select the three bills listed to pay.
- Select Payment Account: **[your name] Checking**.
- Select Payment Method: **Check**.
- Select **To be printed**.
- Payment Date: **02/04/2008**.

Step 3: Click **Pay & Close** to record the bills selected for payment and close the *Pay Bills* window.

> You can buy preprinted check forms to use with QuickBooks software.

PRINT CHECKS

After using the *Pay Bills* windows to select bills for payment, the next step is to print checks.

▣ To **print** checks for the bills selected for payment:

Step 1: From the **File** menu, select: **Print Forms | Checks**.

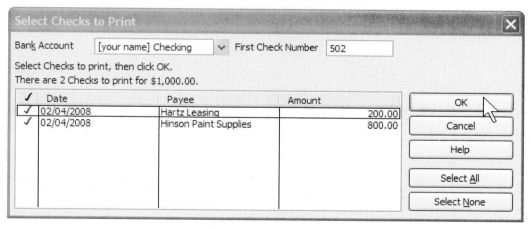

Step 2: When the above *Select Checks to Print* window appears:

- Select Bank Account: **[your name] Checking**.
- First Check Number: **502**.
- Click the **Select All** button.
- Click **OK**.
- Select print settings and standard checks, then click **Print**.

> ✓ **Notice that QuickBooks combined the amounts due Hinson Paint Supplies and printed only one check for the total $800 due ($500 plus $300).**
>
> ✓ **After these bills are paid, QuickBooks reduces the accounts payable balance to zero.**

ADDITIONAL PURCHASE TRANSACTIONS

See **Exercise 9.1** for additional purchase transactions for Fearless Painting Service.

RECORD SALES TRANSACTIONS

When using QuickBooks, sales transactions are recorded using three steps.

	Action	Record Using...	Result
1	**Prepare invoice to record charges for services provided customer**	*Invoice* Window	The invoice is used to bill the customer for services. QuickBooks records the services provided on credit as an Account Receivable (an amount to be received in the future).
2	**Receive customer payment**	*Receive Payments* Window	QuickBooks reduces Accounts Receivable and increases undeposited funds.
3	**Record bank deposit**	*Make Deposits* Window	QuickBooks transfers the amount from undeposited funds to the bank account.

To create an invoice to record painting services provided by Fearless Painting to Katrina Beneficio during January:

Step 1: Click the **Invoices** icon in the Customer section of the Home page.

Step 2: Select Customer & Job: **Beneficio, Katrina: Dining Room**.

Step 3: When the *Billable Time/Costs* window appears to remind you the job has outstanding billable time or costs, click **OK.**

Step 4: Select Form Template: **Intuit Service Invoice**.

Step 5: Enter Date: **01/31/2008**.

Step 6: Click the **Time/Costs** button.

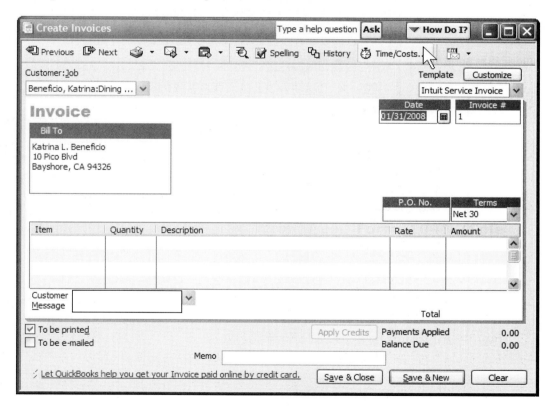

Step 7: Select billable costs to apply to the Beneficio invoice as follows:

> Be sure to enter %, otherwise $40 will be the markup.

- Click the **Expenses** tab.

- Enter Markup Amount: **40%**. Select Markup Account: **4050 – Sales**.

- Check ✓ to select: **Hinson Paint Supplies**.

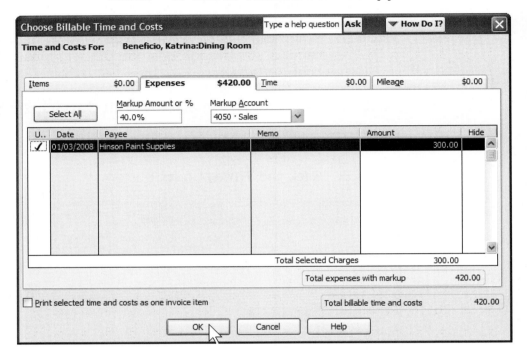

- Click **OK** to bill the Paint Supplies cost.

Step 8: The Beneficio Invoice will now list Total Reimbursable Expenses of $420.00. Enter the service provided in the *Create Invoices* window as follows:

- Select Item: **Labor Mural**.

> The Amount column will automatically display 3,280.00.

- Enter Quantity: **82** (hours).

Step 9: Click the **Print** button and print the invoice.

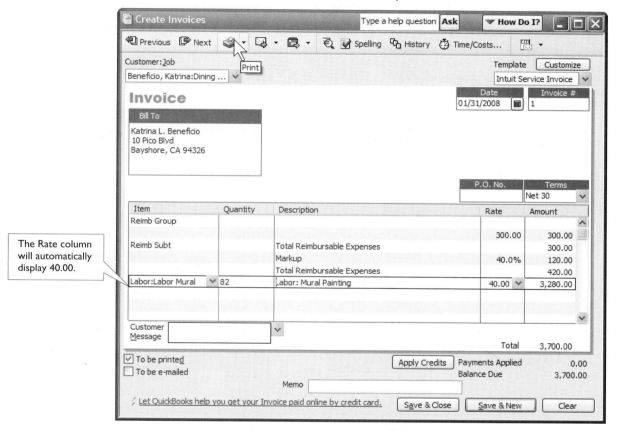

> The Rate column will automatically display 40.00.

Step 10: To E-mail an invoice:

- Click the **Send** arrow at the top of the *Invoices* window. Select **E-mail Invoice**.

> For purposes of this exercise, E-mail the invoice to yourself.

- Select Send by: **E-mail**.
- In the *To* field, enter your E-mail address.
- In the *From* field, enter your E-mail address.
- Click **Send Now**.
- If necessary, complete the registration and password for free online billing.

Step 11: Click **Save & Close** to record the invoice and close the *Create Invoices* window.

To record Katrina Beneficio's payment for the $3,700.00 invoice:

Step 1: From the Customer section of the Home page, click the **Receive Payments** icon.

Step 2: Select Received From: **Beneficio, Katrina: Dining Room**.

Step 3: Select Date: **02/04/2008**.

> QuickBooks automatically applies the payment to the outstanding invoice.

Step 4: Enter Amount: **$3700.00**. A check mark will appear by the outstanding invoice listed.

Step 5: Select Payment Method: **Check**.

> Invoice No. 1 for $3,700 should appear as an outstanding invoice.

Step 6: Enter Check No. **555**.

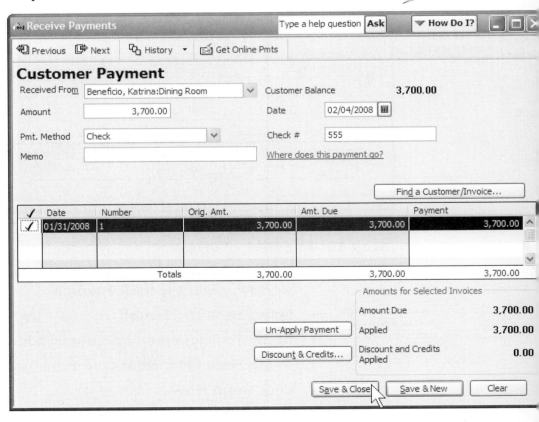

Step 7: Click **Save & Close** to record the payment and close the *Receive Payments* window.

When a customer makes a payment, the customer's account receivable is reduced by the amount of the payment. In this case, Beneficio's account receivable is reduced by $3,700.00.

To record the deposit of the customer's payment in the bank:

Step 1: From the Customer section of the Home page, click the **Record Deposits** icon. The following *Payments to Deposit* window will appear.

The *Payments to Deposit* window lists undeposited funds that have been received, but not yet deposited in the bank.

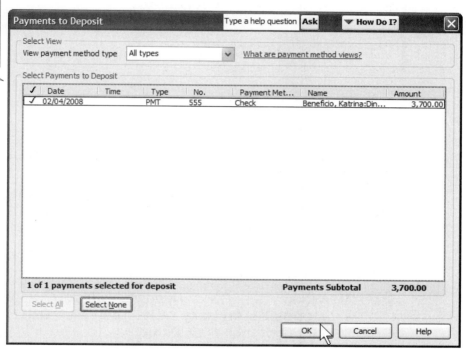

Step 2: Select the payment from Katrina Beneficio for deposit.

Step 3: Click **OK** and the following *Make Deposits* window appears.

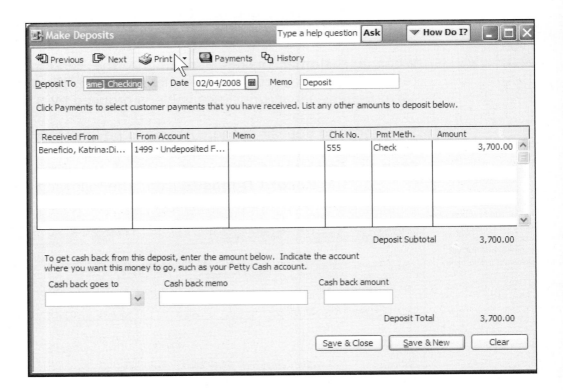

Step 4: Select Deposit To: **[your name] Checking**.

Step 5: Select Date: **02/04/2008**.

Step 6: Click **Print**.

Step 7: When the *Print Deposits* window appears, select **Deposit summary only**. Then click **OK**. Select printer settings, then click **Print**.

Step 8: Click **Save & Close** to record the deposit and close the *Make Deposits* window.

ADDITIONAL SALES TRANSACTIONS

See **Exercise 9.2** for additional sales transactions for Fearless Painting Service.

MAKE ADJUSTING ENTRIES

At the end of Fearless Painting's accounting period, December 31, 2008, it is necessary to record adjustments to bring the company's accounts up to date as of year-end.

The following adjustments are necessary for Fearless Painting at December 31, 2008:

1. Record depreciation expense for the computer for the year.

2. Record depreciation expense for the painting equipment for the year. (Complete in **Exercise 9.3**.)

3. Record the amounts of paint supplies that are still on hand at year-end. Unused paint supplies should be recorded as assets because they have future benefit. (Complete in **Exercise 9.3**.)

Use the General Journal to record the adjusting entry for depreciation expense on the computer for Fearless Painting at December 31, 2008. The $1,500 computer cost will be depreciated over a useful life of three years.

Step 1: From the **Company** menu, select **Make General Journal Entries**.

Step 2: Record the entry for depreciation on the computer equipment in the General Journal.

- Select Date: **12/31/2008**.

- Entry No.: **ADJ 1**.

- Enter Account: **6430**. Press the **Tab** key to advance the cursor to the Debit column.

- Next, use QuickMath calculator to calculate the amount of depreciation expense.

  - With the cursor in the Debit column, press the = key to display the QuickMath calculator.

  - Enter **1500.00**.

  - Press **/**.

  - Enter **3** to divide by the 3-year useful life.

  - Press the **Enter** key. $500 should now appear in the Debit column.

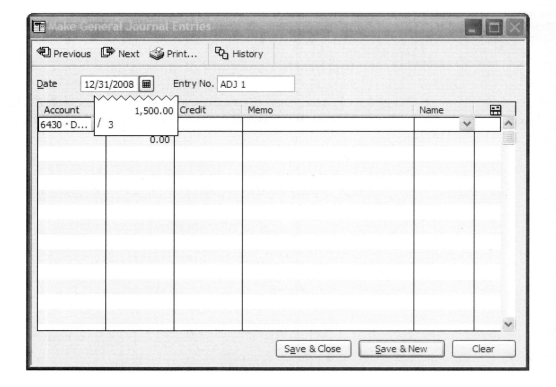

- Enter Account: **1430**. Credit: **500.00**. Your journal entry should appear as shown below.

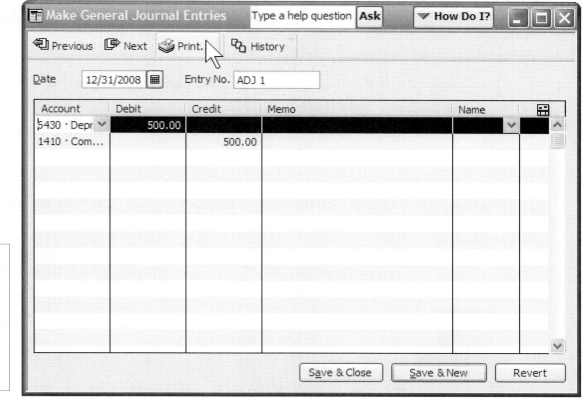

To print the entire journal instead of just one entry:
1. Click **Reports** to open the Report Navigator.
2. Select Type of Report: **Accountant & Taxes**.
3. Select **Journal**.

Step 3: To **print** the adjusting journal entry, click the **Print** button.

Step 4: Click **Save & Close** to close the *Make General Journal Entries* window.

PRINT REPORTS

The next step in the accounting cycle is to print financial reports. Usually, a company prints the following financial reports for the year:

- General Ledger
- Profit & Loss (also known as the P & L or Income Statement)
- Balance Sheet
- Statement of Cash Flows

> To print financial statements, select **Report Center**, select **Company & Financial.**

The General Ledger is accessed from the Report Center (click **Report Center** in the Navigation Bar, then select **Accountant & Taxes**).

The Profit & Loss, the Balance Sheet, and the Statement of Cash Flows are financial statements typically given to external users, such as bankers and investors.

You will print financial statements for Fearless Painting Service for the year 2008 in **Exercise 9.4**.

CLOSE THE ACCOUNTING PERIOD

When using a manual accounting system, closing entries are made in the general journal to close the temporary accounts (revenues, expenses, and withdrawals or dividends). In a manual system, closing entries are used in order to start the new year with a zero balance in the temporary accounts.

QuickBooks automatically closes temporary accounts to start each new year with $-0- balances in all temporary accounts (revenues, expenses, and dividends).

To prevent changes to prior periods, QuickBooks permits you to restrict access to the accounting records for past periods that have been closed. See **Exercise 9.5** for instructions on closing the accounting period in QuickBooks.

SAVE CHAPTER 9

Save Chapter 9 as a portable QuickBooks file to the location specified by your instructor.

Step 1: If necessary, insert a removable disk.

Step 2: From the menu bar, click **File | Portable Company File | Create File**.

Step 3: When the *Close and Reopen* window appears, click **OK**.

Step 4: When the following *Create Portable Company File* window appears, enter the filename: **[your name] Chapter 9** and the appropriate location. Then click **Save**.

Step 5: Click **OK** after the portable file has been created successfully.

Step 6: Close the company file by clicking **File** (Menu), **Close Company**.

ASSIGNMENTS

> *NOTE: See the Quick Reference Guide in Part 3 for step-by-step instructions to frequently used tasks.*

EXERCISE 9.1: PURCHASE TRANSACTIONS

In this Exercise, you will enter purchase transactions for Fearless Painting Service.

TASK 1: OPEN PORTABLE COMPANY FILE

To open the portable company file (.QBM) file, convert the portable file to a regular company file with a .QBW extension as follows:

Step 1: From the menu bar, click **File | Portable Company File | Open File**.

Step 2: Identify the filename and location for the portable company file:

- Click the **Browse** button to find the location of the portable company file on the hard drive or removable media.

- Select the file: **[your name] Chapter 9.QBM**.

Step 3: Identify the name and location of the new company file (.QBW) file to use for completing Exercise 9.1 to 9.5:

- Filename: **[your name] Exercise 9.1 to 9.5**. The **.QBW** extension should appear automatically based upon your Windows settings.

- Location: **C:\Program Files\Intuit\QuickBooks 2006**. This is the location of the .QBW file on the hard drive of your computer. Click the Browse button to specify another location.

Step 4: Click **Open** to open the portable company file.

Step 5: Click **Cancel** when the *Create a Backup* window appears.

Step 6: If prompted, enter your **User Name** and **Password**, then click **OK**.

Step 7: Click **OK** when the QuickBooks sample company message appears.

Step 8: Change the company name to: **[your name] Exercise 9.1 to 9.5 Fearless Painting Service**.

TASK 2: RECORD PURCHASE TRANSACTIONS

Record the following purchase transactions for Fearless Painting Service during the year 2008. Print checks as appropriate.

> Memorized Transaction:
> 1. Lists (menu)
> 2. Memorized Transactions List
> 3. Double-click: Hartz Leasing

> To view the van lease bill, select **Show All Bills** in the *Pay Bills* window.

> Print Checks:
> 1. **File** (menu)
> 2. **Print Forms**
> 3. **Checks**

Date	Purchase Transaction
02/01/2008	Use the memorized transaction to record the $200 bill for the February van lease.
02/28/2008	Paid van lease for February.
03/01/2008	Received $200 bill for van lease for March.
03/30/2008	Paid van lease for March. (Due: 03/31/2008)
04/01/2008	Received $200 bill for van lease for April.
04/04/2008	Purchased $50 of paint supplies on account from Hinson Paint Supplies. Record as Paint Supplies Expense.

04/30/2008	Paid van lease for April. (Due: 05/01/2008) Paid for paint supplies purchased on April 4.
05/01/2008	Received $200 bill for van lease for May.
05/30/2008	Paid van lease for May. (Due: 05/31/2008)
06/01/2008	Received $200 bill for van lease for June.
06/30/2008	Paid van lease for June. (Due: 07/01/2008)
07/01/2008	Purchased $100 of paint supplies on account from Hinson Paint Supplies.
07/01/2008	Received $200 bill for van lease for July.
07/30/2008	Paid van lease for July. (Due: 07/31/2008) Paid for paint supplies purchased on July 1.
08/01/2008	Received $200 bill for van lease for August.
08/30/2008	Paid van lease for August. (Due: 08/31/2008)
09/01/2008	Received $200 bill for van lease for September.
09/02/2008	Purchased $75 of paint supplies on account from Hinson Paint Supplies.
09/30/2008	Paid van lease for September. (Due: 10/01/2008). Paid for paint supplies purchased on 09/02/2008.
10/01/2008	Received $200 bill for van lease for October.
10/30/2008	Paid van lease for October. (Due: 10/31/2008)
11/01/2008	Received $200 bill for van lease for November.

Record as **Paint Supplies Expense**. These items are not chargeable to a specific job.

11/30/2008	Paid van lease for November. (Due: 12/01/2008)
12/01/2008	Received $200 bill for van lease for December.
12/20/2008	Purchased $50 of paint supplies on account from Hinson Paint Supplies.
12/30/2008	Paid van lease for December. (Due: 12/31/2008)

Leave the company file open for the next Exercise.

EXERCISE 9.2: SALES TRANSACTIONS

In this Exercise, you will record sales transactions for Fearless Painting Service.

TASK 1:
SALES TRANSACTIONS AND DEPOSIT SUMMARIES

When necessary, add a new job. For more information, see Chapter 3.

🖬 **Print** invoices and deposit summaries for the following sales transactions for Fearless Painting Service during the year 2008.

Date	02/28/2008
Customer	Katrina Beneficio
Job	Dining Room
Item	Labor: Mural
Hours	86
Payment Received & Deposited	03/15/2008
Check No.	675

Date	03/31/2008
Customer	Katrina Beneficio
Job	Dining Room
Item	Labor: Mural
Hours	84
Payment Received & Deposited	04/15/2008
Check No.	690

Date	04/30/2008
Customer	Tom Whalen
Job	Foyer
Item	Labor: Faux
Hours	80
Payment Received & Deposited	05/15/2008
Check No.	432

Date	05/31/2008
Customer	Tom Whalen
Job	Foyer
Item	Labor: Faux
Hours	75
Payment Received & Deposited	06/15/2008
Check No.	455

Date	06/30/2008
Customer	Katrina Beneficio
Job	Vaulted Kitchen
Item	Labor: Mural
Hours	100
Payment Received & Deposited	07/15/2008
Check No.	733

Date	07/31/2008
Customer	Katrina Beneficio
Job	Vaulted Kitchen
Item	Labor: Mural
Hours	90
Payment Received & Deposited	08/15/2008
Check No.	750

Date	08/31/2008
Customer	Katrina Beneficio
Job	Vaulted Kitchen
Item	Labor: Mural
Hours	92
Payment Received & Deposited	09/15/2008
Check No.	782

Date	10/31/2008
Customer	Tom Whalen
Job	Screen Porch
Item	Labor: Mural
Hours	85
Payment Received & Deposited	11/15/2008
Check No.	685

Date	11/30/2008
Customer	Tom Whalen
Job	Screen Porch
Item	Labor: Mural
Hours	87
Payment Received & Deposited	12/15/2008
Check No.	725

Leave the company file open for the next Exercise.

EXERCISE 9.3: YEAR-END ADJUSTMENTS

> The purpose of the trial balance is to determine whether the accounting system is in balance (debits equal credits).

In this Exercise, you will first print a trial balance and then record adjusting entries for Fearless Painting Service.

TASK 1: PRINT TRIAL BALANCE

🖨 **Print** a trial balance for Fearless Painting at December 31, 2008.

Step 1:   Click the **Report Center** icon in the Navigation Bar.

Step 2:   Select: **Accountant & Taxes**.

Step 3:   Select Report: **Trial Balance**.

Step 4:   Select Dates From: **01/01/2008** To: **12/31/2008**.

Step 5:   🖨 **Print** the trial balance for Fearless Painting.

Step 6:   **Close** the *Trial Balance* window.

✓   ***Total debits equal $41,110.***

TASK 2: RECORD ADJUSTING ENTRIES

At the end of the accounting period, it is necessary to make adjusting entries to bring a company's accounts up to date as of year-end. Two adjusting entries are needed for Fearless Painting as of December 31, 2008:

This adjusting entry was recorded in Chapter 9.

1. Record depreciation expense for the computer for the year.

2. Record depreciation expense for the painting equipment for the year. The $500 paint equipment cost is depreciated using straight-line depreciation over five years with no salvage value.

Make the adjusting entry at 12/31/2008 to record depreciation expense for the painting equipment for the year.

TASK 3: PRINT ADJUSTING ENTRIES

🖨 **Print** the adjusting entries recorded on December 31, 2008, for Fearless Painting.

Step 1: Click the **Report Center** icon in the Navigation Bar.

Step 2: Select: **Accountant & Taxes**.

Step 3: Select Report: **Journal**.

Step 4: Select Dates From: **12/31/2008** To: **12/31/2008**.

Step 5: 🖨 **Print** the Journal using **Portrait** orientation.

Step 6: **Close** the *General Journal Entry* window.

> An adjusted trial balance is printed after adjusting entries are made.

TASK 4: PRINT ADJUSTED TRIAL BALANCE

Step 1: 🖨 **Print** an adjusted trial balance at December 31, 2008. Change the report title to: **Adjusted Trial Balance**. Use **Portrait** orientation.

Step 2: ✐ On the adjusted trial balance, **circle** the accounts affected by the adjusting entries.

Leave the company file open for the next Exercise.

EXERCISE 9.4: FINANCIAL REPORTS

> To eliminate the 0.00 appearing for accounts with zero balances, from the *General Ledger* report window, click the **Modify Reports** button, **Advanced**, **In Use**, **Report Date**.

In this Exercise, you will print out financial statements for Fearless Painting Service for the year 2008.

TASK 1: GENERAL LEDGER

🖨 **Print** the General Ledger for Fearless Painting Service for the year 2008.

TASK 2: FINANCIAL STATEMENTS

Print the following financial statements for Fearless Painting Service for the year 2008.

📄 Profit & Loss, Standard

📄 Balance Sheet, Standard

📄 Statement of Cash Flows

> ✓ **Net income for the year 2008 is $31,285.**

Leave the company file open for the next Exercise.

EXERCISE 9.5:
CLOSE THE ACCOUNTING PERIOD

The QuickBooks Administrator has access to all areas of QuickBooks and is established when a new company is set up. For more information about the QuickBooks Administrator, see Chapter 2.

To prevent changes to prior periods, QuickBooks permits you to restrict access to the accounting records for past periods that have been closed.

The QuickBooks Administrator can restrict user access to closed periods either at the time a new user is set up or later.

IMPORTANT! DO NOT COMPLETE THIS EXERCISE UNTIL AFTER YOU HAVE COMPLETED EXERCISE 9.4.

TASK 1: CLOSE THE ACCOUNTING PERIOD

To enter the closing date in QuickBooks:

Step 1: Click **Company** on the menu bar.

Step 2: Click **Set up Users** from the *Company* menu.

Step 3: Enter information for the QuickBooks Administrator, then click **OK**.

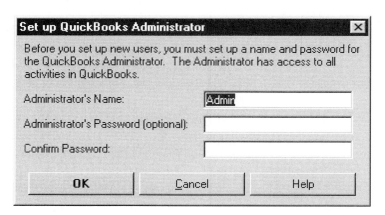

Step 4: When the following *User List* window appears, click the **Closing Date** button.

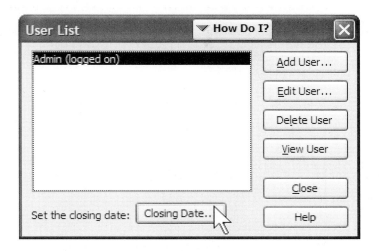

Step 5: Enter the closing date: **12/31/2008**.

Step 6: Click **OK** to close the *Preferences* window.

If you wanted to track the time that your friend Ed helps you with your business, you could permit Ed to access the time tracking features of QuickBooks but restrict his access to other areas and to closed periods.

> If the *User List* window is not open, open the *User List* window by clicking **Company, Set up Users**.

To restrict access when setting up a new user (Ed):

Step 1: From the *User List* window, click **Add** User.

Step 2: Enter User Name: **Ed**.

Step 3: Enter Password: **Time**. Click **Next**.

Step 4: Select: **Selected areas of QuickBooks**. Click **Next**. If necessary, answer no to questions until you arrive at the *Time Tracking* window.

Step 5: For Time Tracking, make the following selections.

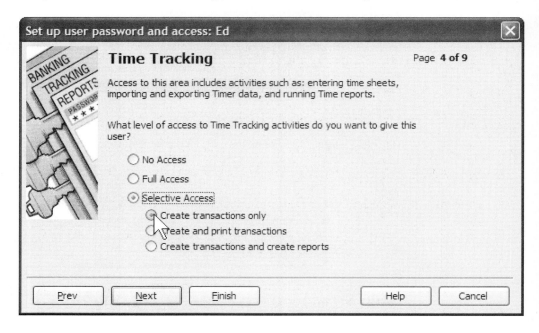

Step 6: To restrict access to closed periods, when the following window appears, select: **No**.

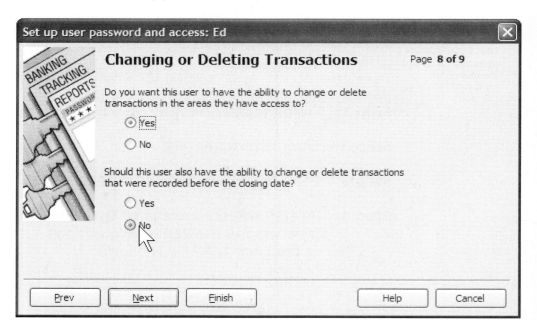

Step 7: Click **Finish** to set up Ed as a new user.

Step 8: **Close** the *User List* window.

Ed will have access to time tracking only and will not have access to other accounting functions or accounting periods prior to the closing date.

TASK 2: SAVE EXERCISE 9.1 – EXERCISE 9.5

Save Exercises 9.1 through Exercise 9.5 as a portable QuickBooks file to the location specified by your instructor.

Step 1: If necessary, insert a removable disk.

Step 2: From the menu bar, click **File | Portable Company File | Create File**.

Step 3: When the *Close and Reopen* window appears, click **OK**.

Step 4: When the following *Create Portable Company File* window appears, enter the filename: **[your name] Exercise 9.1 to 9.5** and the appropriate location. Then click **Save**.

Step 5: Click **OK** after the portable file has been created successfully.

Step 6: Close the company file by clicking **File** (Menu), **Close Company**.

EXERCISE 9.6:
VILLA FLOOR & CARPET TRANSACTIONS

This Exercise is a continuation of Exercise 8.2. You must have completed Exercise 8.2 in order to complete this exercise.

In Exercise 8.2 you created a new company file for Villa Floor & Carpet. In this Exercise, you will enter transactions for the new company.

TASK 1: OPEN PORTABLE COMPANY FILE

To open the portable company file (.QBM) file, convert the portable file to a regular company file with a .QBW extension as follows:

Step 1: From the menu bar, click **File | Portable Company File | Open File**.

Step 2: Identify the filename and location for the portable company file:

- Click the **Browse** button to find the location of the portable company file on the hard drive or removable media.

- Select the file: **[your name] Exercise 8.2.QBM**.

Step 3: Identify the name and location of the new company file (.QBW) file to use for completing Exercise 9.6:

- Filename: **[your name] Exercise 9.6**. The **.QBW** extension should appear automatically based upon your Windows settings.

- Location: **C:\Program Files\Intuit\QuickBooks 2006**. This is the location of the .QBW file on the hard drive of your computer. Click the Browse button to specify another location.

Step 4: Click **Open** to open the portable company file.

Step 5: Click **Cancel** when the *Create a Backup* window appears.

Step 6: If prompted, enter your **User Name** and **Password**, then click **OK**.

Step 7: Click **OK** when the QuickBooks sample company message appears.

Step 8: Change the company name to: **[your name] Exercise 9.6 Villa Floor & Carpet**.

TASK 2: RECORD PURCHASE TRANSACTIONS

During January, Villa Floor & Carpet entered into the transactions listed below. Record the transactions. 🖨 **Print** invoices, checks, and deposit summaries as appropriate.

Use *Record Deposits* window.

Use *Enter Bills* window.

Use *Write Checks* window.

Record Supplies Expense.

Date	Transaction
01/01/2008	Marc Villa invested $5,000 cash in the business.
01/02/2008	Purchased cleaning equipment for $900 from Griffin Cleaning Supplies (Check No. 5001).
01/05/2008	Purchased $100 of cleaning supplies on account from Griffin Cleaning Supplies.
01/09/2008	Cleaned oriental rugs for David Allison on account: ▪ (2) 3 x 5 ▪ (3) 5 x 7 ▪ (4) 8 x 10
01/20/2008	Paid Griffin Cleaning Supply bill.
01/29/2008	Collected David Allison payment for cleaning services.

TASK 3: ADJUSTING ENTRIES

Step 1: Make an adjusting entry for Villa Floor & Carpet at January 31, 2008 to record one month of depreciation for the cleaning equipment. The cleaning equipment cost $900 and has a three-year life (36 month life) and no salvage value.

Step 2: **Print** the Journal for the year to date.

TASK 4: FINANCIAL REPORTS

Print the following reports for Villa Floor & Carpet for January.

- Adjusted Trial Balance
- General Ledger (remember to eliminate unused accounts with zero balances from the printout)
- Profit & Loss, Standard
- Balance Sheet, Standard
- Statement of Cash Flows

TASK 5: SAVE EXERCISE 9.6

Save Exercise 9.6 as a portable QuickBooks file to the location specified by your instructor.

Step 1: If necessary, insert a removable disk.

Step 2: From the menu bar, click **File | Portable Company File | Create File**.

Step 3: When the *Close and Reopen* window appears, click **OK**.

Step 4: When the following *Create Portable Company File* window appears, enter the filename: **[your name] Exercise 9.6** and the appropriate location. Then click **Save**.

Step 5:   Click **OK** after the portable file has been created successfully.

EXERCISE 9.7 WEB QUEST

The Internal Revenue Service (IRS) provides tax information useful for the small business. A sole proprietorship must file Form 1040 Schedule C for the annual tax return. If a sole proprietorship meets certain criteria, it may file a simplified Schedule C-EZ.

Step 1:   Go to the www.irs.gov web site.

Step 2:   Search for Schedule C-EZ on the IRS web site. ▣ **Print** the Schedule C-EZ.

Step 3:   ✐ **Circle** the information about whether you may use Schedule C-EZ instead of Schedule C.

CHAPTER 9 PRINTOUT CHECKLIST
NAME:_____ DATE:_____

INSTRUCTIONS:
1. CHECK OFF THE PRINTOUTS YOU HAVE COMPLETED.
2. STAPLE THIS PAGE TO YOUR PRINTOUTS.

☑ **PRINTOUT CHECKLIST – CHAPTER 9**
☐ Deposit Summary
☐ Check No. 501
☐ Fixed Asset Listing
☐ Check No. 502
☐ Check No. 503
☐ Invoice No. 1
☐ Deposit Summary
☐ Adjusting Entry

☑ **PRINTOUT CHECKLIST – EXERCISE 9.1**
☐ Task 2: Checks

☑ **PRINTOUT CHECKLIST – EXERCISE 9.2**
☐ Task 2: Invoices and Deposit Summaries

☑ **PRINTOUT CHECKLIST – EXERCISE 9.3**
☐ Task 1: Trial Balance
☐ Task 3: Adjusting Entries
☐ Task 4: Adjusted Trial Balance

☑ **PRINTOUT CHECKLIST – EXERCISE 9.4**
☐ Task 1: General Ledger
☐ Task 2: Financial Statements

☑ **PRINTOUT CHECKLIST – EXERCISE 9.6**
☐ Task 2: Villa Floor & Carpet Invoices & Checks
☐ Task 3: Journal
☐ Task 4: Adjusted Trial Balance
☐ Task 4: General Ledger

☐   Task 4: Income Statement
☐   Task 4: Balance Sheet
☐   Task 4: Statement of Cash Flows

☑   ***PRINTOUT CHECKLIST – EXERCISE 9. 7***
☐   Schedule C-EZ

COMPANY PROJECT 9.1

PROJECT 9.1: NEW BEGINNINGS LAWN CARE

SCENARIO

Your friend Ed started a new lawn service business, New Beginnings Lawn Care, to help pay his college expenses. You and Ed reach an agreement: you will help Ed with his accounting records and provide customer referrals, and he will help you with your painting business.

TASK 1: SET UP A NEW COMPANY

Step 1: Create a new company in QuickBooks for New Beginnings Lawn Care. Use the following information.

Company name	[your name] Project 9.1 New Beginnings Lawn Care
Legal name	[your name] Project 9.1 New Beginnings Lawn Care
Tax ID	314-14-7878
Address	2300 Olive Boulevard
City	Bayshore
State	CA
Zip	94326
E-mail	[enter your own email address]
Save in	C:/Program Files/Intuit/QuickBooks 2006
Filename	[your name] Project 9.1
Industry	Landscaping Services

What do you sell?	Services only
Sales tax	No
Estimates	No
Sales receipts	Yes
Billing statements	No
Invoices	Yes
Progress billing	No
Track bills you owe	Yes
Accept credit cards	I don't currently accept credit cards and I don't plan to.
Track time	Yes
Employees	No
Start date	01/01/2008
Add a bank account?	Yes
Bank account name	[your name] Checking
Bank account opened	On or after 01/01/2008
Use recommended expense accounts?	Yes
Use recommended Income accounts?	Yes

Step 2: Click **Finish** to exit the EasyStep Interview.

Step 3: Select tax form: Form 1040 (Sole Proprietor). (From the **Company** menu, select **Company Information**. Select Income Tax Form Used: **Form 1040 (Sole Proprietor)**.

To display account numbers:
1. Click **Edit** on the menu bar.
2. **Preferences.**
3. **Accounting.**
4. **Company Preferences.**
5. **Use account numbers.**

TASK 2: CUSTOMIZE THE CHART OF ACCOUNTS

Customize the Chart of Accounts for New Beginnings Lawn Service as follows:

Step 1: Display account numbers in the Chart of Accounts.

Step 2: Add the following accounts to the Chart of Accounts. Abbreviate account titles as necessary.

Account No.	1700
Account Type	Fixed Asset
Account Name	Mower
Account Description	Mower
Tax Line	Unassigned
Opening Balance	0 as of 01/01/2008

Account No.	1710
Account Type	Fixed Asset
Account Name	Mower Cost
Subaccount of	Mower
Account Description	Mower Cost
Tax Line	Unassigned
Opening Balance	0 as of 01/01/2008

Account No.	1720
Account Type	Fixed Asset
Account Name	Accumulated Depreciation-Mower
Account Description	Accumulated Depreciation-Mower
Subaccount of	Mower
Tax Line	Unassigned
Opening Balance	0 as of 01/01/2008

Account No.	1800
Account Type	Fixed Asset
Account Name	Trimmer Equipment
Account Description	Trimmer Equipment
Tax Line	Unassigned
Opening Balance	0 as of 01/01/2008

Account No.	1810
Account Type	Fixed Asset
Account Name	Trimmer Equipment Cost
Account Description	Trimmer Equipment Cost
Subaccount of	Trimmer Equipment
Tax Line	Unassigned
Opening Balance	0 as of 01/01/2008

Account No.	1820
Account Type	Fixed Asset
Account Name	Accumulated Depr Trimmer
Account Description	Accumulated Depr Trimmer
Subaccount of	Trimmer Equipment
Tax Line	Unassigned
Opening Balance	0 as of 01/01/2008

Account No.	6551
Account Type	Expense
Account Name	Supplies Expense
Account Description	Supplies Expense
Tax Line	Sch C: Supplies (not from COGS)

Step 3: ⊟ **Print** the Chart of Accounts for New Beginnings Lawn Care.

TASK 3: CUSTOMER LIST

Step 1: Create a Customer List for New Beginnings Lawn Care using the following information.

Customer	Beneficio, Katrina
Opening Balance	0.00 as of 01/01/2008
Address Info:	
First Name	Katrina
Last Name	Beneficio
Contact	Katrina Beneficio
Phone	415-555-1818
Alt. Ph.	415-555-3636
Address	10 Pico Blvd Bayshore, CA 94326

Select **Add New**.

Additional Info:	
Type	Residential
Terms	Net 30

Payment Info:	
Account No.	3001
Preferred Payment Method	Check

Step 2: Add a job for Katrina Beneficio.

Select **Add New**.

Job Info:	
Job Status	Awarded
Job Description	Mow/Trim Lawn
Job Type	Lawn

Step 3:   Add another customer.

Customer	Whalen, Tom
Opening balance	0.00 as of 01/01/2008
Address Info:	
First Name	Tom
Last Name	Whalen
Contact	Tom Whalen
Phone	415-555-1234
Alt. Ph.	415-555-5678
Alt. Contact	Work phone
Address	100 Sunset Drive Bayshore, CA 94326

Additional Info:	
Type	Residential
Terms	Net 30

Payment Info:	
Account	3002
Preferred Payment Method	Check

Step 4:   Add a job for Tom Whalen.

Job Info:	
Job Status	Awarded
Job Description	Mow/Trim Lawn
Job Type	Lawn

Step 5: Add a new customer.

Customer	Rock Castle Construction
Opening balance	0.00 as of 01/01/2008
Address Info:	
Company Name	Rock Castle Construction
First Name	Rock
Last Name	Castle
Contact	Rock Castle
Phone	415-555-7878
Alt. Ph.	415-555-5679
Address	1735 County Road Bayshore, CA 94326

Additional Info:	
Type	Commercial
Terms	Net 30

Payment Info:	
Account No.	3003
Preferred Payment Method	Check

Step 6: Add a new job for Rock Castle Construction.

Job Info:	
Job Status	Awarded
Job Description	Mow/Trim Lawn & Shrubs
Job Type	Lawn & Shrubs

Step 7: 🖨 **Print** the Customer List.

TASK 4: VENDOR LIST

Step 1: Create a Vendor List for New Beginnings Lawn Care using the following information.

Vendor	KC Gas Station
Opening Balance	0 as of 01/01/2008
Address Info:	
Company Name	KC Gas Station
Address	100 Manchester Road Bayshore, CA 94326
Contact	Norm
Phone	415-555-7844
Print on Check as	KC Gas Station

Additional Info:	
Account	4001
Type	Fuel
Terms	Net 30
Credit Limit	500.00
Tax ID	37-8910541

Vendor	Mower Sales & Repair
Opening Balance	0.00 as of 01/01/2008
Address Info:	
Company Name	Mower Sales & Repair
Address	650 Manchester Road Bayshore, CA 94326
Contact	Carol
Phone	415-555-8222
Print on Check as	Mower Sales & Repair

Additional Info:	
Account	4002
Type	Mower
Terms	Net 30
Credit Limit	1000.00
Tax ID	37-6510541

Step 2: 🖨 **Print** the Vendor List.

TASK 5: ITEM LIST

Step 1: Create an Item List for New Beginnings Lawn Care using the following information.

Item Type	Service
Item Name	Mowing
Description	Lawn Mowing
Rate	25.00
Account	4070 – Services

Item Type	Service
Item Name	Trim Shrubs
Description	Trim Shrubs
Rate	30.00
Account	4070 – Services

Step 2: 🖶 **Print** the Item List.

TASK 6: CUSTOM INVOICE TEMPLATE

Create a Custom Invoice Template with a *Service Date* column. This permits New Beginnings to bill customers once a month for all services provided during the month, listing each service date separately on the invoice.

To create a custom invoice, complete the following steps:

Step 1: Click the **Invoices** icon in the Customer section of the Home page.

Step 2: Click the **Customize** button on the upper right of the *Create Invoices* window.

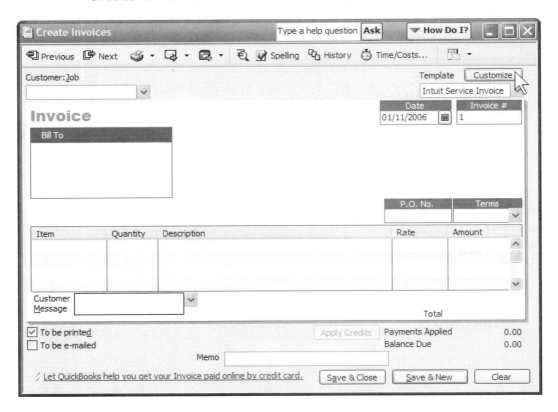

Step 3: Select **Intuit Service Invoice**. Then click **New**.

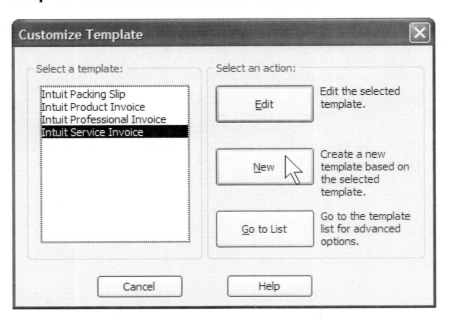

Step 4: To add a *Service Date* column to the custom invoice, when the following *Customize Invoice* window appears:

- Enter Template Name: **Service Date Invoice**.
- Click the **Columns** tab.

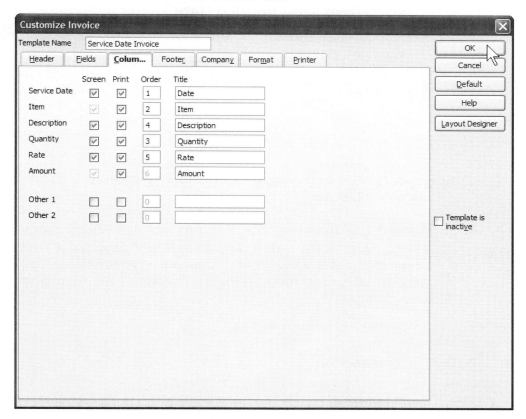

- ✓ Check **Service Date: Screen**.
- ✓ Check **Service Date: Print**.
- ✓ Check **Item: Print**.
- Enter Title for Service Date: **Date**.
- Renumber the Order so they appear as shown above.
- Click **OK** to close the *Customize Invoice* window.

Step 5: To view the custom invoice:

- If the *Create Invoices* window is not still open, click **Invoice** icon in the Customer section of the Home page to open the *Create Invoices* window.

- If necessary, from the *Create Invoices* window, select Template: **Service Date Invoice**.

- Notice that the first column of the invoice is now the *Date* column.

Step 6: **Close** the *Create Invoices* window.

TASK 7: RECORD TRANSACTIONS

During the year, New Beginnings Lawn Service entered into the transactions listed below.

Step 1: Record the following transactions for New Beginnings Lawn Care. Customers are billed monthly. 🖨 **Print** invoices, checks, and deposit summaries as appropriate. Use memorized transactions for recurring transactions.

Date	Transaction
01/01/2008	Ed Norman invested $1,500 cash in the business.
02/01/2008	Purchased a mower for $800 cash from Mower Sales & Repair (Check No. 501).
02/20/2008	Purchased trimming equipment from Mower Sales & Repair for $200 on account.
03/01/2008	Purchased $100 of gasoline and supplies on account from KC Gas Station.
03/20/2008	Paid $200 on your account with Mower Sales & Repair. Paid $100 on your account with KC Gas Station.

Use *Make Deposits* window.

Use *Write Checks* window.

Use *Enter Bills* window.

Record Supplies Expense.

Select **Show All Bills** in the *Pay Bills* window.

04/30/2008	Printed and mailed invoices to customers for the following work performed in April. Use the Intuit Service Date Invoice to record all work performed for the same customer on **one** invoice, indicating the date of service in the DATE column.	
	04/01/2008 Mowed Katrina Beneficio's lawn 04/15/2008 Mowed Katrina Beneficio's lawn	6 hrs 6 hrs
	04/04/2008 Mowed R.C. Construction's lawn 04/19/2008 Mowed R.C. Construction's lawn	8 hrs 8 hrs
	04/08/2008 Mowed Tom Whalen's lawn 04/22/2008 Mowed Tom Whalen's lawn	4 hrs 4 hrs
05/01/2008	Purchased $100 of gasoline and supplies on account from KC Gas Station.	
05/15/2008	Received payments from Beneficio (Check No. 755), Whalen (Check No. 645), and Rock Castle Construction (Check No. 1068) for April invoices.	
05/30/2008	Paid KC Gas Station bill.	
05/30/2008	Mailed invoices to customers for the following services provided during May.	
	05/01/2008 Mowed Katrina Beneficio's lawn 05/15/2008 Mowed Katrina Beneficio's lawn	6 hrs 6 hrs
	05/04/2008 Mowed R.C. Construction's lawn 05/19/2008 Mowed R.C. Construction's lawn	8 hrs 8 hrs
	05/08/2008 Mowed Tom Whalen's lawn 05/22/2008 Mowed Tom Whalen's lawn	4 hrs 4 hrs
06/01/2008	Purchased $100 of gasoline and supplies on account from KC Gas Station.	
06/15/2008	Received payments from Beneficio (Check No. 895), Whalen (Check No. 698), and Rock Castle Construction (Check No. 1100) for May services.	
06/30/2008	Paid KC Gas Station bill.	

Check **To be printed** on the *Invoice* window. Then print the invoices by selecting **File**, **Print Forms**, **Invoices**.

06/30/2008	Mailed invoices to customers for the following services provided during June.		
	06/01/2008 06/02/2008 06/15/2008	Mowed Katrina Beneficio's lawn Trimmed Katrina Beneficio's shrubs Mowed Katrina Beneficio's lawn	6 hrs 7 hrs 6 hrs
	06/04/2008 06/05/2008 06/19/2008	Mowed R. C. Construction's lawn Trimmed R.C. Construction's shrubs Mowed R. C. Construction's lawn	8 hrs 9 hrs 8 hrs
	06/08/2008 06/09/2008 06/22/2008	Mowed Tom Whalen's lawn Trimmed Tom Whalen's shrubs Mowed Tom Whalen's lawn	4 hrs 3 hrs 4 hrs
07/01/2008	Purchased $100 of gasoline and supplies on account from KC Gas Station.		
07/15/2008	Received payments from Beneficio (Check No. 910), Whalen (Check No. 715), and Rock Castle Construction (Check No. 1200) for June services.		
07/31/2008	Paid KC Gas Station bill.		
07/31/2008	Mailed invoices to customers for the following services provided during July.		
	07/01/2008 07/15/2008	Mowed Katrina Beneficio's lawn Mowed Katrina Beneficio's lawn	6 hrs 6 hrs
	07/04/2008 07/19/2008	Mowed R.C. Construction's lawn Mowed R.C. Construction's lawn	8 hrs 8 hrs
	07/08/2008 07/22/2008	Mowed Tom Whalen's lawn Mowed Tom Whalen's lawn	4 hrs 4 hrs
08/01/2008	Purchased $100 of gasoline and supplies on account from KC Gas Station.		
08/15/2008	Received payments from Beneficio (Check No. 935), Whalen (Check No. 742), and Rock Castle Construction (Check No. 1300) for July services.		

08/31/2008	Paid KC Gas Station bill.		
08/31/2008	Mailed invoices to customers for the following services provided during August.		
	08/01/2008 08/15/2008	Mowed Katrina Beneficio's lawn Mowed Katrina Beneficio's lawn	6 hrs 6 hrs
	08/04/2008 08/19/2008	Mowed R.C. Construction's lawn Mowed R.C. Construction's lawn	8 hrs 8 hrs
	08/08/2008 08/22/2008	Mowed Tom Whalen's lawn Mowed Tom Whalen's lawn	4 hrs 4 hrs
09/01/2008	Purchased $100 of gasoline and supplies on account from KC Gas Station.		
09/15/2008	Received payments from Beneficio (Check No. 934), Whalen (Check No. 746), and Rock Castle Construction (Check No. 1400) for August services.		
09/30/2008	Paid KC Gas Station bill.		
09/30/2008	Mailed invoices to customers for the following service provided during September.		
	09/01/2008 09/15/2008	Mowed Katrina Beneficio's lawn Mowed Katrina Beneficio's lawn	6 hrs 6 hrs
	09/04/2008 09/19/2008	Mowed R.C. Construction's lawn Mowed R.C. Construction's lawn	8 hrs 8 hrs
	09/08/2008 09/22/2008	Mowed Tom Whalen's lawn Mowed Tom Whalen's lawn	4 hrs 4 hrs
10/01/2008	Purchased $50 of gasoline on account from KC Gas Station.		
10/15/2008	Received payments from Beneficio (Check No. 956), Whalen (Check No. 755), and Rock Castle Construction (Check No. 1500) for September services.		
10/31/2008	Paid KC Gas Station bill.		

10/31/2008	Mailed invoices to customers for the following services provided during October.		
	10/01/2008 10/02/2008 10/15/2008	Mowed Katrina Beneficio's lawn Trimmed Katrina Beneficio's shrubs Mowed Katrina Beneficio's lawn	6 hrs 7 hrs 6 hrs
	10/04/2008 10/05/2008 10/19/2008	Mowed R. C. Construction's lawn Trimmed R.C. Construction's shrubs Mowed R. C. Construction's lawn	8 hrs 9 hrs 8 hrs
	10/08/2008 10/09/2008 10/22/2008	Mowed Tom Whalen's lawn Trimmed Tom Whalen's shrubs Mowed Tom Whalen's lawn	4 hrs 3 hrs 4 hrs
11/15/2008	Received payments from Beneficio (Check No. 967), Whalen (Check No. 765), and Rock Castle Construction (Check No. 1600) for October services.		

Step 2: 🖨 **Print** the Check Register for January 1, 2008, to December 31, 2008.

TASK 8: ADJUSTING ENTRIES

Step 1: Make adjusting entries for New Beginnings Lawn Care at December 31, 2008, using the following information.

- The mowing equipment cost $800 and has a four-year life and no salvage value.

- The trimming equipment cost $200 and has a two-year life and no salvage value.

Step 2: 🖨 **Print** the Journal for the year.

TASK 9: FINANCIAL REPORTS

⌨ **Print** the following reports for New Beginnings Lawn Care.

📄 General Ledger (remember to omit unused accounts with zero balances from the printout)

📄 Profit & Loss, Standard

📄 Balance Sheet, Standard

📄 Statement of Cash Flows

✓   *Net income is $6,490.00.*

TASK 10: SAVE PROJECT 9.1

Save Project 9.1 as a portable QuickBooks file to the location specified by your instructor.

Step 1: If necessary, insert a removable disk.

Step 2: From the menu bar, click **File | Portable Company File | Create File**.

Step 3: When the *Close and Reopen* window appears, click **OK**.

Step 4: When the following *Create Portable Company File* window appears, enter the filename: **[your name] Project 9.1** and the appropriate location. Then click **Save**.

Step 5: Click **OK** after the portable file has been created successfully.

TASK 11: ANALYSIS AND RECOMMENDATIONS

Step 1: Analyze the financial performance of New Beginnings Lawn Care.

Step 2: What are your recommendations to improve the company's financial performance in the future?

PROJECT 9.1 PRINTOUT CHECKLIST
NAME:_____ DATE:_____

INSTRUCTIONS:
1. CHECK OFF THE PRINTOUTS YOU HAVE COMPLETED.
2. STAPLE THIS PAGE TO YOUR PRINTOUTS.

☑ **PRINTOUT CHECKLIST – PROJECT 9.1**
☐ Chart of Accounts
☐ Customer List
☐ Vendor List
☐ Item List
☐ Invoices
☐ Checks
☐ Deposit Summaries
☐ Check Register
☐ General Journal
☐ General Ledger
☐ Profit & Loss
☐ Balance Sheet
☐ Statement of Cash Flows

NOTES:

CHAPTER 10
MERCHANDISING CORPORATION: SALES, PURCHASES & INVENTORY

SCENARIO

After only one year of operation, your painting service is growing as more customers learn of your custom murals. You often suggest that your customers buy their paint from a small paint store owned and operated by Wil Miles because he provides excellent customer service. In addition, Wil will deliver paint to a job when you run short.

To your dismay, you discover that Wil Miles is planning to sell the store and retire, taking his first vacation since he opened the store 15 years ago. After your initial disappointment, however, you see a business opportunity.

Lately, you've noticed increased demand for custom paint colors to coordinate with furniture, fabrics, and various decorating accessories. If you owned the paint store, you could make a profit on the markup from paint sales made to Fearless Painting Service customers. In addition, you are certain you could land three large commercial customers for whom you have worked: Custom Interiors, The Decorating Center, and Rock Castle Construction. You could also sell paint to other customers, including paint contractors and homeowners.

Convinced there is a profitable market for custom-mixed paint, you approach Wil Miles about purchasing his store. Wil agrees to sell the business to you for $11,000 cash. In addition, you agree to assume a $1,000 bank loan as part of the purchase agreement. You have some extra cash you can invest, and you decide to seek other investors to finance the remainder.

Two of Rock Castle Construction's subcontractors, Nic of Nic's Window & Door, and Patrick of Rishe's Racks are long-time customers of the paint store. When they learn of your plans to buy the paint store, both eagerly offer to invest.

Nic suggests that you investigate incorporating the new business to provide limited liability to the owners. You vaguely recall discussion of limited liability in your college accounting class and decide to E-mail your college accounting professor, Troy Luh, for more information.

Professor Luh's E-mail reply:

SUBJECT:RE:Limited Liability

Corporations provide investors with limited liability; the most the investor can lose is the amount invested in the corporation's stock. If you invest in a corporation, your personal assets are protected from claims against the paint store.

For tax purposes, there are two different types of corporations: (1) subchapter S corporation and (2) C corporation. A C corporation's earnings are subject to double taxation: the profits of the corporation are taxed (Form 1120) and then the dividends received by investors are taxed on their 1040s.

To avoid double taxation, use an S Corporation. (It appears you meet the requirements.) An S Corporation files a Form 1120S and its earnings appear on your personal 1040 tax return, taxed at your personal income tax rate.

Good Luck with your new business venture!

Nic, Patrick, and you form an S Corporation. Nic and Patrick each buy $3,000 of stock, and you buy $5,000 of stock. The stock proceeds are used to purchase the business from Wil Miles. Until you can hire a store manager, you will manage the store.

You prepare the following list of planned expenditures to launch the business:

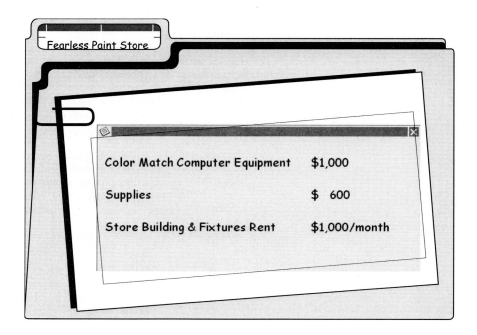

Fearless Paint Store

Color Match Computer Equipment	$1,000
Supplies	$ 600
Store Building & Fixtures Rent	$1,000/month

Fearless Paint Store opens for business on January 1, 2009.

CHAPTER 10
LEARNING OBJECTIVES

In Chapter 10, you will learn the following QuickBooks activities:

INTRODUCTION

A company can sell customers either (1) a product or (2) a service.

In Chapters 8 and 9, you maintained accounting records for a company that sells a service to customers. In this chapter, you will maintain an accounting system for a company that sells a product. In Chapter 10, you will complete the following:

---

1. Easy Step Interview

Use the EasyStep Interview to enter information and preferences for the new company. Based on the information entered, QuickBooks automatically creates a chart of accounts.

---

2. Edit the Chart of Accounts

Modify the chart of accounts to customize it for your business. Enter beginning account balances.

---

3. Create Lists

Enter information in the following lists:
- Customer List: Enter information about customers to whom you sell.
- Vendor List: Enter information about vendors from whom you buy.
- Item List: Enter information about products (inventory) you buy and resell to customers.
- Employee List: Enter information about employees.

---

4. Record Transactions

Enter business transactions in QuickBooks using onscreen forms and the onscreen journal.

---

5. Reports

After preparing adjusting entries, print financial reports.

To begin Chapter 10, start QuickBooks software by clicking on the QuickBooks desktop icon or click **Start**, **Programs**, **QuickBooks Pro**, **QuickBooks Pro 2006**.

CREATE A NEW COMPANY

To create a new company data file in QuickBooks, use the EasyStep Interview. The EasyStep Interview will ask you a series of questions about your business. QuickBooks then uses the information to customize QuickBooks to fit your business needs.

Open the EasyStep Interview as follows:

> If you are familiar with accounting, you can create a company in QuickBooks but skip the interview questions, by clicking **Skip Interview**.

Step 1: Select **File** (menu).

Step 2: Select **New Company**.

Step 3: Click **Start Interview.** Enter the following information for Fearless Paint Store in the EasyStep Interview.

Company name	[your name] Chapter 10 Fearless Paint Store
Legal name	[your name] Chapter 10 Fearless Paint Store
Federal tax ID	37-9875602
Address	2301 Olive Boulevard
City	Bayshore
State	CA
Zip	94326
E-mail	[enter your own email address]
Save in	C:/Program Files/Intuit/QuickBooks 2006
Filename	[your name] Chapter 10
Industry	Retail Establishments
What do you sell?	Products only
Enter sales	Record each sale individually
Sell products online?	I don't sell online and I am not interested in doing so.

Sales tax	Yes
Estimates	No
Sales receipts	Yes
Billing statements	No
Invoices	Yes
Progress billing	No
Track bills you owe	Yes
Track inventory in QuickBooks?	Yes
Accept credit cards	I accept credit cards and debit cards.
Track time	Yes
Employees	No
Start date	01/01/2009
Add a bank account?	Yes
Bank account name	[your name] Checking
Bank account opened	On or after 01/01/2009
Use recommended expense accounts?	Yes
Use recommended Income accounts?	Yes

Step 4: Click **Finish** to exit the EasyStep Interview.

COMPLETE COMPANY SETUP

After the EasyStep Interview is finished, use the following checklist to complete the company setup:

- Select tax form
- Edit the chart of accounts
- Add customers
- Add vendors
- Add products and services as items

SELECT TAX FORM

To complete the company information:

Step 1: From the Company menu, select **Company Information**.

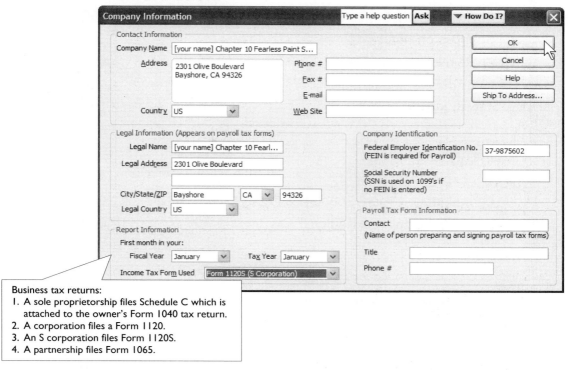

Business tax returns:
1. A sole proprietorship files Schedule C which is attached to the owner's Form 1040 tax return.
2. A corporation files a Form 1120.
3. An S corporation files Form 1120S.
4. A partnership files Form 1065.

Step 2: Select Income Tax Form Used: **Form 1120S (S Corporation)**.

Step 3: Click **OK** to close the *Company Information* window.

EDIT CHART OF ACCOUNTS

Based on your answers in the EasyStep Interview, QuickBooks automatically creates a chart of accounts for Fearless Paint Store. You can customize the chart of accounts to suit your specific business needs.

Because you are purchasing an existing business, some accounts have opening balances. The balance sheet with opening balances for Fearless Paint Store at January 1, 2009, appears as follows.

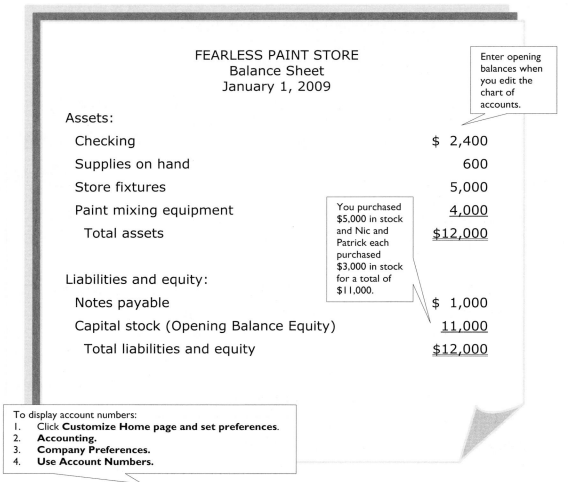

FEARLESS PAINT STORE
Balance Sheet
January 1, 2009

Enter opening balances when you edit the chart of accounts.

Assets:

Checking	$ 2,400
Supplies on hand	600
Store fixtures	5,000
Paint mixing equipment	4,000
Total assets	$12,000

You purchased $5,000 in stock and Nic and Patrick each purchased $3,000 in stock for a total of $11,000.

Liabilities and equity:

Notes payable	$ 1,000
Capital stock (Opening Balance Equity)	11,000
Total liabilities and equity	$12,000

To display account numbers:
1. Click **Customize Home page and set preferences**.
2. **Accounting.**
3. **Company Preferences.**
4. **Use Account Numbers.**

Edit the Chart of Accounts and enter opening balances as follows:

Step 1: Display account numbers in the Chart of Accounts.

Step 2: Enter the opening balance for the company Checking account:

- To open the Chart of Accounts, click the **Chart of Accounts** icon in the Company section of the Home page.

- Select **[your name] Checking** account. **Right-click** to display the popup menu.

- Select **Edit Account**.

- When the *Edit Account* window for the Checking account appears, enter Account Number: **1100**.

- Enter Opening Balance: **$2,400** as of **01/01/2009**.
- Click **OK**.

Step 3: Add the following accounts and opening balances to the Chart of Accounts. Abbreviate account titles as necessary.

Account No.	2600
Account Type	Other Current Liability
Account Name	Notes Payable
Account Description	Notes Payable
Tax Line	B/S-Liabs/Eq.: Other current liabilities
Opening Balance	$1,000 as of 01/01/2009

Account No.	1250
Account Type	Other Current Asset
Account Name	Supplies on Hand
Account Description	Supplies on Hand
Tax Line	B/S-Assets: Other current assets
Opening Balance	$600 as of 01/01/2009

Account No.	1600
Account Type	Fixed Asset
Account Name	Store Fixtures
Account Description	Store Fixtures
Tax Line	B/S-Assets: Buildings/oth. depr. assets
Opening Balance	$0 as of 01/01/2009

Account No.	1610
Account Type	Fixed Asset
Account Name	Store Fixtures Cost
Subaccount of	Store Fixtures
Account Description	Store Fixtures Cost
Tax Line	B/S-Assets: Buildings/oth. depr. assets
Opening Balance	$5,000 as of 01/01/2009

Account No.	1620
Account Type	Fixed Asset
Account Name	Accumulated Depr-Store Fixtures
Subaccount of	Store Fixtures
Account Description	Acc Depr-Store Fixtures
Tax Line	B/S-Assets: Buldings/oth. depr. assets
Opening Balance	$0 as of 01/01/2009

Account No.	1700
Account Type	Fixed Asset
Account Name	Paint Mixing Equipment
Account Description	Paint Mixing Equipment
Tax Line	B/S-Assets: Buldings/oth. depr. assets
Opening Balance	$0 as of 01/01/2009

Account No.	1710
Account Type	Fixed Asset
Account Name	Paint Mixing Equipment Cost
Subaccount of	Paint Mixing Equipment
Account Description	Paint Mixing Equipment Cost
Tax Line	B/S-Assets: Buldings/oth. depr. assets
Opening Balance	$4,000 as of 01/01/2009

Account No.	1720
Account Type	Fixed Asset
Account Name	Accum Depr- Paint Mixing Equip
Subaccount of	Paint Mixing Equipment
Account Description	Accum Depr- Paint Mixing Equip
Tax Line	B/S-Assets: Buldings/oth. depr. assets
Opening Balance	$0 as of 01/01/2009

Account No.	1800
Account Type	Fixed Asset
Account Name	Color Match Equipment
Account Description	Color Match Equipment
Tax Line	B/S-Assets: Buldings/oth. depr. assets
Opening Balance	$0 as of 01/01/2009

Account No.	1810
Account Type	Fixed Asset
Account Name	Color Match Equipment Cost
Subaccount of	Color Match Equipment
Account Description	Color Match Equipment Cost
Tax Line	B/S-Assets: Buldings/oth. depr. assets
Opening Balance	$0 as of 01/01/2009

Account No.	1820
Account Type	Fixed Asset
Account Name	Accum Depr-Color Match Equip
Subaccount of	Color Match Equipment
Account Description	Accum Depr-Color Match Equip
Tax Line	B/S-Assets: Buldings/oth. depr. assets
Opening Balance	$0 as of 01/01/2009

Account No.	6550
Account Type	Expense
Account Name	Supplies Expense
Account Description	Supplies Expense
Tax Line	Deductions: Other Deductions

Step 4: 🖨 **Print** the Chart of Accounts with opening balances for Fearless Paint Store.

Step 5: 🖨 **Print** a trial balance for Fearless Paint Store dated **01/01/2009**. Compare your printout to the following to verify your account balances are correct.

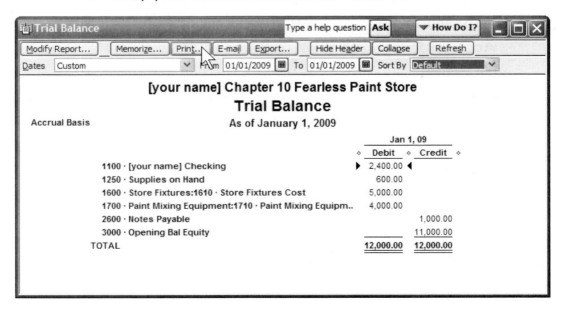

Step 6:   🖨 **Print** a balance sheet (standard) for Fearless Paint Store dated **01/01/2009**. Compare your printout to the balance sheet that appears on page 10.

CREATE A CUSTOMER LIST

Next, enter customer information in the Customer List. When using QuickBooks to account for a merchandising company that sells a product to customers, you must indicate whether the specific customer is charged sales tax.

Fearless Paint Store will sell to:

1. Retail customers, such as homeowners who must pay sales tax.

2. Wholesale customers, such as The Decorating Center, who resell the product and do not pay sales tax.

Step 1:   Create a Customer List for Fearless Paint Store using the following information.

Customer	Beneficio, Katrina
Opening Balance	$0.00 as of 01/01/2009
Address Info:	
Mr./Ms./...	Mrs.
First Name	Katrina
Last Name	Beneficio
Contact	Katrina Beneficio
Phone	415-555-1818
Alt. Ph.	415-555-3636
Address	10 Pico Blvd Bayshore, CA 94326

NOTE: If customers had opening balances, you can also enter the opening balances using the *Create Invoices* window (select Item: **Opening Balance**).

Additional Info:	
Type	Residential
Terms	Net 30
Tax Code	Tax
Tax Item	State Tax

Select **Add New**.

Payment Info:	
Account	3001

Job Info:	
Job Status	Awarded
Job Description	Custom Paint
Job Type	Custom Paint

Select **Add New**.

Customer	Decor Centre
Opening Balance	$0.00 as of 01/01/2009
Address Info:	
Company Name	Decor Centre
Contact	Sara
Phone	415-555-9898
Address	750 Clayton Road Bayshore, CA 94326

Additional Info:	
Type	Commercial
Terms	Net 30
Tax Code	Non

Payment Info:	
Account	3005

Job Info:	
Job Status	Awarded
Job Description	Custom & Stock Paint
Job Type	Custom & Stock Paint

Customer	Rock Castle Construction
Opening Balance	$0.00 as of 01/01/2009
Address Info:	
Company Name	Rock Castle Construction
Mr./Ms./...	Mr.
First Name	Rock
Last Name	Castle
Contact	Rock Castle
Phone	415-555-7878
Alt. Ph.	415-555-5679
Address	1735 County Road Bayshore, CA 94326

Additional Info:	
Type	Commercial
Terms	Net 30
Tax Code	Non

Payment Info:	
Account	3003

Job Info:	
Job Status	Awarded
Job Description	Custom Paint
Job Type	Custom Paint

Customer	Three French Hens Interiors
Opening Balance	$0.00 as of 01/01/2009
Address Info:	
Company Name	Three French Hens Interiors
Contact	Cheryl
Phone	415-555-4356
Address	120 Ignatius Drive Bayshore, CA 94326

Additional Info:	
Type	Commercial
Terms	Net 30
Tax Code	Non

Payment Info:	
Account	3004

Job Info:	
Job Status	Awarded
Job Description	Custom & Stock Paint
Job Type	Custom & Stock Paint

Customer	Whalen, Tom
Opening Balance	$0.00 as of 01/01/2009
Address Info:	
Mr./Ms./...	Mr.
First Name	Tom
Last Name	Whalen
Contact	Tom Whalen
Phone	415-555-1234
Address	100 Sunset Drive Bayshore, CA 94326

Additional Info:	
Type	Residential
Terms	Net 30
Tax Code	Tax
Tax Item	State Tax

Payment Info:	
Account	3002

Job Info:	
Job Status	Awarded
Job Description	Custom Paint
Job Type	Custom Paint

Step 2: 🖶 **Print** the Customer List for Fearless Paint Store.

CREATE A VENDOR LIST

Step 1: Create a Vendor List for Fearless Paint Store using the following information.

Vendor	Hinson Paint Supplies
Opening Balance	$0 as of 01/01/2009
Address Info:	
Company Name	Hinson Paint Supplies
Address	200 Garden Street Bayshore, CA 94326
Contact	Steve Hinson
Phone	415-555-6070
Print on Check as	Hinson Paint Supplies

Additional Info:	
Account	4001
Type	Paint
Terms	Net 30
Credit Limit	15,000.00
Tax ID	37-7832541

Vendor	Hartz Leasing
Opening Balance	$0 as of 01/01/2009
Address Info:	
Company Name	Hartz Leasing
Address	13 Appleton Drive Bayshore, CA 94326
Contact	Joseph
Phone	415-555-0412

Select **Add New**.

Additional Info:	
Account	4002
Type	Leasing
Terms	Net 30
Tax ID	37-1726354

Vendor	Shades of Santiago
Opening Balance	$0 as of 01/01/2009
Address Info:	
Company Name	Shades of Santiago
Address	650 Chile Avenue Bayshore, CA 94326
Contact	Elke
Phone	415-555-0444

Additional Info:	
Account	4003
Type	Inventory
Terms	Net 30
Tax ID	37-1726355

Select **Add New**.

Step 2: 🖨 **Print** the Vendor List for Fearless Paint Store.

CREATE AN INVENTORY LIST

Each of the inventory items that Fearless sells is entered in the QuickBooks Item List. Fearless Paint Store will stock and sell paint inventory to both retail and wholesale customers. Fearless will charge retail customers the full price and charge wholesale customers a discounted price for the paint. Because the sales price varies depending upon the type of customer, instead of entering the sales price in the Item List, you will enter the sales price on the invoice at the time of sale.

Step 1: Create an Item List for Fearless Paint Store inventory using the following information.

Item Type	Inventory Part
Item Name	Paint Base
Description	Paint Base
COGS Account	5000 – Cost of Goods Sold
Income Account	4010 – Sales
Asset Account	1300 – Inventory Asset
Qty on Hand	$0 as of 01/01/2009

Item Type	Inventory Part
Item Name	IntBase 1 gal
Subitem of	Paint Base
Description	Interior Paint Base (1 gallon)
Cost	10.00
COGS Account	5000 – Cost of Goods Sold
Taxable	Tax
Income Account	4010 – Sales
Asset Account	1300 – Inventory Asset
Qty on Hand	$0 as of 01/01/2009

Item Type	Inventory Part
Item Name	ExtBase 1 gal
Subitem of	Paint Base
Description	Exterior Paint Base (1 gallon)
Cost	10.00
COGS Account	5000 – Cost of Goods Sold
Taxable	Tax
Income Account	4010 – Sales
Asset Account	1300 – Inventory Asset
Qty on Hand	$0 as of 01/01/2009

Item Type	Inventory Part
Item Name	Paint Color
Description	Paint Color
COGS Account	5000 – Cost of Goods Sold
Income Account	4010 – Sales
Asset Account	1300 – Inventory Asset
Qty on Hand	$0 as of 01/01/2009

Item Type	Inventory Part
Item Name	Stock Color
Subitem of	Paint Color
Description	Stock Paint Color
Cost	2.00
COGS Account	5000 – Cost of Goods Sold
Taxable	Tax
Income Account	4010 – Sales
Asset Account	1300 – Inventory Asset
Qty on Hand	$0 as of 01/01/2009

Item Type	Inventory Part
Item Name	Custom Color
Subitem of	Paint Color
Description	Custom Paint Color
Cost	8.00
COGS Account	5000 – Cost of Goods Sold
Taxable	Tax
Income Account	4010 – Sales
Asset Account	1300 – Inventory Asset
Qty on Hand	$0 as of 01/01/2009

Step 2: ⊟ **Print** the Item List for inventory.

CREATE A SALES TAX ITEM

A merchandiser selling products to consumers must charge sales tax. A sales tax item is created in the Item List with the rate and tax agency information.

To enter a sales tax item:

Step 1: From the Item List, double-click on **State Tax**.

Step 2: When the *Edit Item* window appears:

- Enter Tax Rate: **7.75**%.

- Enter Tax Agency: **California State Board of Equalization**.

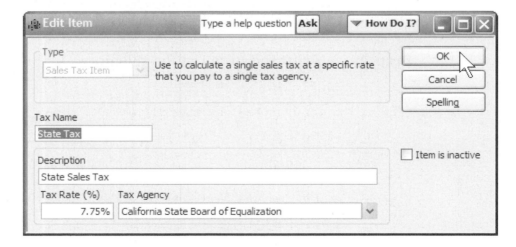

Step 3: Click **OK**.

Step 4: When the *Vendor Not Found* window appears, select: **Quick Add**. If necessary, click **OK** again to close the *Edit Item* window.

RECORD PURCHASE TRANSACTIONS

EQUIPMENT PURCHASES

On January 1, 2009, Fearless Paint Store purchased computerized paint color matching equipment from Hinson Paint Supplies for $1,000 cash.

Step 1: Record the purchase using the *Write Checks* window. Record the color match equipment in account No. 1810. If asked, add the equipment to the Fixed Asset List.

Step 2: ⎙ **Print** the check (Check No. 401) using the standard check style.

THE PURCHASING CYCLE

The purchasing cycle for a merchandising company consists of the following transactions:

1. Create a purchase order to order inventory.
2. Receive the inventory items ordered and record in the inventory account.
3. Enter the bill in QuickBooks when the bill is received.
4. Pay the bill.
5. Print the check.

Next, you will record each of the above transactions in the purchasing cycle for Fearless Paint Store.

CREATE A PURCHASE ORDER

The first step in the purchasing cycle is to create a Purchase Order which is sent to the vendor to order inventory. The Purchase Order provides a record of the type and quantity of item ordered.

Fearless Paint Store needs to order 50 gallons of Interior Base Paint. To order the paint, Fearless must create a purchase order indicating the item and quantity desired.

To create a Purchase Order in QuickBooks:

Step 1: Click the **Purchase Orders** icon in the Vendor section of the Home page.

Step 2: Select Vendor: **Hinson Paint Supplies**.

Step 3: Select Template: **Custom Purchase Order**.

Step 4: Enter Date: **01/03/2009**.

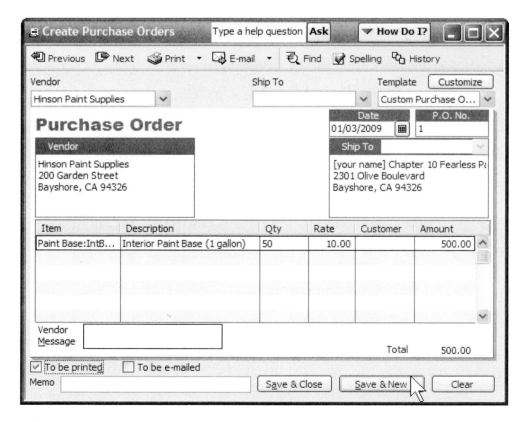

Step 5: Enter the item ordered:

After entering 50 in the Quantity column, $500.00 will appear in the *Amount* column.

$10.00 will automatically appear in the *Rate* column.

- Select Item: **Interior Paint Base (1 gallon)**.

- Enter Quantity: **50**.

Step 6: Select: **To be printed**.

Step 7: Click **Save & New** to record the purchase order and advance to a blank purchase order.

Step 8: Create purchase orders for the following inventory items for Fearless Paint Store.

Vendor	Hinson Paint Supplies
Date	01/05/2009
Item	Exterior Paint Base (1 gallon)
Quantity	40

If prompted to assign classes, select **Save Anyway**. To eliminate this prompt in the future:
1. From the **Edit** menu, select **Preferences**.
2. Click the **Accounting** icon on the left scrollbar.
3. Click the **Company Preferences** tab.
4. Under Use Class Tracking, uncheck **Prompt to Assign Classes**.

Vendor	Shades of Santiago
Date	01/10/2009
Item	Custom Color
Quantity	25 (cartons)
Item	Stock Color
Quantity	5 (cartons)

Vendor	Hinson Paint Supplies
Date	01/12/2009
Item	Stock Color
Quantity	10 (cartons)

Step 9: Click **Save & Close** to record the last purchase order and close the *Purchase Order* window.

Step 10: 🖨 **Print** the Purchase Orders as follows:

- Click **File** (menu).
- Click **Print Forms**.
- Click **Purchase Orders**.
- Select the purchase orders to print and click **OK**.

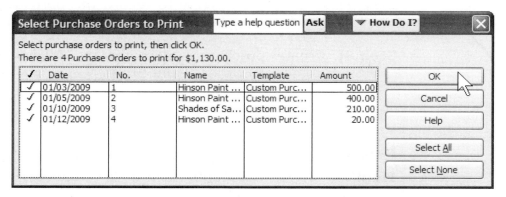

- Select print settings: **Blank paper** and **Print lines around each field**.
- Click **Print**.

RECEIVE INVENTORY ITEMS

When the inventory items that have been ordered are received, record their receipt in QuickBooks. QuickBooks will then add the items received to the Inventory account.

On January 12, 2009, Fearless Paint Store received 40 gallons of interior paint base from Hinson Paint Supplies.

To record the inventory items received from Hinson Paint Supplies:

Step 1: Click the **Receive Inventory** icon in the Vendor section of the Home page. Select **Receive Inventory without Bill**.

Step 2: When the *Create Item Receipts* window appears, select Vendor: **Hinson Paint Supplies**.

Step 3: If a purchase order for the item exists, QuickBooks displays the following *Open PO's Exist* window.

- Click **Yes** to receive against an open purchase order for Hinson Paint Supplies.

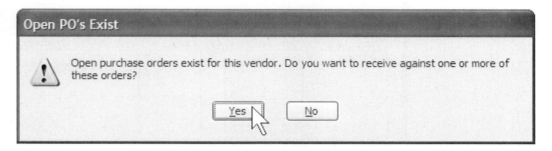

- When the following *Open Purchase Orders* window appears, select **Purchase Order No. 1** dated **01/03/2009**, then click **OK**.

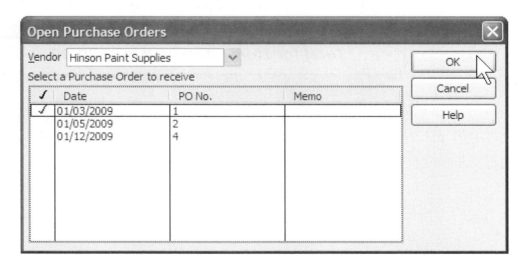

Step 4: The following *Create Item Receipts* window will appear. The quantity received (40 gallons) differs from the quantity ordered (50 gallons). Enter Quantity: **40**.

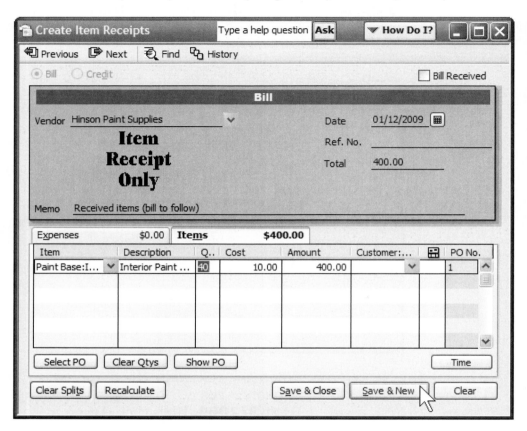

✓ *Total for Items Received is $400.00.*

Step 5: Click **Save & New** on the *Create Item Receipts* window to record the paint received and advance to a blank screen.

Step 6: Record the following inventory items received.

Vendor	Hinson Paint Supplies
Date	01/13/2009
PO No.	2
Item	1 gallon Exterior Paint Base
Quantity	40

Vendor	Hinson Paint Supplies
Date	01/14/2009
PO No.	4
Item	Stock Color
Quantity	10 (cartons)

Vendor	Shades of Santiago
Date	01/15/2009
PO No.	3
Item	Custom Color
Quantity	25 (cartons)
Item	Stock Color
Quantity	5 (cartons)

Step 7: Click **Save & Close** to record the items received and close the *Create Item Receipts* window.

Step 8: 🖶 **Print** the Item List showing the quantity on hand for each item in inventory.

ENTER BILLS

Bills can be entered in QuickBooks when the bill is received or when the bill is paid. (For more information, see Chapter 5.)

Fearless Paint Store will enter bills in QuickBooks when bills are received. At that time, QuickBooks records an obligation to pay the bill later (account payable). QuickBooks tracks bills due. If you use the reminder feature, QuickBooks will even remind you when it is time to pay bills.

Fearless Paint Store previously received 40 1-gallon cans of Interior Paint Base and received the bill later.

To record the bill received:

Step 1: Click the **Enter Bills Against Inventory** icon in the Vendor section of the Home page.

> If the items and the bill were received at the same time, use the *Receive Item with Bill* window.

Step 2: The following *Select Item Receipt* window will appear.

- Select Vendor: **Hinson Paint Supplies**.
- Select Item Receipt corresponding to the bill (**Date: 01/12/2009**).
- Click **OK**.

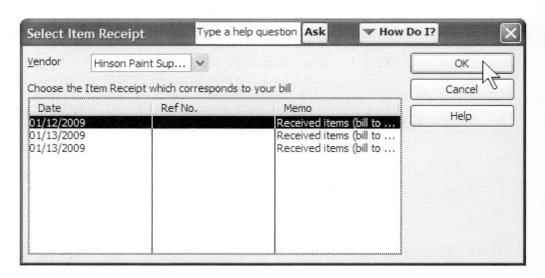

Step 3: When the following *Enter Bills* window appears, make any necessary changes. In this case, change the date to **01/14/2009** (the date the bill was received).

NOTE: The *Enter Bills* window is the same as the *Create Item Received* window except:
1. There is no *Item Receipt Only* stamp.
2. *Bill Received* in the upper right corner is checked.

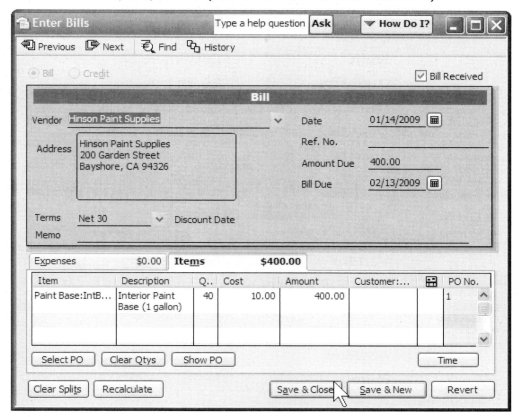

Step 4: The Amount Due of $400.00 should agree with the amount shown on the vendor's bill received.

Step 5: Click **Save & Close**.

Step 6: Record the following bills that Fearless Paint Store received.

Vendor	Hinson Paint Supplies
Date Bill Received	01/16/2009
Terms	Net 30
PO No.	2
Item	Exterior Paint Base (1 gallon)
Quantity	40

Vendor	Shades of Santiago
Date Bill Received	01/16/2009
Terms	Net 30
PO No.	3
Item	Custom Color
Quantity	25 cartons
Item	Stock Color
Quantity	5 cartons

> You could also use the *Enter Bills* window because there was no purchase order for the transaction.

Step 7: Click **Next** to enter the Hartz Leasing bill for January rent.

Vendor	Hartz Leasing
Date Bill Received	01/16/2009
Terms	Net 30
Amount Due	$1,000.00
Account	6600 Rent Expense
Memo	Rent

> Click the **Expenses** tab to record.

> With the *Enter Bills* window still open, click **Edit**, **Memorize Bill**.

Step 8: Record the bill for rent as a memorized transaction.

Step 9: Click **Save & Close** to record the bill and close the *Enter Bills* window.

When you enter bills, QuickBooks automatically adds the amount of the bill to Accounts Payable, reflecting your obligation to pay the bills later.

PAY BILLS

After receiving an inventory item and entering the bill in QuickBooks, the next step is to pay the bill when due. To pay the bill, select bills to pay, then 🖨 **print** the checks.

Fearless Paint Store will pay the bills for paint and paint color that have been received and recorded.

To pay bills in QuickBooks:

Step 1: Click the **Pay Bills** icon in the Vendor section of the Home page.

Step 2: When the *Pay Bills* window appears:

- Select: **Show All Bills**.
- Select bills from **Hinson Paint Supply** and **Shades of Santiago**.
- Select **Checking** account.
- Select Pay By: **Check To be Printed**.
- Select Payment Date: **01/31/2009**.

Step 3: Click **Pay & Close** to close the *Pay Bills* window.

PRINT CHECKS

After selecting bills to pay, you can prepare checks in two different ways:

1. Write the checks manually, or

> If using QuickBooks to print checks, insert preprinted check forms in your printer.

2. 🖨 **Print** the checks using QuickBooks.

To print checks:

Step 1: Select **File** (menu).

Step 2: Select **Print Forms**.

Step 3: Select **Checks**.

> QuickBooks prints one check for each vendor, combining all amounts due the same vendor.

Step 4: Select **Checking** account.

Step 5: First Check Number: **402**.

Step 6: Select checks to print: **Hinson Paint Supplies** and **Shades of Santiago**. Then click **OK**.

Step 7: Select printer settings, then click **Print**.

RECORD SALES TRANSACTIONS

The sales cycle for a merchandising company consists of the following transactions:

1. Create an invoice to record the sale and bill the customer.

2. Receive the customer payments.

3. Deposit the customer payments in the bank.

Next, you will record each of these transactions in QuickBooks for Fearless Paint Store.

CREATE INVOICES

> If prompted to assign classes, select **Save Anyway**. To eliminate this prompt in the future:
> 1. From the **Edit** menu, select **Preferences**.
> 2. Click the **Accounting** icon on the left scrollbar.
> 3. Click the **Company Preferences** tab.
> 4. Under Use Class Tracking, uncheck **Prompt to Assign Classes**.

When inventory is sold to a customer, the sale is recorded on an invoice in QuickBooks. The invoice lists the items sold, the quantity, and the price. In addition, if the product is sold to a retail customer, sales tax is automatically added to the invoice.

To create an invoice:

Step 1: Click the **Invoices** icon in the Customer section of the Home page.

Step 2: Create and 🖨 **print** invoices for the following sales made by Fearless Paint Store.

Sale of 3 gallons of custom color interior paint to Katrina Beneficio:

Date	01/20/2009
Customer	Katrina Beneficio
Terms	Net 30
Quantity	3 gallons
Item Code	Interior Paint Base (1 gallon)
Price Each	25.00
Quantity	3
Item Code	Custom Color
Price Each	6.00
To Be Printed	Yes
Tax Code	Tax

> ✓   ***The Invoice total for Katrina Beneficio is $100.21.***

Sale of 10 gallons of stock color interior paint to Décor Centre.

Date	01/22/2009
Customer	Decor Centre
Terms	Net 30
Quantity	10 gallons
Item Code	Interior Paint Base (1 gallon)
Price Each	20.00
Quantity	10
Item Code	Stock Color
Price Each	3.50
To Be Printed	Yes
Tax Code	Non

Sale of 5 gallons stock color interior paint and 2 gallons customer color exterior paint to Three French Hens Interiors:

> If a customer pays cash at the time of sale, it is recorded using the *Sales Receipts* window.

Date	01/25/2009
Customer	Three French Hens Interiors
Terms	Net 30
Quantity	5 gallons
Item Code	Interior Paint Base (1 gallon)
Price Each	20.00
Quantity	5
Item Code	Stock Color
Price Each	3.50
Quantity	2 gallons
Item Code	Exterior Paint Base (1 gallon)
Price Each	22.00
Quantity	2
Item Code	Custom Color
Price Each	5.00
To Be Printed	Yes
Tax Code	Non

RECEIVE PAYMENTS

When a credit sale is recorded, QuickBooks records an account receivable at the time the invoice is created. The account receivable is the amount that Fearless Paint Store expects to receive from the customer later.

To record a payment received from a customer:

Step 1: Click the **Receive Payments** icon in the Customer section of the Home page.

Step 2: Record the following payments received by Fearless Paint Store from customers.

Date Received	01/30/2009
Customer	Katrina Beneficio
Amount Received	100.21
Payment Method	Check
Check No.	1001

Date Received	01/31/2009
Customer	Three French Hens Interiors
Amount Received	171.50
Payment Method	Check
Check No.	4567

MAKE DEPOSITS

When the customer's payment is deposited in Fearless Painting's checking account, record the bank deposit in QuickBooks.

To record a bank deposit:

Step 1: Click the **Record Deposits** icon in the Customer section of the Home page.

Step 2: On January 31, 2009, record the deposit of customer payments received from **Katrina Beneficio** and **Three French Hens Interiors**. Select Deposit To: **[Your Name] Checking**.

Step 3: 🖶 **Print** the deposit summary.

MAKE ADJUSTING ENTRIES

Before preparing financial statements for Fearless Paint Store for January, print a trial balance and make adjusting entries to bring the accounts up to date.

Step 1: 🖨 **Print** the trial balance for Fearless Paint Store at January 31, 2009.

Step 2: Make adjusting entries for Fearless Paint Store at January 31, 2009, using the following information:

- The store fixtures cost of $5,000 will be depreciated over a 10-year useful life with no salvage value. Depreciation expense is $42 per month.

- The paint mixing equipment cost of $4,000 will be depreciated over a 5-year useful life with no salvage value. Depreciation expense is $67 per month.

- The computer paint color match equipment cost $1,000 and has a useful life of four years with no salvage value. Depreciation expense is $21 per month.

> Supplies on hand have future benefit and are recorded in an asset account (No. 1250). Supplies that have been used and the benefits expired are recorded in the Supplies Expense account (No. 6550).

- A count of supplies on hand at the end of January totaled $400. The Supplies on Hand account balance before adjustment is $600. Therefore, reduce (credit) the Supplies on Hand account by $200 and increase (debit) Account No. 6550 Supplies Expense by $200.

Step 3: 🖨 **Print** the Journal (including adjusting entries) for Fearless Paint Store for January 2009.

Step 4: 🖨 **Print** the adjusted trial balance for Fearless Paint Store at January 31, 2009.

Step 5: ✐ On the adjusted trial balance, **circle** the account balances affected by the adjusting entries.

✓ ***Total debits on the adjusted trial balance equal $13,656.71.***

PRINT REPORTS

To eliminate the 0.00 for accounts with zero balances, from the *General Ledger* report:
1. Click **Modify Reports.**
2. Click the **Display** tab.
3. Click the **Advanced** button.
4. Select **In Use**.

🖨 **Print** the following reports for Fearless Paint Store for the month of January 2009.

- General Ledger
- Profit and Loss, Standard
- Balance Sheet, Standard
- Statement of Cash Flows

After reviewing the financial statements for Fearless Paint Store, what are your recommendations to improve financial performance?

SAVE CHAPTER 10

Save Chapter 10 as a portable QuickBooks file to the location specified by your instructor.

Step 1: If necessary, insert a removable disk.

Step 2: From the menu bar, click **File | Portable Company File | Create File**.

Step 3: When the *Close and Reopen* window appears, click **OK**.

Step 4: When the following *Create Portable Company File* window appears, enter the filename: **[your name] Chapter 10** and the appropriate location. Then click **Save**.

Step 5: Click **OK** after the portable file has been created successfully.

Step 6: Close the company file by clicking **File** (Menu), **Close Company**.

ASSIGNMENTS

> **NOTE: See the Quick Reference Guide in Part 3 for step-by-step instructions to frequently used tasks.**

EXERCISE 10.1: MUJERES' YARNS

Chel, owner of Mujeres' Yarns, has asked you if you would be interested in maintaining the accounting records for her yarn shop. She would like to begin using accounting software for her accounting records, converting from her current manual accounting system. After reaching agreement on your fee, Chel gives you the following information to enter into QuickBooks.

TASK 1: NEW COMPANY SETUP

Step 1: Create a new company in QuickBooks for Mujeres' Yarns using the following information.

Company name	[your name] Exercise 10.1 Mujeres' Yarns
Legal name	[your name] Exercise 10.1 Mujeres' Yarns
Federal tax ID	37-1872613
Address	13 Isla Boulevard
City	Bayshore
State	CA
Zip	94326
E-mail	[enter your own email address]
Save in	C:/Program Files/Intuit/QuickBooks 2006
Filename	[your name] Exercise 10.1

Industry	Retail Establishments
What do you sell?	Products only
Enter sales	Record each sale individually
Sell products online?	I don't sell online, but I may want to someday.
Sales tax	Yes
Estimates	No
Sales receipts	Yes
Billing statements	No
Invoices	Yes
Progress billing	No
Track bills you owe	Yes
Track inventory in QuickBooks?	Yes
Accept credit cards	I accept credit cards and debit cards.
Track time	Yes
Employees	No
Start date	01/01/2009
Add a bank account?	Yes
Bank account name	[your name] Checking
Bank account opened	On or after 01/01/2009
Use recommended expense accounts?	Yes
Use recommended Income accounts?	Yes

Step 2: Click **Finish** to exit the EasyStep Interview.

Step 3: From the **Company** menu, select **Company Information**. Select Income Tax Form Used: **Form 1120S (S Corporation)**.

> To display account numbers:
> 1. Click **Customize Home page and set preferences**.
> 2. **Accounting.**
> 3. **Company Preferences.**
> 4. **Use Account Numbers.**

TASK 2: EDIT CHART OF ACCOUNTS

Edit the Chart of Accounts and enter opening balances as follows:

Step 1: Display account numbers in the Chart of Accounts.

Step 2: Enter the opening balance of $1,300 for the company Checking account:

- To open the Chart of Accounts, click the **Chart of Accounts** icon in the Company section of the Home page.

- Select **[your name] Checking** account. **Right-click** to display the popup menu.

- Select **Edit Account**.

- When the *Edit Account* window for the Checking account appears, enter Account Number: **1100**.

- Enter Opening Balance: **$1,300** as of **01/01/2009**.

- Click **OK**.

Step 3: Enter the opening balance of **$1,800** for the Inventory account.

Step 4: Add the following Notes Payable account and opening balance of $800 to the Chart of Accounts.

Account No.	2600
Account Type	Other Current Liability
Account Name	Notes Payable
Account Description	Notes Payable
Tax Line	B/S-Liabs/Eq.: Other current liabilities
Opening Balance	$800 as of 01/01/2009

Step 5: **Print** the Chart of Accounts with opening balances for Mujeres' Yarns.

Step 6: 🖨 **Print** a trial balance for Mujeres' Yarns dated **01/01/2009**. Compare your printout to the following to verify your account balances are correct.

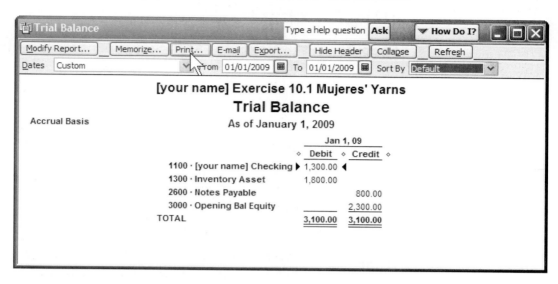

TASK 3: ADD CUSTOMER & JOB

Step 1: Add Ella Brewer to Mujeres' Yarns Customer List.

Customer	Brewer, Ella
Address Info:	
First Name	Ella
Last Name	Brewer
Contact	Ella Brewer
Phone	415-555-3600
Address	18 Spring Street Bayshore, CA 94326

Additional Info:	
Terms	Net 15
Tax Code	Tax
Tax Item	State Tax

Payment Info:	
Account	10000
Preferred Payment	Check

Step 2: Click **Next** to add Sue Counte to Mujeres' Yarns Customer List.

Customer	Counte, Suzanne
Address Info:	
First Name	Suzanne
Last Name	Counte
Contact	Suzanne Counte
Phone	415-555-2160
Address	220 Johnson Avenue Bayshore, CA 94326

Additional Info:	
Terms	Net 15
Tax Code	Tax
Tax Item	State Tax

Payment Info:	
Account	12000
Preferred Payment	Check

Step 3: Click **OK**.

Step 4: 🖨 **Print** the Customer List.

- Click the **Print** button at the top of the Customer Center.

- Click **Customer & Job List**.

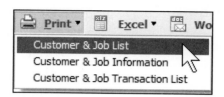

- Select **Portrait** Orientation.

- Click **Print**.

Step 5: **Close** the Customer Center.

TASK 4: ADD VENDORS

Step 1: Add the following vendors to the Vendor List for Mujeres' Yarns.

Vendor	Hayveyah Enterprises
Opening balance	$0.00 as of 01/01/2009
Address Info:	
Company Name	Hayveyah Enterprises
Address	720 Ngozi Avenue Bayshore, CA 94326
Contact	Hayveyah
Phone	415-555-1270
Additional Info:	
Account	2400
Terms	Net 30
Tax ID	37-3571595

Vendor	Hartz Leasing
Opening balance	$0.00 as of 01/01/2009
Address Info:	
Company Name	Hartz Leasing
Address	13 Appleton Drive Bayshore, CA 94326
Contact	Joe Hartz
Phone	415-555-0412
Additional Info:	
Account	2500
Type	Leasing
Terms	Net 30
Tax ID	37-1726354

Select **Add New**.

Vendor	Roxanne's Supplies
Opening balance	$0.00 as of 01/01/2009
Address Info:	
Company Name	Roxanne's Supplies
Address	5 Austin Drive Bayshore, CA 94326
Contact	Roxanne
Phone	415-555-1700
Additional Info:	
Account	2600
Terms	Net 30
Tax ID	37-1599515

Step 2: 🖨 **Print** the Vendor List.

TASK 5: ADD ITEMS

Step 1: Add the following items to Mujeres' Yarns. Click **Next** after entering each item.

Item Type	Inventory Part
Item Name	Alpaca Yarn
Description	Alpaca Yarn 3 ply
Income Account	4010 – Sales

Item Type	Inventory Part
Item Name	Alpaca Yarn-Creme Color
Subitem of	Alpaca Yarn
Description	Alpaca Yarn-Creme Color
Sales Price	10.00 (per skein)
Income Account	4010 – Sales

Item Type	Inventory Part
Item Name	Alpaca Yarn-Earthen Tweed
Subitem of	Alpaca Yarn
Description	Alpaca Yarn-Earthen Tweed Color
Sales Price	12.00 (per skein)
Income Account	4010 – Sales

Item Type	Inventory Part
Item Name	Peruvian Wool
Description	Peruvian Wool Yarn-4 ply
Income Account	4010 – Sales

Item Type	Inventory Part
Item Name	Peruvian Wool Yarn-Charcoal
Subitem of	Peruvian Wool
Description	Peruvian Wool Yarn-Charcoal Color
Sales Price	20.00 (per skein)
Income Account	4010 – Sales

Item Type	Inventory Part
Item Name	Peruvian Wool Yarn-Black
Subitem of	Peruvian Wool
Description	Peruvian Wool Yarn-Black Color
Sales Price	25.00 (per skein)
Income Account	4010 – Sales

Step 2: From the Item List, enter the 7.75% sales tax rate as follows:

- **Double-click** on **State Tax** in the Item List.
- Enter Tax Rate: **7.75%**.
- Enter Tax Agency: **California State Board of Equalization**.

Step 3: 🖳 **Print** the Item List.

TASK 6: ENTER TRANSACTIONS

Mujeres' Yarns entered into the following transactions during January 2009.

- Record all deposits to: [Your Name] Checking.
- 🖳 **Print** invoices, checks, purchase orders, and deposit summaries as appropriate. Use memorized transactions for recurring transactions.

Record the following transactions for Mujeres' Yarns.

Use *Write Checks* window, then create a memorized transaction.

Use *Enter Bills* window to record as Office Supplies Expense.

Click **Yes** if asked to update cost.

Use *Create Invoices* window.

Date	Transaction
01/01/2009	Chel paid $600 store rent to Hartz Leasing (Check No. 1001).
01/02/2009	Purchased $300 in office supplies on account from Roxanne's Supplies.
01/13/2009	Placed the following order with Hayveyah Enterprises. ▪ 10 skeins of Alpaca creme yarn at a cost of $4 each ▪ 20 skeins of Alpaca earthen tweed yarn at a cost of $4.80 each
01/15/2009	Received Alpaca yarn ordered on 01/13/2009.
01/19/2009	Sold 6 skeins of Alpaca creme yarn to Suzanne Counte on account and 8 skeins of Alpaca earthen tweed yarn.
01/19/2009	Received bill from Hayveyah Enterprises for Alpaca yarn received on 01/15/2009.
01/21/2009	Ordered the following yarn from Hayveyah Enterprises on account. ▪ 20 skeins of Peruvian Wool in Charcoal @ $8 each ▪ 12 skeins of Peruvian Wool in Black @ $10 each
01/23/2009	Received the Peruvian Wool yarn ordered on 01/21/2009.
01/25/2009	Sold 13 skeins of Peruvian Wool Charcoal and 5 skeins of Peruvian Wool Black to Ella Brewer on account.
01/25/2009	Paid Hayveyah Enterprises for bill received on 01/19/2009 for Alpaca yarn (Check No. 1002).
01/25/2009	Received and deposited to your Checking account the customer payment from Suzanne Counte for sale of Alpaca yarn on 01/19/2009 (Check No. 1200).
01/27/2009	Paid $300 bill received from Roxanne's Supplies.

TASK 7: ADJUSTING ENTRIES

Step 1: 🖨 **Print** the trial balance for Mujeres' Yarns at January 31, 2009.

Step 2: Make an adjusting entry for Mujeres' Yarns at January 31, 2009 using the following information.

- A count of supplies revealed $180 of supplies on hand. Since $300 of supplies were recorded as Office Supplies Expense when purchased and $180 still remain on hand unused, it is necessary to transfer $180 into an asset account, Supplies on Hand.

- Add a new account: **1370 Supplies on Hand**. Account Type: **Other Current Asset**.

- Make the adjusting entry to transfer $180 from the Office Supplies Expense account to the Supplies on Hand, an asset account.

Step 3: 🖨 **Print** the Journal for January 2009, including the adjusting journal entry.

Step 4: 🖨 **Print** the adjusted trial balance for Mujeres' Yarns at January 31, 2009.

Step 5: ✐ On the adjusted trial balance, **circle** the accounts affected by the adjusting entry.

TASK 8: FINANCIAL REPORTS

🖨 **Print** the following reports for Mujeres' Yarns.

📑 General Ledger (remember to omit unused accounts with zero balances from the printout)

📑 Profit & Loss, Standard

📑 Balance Sheet, Standard

📑 Statement of Cash Flows

TASK 9: SAVE EXERCISE 10.1

Save Exercise 10.1 as a portable QuickBooks file to the location specified by your instructor.

Step 1: If necessary, insert a removable disk.

Step 2: From the menu bar, click **File | Portable Company File | Create File**.

Step 3: When the *Close and Reopen* window appears, click **OK**.

Step 4: When the following *Create Portable Company File* window appears, enter the filename: **[your name] Exercise 10.1** and the appropriate location. Then click **Save**.

Step 5: Click **OK** after the portable file has been created successfully.

Step 6: Close the company file by clicking **File** (Menu), **Close Company**.

EXERCISE 10.2 WHAT'S NEW

To explore new features of QuickBooks Pro 2006:

Step 1: In QuickBooks, click **Help** (menu).

Step 2: Select: **QuickBooks Learning Center | What's New**.

Step 3: From the *What's New* window, select one of the items.

Step 4: 🖨 **Print** the information about the new item that you selected.

EXERCISE 10.3: WEB QUEST

When setting up a chart of accounts for a business, it is helpful to review the tax form that the business will use. Then accounts can be used to track information needed for the business tax return.

The tax form used by the type of organization is listed below.

Type of Organization	Tax Form
Sole Proprietorship	Schedule C (Form 1040)
Partnership	Form 1065 & Schedule K-1
Corporation	Form 1120
S Corporation	Form 1120S

In this exercise, you will download the tax form for a subchapter S corporation from the Internal Revenue Service web site.

Step 1: Go to the Internal Revenue Service web page: www.irs.gov.

Step 2: Using the Search Forms and Publications feature of the IRS web site, find and 🖨 **print** Form 1120S: U.S. Income Tax Return for an S Corporation.

Step 3: ✏ **Circle** Advertising Expense on Form 1120S.

CHAPTER 10 PRINTOUT CHECKLIST
NAME:_____ DATE:_____

INSTRUCTIONS:
1. *CHECK OFF THE PRINTOUTS YOU HAVE COMPLETED.*
2. *STAPLE THIS PAGE TO YOUR PRINTOUTS.*

☑ *PRINTOUT CHECKLIST – CHAPTER 10*
☐ Chart of Accounts
☐ Trial Balance
☐ Balance Sheet
☐ Customer List
☐ Vendor List
☐ Item List
☐ Check
☐ Purchase Orders
☐ Item List: Quantity on Hand
☐ Checks
☐ Invoices
☐ Deposit Summary
☐ Trial Balance
☐ Journal
☐ Adjusted Trial Balance
☐ General Ledger
☐ Profit & Loss
☐ Balance Sheet
☐ Statement of Cash Flows

☑ *PRINTOUT CHECKLIST – EXERCISE 10.1*
☐ Chart of Accounts
☐ Trial Balance
☐ Customer List
☐ Vendor List
☐ Item List
☐ Purchase Orders
☐ Checks
☐ Invoices
☐ Deposit Summary

- ☐ Trial Balance
- ☐ Journal
- ☐ Adjusted Trial Balance
- ☐ General Ledger
- ☐ Profit & Loss
- ☐ Balance Sheet
- ☐ Statement of Cash Flows

- ☑ ***PRINTOUT CHECKLIST – EXERCISE 10.2***
- ☐ What's New

- ☑ ***PRINTOUT CHECKLIST – EXERCISE 10.3***
- ☐ Form 1120S: U.S. Income Tax Return for an S Corporation

COMPANY PROJECT 10.1

PROJECT 10.1: SCOTT'S MOWERS & MORE

SCENARIO

On March 1, 2009, your friend Drake Scott approaches you with another investment opportunity. He asks if you would like to buy stock in a business that sells lawn mowers and equipment. Drake would like to buy the business but needs additional investors.

Drake plans to invest $10,000 and you agree to invest $5,000 in the business. You also enter into an arrangement with Drake whereby you agree to help Drake with the accounting records for his new business in exchange for free lawn service for your paint store.

TASK 1: SET UP A NEW COMPANY

Step 1: Create a new company in QuickBooks for Scott Mowers & More using the following information.

Company name	[your name] Project 10.1 Scott's Mowers & More
Legal name	[your name] Project 10.1 Scott's Mowers & More
Federal tax ID	37-7879146
Address	2300 Olive Boulevard
City	Bayshore
State	CA

Zip	94326
E-mail	[enter your own email address]
Save in	C:/Program Files/Intuit/QuickBooks 2006
Filename	[your name] Project 10.1
Industry	Retail Establishments
What do you sell?	Products only
Enter sales	Record each sale individually
Sell products online?	I don't sell online, and I am not interested in doing so.
Sales tax	Yes
Estimates	No
Sales receipts	Yes
Billing statements	No
Invoices	Yes
Progress billing	No
Track bills you owe	Yes
Track inventory in QuickBooks?	Yes
Accept credit cards	I accept credit cards and debit cards.
Track time	Yes
Employees	No
Start date	03/01/2009
Add a bank account?	Yes
Bank account name	[your name] Checking
Bank account opened	On or after 03/01/2009
Use recommended expense accounts?	Yes
Use recommended Income accounts?	Yes

Step 2: Click **Finish** to exit the EasyStep Interview.

Step 3: From the **Company** menu, select **Company Information**. Select Income Tax Form Used: **Form 1120 (Corporation)**.

To display account numbers:
. Click **Customize Home page and set preferences** on the Home page.
. **Accounting.**
. **Company Preferences.**
. **Use account numbers.**

TASK 2: EDIT THE CHART OF ACCOUNTS

Edit the Chart of Accounts for Scott Mowers & More as follows:

Step 1: Display account numbers in the Chart of Accounts.

Step 2: Enter the opening balance for the company Checking account:

- To open the Chart of Accounts, click the **Chart of Accounts** icon in the Company section of the Home page.

- Select **[your name] Checking** account. **Right-click** to display the popup menu.

- Select **Edit Account**.

- When the *Edit Account* window for the Checking account appears, enter Account Number: **1100**.

- Enter Opening Balance: **$2,400** as of **01/01/2009**.

- Click **OK**.

Step 3: Add the following accounts and opening balances to the Chart of Accounts. Abbreviate account titles as necessary.

This loan will not be paid in one year; therefore, it is a long-term liability.

Account No.	2600
Account Type	Long Term Liability
Account Name	Notes Payable
Account Description	Notes Payable
Tax Line	B/S-Liabs/Eq.:L-T Mortgage/note/bond pay.
Opening Balance	$2,000 as of 03/01/2009

Account No.	1250
Account Type	Other Current Asset
Account Name	Supplies on Hand
Account Description	Supplies on Hand
Tax Line	B/S-Assets: Other current assets
Opening Balance	$500.00 as of 03/01/2009

Account No.	1600
Account Type	Fixed Asset
Account Name	Store Fixtures
Account Description	Store Fixtures
Tax Line	B/S-Assets: Buildings/oth.depr. assets
Opening Balance	$0 as of 03/01/2009

Account No.	1610
Account Type	Fixed Asset
Account Name	Store Fixtures Cost
Subaccount of	Store Fixtures
Account Description	Store Fixtures Cost
Tax Line	B/S-Assets: Buildings/oth.depr. assets
Opening Balance	$2500.00 as of 03/01/2009

Account No.	1620
Account Type	Fixed Asset
Account Name	Accum Depr - Store Fixtures
Subaccount of	Store Fixtures
Account Description	Accum Depr - Store Fixtures
Tax Line	B/S-Assets: Buildings/oth.depr. assets
Opening Balance	$0 as of 03/01/2009

Account No.	6550
Account Type	Expense
Account Name	Supplies Expense
Account Description	Supplies Expense
Tax Line	Deductions: Other Deductions

Step 4: 🖨 **Print** the Chart of Accounts for Scott's Mowers & More.

TASK 3: CUSTOMER LIST

Create and 🖶 **print** a Customer List for Scott Mowers & More.

Customer	Fowler, Gerry
Opening Balance	$200.00 as of 03/01/2009
Address Info:	
First Name	Gerry
Last Name	Fowler
Contact	Gerry Fowler
Phone	415-555-9797
Alt. Ph.	415-555-0599
Address	500 Lindell Blvd Bayshore, CA 94326
Additional Info:	
Type	Residential
Terms	Net 30
Tax Code	Tax
Tax Item	State Tax
Payment Info:	
Account	3001

Select **Add New**.

Customer	Stanton, Mike
Opening Balance	$0.00 as of 03/01/2009
Address Info:	
First Name	Mike
Last Name	Stanton
Contact	Mike Stanton
Phone	415-555-7979
Alt. Ph.	415-555-0596
Alt. Contact	Work phone
Address	1000 Grand Avenue Bayshore, CA 94326

Additional Info:	
Type	Residential
Terms	Net 30
Tax Code	Tax
Tax Item	State Tax
Payment Info:	
Account	3002

Customer	Grady's Bindery
Opening Balance	$0.00 as of 03/01/2009
Address Info:	
Company Name	Grady's Bindery
First Name	Mike
Last Name	Grady
Contact	Mike Grady
Phone	415-555-7777
Address	700 Laclede Avenue Bayshore, CA 94326
Additional Info:	
Type	Commercial
Terms	Net 30
Tax Code	Tax
Tax Item	State Tax
Payment Info:	
Account	3003

TASK 4: VENDOR LIST

Create and 🖨 **print** a Vendor List for Scott Mowers & More.

Vendor	Wooley Supply
Address Info:	
Company Name	Wooley Supply
Address	100 Collinsville Road Bayshore, CA 94326
Contact	Bill
Phone	415-555-0500
Print on Check as	Wooley Supply

Additional Info:	
Account	4001
Type	Mowers
Terms	Net 30
Credit Limit	20,000.00
Tax ID	37-4327651
Opening Balance	$0 as of 03/01/2009

Vendor	Mower Sales & Repair
Address Info:	
Company Name	Mower Sales & Repair
Address	650 Manchester Road Bayshore, CA 94326
Contact	Dan
Phone	415-555-8222
Print on Check as	Mower Sales & Repair

Additional Info:	
Account	4002
Type	Mowers
Terms	Net 30
Credit Limit	10,000.00
Tax ID	37-6510541
Opening Balance	$0 as of 03/01/2009

Vendor	Hartz Leasing
Address Info:	
Company Name	Hartz Leasing
Address	13 Appleton Drive Bayshore, CA 94326
Contact	Joe
Phone	415-555-0412
Print on Check as	Hartz Leasing

Additional Info:	
Account	4003
Type	Leasing
Terms	Net 30
Tax ID	37-1726354
Opening Balance	$0 as of 03/01/2009

TASK 5: ITEM LIST

Step 1: From the Item List, enter the 7.75% sales tax rate as follows:

- **Double-click** on **State Tax** in the Item List.

- Enter Tax Rate: **7.75%.**

- Enter Tax Agency: **California State Board of Equalization**.

Step 2: Enter the following items in the Item List for Scott Mowers & More.

Item Type	Inventory Part
Item Name	Mowers
Description	Lawn Mowers
COGS Account	5000 – Cost of Goods Sold
Tax Code	Tax
Income Account	4010 – Sales
Asset Account	1300 – Inventory Asset
Quantity on Hand	$0 as of 03/01/2009

Item Type	Inventory Part
Item Name	Riding Mower
Subitem of	Mowers
Description	48" Riding Mower
Cost	2,000.00
COGS Account	5000 – Cost of Goods Sold
Tax Code	Tax
Sales Price	3800.00
Income Account	4010 – Sales
Asset Account	1300 – Inventory Asset
Quantity on Hand	$0 as of 03/01/2009

Item Type	Inventory Part
Item Name	Push Mower
Subitem of	Mowers
Description	Push Mower
Cost	400.00
COGS Account	5000 – Cost of Goods Sold
Tax Code	Tax
Sales Price	780.00
Income Account	4010 – Sales
Asset Account	1300 – Inventory Asset
Quantity on Hand	$0 as of 03/01/2009

Item Type	Inventory Part
Item Name	Propel Mower
Subitem of	Mowers
Description	Self-Propelled Mower
Cost	600.00
COGS Account	5000 – Cost of Goods Sold
Tax Code	Tax
Sales Price	1150.00
Income Account	4010 – Sales
Asset Account	1300 – Inventory Asset
Quantity on Hand	$0 as of 03/01/2009

Item Type	Inventory Part
Item Name	Trimmer
Description	Lawn Trimmer
COGS Account	5000 – Cost of Goods Sold
Tax Code	Tax
Income Account	4010 – Sales
Asset Account	1300 – Inventory Asset
Quantity on Hand	$0 as of 03/01/2009

Item Type	Inventory Part
Item Name	Gas Trimmer
Subitem of	Trimmer
Description	Gas-Powered Trimmer
Cost	300.00
COGS Account	5000 – Cost of Goods Sold
Tax Code	Tax
Sales Price	570.00
Income Account	4010 - Sales
Asset Account	1300 – Inventory Asset
Quantity on Hand	$0 as of 03/01/2009

Item Type	Inventory Part
Item Name	Battery Trimmer
Subitem of	Trimmer
Description	Rechargeable Battery-Powered Trimmer
Cost	200.00
COGS Account	5000 – Cost of Goods Sold
Tax Code	Tax
Sales Price	390.00
Income Account	4010 - Sales
Asset Account	1300 – Inventory Asset
Quantity on Hand	$0 as of 03/01/2009

Step 3: 🖶 **Print** an Item List for Scott's Mowers & More.

TASK 6: RECORD TRANSACTIONS

Scott Mowers & More entered into the following transactions during March 2009.

Step 1: Record the following transactions for Scott Mowers & More. Customers are billed monthly. 🖶 **Print** checks, purchase orders, invoices, and deposit summaries as appropriate. Use memorized transactions for recurring transactions.

Use *Record Deposits* window.

Use *Write Checks* window, then create a memorized transaction.

Use *Enter Bills* window. Record as Supplies Expense.

Date	Transaction
03/01/2009	Drake Scott invested $10,000 cash in stock of Scott Mowers & More. You invested $5,000 cash in the stock of the business. Deposit the funds into the company Checking account.
03/01/2009	Paid $800 store rent to Hartz Leasing (Check No. 601).
03/02/2009	Purchased $300 in supplies on account from Mower Sales & Repair.
03/02/2009	Ordered (2) 48" riding mowers, 2 gas-powered trimmers, and 3 battery-powered trimmers from Wooley Supply.
03/04/2009	Received items ordered from Wooley Supply on 03/02/2009.
03/05/2009	Sold a 48" riding mower and a gas-powered trimmer to Grady's Bindery on account.
03/07/2009	Received bill from Wooley Supply.
03/09/2009	Ordered 2 self-propelled mowers and 1 push mower from Wooley Supply.

03/12/2009	Received the self-propelled mowers ordered on 03/09/2009 from Wooley Supply.
03/13/2009	Received the bill from Wooley Supply for the self-propelled mowers.
03/15/2009	Sold 1 self-propelled mower and 1 battery-powered trimmer to Mike Stanton on account.
03/16/2009	Sold a 48" riding mower to Gerry Fowler on account.
03/16/2009	Ordered (2) 48" riding mowers from Wooley Supply to restock inventory.
03/20/2009	Received and deposited the customer payment from Grady's Bindery (Check No. 401).
03/29/2009	Paid bill from Wooley Supply received on 03/07/2009 and due 04/06/2009. Paid $300 bill from Mower Sales & Repairs.
03/31/2009	Received and deposited payment from Mike Stanton (Check No. 3001).
03/31/2009	Paid bill for self-propelled mowers due 04/12/2009.
03/31/2009	Paid $800 store rent to Hartz Leasing.

Step 2: 🖨 **Print** the Check Register for March 2009.

TASK 7: ADJUSTING ENTRIES

Step 1: 🖶 **Print** the trial balance for Scott Mowers & More at March 31, 2009.

Step 2: Make adjusting entries for Scott Mowers & More at March 31, 2009 using the following information.

- A count of supplies revealed $350 of supplies on hand.
- March depreciation expense for store fixtures was $35.

Step 3: 🖶 **Print** the Journal for March 2009, including the adjusting journal entries.

Step 4: 🖶 **Print** the adjusted trial balance for Scott Mowers & More at March 31, 2009.

Step 5: 🖉 On the adjusted trial balance, **circle** the accounts affected by the adjusting entries.

TASK 8: FINANCIAL REPORTS

Step 1: 🖶 **Print** the following reports for Scott Mowers & More.

- General Ledger (remember to omit unused accounts with zero balances from the printout)
- Profit & Loss, Standard
- Balance Sheet, Standard
- Statement of Cash Flows
- Accounts Receivable Aging Summary

Step 2: Using the financial statements, determine the balance of the Supplies Expense account and explain how the account balance was calculated. $_____

Step 3: Using the balance sheet, determine the amount of sales tax that Scott Mowers & More collected and owes to the State Board of Equalization. $_____

Step 4: Discuss how the aging summary for accounts receivable might be used by a small business.

TASK 9: SAVE PROJECT 10.1

Save Project 10.1 as a portable QuickBooks file to the location specified by your instructor.

Step 1: If necessary, insert a removable disk.

Step 2: From the menu bar, click **File | Portable Company File | Create File**.

Step 3: When the *Close and Reopen* window appears, click **OK**.

Step 4: When the following *Create Portable Company File* window appears, enter the filename: **[your name] Project 10.1** and the appropriate location. Then click **Save**.

Step 5: Click **OK** after the portable file has been created successfully.

Step 6: Close the company file by clicking **File** (Menu), **Close Company**.

TASK 10: ANALYSIS AND RECOMMENDATIONS

Step 1: Analyze the financial performance of Scott Mowers & More.

Step 2: What are your recommendations to improve the company's financial performance in the future?

PROJECT 10.1 PRINTOUT CHECKLIST
NAME:_____DATE:_____

INSTRUCTIONS:
1. *CHECK OFF THE PRINTOUTS YOU HAVE COMPLETED.*
2. *STAPLE THIS PAGE TO YOUR PRINTOUTS.*

☑ *PRINTOUT CHECKLIST – PROJECT 10.1*
☐ Chart of Accounts
☐ Customer List
☐ Vendor List
☐ Item List
☐ Invoices
☐ Purchase Orders
☐ Checks
☐ Deposit Summaries
☐ Check Register
☐ Trial Balance
☐ General Journal
☐ Adjusted Trial Balance
☐ General Ledger
☐ Profit & Loss
☐ Balance Sheet
☐ Statement of Cash Flows
☐ Accounts Receivable Aging Summary

Chapter 11
Merchandising Corporation: Payroll

Scenario

After returning from his vacation, Wil Miles drops by the paint store to visit you and his former business. While the two of you are talking, customers in the store begin asking him for assistance. In cheerful good humor, he offers to tend the store for you while you go to lunch.

When you return after lunch, Wil tells you that Katrina Beneficio called, asking when you will have time to finish a paint job for her. Always ready to help, Wil suggests that you finish the Beneficio job while he watches the store.

When you return later that afternoon, Wil appears to be thoroughly enjoying himself as he restocks the shelves and waits on customers. By closing time, you and Wil have reached an agreement: you will hire him to manage the store full-time, freeing you to return to your painting. Wil has only one condition—he wants one month of vacation every year.

CHAPTER 11
LEARNING OBJECTIVES

In Chapter 11, you will learn the following QuickBooks activities:

INTRODUCTION

In Chapter 11, you will account for payroll for Fearless Paint Store. In Chapter 10, you set up a new merchandising company, Fearless Paint Store, in QuickBooks. In this chapter, you will record a bank loan. Then you will set up payroll and record payroll transactions for Fearless Paint Store.

OPEN PORTABLE COMPANY FILE

> Chapter 10 must be completed before starting Chapter 11 or use the Chapter 10 Instructor backup for Chapter 11.

To begin Chapter 11, first start QuickBooks software and then open the portable QuickBooks file for Fearless Paint Store, the company file you created in Chapter 10.

Step 1: Start QuickBooks by clicking on the **QuickBooks** desktop icon or click **Start, Programs, QuickBooks, QuickBooks Pro 2006**.

Step 2: To open the portable company file (.QBM) file and convert the portable file to a regular company file with a .QBW extension, from the menu bar, click **File | Portable Company File | Open File**.

Step 3: Identify the filename and location for the portable company file:

- Click the **Browse** button to find the location of the portable company file on the hard drive or removable media.

- Select the file: **[your name] Chapter 10**. The .QBM may appear automatically based upon your Windows settings, but if it does not appear automatically, do **not** type it.

Step 4: Identify the name and location of the new company file (.QBW) file to use for Chapter 11:

- Filename: **[your name] Chapter 11**. The **.QBW** extension should appear automatically based upon your Windows settings. The .QBW identifies this as a QuickBooks working file.

- Location: **C:\Program Files\Intuit\QuickBooks 2006**. This is the location of the .QBW file on the hard drive of your computer.

Step 5: Click **Open** to open the portable company file.

Step 6: Click **Cancel** when the *Create a Backup* window appears.

Step 7: If prompted, enter your **User ID** and **Password**.

Step 8: Click **OK** when the sample company window appears.

Step 9: Change the company name to: **[your name] Chapter 11 Fearless Paint Store.** If necessary, change the Checking account title to include your name.

The portable company file (.QBM) should now be converted to a regular company file (Chapter 11.QBW) that can be used to complete the assignments for Chapter 11.

BANK LOAN

Although Fearless Paint Store sales appear to be improving, business has been slower than you anticipated. As a result, you need an operating loan in order to pay your bills and Wil's salary.

Fearless Paint Store takes out a $4,000 operating loan from National Bank. You intend to repay the loan within one year.

Step 1: Create a new loan account: Note Payable: National Bank.

A loan to be repaid within 1 year is classified as Other Current Liability.

- Display the **Chart of Accounts**.
- Right-click to display the popup menu. Select **New**.
- Select Account Type: **Other Current Liability**.
- Enter Account Number: **2610**.
- Enter Account Name: **Note Payable-National Bank**.
- Enter Description: **Note Payable – National Bank**.

- Enter Tax Line: **B/S-Liabs/Eq.: Other current liabilities**.
- Enter Opening Balance: **$0.00** as of **02/01/2009**.
- Click **OK** to save.

Step 2: When the bank deposits the $4,000 loan amount in your checking account, record the loan as follows:

- From the Banking section of the Home page, select **Record Deposits**.
- Select Deposit To: **[your name] Checking**.
- Select Date: **02/01/2009**.
- Select From Account: **2610: Note Payable-National Bank**.
- Enter Amount: **4,000.00**.
- 🖨 **Print** the **deposit summary**.
- Click **Save & Close**.

ENABLE PAYROLL

To enable QuickBooks payroll for Fearless Paint Store, complete the following steps:

Step 1: From the Home page, click **Customize Home page and set preferences**.

Step 2: Click **Payroll & Employees** on the left scrollbar of the *Preferences* window.

> Intuit provided tax tables with QuickBooks 6.0 and 99; however to receive updated tax tables with later versions of QuickBooks, you must subscribe to one of Intuit's payroll services.

> Set employee defaults for information common to all employees, such as deductions for health insurance.

Step 3:   Click the **Company Preferences** tab.

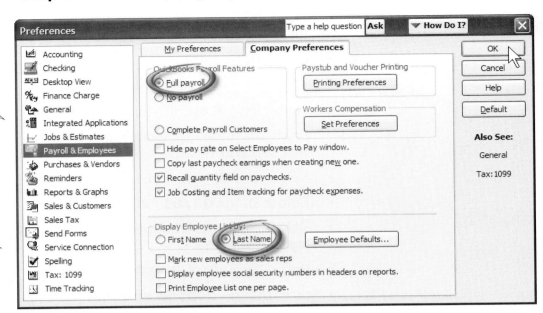

Step 4:   Select **Full payroll features** to enable QuickBooks Payroll.

Step 5:   Select Display Employee List by: **Last Name**.

Step 6:   Click **OK** to close the *Preferences* window.

SET UP PAYROLL

QuickBooks Pro and QuickBooks Premier provide various ways to process payroll. There are two general ways that a company can perform payroll calculations.

1. Use QuickBooks Payroll Services.

2. Manually calculate payroll taxes.

Information about each option appears below.

QUICKBOOKS PAYROLL SERVICE

When you subscribe to a payroll service, QuickBooks automatically calculates tax deductions, requiring an Internet connection. QuickBooks offers several different levels of payroll services:

- **QuickBooks Standard/Enhanced Payroll** provides automatic payroll tax updates and automatically calculates the payroll deductions.

- **QuickBooks Assisted Payroll** offers the additional feature of preparing federal and state payroll forms and electronically paying federal and state payroll taxes.

- **Complete Payroll** offers a full-service payroll service.

To view more information about each of the QuickBooks Payroll Services from the **Employee** menu, select: **Add Payroll Service | Learn About Payroll Options**.

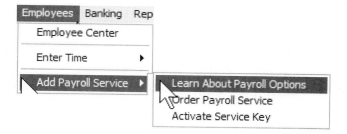

CALCULATE PAYROLL MANUALLY

If you do not use one of the payroll tax services, you can calculate tax withholdings and payroll taxes manually using IRS Circular E. Then enter the amounts in QuickBooks to process payroll.

In Chapter 6, you processed payroll with tax deductions calculated automatically by QuickBooks. In this chapter, you will learn how to enter payroll tax amounts manually instead of using a payroll tax service.

To enable manual paycheck entry:

Step 1: In the Employees section of the Home page, click **Learn about Payroll Options**. Click **OK** to open your web browser.

Step 2: When the following QuickBooks Payroll Services window appears, if necessary scroll down and select: **Learn More**.

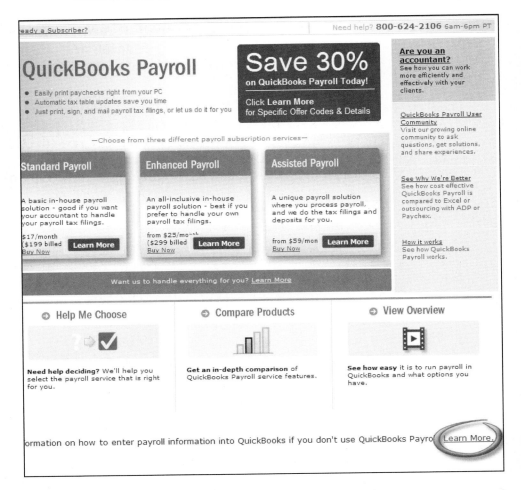

Step 3: Select: **Set QuickBooks to Enable Manual Paycheck Entry**.

Step 4: Click **OK** when the following message appears that your company file is now enabled to process payroll manually.

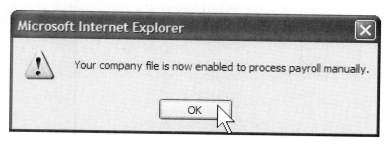

Step 5: Click **OK** when the following QuickBooks information window appears.

> Or you can access payroll setup from the Employee menu, select **Payroll Setup**.

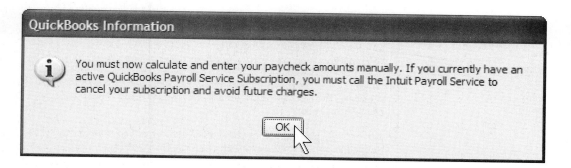

Step 6: The Employee section of the Home page should now appear as below.

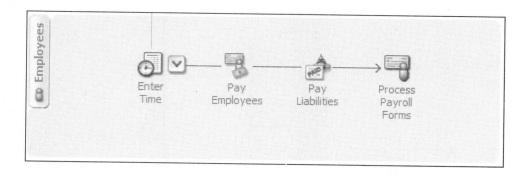

Step 7: From the Employees section of the Home page, select: **Pay Employees**.

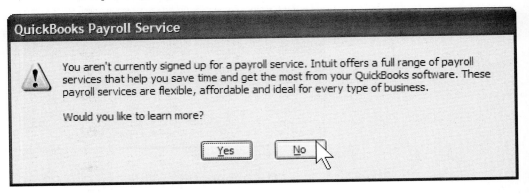

Step 8: Select: **Go to Payroll Setup**.

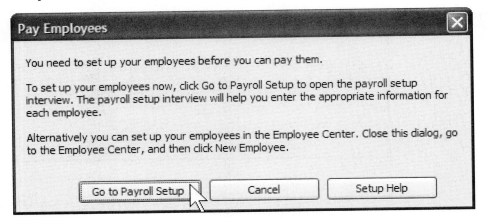

Step 9: After reading the *Welcome to QuickBooks Payroll Setup* window, click **Continue**.

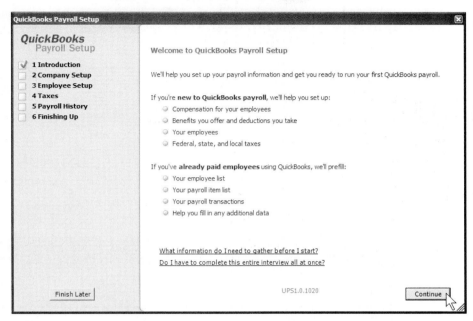

Step 10: When the *Company Setup: Compensation and Benefits* window appears, click **Continue**.

Step 11: When the *Add New* window appears, select the following options, then click **Finish**.

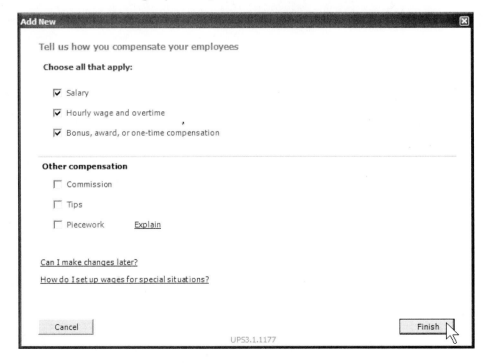

Step 12: Click **Continue** when the *Compensation List* window
appears.

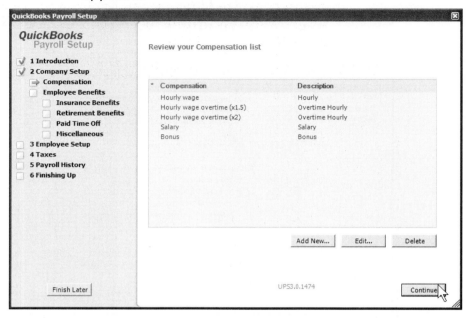

Step 13: Click **Continue** when the *Set up Employee Benefits*
window appears.

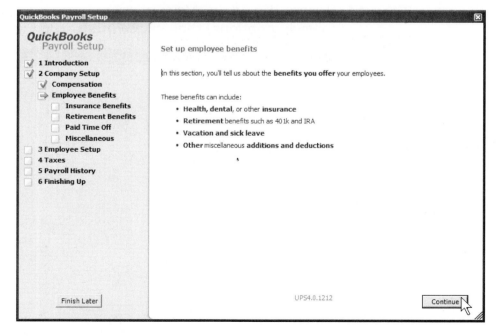

Step 14: If you needed to set up insurance benefits, you would select the appropriate items on this screen. Since you are not providing insurance benefits to your employee, select: **My company does not provide insurance benefits**. Click **Finish**.

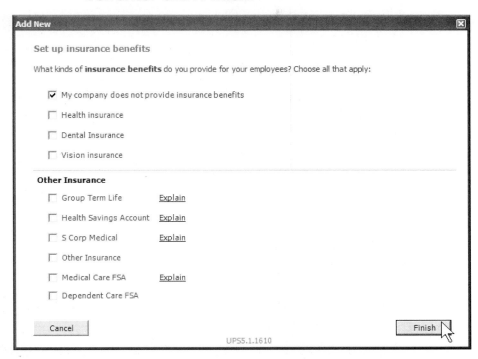

Step 15: Click **Continue** when the *Review your Insurance Benefits* window appears.

Step 16: If your payroll included retirement plan deductions, you would indicate those items on the following screen. Since your company does not, select: **My company does not provide retirement benefits**. Click **Finish**.

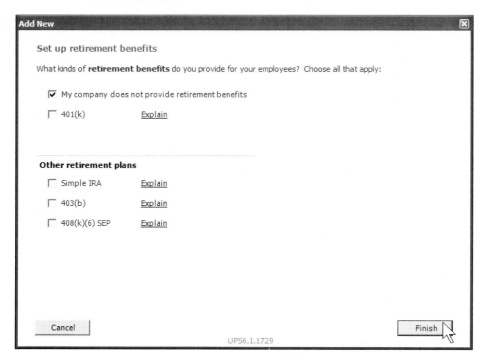

Step 17: Click **Continue** when the *Review your Retirement Benefits List* window appears.

Step 18: When the *Set up Paid Time Off* window appears, select: **My employees do not get paid time off**. Click **Finish**.

Step 19: Click **Continue** when the *Review Your Paid Time Off List* window **appears.**

Step 20: When the *Set Up Additions and Deductions* window appears, select: **Donation to charity**. Click **Finish**.

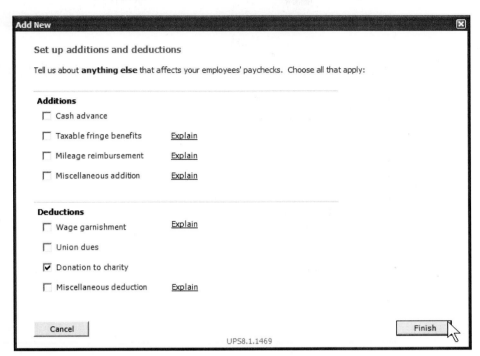

Step 21: Click **Continue** when the *Review Your Additions and Deductions List* window appears.

Step 22: Click **Continue** when the *Set up Employees* window appears.

Step 23: When the *New Employee* window appears, enter the following information for Wil Miles.

Step 24: Enter Wil Miles hiring information as shown below. Click **Next**.

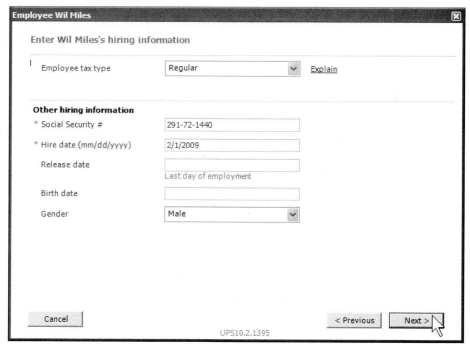

Step 25: Enter Wil Miles compensation information as shown below. Click **Next**.

Employee Wil Miles

Tell us about wages and compensation for **Wil Miles**

Pay frequency | Every other week (Biweekly)

What regular compensation does Wil Miles receive?
- ○ Employee is paid hourly
- ● **Employee is paid on salary**
- ○ Employee does not have any base compensation

Salary amount | 25,000.00 | Per | Year

	Regular wages	Amount	Description
☐	Hourly wage overtime (x1.5)		$ per hour
☐	Hourly wage overtime (x2)		$ per hour
☐	Bonus		default amount

One of the ways I pay this employee isn't on this list. What should I do?

Cancel   < Previous   Next >

UPS10.3.1174

Step 26: When the *Tell Us About Benefits for Wil Miles* window appears, enter the information as shown below. Click **Next**.

Employee Wil Miles

Tell us about benefits for **Wil Miles**

Select items and specify the amount **per paycheck** . Then enter the annual maximum amount.

#	Use	Item	Description	Amount	Annual Limit
1	✔	Charity Donation		$10.00	

One of the ways I compensate this employee isn't on this list. What should I do?

Cancel   < Previous   Next >

UPS10.4.1581

Step 27: When the Wil Miles Direct Deposit window appears, leave it **unchecked**, and click **Next**.

Step 28: When the *Tell Us Where Wil Miles Lives and Works* window appears, enter the information as shown below. Click **Next**.

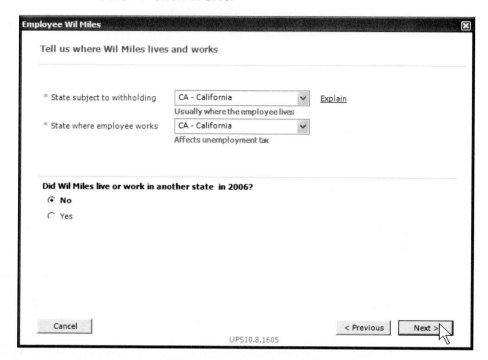

Step 29: Enter Wil Miles federal tax information as shown below. Click **Next**.

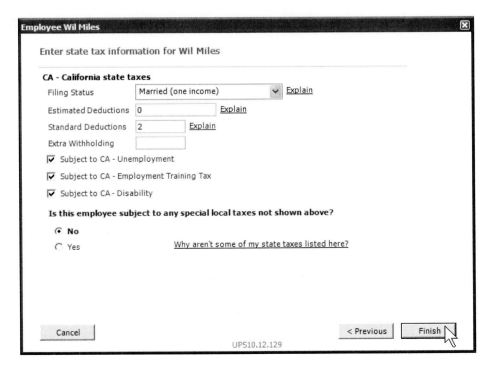

Step 30: Enter Wil Miles state income tax information as shown below. Click **Finish**.

Step 31: Review the Employee List, and then click **Continue**.

Step 32: When the *Set Up Your Payroll Taxes* window appears, click **Continue**.

Step 33: Click **Continue** when the *Review Your Federal Taxes* window appears.

Step 34: When the *Set up State Payroll Taxes* window appears enter the information shown below. Click **Finish**.

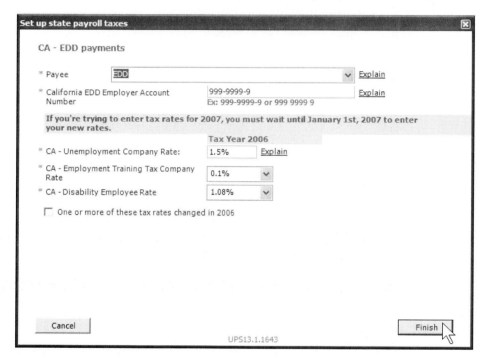

Step 35: Click **Continue** when the *Review your State Taxes* window appears.

Step 36: Click **Continue** when the *Enter Payroll History for the Current Year* window appears.

Step 37: Click **No** when asked if you have issued paychecks in 2006. Click **Continue**.

Step 38: Click **Continue** when the following *Congratulations* window appears.

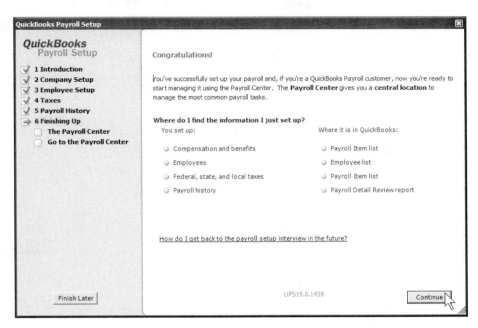

Step 39: Click **Continue** when the following *Payroll Center* window appears.

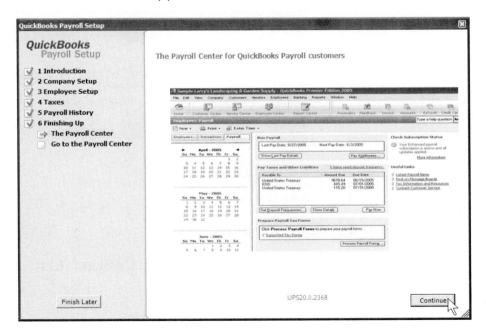

Step 40: Click **Go to the Payroll Center**. The Employee Center should appear.

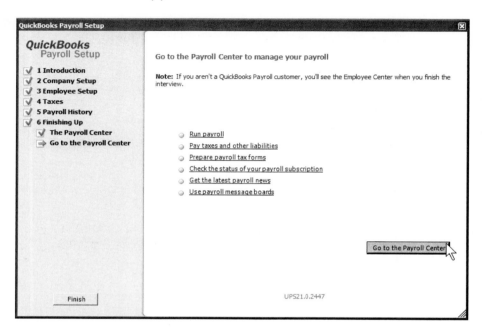

PRINT EMPLOYEE LIST

Print the Employee List as follows:

Step 1: From the Employee Center, click the **Print** button.

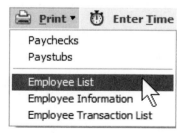

Step 2: Select **Employee List**.

Step 3: **Print** the **Employee Contact List**. Use **Portrait** orientation.

Step 4: **Close** the Employee Center.

PRINT PAYCHECKS

As you may recall from Chapter 6, processing payroll using QuickBooks involves the following steps:

1. Create paychecks for the employees.

2. Print the paychecks.

3. Pay payroll liabilities, such as federal and state income tax withheld.

4. Print payroll reports.

When you create paychecks using QuickBooks, you must deduct (withhold) from employees' pay for the following items:

- Federal income taxes.
- State income taxes.
- Social security (employee portion).
- Medicare (employee portion).

The amounts withheld for taxes are determined by tax tables that change periodically. Intuit offers two different ways for a company to perform payroll calculations:

1. Use a QuickBooks Payroll Service. For more information about QuickBooks Payroll Services, click **Employees** (menu bar), select **Payroll Services**, then select **Learn about Payroll Options**.

2. Manually calculate payroll taxes. You can manually calculate tax withholdings and payroll taxes using IRS Circular E. Then enter the amounts in QuickBooks to process payroll.

In this chapter, you will learn how to enter payroll tax amounts manually.

Wil Miles was hired by Fearless Paint Store on February 1, 2009. He is paid an annual salary of $25,000. Wil will be paid biweekly, receiving a paycheck every two weeks. Therefore, the first pay period ends on February 14th and Wil is paid February 15th.

QuickBooks provides a free trial of the Payroll Tax Service. You can continue to use the latest update to calculate payroll without subscribing to the service until February 15 of the following year. After February 15, the tax tables will not function. If you continue to use the trial version, you will not receive online tax table updates after the 30-day trial period and your tax tables could be incorrect.

The Check Date (payday) is the day the check is prepared; the Pay Period Ends date is the last day the employee works during the pay period.

To create a paycheck for Wil Miles:

Step 1: From the Employee section of the Home page, click the **Pay Employees** icon.

Step 2: If the following window appears, click **No**.

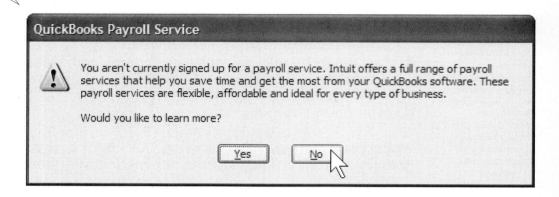

If the following window appears, select: **Pay Employees anyway**.

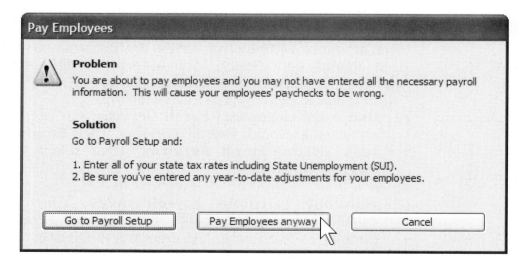

Step 3: When the following *Select Employees to Pay* window appears:

- Select Bank Account: **[your name] Checking**.

- Select: **To be printed**.

- Select: **Enter hours and tax amounts before creating paychecks**.

- Enter Check Date: **02/15/2009**.

- Enter Pay Period Ends: **02/14/2009**.

- Select Employee: **Wil Miles**.

- Click **Create**.

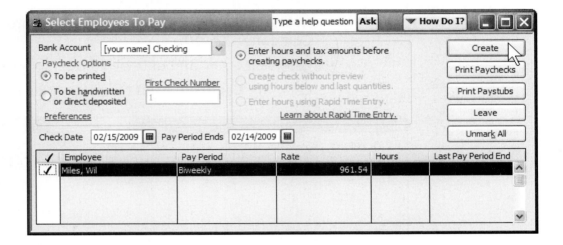

Step 4: When the following *Preview Paycheck* window appears:

- In the *Employee Summary* section, the Salary amount of $961.54 will automatically appear.

- In the *Employee Summary* section, enter Federal Withholding: **75.00**.

- In the *Employee Summary* section, enter Social Security Employee: **60.00**.

- In the *Employee Summary* section, enter Medicare Employee: **14.00**.

- In the *Company Summary* section, enter Social Security Company: **60.00**.

- In the *Company Summary* section, enter Medicare Company: **14.00**.

- Leave all other amounts at $0.00.

- Click the **Create** button to create Wil's paycheck.

When voucher checks are used, paystub information is printed on the voucher. If standard checks are used, print paystubs by clicking **File**, **Print Forms**, **Paystubs**.

Step 5: When the *Select Employees to Pay* window reappears, click **Print Paychecks**.

Step 6: When the *Select Paychecks to Print* window appears, select **Wil Miles**, then click **OK**.

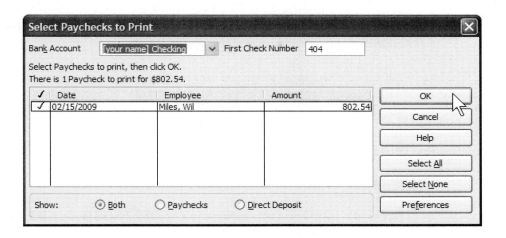

Step 7: Select the following print settings:

- Select **Voucher Checks**.
- Select **Print company name and address**.
- 🖨 Click **Print**.

Step 8: Create and 🖨 **print** paychecks to pay Wil Miles through the end of March 2009.

Check Date	Pay Period
03/01/2009	02/15/2009 – 02/28/2009
03/15/2009	03/01/2009 – 03/14/2009
03/29/2009	03/15/2009 – 03/28/2009

Step 9: Click **Leave** to close the *Select Employee to Pay* window.

QuickBooks records gross pay (the total amount the employee earned) as salaries expense and records the amounts due tax agencies as payroll tax liabilities.

PRINT PAYROLL ENTRIES IN THE JOURNAL

> Notice that Wil Miles' wages are recorded as payroll expense. Withholdings from his paycheck are recorded as payroll liabilities, amounts owed tax agencies.
>
> Payroll taxes that the company must pay, such as the employer share of social security and Medicare, are recorded as payroll expense.

When QuickBooks records paychecks and payroll tax liabilities, it converts the transaction to a journal entry with debits and credits.

To view the payroll entry in the Journal:

Step 1: Click the **Report Center** in the Navigation Bar.

Step 2: Select: **Accountant & Taxes**.

Step 3: Select Report: **Journal**.

Step 4: Select Dates From: **02/01/2009** To: **02/15/2009**.

Step 5: To view only payroll entries, use a filter:

- Click the **Modify Report** button in the upper left corner of the *Reports* window.
- Click the **Filters** tab.
- Choose filter: **Transaction Type**.
- Select Transaction Type: **Paycheck**.
- Click **OK**.

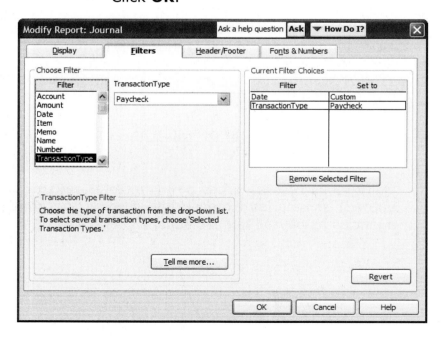

Step 6: 🖶 **Print** the Journal report.

Step 7: **Close** the *Journal* window, and then close the Report Center.

PAY PAYROLL LIABILITIES

Payroll liabilities include amounts Fearless Paint Store owes to outside agencies including:

- Federal income taxes withheld from employee paychecks.
- State income taxes withheld from employee paychecks.
- FICA (Social Security and Medicare), both the employee and the employer portions.
- Unemployment taxes.

Typically, a company deposits payroll withholdings and payroll taxes with a local bank. The local bank then remits the amount to the Internal Revenue Service on behalf of the company.

Fearless Paint Store will pay federal income tax withheld and the employee and employer portions of Social Security and Medicare. Fearless Paint Store will make monthly deposits of these federal taxes by the 10th of the following month.

To pay payroll taxes:

Step 1: Click the **Pay Liabilities** icon in the Employee section of the Home page.

Step 2: When the *Select Date Range for Liabilities* window appears, enter dates from **02/01/2009** through **02/28/2009**. Click **OK**. *Note that QuickBooks calculates payroll liabilities based on check dates rather than the pay period. Accordingly, the March 10 payroll liability check covers obligations arising only from the payroll check dated 02/15/2009.*

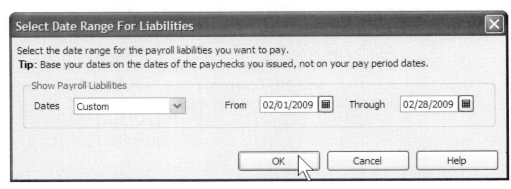

Step 3: When the *Pay Liabilities* window appears:

- Select Checking Account: [your name] **Checking**.
- Select Check Date: **03/10/2009**.
- Check: **To be printed**.
- Select the following amounts to pay:
  - ✓ Federal Withholding
  - ✓ Medicare Company
  - ✓ Medicare Employee
  - ✓ Social Security Company
  - ✓ Social Security Employee
- Select: **Review liability check to enter expenses/penalties**.

Step 4: Click **Create** to view the check to pay the payroll liabilities selected.

Step 5: To 🖨 **print** the check:

- Click the **Print** button at the top of the *Liability Check* window.
- Enter the check number: **408**, then click **OK**.
- Select **Voucher** checks.
- Select **Print company name and address**.
- Click **Print**.

Step 6: Record and 🖨 **print** the check to pay the above payroll liabilities for the pay period **03/01/2009** to **03/31/2009** to be paid on **04/10/2009**. *Note that QuickBooks calculates payroll liabilities based on check dates rather than the pay period. Accordingly, the April 10 payroll liability check covers obligations arising from the payroll checks dated 03/01/2009, 03/15/2009, and 03/29/2009.*

When Fearless Paint Store pays federal payroll taxes, it must file a Form 941 to report the amount of federal income tax, social security, and Medicare for the quarter. QuickBooks tracks the amounts to report on the Form 941.

To ▣ **print** Form 941 (Employer's Quarterly Federal Tax Return) for Fearless Paint Store for the first quarter of 2009:

Step 1: Click the **Process Payroll Forms** icon in the Employees section of the Home page.

Step 2: Select Payroll Form: **Federal Form**.

Step 3: When the *Select Payroll Form* window appears:
- Select: **Quarterly Form 941/Schedule B**.
- Select Quarter Ending: **03/31/2009**. If necessary, press **Tab**.
- Click **OK**.

Step 4: If the message appears that QuickBooks must close all windows, click **OK**.

Step 5: When asked if you need to file a Schedule B, select **No**.

Step 6: Enter the state code for California: **CA**. Click **Next**.

Step 7: On Form 941 Line 1, enter number of employees: **1**.

Step 8: On Form 941, Line 13 Overpayment, select: **Apply to next return**.

Step 9: Click **Check for errors**. If QuickBooks tells you there are no errors, then click **Print forms** to print Form 941.

Step 10: Select: **Tax form(s) and filing instructions**. Click **Print**.

Step 11: Click **Save & Close** to close the *Form 941* window. Read **Next Steps** if any, then click **OK** to close the *Next Steps* window.

Form 941 is filed with the IRS to report the amount of federal income tax, Medicare and social security associated with the company's payroll for the first quarter of the year. Form 941 for the first quarter of the year must be filed by April 30.

PRINT PAYROLL REPORTS

QuickBooks provides payroll reports that summarize amounts paid to employees and amounts paid in payroll taxes. Payroll reports can be accessed using the Report Center.

▣ **Print** the Payroll Summary report:

Step 1: Click the **Report Center** icon in the Navigation Bar.

Step 2: Select: **Employees & Payroll**.

Step 3: Select Report: **Payroll Summary**.

Step 4: Select Dates From: **02/01/2009** To: **02/28/2009**.

Step 5: ▣ **Print** the Payroll Summary report using **Portrait** orientation.

SAVE CHAPTER 11

Save Chapter 11 as a portable QuickBooks file to the location specified by your instructor.

Step 1: If necessary, insert a removable disk.

Step 2: From the menu bar, click **File | Portable Company File | Create File**.

Step 3: When the *Close and Reopen* window appears, click **OK**.

Step 4: When the following *Create Portable Company File* window appears, enter the filename: **[your name] Chapter 11** and the appropriate location. Then click **Save**.

Step 5: Click **OK** after the portable file has been created successfully.

Step 6: Close the company file by clicking **File** (Menu), **Close Company**.

ASSIGNMENTS

> **NOTE: See the Quick Reference Guide in Part 3 for step-by-step instructions to frequently used tasks.**

EXERCISE 11.1: WEB QUEST

Clayton Café is a trendy, new restaurant serving rich, black coffee, smelly, but tasty cheeses, caper berries, and cheap, but interesting wines including Chilean, Australian, Argentine, and Spanish varieties. The café is known for its live, progressive folk music with different performers nightly. Three of their star performers are David Surkamp, Sara Surkamp, and Saylor Surkamp.

Mr. Bill Yavitz, the owner of Clayton Café, has asked you to keep his accounting records using QuickBooks. Since the Surkamps are regular performers, he is not certain if they are considered employees or independent contractors for tax purposes. Also, Mr. Bill has two servers, Pebbles Lizzardo and Millie Sonneshine. Since the servers are considered employees, he assumes that the Surkamps should be considered employees also, but he is seeking your advice on this matter.

Step 1: Use QuickBooks Decision Tool to determine whether the Surkamps would be considered employees or independent contractors for tax purposes. (From the Company menu, select **Planning & Budgeting | Decision Tools | Employee, Contractor or Temp?**.)

Step 2: Go to the www.irs.gov web site. Research the requirements for employee versus independent contractor status.

Step 3: Prepare and 🖶 **print** an email to Mr. Bill summarizing your recommendation regarding employee versus independent contractor status for the three Surkamps. Include support for your recommendation and which tax forms Mr. Bill should provide the Surkamps (W-2 or 1099).

EXERCISE 11.2: WEB QUEST

Learn more about filing payroll Forms 940 and 941 by visiting the IRS web site.

Step 1: Go to the www.irs.gov web site.

Step 2: 🖶 **Print** instructions for preparing and filing Form 940.

Step 3: 🖶 **Print** instructions for preparing and filing Form 941.

Step 4: On Form 941, **circle** the address to which Rock Castle Construction located in California would send payroll taxes.

EXERCISE 11.3: WEB QUEST

Employers must give employees Form W-2 each year summarizing wages and withholdings for tax purposes. In addition, employers must file Form W-3 with the IRS. Form W-3 summarizes the payroll information provided on the W-2 forms.

To learn more about filing Forms W-2 and W-3, visit the IRS web site.

Step 1: Go to www.irs.gov web site.

Step 2: 🖶 **Print** instructions for preparing and filing Form W-2.

Step 3: 🖶 **Print** instructions for preparing and filing Form W-3.

CHAPTER 11 PRINTOUT CHECKLIST
NAME:_____DATE:_____

INSTRUCTIONS:
1. CHECK OFF THE PRINTOUTS YOU HAVE COMPLETED.
2. STAPLE THIS PAGE TO YOUR PRINTOUTS.

☑ *PRINTOUT CHECKLIST – CHAPTER 11*
☐ Deposit Summary
☐ Employee List
☐ Voucher Paychecks
☐ Journal
☐ Payroll Liability Checks
☐ Form 941
☐ Payroll Summary Report

☑ *PRINTOUT CHECKLIST – EXERCISE 11.1*
☐ E-mail to Mr. Bill

☑ *PRINTOUT CHECKLIST – EXERCISE 11.2*
☐ Form 940 and Form 941 Instructions

☑ *PRINTOUT CHECKLIST – EXERCISE 11.3*
☐ Form W-2 and Form W-3 Instructions

COMPANY PROJECT 11.1

PROJECT 11.1:
SCOTT'S MOWERS & MORE: PAYROLL

SCENARIO

Scott's Mowers & More hired Susy N. Bradford as a sales clerk for evenings and weekends. You maintain the payroll records for Scott's Mowers & More and print Susy's payroll checks.

> Project 10.1 must be completed before starting Project 11.1 or use the Instructor backup file for Project 10.1.

TASK 1: OPEN PORTABLE COMPANY FILE

To open the portable company file (.QBM) file, convert the portable file to a regular company file with a .QBW extension as follows:

Step 1:   From the menu bar, click **File | Portable Company File | Open File**.

Step 2:   Identify the filename and location for the portable company file:

- Click the **Browse** button to find the location of the portable company file on the hard drive or removable media.

- Select the file: **[your name] Project 10.1.QBM**.

Step 3: Identify the name and location of the new company file (.QBW) file to use for completing Project 11.1:

- Filename: **[your name] Project 11.1**. The **.QBW** extension should appear automatically based upon your Windows settings.

- Location: **C:\Program Files\Intuit\QuickBooks 2006**. This is the location of the .QBW file on the hard drive of your computer. Click the Browse button to specify another location.

Step 4: Click **Open** to open the portable company file.

Step 5: Click **Cancel** when the *Create a Backup* window appears.

Step 6: If prompted, enter your **User Name** and **Password**, then click **OK**.

Step 7: Click **OK** when the QuickBooks sample company message appears.

Step 8: Change the company name to: **[your name] Project 11.1 Scott's Mowers & More.**

TASK 2: SET UP PAYROLL

Set up QuickBooks Payroll for Scott's Mowers & More by completing the following steps.

Step 1: Enable QuickBooks Payroll for Scott's Mowers & More. (From the Home page, select **Customize Home page and set preferences**, click **Payroll & Employees**, **Company Preferences**, **Full Payroll Features**.)

Step 2: Set up payroll for Scott's Mowers & More using the employee information on the following page.

First Name	Susy
Middle Initial	N.
Last Name	Bradford
SS No.	343-21-6767
Address and Contact:	
Address	513 Ali Drive
City	Bayshore
State	CA
ZIP	94326
Phone	415-555-9876
Payroll Info:	
Hourly Regular Rate	$8.00
Pay Period	Weekly
Hired	03/01/2009
Federal and State Filing Status	Single
Allowances	1
State Tax	CA
Federal ID Number	37-7879146
State ID Number	888-8888-8
State Allowances	1
Subject to CA Training Tax?	No

TASK 3: PRINT EMPLOYEE LIST

🖨 **Print** the Employee List.

TASK 4: PRINT PAYCHECKS

To print paystubs, click:
1. **File**
2. **Print Forms**
3. **Paystubs**

Using the following information, create and 🖨 **print** paychecks for Scott's Mowers & More employee, Susy N. Bradford. Use standard checks and paystubs.

To display the QuickMath Calculator:
1. Place your cursor in the federal withholding field, then press the **=** key.
2. Enter calculations. Use the ***** key to multiply.
3. Press **Enter** to enter the amount into the field.

Check Date	Payroll Period	Hours Worked*
March 5	March 1-3	12
March 12	March 4-10	30
March 19	March 11-17	32
March 26	March 18-24	28
April 2	March 25-31	31

*Enter hours worked in the *Preview Paycheck* window.

Assume the following rates for withholdings:

Federal income tax	20.00%
Social security (employee)	6.20%
Social security (company)	6.20%
Medicare (employee)	1.45%
Medicare (company)	1.45%
State (CA) income tax	5.00%

Note that the wage base limit will not be exceeded for social security.

✓ **Susy Bradford's March 12th paycheck is $161.64.**

TASK 5: PAY PAYROLL LIABILITY

On April 10, pay the payroll tax liability for federal income tax, Social Security, Medicare, and state income tax as of 03/31/2009.

TASK 6: PRINT FORM 941

⌨ **Print** Form 941 for the first quarter of 2009 for Scott's Mowers & More. Using Form 941, determine the following:

1.   Total taxes after adjustment as listed on Form 941: $_____

2.   Total deposits for taxes for the quarter: $_____

3.   Balance due: $_____

4.   The overpayment for the quarter: $_____

TASK 7: SAVE PROJECT 11.1

Save Project 11.1 as a portable QuickBooks file to the location specified by your instructor.

Step 1:   If necessary, insert a removable disk.

Step 2:   From the menu bar, click **File | Portable Company File | Create File**.

Step 3:   When the *Close and Reopen* window appears, click **OK**.

Step 4:   When the following *Create Portable Company File* window appears, enter the filename: **[your name] Project 11.1** and the appropriate location. Then click **Save**.

Step 5: Click **OK** after the portable file has been created successfully.

Step 6: Close the company file by clicking **File** (Menu), **Close Company**.

PROJECT 11.1 PRINTOUT CHECKLIST
NAME:_____DATE:_____

INSTRUCTIONS:
1. CHECK OFF THE PRINTOUTS YOU HAVE COMPLETED.
2. STAPLE THIS PAGE TO YOUR PRINTOUTS.

☑ ***PRINTOUT CHECKLIST – PROJECT 11.1***
☐ Employee List
☐ Paychecks and Paystubs
☐ Payroll Liability Check
☐ Form 941

CHAPTER 12
ADVANCED TOPICS

SCENARIO

During the month of January 2009 you continue to operate your painting service while still managing Fearless Paint Store. You know that you need to budget for the coming year, providing you an opportunity to develop a business plan for the company.

In the new year, several commercial customers have approached you about custom painting for their offices and restaurants. Moreover, you continue to get referrals from your satisfied customers. The new customers want bids and estimates before they award contracts. Also, since some of these new jobs would require months to complete, you want to use progress billing (bill customers as the job progresses) in order to bring in a steady cash flow for your business.

CHAPTER 12
LEARNING OBJECTIVES

In Chapter 12, you will learn the following QuickBooks activities:

INTRODUCTION

This chapter covers some of the more advanced features of QuickBooks software using Fearless Painting Service company files.

OPEN PORTABLE COMPANY FILE

To begin Chapter 12, first start QuickBooks software and then open the portable QuickBooks file for Fearless Painting Service, the company file you created in Chapters 8 and 9.

> **Exercise 9 must be completed before starting Chapter 12 or ask your instructor about using the backup files that accompany the text.**

Step 1: Start QuickBooks by clicking on the **QuickBooks** desktop icon or click **Start**, **Programs**, **QuickBooks**, **QuickBooks Pro 2006**.

Step 2: To open the portable company file (.QBM) file and convert the portable file to a regular company file with a .QBW extension, from the menu bar, click **File | Portable Company File | Open File**.

Step 3: Identify the filename and location for the portable company file:

- Click the **Browse** button to find the location of the portable company file on the hard drive or removable media.

- Select the file: **[your name] Exercise 9.1 to 9.5**. The .QBM may appear automatically based upon your Windows settings, but if it does not appear automatically, do ***not*** type it.

Step 4: Identify the name and location of the new company file (.QBW) file to use for Chapter 12:

- Filename: **[your name] Chapter 12**. The **.QBW** extension should appear automatically based upon your Windows settings. The .QBW identifies this as a QuickBooks working file.

- Location: **C:\Program Files\Intuit\QuickBooks 2006**. This is the location of the .QBW file on the hard drive of your computer.

Step 5:   Click **Open** to open the portable company file.

Step 6:   Click **Cancel** when the *Create a Backup* window appears.

Step 7:   If prompted, enter your **User ID** and **Password**.

Step 8:   Click **OK** when the sample company window appears.

Step 9:   Change the company name to: **[your name] Chapter 12 Fearless Painting Service.** If necessary, change the Checking account title to include your name.

The portable company file (.QBM) should now be converted to a regular company file (Chapter 12.QBW) that can be used to complete the assignments for Chapter 12.

BUDGETS

As Fearless Painting Service enters its second year of operation, planning for future expansion is important to its continued success. You develop the following budget for 2009.

- January sales are expected to be $3,000. Sales are expected to increase by 5% each month thereafter.

- Paint supplies expense is budgeted at $60 per month.

- The van lease will increase to $300 per month. (Use Account No. 6290.)

To prepare budgets for Fearless Painting Service using QuickBooks:

Step 1: From the **Company** menu, select: **Planning & Budgeting | Set Up Budgets**.

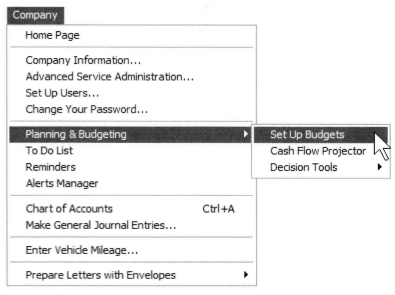

Step 2: On the *Create New Budget* window, select the year: **2009**.

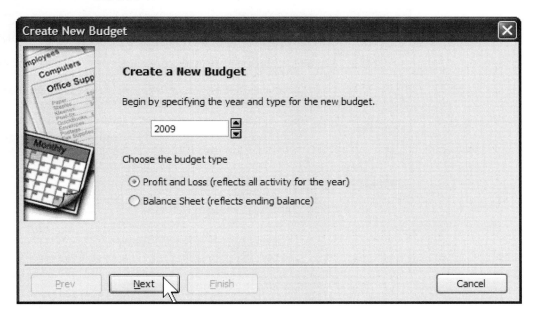

Step 3: Choose the budget type: **Profit and Loss**. Click **Next**.

Step 4: Select **No additional criteria**. Click **Next**.

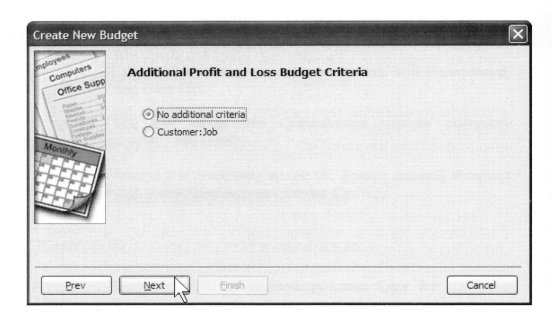

Step 5: Select **Create budget from scratch**. Click **Finish**.

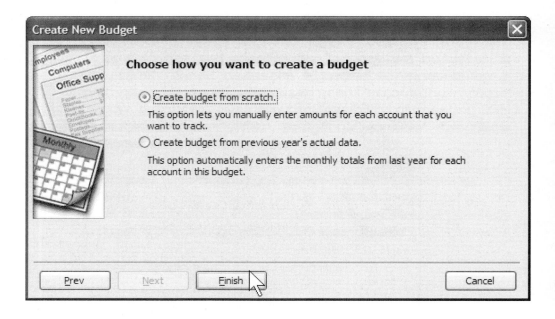

Step 6: When the following *Set Up Budgets* window appears, enter **3000.00** for 4050 Sales account in the Jan09 column.

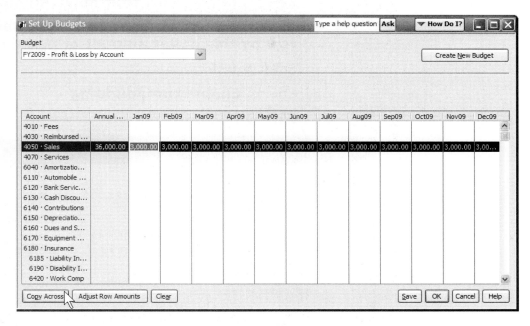

Step 7: Click the **Copy Across** button.

Step 8: Click the **Adjust Row Amounts** button.

Step 9: When the following *Adjust Row Amounts* window appears:

- Select Start at: **Currently selected month**.
- Select: **Increase each monthly amount in this row by this dollar amount or percentage**.
- Enter **5.0%**.
- Check: **Enable compounding**.
- Click **OK**.

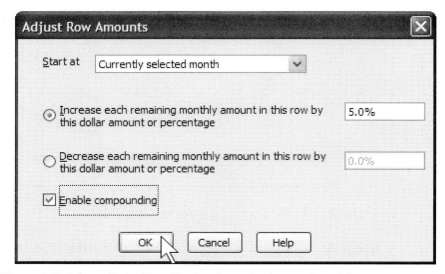

Step 10: The *Set Up Budgets* window should now appear as follows.

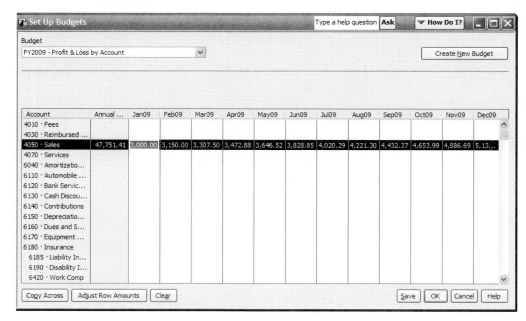

TIP: Use the **Copy Across** button to fill in the budget amounts for each month.

Step 11: Enter budget amounts for paint supplies expense ($60 per month) and then equipment rental expense for the van ($300 per month).

Step 12: Click **OK** to close the *Set Up Budgets* window.

🖨 **Print** the budgets you have created for Fearless Painting Service:

Step 1: From the Report Center, select: **Budgets**.

Step 2: Select Report: **Budget Overview**.

Step 3: Select **FY2009 – Profit and Loss by Account**. Click **Next**.

Step 4: Select Report Layout: **Account by Month**. Click **Next**, then click **Finish**.

Step 5: Select Dates From: **01/01/2009** To: **12/31/2009**.

Step 6: 🖨 **Print** the Budget Overview report using **Landscape** orientation.

Step 7: **Close** the *Budget Overview* window.

ESTIMATES

NOTE: If the Estimates icon does not appear on your screen, turn on the Estimates preference by clicking **Company**, **Preferences** icon, **Jobs and Estimates** icon, and **Company Preference** tab. Select **Yes** to indicate you create estimates.

Often customers ask for a bid or estimate of job cost before awarding a contract. Fearless Painting Service needs to estimate job costs that are accurate in order not to *overbid* and lose the job or *underbid* and lose money on the job.

To prepare a job cost estimate for Fearless Painting Service:

Step 1: Click the **Estimates** icon in the Customer section of the Home page.

Step 2: When the *Create Estimates* window appears, add a new customer as follows:

- From the drop-down customer list, select: **<Add New>**.
- Enter Customer Name: **Grandprey Cafe**.
- Enter Address: **10 Broadway Blvd., Bayshore, CA 94326**.
- Enter Contact: **Milton**.
- Click the **Job Info** tab, then enter Job Status: **Pending**.
- Click **OK** to close the *New Customer* window.

Step 3: Next, enter estimate information in the *Create Estimates* window:

- Select Template: **Custom Estimate**.
- Select Date: **01/05/2009**.
- Enter Item: **Labor: Exterior Painting**.
- Enter Quantity **40**.
- Enter a second item: **Labor: Interior Painting**.
- Enter Quantity: **65**.

> The estimate can be given to a customer when bidding on a job.

Step 4: 🖨 **Print** the estimate, then click **Save & Close** to close the *Create Estimates* window.

PROGRESS BILLING

When undertaking a job that lasts a long period of time, a business often does not want to wait until the job is completed to receive payment for its work. The business often incurs expenses in performing the job that must be paid before the business receives payment from customers. This can create a cash flow problem. One solution to this problem is progress billing.

Progress billing permits a business to bill customers as the job progresses. Thus, the business receives partial payments from the customer before the project is completed.

After you give Grandprey Cafe your estimate of the paint job cost, Milton awards you the contract. The job will last about three weeks. However, instead of waiting three weeks to bill Milton, you bill Milton every week so that you will have cash to pay your bills.

To use progress billing in QuickBooks, first you must turn on the preference for progress invoicing.

To select the preference for progress invoicing:

Step 1: From the Home page, click **Customize Home page and set preferences**.

Step 2: When the following *Preferences* window appears, click the **Jobs & Estimates** icon on the left scrollbar.

Step 3: Click the **Company Preferences** tab.

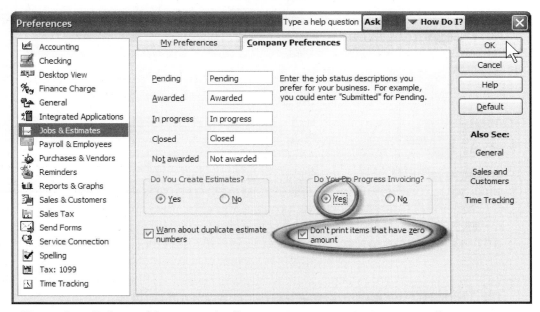

Step 4: Select **Yes** to indicate you want to use Progress Invoicing.

Step 5: ✓ Check **Don't print items that have zero amount**.

Step 6:   Click **OK** to save the Progress Invoicing preference and close the *Preferences* window. If asked if you would like to set a closing date password, click **No**.

After selecting the Progress Invoicing preference, the Progress Invoice template is now available on the *Create Invoices* window.

To create a Progress Invoice:

Step 1:   Click the **Invoices** icon in the Customer section of the Home page.

Step 2:   When the *Create Invoices* window appears, select Customer: **Grandprey Cafe**.

Step 3:   Select the **Grandprey Cafe** estimate to invoice, then click **OK**.

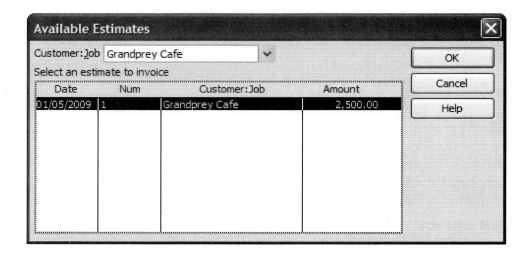

Step 4: When the *Create Progress Invoice Based on Estimate* window appears:

- Select: **Create invoice for the entire estimate (100%)**.

- Click **OK**.

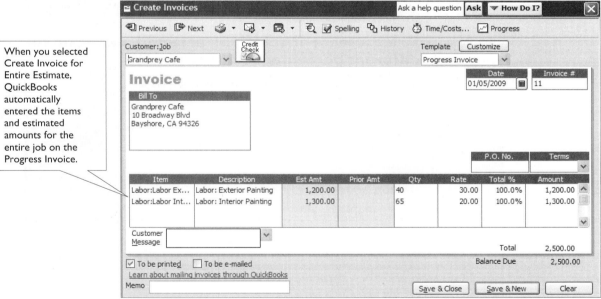

Step 5: When the following *Create Invoices* window appears, the Form Template should now be: **Progress Invoice**.

When you selected Create Invoice for Entire Estimate, QuickBooks automatically entered the items and estimated amounts for the entire job on the Progress Invoice.

Step 6: Enter the number of hours actually worked on the Grandprey Cafe job.

- Enter Exterior Painting Labor Quantity: **24**.

- Enter Interior Painting Labor Quantity: **0**.

Notice the Total % column now shows 60% for Exterior Painting Labor, indicating 60% of estimated hours have been worked.

Step 7: 🖨 **Print** the Progress Invoice.

Step 8: Click **Save & Close** to close the *Create Invoices* window. If a message appears that estimates are linked to the invoices, click **Yes** to record changes to the invoice.

The following week you complete the exterior painting for Grandprey Cafe and work 6.5 hours on interior painting.

Create another progress invoice for Grandprey Cafe by completing the following steps.

Step 1: Display the *Create Invoices* window.

Step 2: Select Customer: **Grandprey Cafe**.

Step 3: Select the **Grandprey Cafe** estimate to invoice, then click **OK**.

Step 4: When the following *Create Progress Invoice Based on Estimate* window appears:

- Select **Create invoice for selected items or for different percentages of each item**.
- Click **OK**.

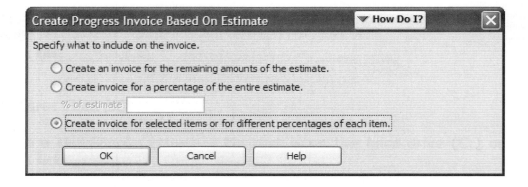

Step 5: When the following *Specify Invoice Amounts for Items on Estimate* window appears:

- ✓ Check: **Show Quantity and Rate**.
- ✓ Check: **Show Percentage**.
- Enter Exterior Painting Quantity: **16**.
- Enter Interior Painting Quantity: **6.5**.
- Click **OK** to record these amounts on the progress invoice.

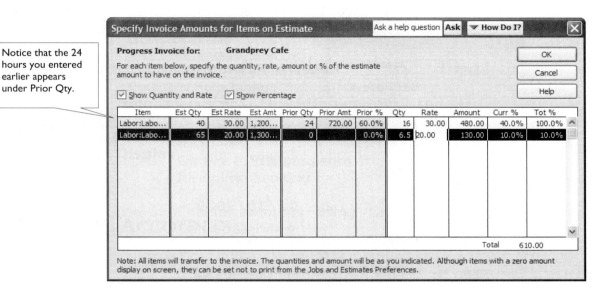

> Notice that the 24 hours you entered earlier appears under Prior Qty.

Specify Invoice Amounts for Items on Estimate   Ask a help question **Ask** ▼ **How Do I?**

Progress Invoice for: **Grandprey Cafe**

For each item below, specify the quantity, rate, amount or % of the estimate amount to have on the invoice.

☑ Show Quantity and Rate   ☑ Show Percentage

Item	Est Qty	Est Rate	Est Amt	Prior Qty	Prior Amt	Prior %	Qty	Rate	Amount	Curr %	Tot %
Labor:Labo...	40	30.00	1,200...	24	720.00	60.0%	16	30.00	480.00	40.0%	100.0%
Labor:Labo...	65	20.00	1,300...	0		0.0%	6.5	20.00	130.00	10.0%	10.0%

Total   610.00

Note: All items will transfer to the invoice. The quantities and amount will be as you indicated. Although items with a zero amount display on screen, they can be set not to print from the Jobs and Estimates Preferences.

Step 6: When the *Create Invoices* window appears, change the date of the Progress Invoice to: **01/12/2009**.

Step 7: 🖶 **Print** the invoice.

✓   ***The invoice total is $610.00.***

Step 8: Click **Save & Close** to record the Progress Invoice and close the *Create Invoices* window.

Customer payments received on Progress Invoices are recorded in the same manner as customer payments for standard invoices (See Chapter 4).

CREDIT CARD SALES

As a convenience to your customers, you agree to accept credit cards as payment for services you provide. Grandprey Cafe would like to make its first payment using a VISA credit card.

In QuickBooks, you record credit card payments in the same manner that you record a payment by check; however, instead of selecting Check as the payment method, you select the type of credit card used.

To record a credit card sale using QuickBooks:

Step 1: Click the **Receive Payments** icon in the Customer section of the Home page.

Step 2: When the *Receive Payments* window appears, select Received From: **Grandprey Cafe**. QuickBooks will automatically display any unpaid invoices for Grandprey Cafe.

> If the specific credit card is not listed on the Payment Method list, select **Add New**, then enter the name of the credit card.

Step 3: Enter the Date: **01/30/2009**.

Step 4: Enter Amount: **720.00**.

Step 5: Select Payment Method: **VISA**.

Step 6: Enter Card No.: **13575757578013**. Enter Exp. Date: **12/2009**.

Step 7: Select outstanding Invoice No. **11**, dated **01/05/2009**.

Step 8: Your *Receive Payments* window should appear as shown below.

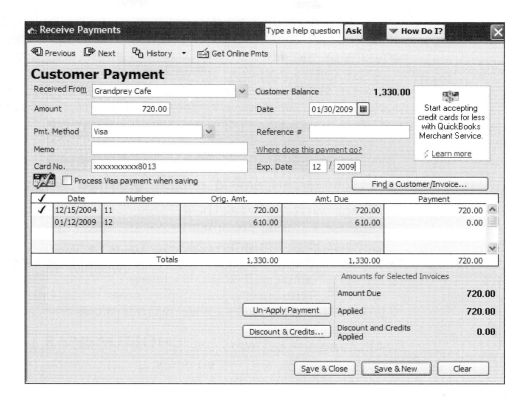

Step 9: Check **Process VISA payment when saving.**

Step 10: Close the *QuickBooks Merchant Account* window. To record the customer payment and close the *Receive Payments* window, click **Save & Close**.

Step 11: Since you are not using the Merchant Account Services, when the credit card payment is deposited at the bank on 01/30/2009, record the deposit just as you would a check or cash deposit.

> Banks will accept bank credit card payments, such as Visa or MasterCard, the same as a cash or check deposit. You can record the credit card payment as a deposit to your checking account.

- Click the **Record Deposits** icon in the Customer section of the Home page.

- Select **Grandprey Cafe credit card payment** for deposit. Click **OK**.

- **Print** the deposit summary.

BAD DEBTS

At the time a credit sale occurs, it is recorded as an increase to sales and an increase to accounts receivable. Occasionally a company is unable to collect a customer payment and must write off the customer's account as a bad debt or uncollectible account. When an account is uncollectible, the account receivable is written off or removed from the accounting records.

There are two different methods that can be used to account for bad debts:

1. **Direct write-off method.** This method records bad debt expense when it becomes apparent that the customer is not going to pay the amount due. If the direct write-off method is used, the customer's uncollectible account receivable is removed and bad debt expense is recorded whenever a specific customer's account becomes uncollectible. The direct write-off method is used for tax purposes.

2. **Allowance method.** The allowance method *estimates* bad debt expense and establishes an allowance or reserve for uncollectible accounts. When using the allowance method, uncollectible accounts expense is estimated in advance of the write-off. The estimate can be calculated as a percentage of sales or as a percentage of accounts receivable. (For example, 2% of credit sales might be estimated to be uncollectible.) This method should be used if uncollectible accounts have a material effect on the company's financial statements used by investors and creditors, and the company must comply with Generally Accepted Accounting Principles (GAAP).

Fearless Painting Service will use the direct write-off method and record the uncollectible accounts expense when an account actually becomes uncollectible.

When Milton paid the bill for $720 for Grandprey Cafe, he tells you that his business has plummeted since a new restaurant opened next door. To your dismay, he tells you his cafe is closing and he will not be able to pay you the remainder that he owes. You decide to write off the Grandprey remaining $610 account balance as uncollectible.

First, create an account for tracking uncollectible accounts expense, and then write off the customer's uncollectible account receivable.

To add a Bad Debt Expense account to the Chart of Accounts for Fearless Painting Service, complete the following steps:

Step 1: Click the **Chart of Accounts** icon in the Company section of the Home page.

Step 2: Add the following account to the chart of accounts.

Account Type	Expense
Account Number	6700
Account Name	Bad Debt Expense
Description	Bad Debt Expense
Tax Line	Sch C: Bad debts from sales/services

Next, record the write-off of the uncollectible account receivable. There are three different methods to record a bad debt using QuickBooks:

1. Make a journal entry to remove the customer's account receivable (credit Accounts Receivable) and debit either Bad Debt Expense or the Allowance for Uncollectible Accounts.

2. Use the *Receive Payments* window (Discount Info button) to record the write-off of the customer's uncollectible account.

3. Use the *Credit Memo* window to record uncollectible accounts.

If you charged sales tax on the transaction, use this method.

To record the write-off of an uncollectible accounts receivable using the *Receive Payments* window, complete the following steps:

Step 1:   Change the preference for automatically calculating payments as follows:

- From the Home page, click **Customize Home page and set preferences.**

- Select the **Sales & Customers** icon in the left scroll bar of the *Preferences* window.

- Click the **Company Preferences** tab.

- **Uncheck** the **Automatically calculate payments** preference.

- Click **OK** to close the *Preferences* window.

Step 2:   Click the **Receive Payments** icon in the Customer section of the Home page.

Step 3:   When the *Receive Payment* window appears, select Received From: **Grandprey Cafe**.

Step 4:   Enter Date: **01/30/2009**.

Step 5:   Leave the Amount as **$0.00**.

Step 6:   Enter Memo: **Write off Uncollectible Account**.

Step 7:   Select the outstanding invoice dated: **01/12/2009**.

Step 8:   Because the Amount field is $0.00, the following warning will appear. Click **OK**.

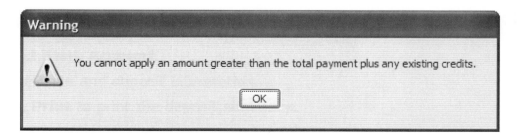

Step 9: Click the **Discounts & Credits** button in the *Receive Payments* window.

Step 10: When the following *Discount and Credits* window appears:

- Enter Amount of Discount: **610.00**.

- Select Discount Account: **6700 Bad Debt Expense**.

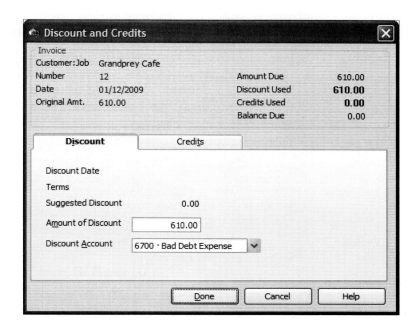

Step 11: Click **Done** to close the *Discount and Credits* window. Click **Save & Close** again to close the *Receive Payments* window.

To view Grandprey Cafe account:

Step 1: Click the **Report Center** in the Navigation Bar.

Step 2: Select: **Customers & Receivables**.

Step 3: Select Report: **Customer Balance Detail**.

Step 4: Select Date: **All**.

Step 5: Customize the Customer Balance Detail report so the Memo field appears on the report:

- Click the **Modify Report** button to display the *Modify Report* window.
- Click the **Display** tab.
- Select Columns: **Memo**.

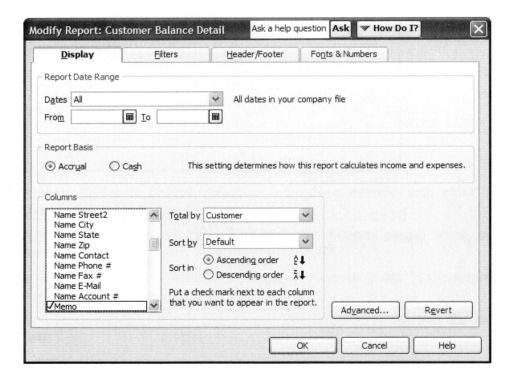

Step 6: Next, create a filter to display only Grandprey Cafe account information.

- Click the **Filters** tab in the *Modify Reports* window.
- Select Filter: **Name**.
- Select Name: **Grandprey Cafe**.
- Click **OK** to close the *Modify Report* window.

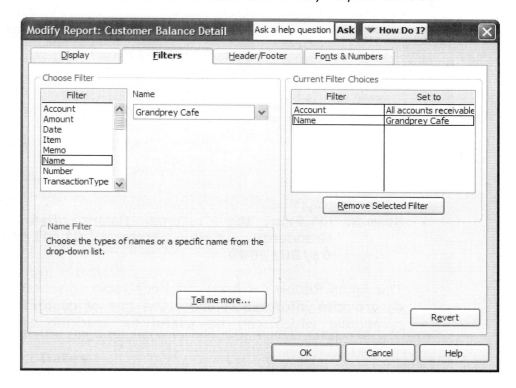

Step 7: The *Customer Balance Detail* window should now appear as shown below. Double-click on the entry for 01/30/2009 to drill down to the *Receive Payments* window that displays the entry to write-off $610 of Grandprey account. **Close** the *Receive Payments* window.

The write-off on 01/30/2009 reduced the account receivable balance by $610.

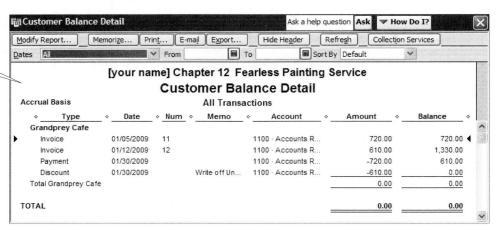

Step 8: 🖨 **Print** the *Customer Balance Detail* report for Grandprey Cafe From: **01/01/2009** To: **01/30/2009**.

The Aging Report for Accounts Receivable (discussed in Chapter 4) provides information about the age of customers' accounts receivable which can be useful for tracking and managing collections.

To reduce uncollectible customer accounts, some companies adopt a policy that requires customers to make a deposit or advance payment before beginning work on a project. In addition, companies often evaluate the creditworthiness of customers before extending credit.

MEMORIZED REPORTS

On March 1, 2009, a potential buyer contacts you, expressing an interest in purchasing your painting service business. The potential buyer offers to purchase your business for a price equal to five times the operating income of the business.

The buyer asks for a copy of the prior year financial statements for his accountant to review.

- Profit & Loss (P&L)
- Balance Sheet
- Statement of Cash Flows

When you prepare the reports, you create memorized reports for future use. To memorize a report, first create the report and then use the memorize feature of QuickBooks.

To create a memorized Profit & Loss report for Fearless Painting Service:

Step 1: Click the **Report Center** in the Navigation Bar.

Step 2: Select: **Company & Financial**.

Step 3: Select Report: **Profit & Loss Standard**.

Step 4: Select Date: From: **01/01/2008** To: **12/31/2008**.

✓ *Income for Fearless Painting Service was $31,285. Therefore, the purchase price of the business would be $156,425 (five times income of $31,285).*

Step 5: To memorize the report:

- Click the **Memorize** button at the top of *the Profit and Loss* window.

- When the following *Memorize Report* window appears, enter Memorized Report Name: **Profit & Loss**. Click **OK**.

Step 6: **Close** the *Profit & Loss* window.

Step 7: To use a memorized report:

- Click **Reports** (menu).

- Click **Memorized Reports**.

- Click **Memorized Report List**.

- When the following *Memorized Report List* window appears, double-click on **Profit & Loss** to display the Profit & Loss report.

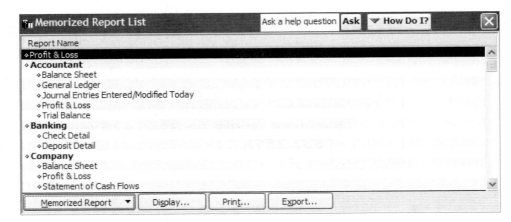

Step 8: Print the Profit & Loss statement.

Step 9: Leave the *Profit & Loss* window open to export the report.

EXPORT REPORTS

In Chapter 7, you learned how to export reports to Excel spreadsheet software. Now, you will export to Excel the Profit & Loss statement you just created.

To export the Profit & Loss statement to Excel:

Step 1: Click the **Export** button at the top of the *Profit and Loss* report window.

Step 2: When the *Export Report* window appears, select Export QuickBooks report to: **a new Excel workbook**.

Step 3: Click **Export** to export the Profit & Loss statement to an Excel spreadsheet.

Step 4: Save the Excel spreadsheet as follows:
- In Excel, click **File** on the menu bar.
- Select **Save As**.
- Select the drive (A drive, C drive, or USB drive).
- Enter the filename: **Profit & Loss**.
- Click **Save** to save the Profit & Loss Report to a disk as an Excel spreadsheet file.

Step 5: **Close** the Excel software by clicking the ⊠ in the upper right corner of the *Excel* window.

Step 6: **Close** the QuickBooks *Profit & Loss Report* window.

In addition to exporting reports to Excel from the *Reports* window, QuickBooks can save reports as a file to a disk. QuickBooks permits you to select from the following file formats:

- **ASCII text file**. After saving as a text file, the file can be used with word processing software.
- **Comma delimited file.** Comma delimited files can be used with word processing software or database software.

- **Tab delimited file.** Tab delimited files can be used with word processing or database software, such as Microsoft® Access®.

Next, you will create a balance sheet for Fearless Painting Service and then save the balance sheet as an ASCII text file.

Step 1: Create and memorize a balance sheet for Fearless Painting Service at December 31, 2008.

Step 2: Save the balance sheet as an ASCII text file to a disk.

- Click the **Print** button near the top of *the Balance Sheet* window.

- When the *Print Reports* window appears, select Print to: **File**.

- Select File Format: **ASCII text file**.

- Click **Print** to save the text file on your floppy disk, specifying the filename: **Balance Sheet**.

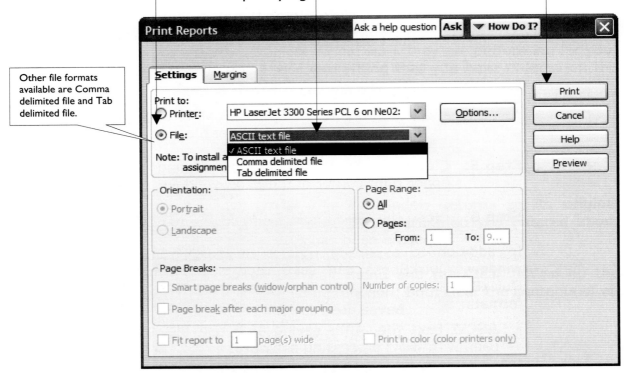

Other file formats available are Comma delimited file and Tab delimited file.

Step 3: Create and memorize a statement of cash flows for Fearless Painting Service for the year 2008. Export the report to Excel as follows:

In QuickBooks Pro 2006, you can also E-mail reports. Click the **E-mail** button at the top of the Report window.

- With the *Statement of Cash Flows* window still open, click the **Export** button at the top of the report window.

- Select **a new Excel workbook**, then click **Export** to export the report to Excel software.

- **Close** the Excel software without saving the changes, then **close** the *Statement of Cash Flows* window.

Step 4: Based on the financial statement results for Fearless Painting Service, decide whether to sell the painting service business.

Sell painting service?	Yes	No
If you sell, the selling price you will accept:	$_____	
Reason(s) for decision:		

AUDIT TRAIL

The Audit Trail feature of QuickBooks permits you to track all changes (additions, modifications, and deletions) made to your QuickBooks records. This feature is especially important in tracking unauthorized changes to accounting records.

The Audit Trail report consists of two sections:

1. One section of the audit trail report shows all transactions that are currently active.

2. A second section of the report lists all deleted transactions.

> The employee might also try to write off the customer's account as uncollectible in order to ensure the customer does not receive another bill.

To illustrate how an accounting clerk, Ima M. Bezler, might attempt to embezzle funds, assume Ima pockets a customer's cash payment and deletes any record of the customer's bill from QuickBooks.

To test the audit trail, first record a customer invoice to Katrina Beneficio for $80.

Step 1: Using the *Create Invoices* window, on **02/01/2009** record **2** hours of **mural painting** on the **Katrina Beneficio Kitchen job**. **Print** the invoice.

Step 2: On 02/02/2009, Katrina Beneficio pays her bill in cash. If Ima decides to keep the cash and delete the invoice (so that Beneficio would not receive another bill), the audit trail maintains a record of the deleted invoice.

To delete the invoice on **02/02/2009**, open the Beneficio invoice for $80, click **Edit** (menu), then select **Delete Invoice**.

The audit trail report lists the original transaction and all changes made later. The audit trail report will list the above change that was made to delete the customer's invoice.

Print an audit trail report:

Step 1: Click the **Report Center** in the Navigation Bar.

Step 2: Select: **Accountant & Taxes**.

Step 3: Select Report: **Audit Trail**.

Step 4: Select Date: From: **01/01/2009** To: **02/02/2009**.

Step 5: **Print** the Audit Trail Report.

Step 6: 🖉 **Circle** the record of the deleted invoice dated 02/01/2009.

The audit trail report is especially useful if you have more than one user for QuickBooks. This report permits you to determine which user made which changes. The audit trail should usually be turned on if someone other than the owner of the business has access to the QuickBooks company accounting data.

> **IMPORTANT!** Access to the audit trail should be restricted to only the QuickBooks Administrator.

The audit trail feature improves internal control by tracking unauthorized changes to accounting records. The owner (or manager) should periodically review the audit trail for discrepancies or unauthorized changes.

The audit trail feature requires more storage for larger files because both original transactions and changed transactions are saved. In addition, the audit trail feature may slow processing time.

To facilitate tracking of changes made by users, export the audit trail report to Excel using the Autofilter feature:

Step 1: With the *Audit Trail* window open, click the **Export** button at the top of the report window.

Step 2: Select: **a new Excel workbook**.

Step 3: Click the **Advanced** tab on the *Export Report* window.

Step 4: ✓ Check **Auto Filtering**, then click **Export** to close the *Export Report* window and export the report to Excel.

> Use the Auto Filter to show all items recorded by a specific user.

Step 5: The Audit Trail report is exported to Excel with the Auto Filter feature. Each column heading is a drop-down list to use for filtering. Select a filter of your choice from one of the drop-down lists.

Step 6: **Close** Excel software without saving your changes.

Step 7: **Close** the *Audit Trail* window.

ACCOUNTANT'S REVIEW COPY

If you use an accountant to make adjustments for you, QuickBooks can create a copy of your company data files for your accountant to use (Accountant's Review Copy). The accountant can make adjustments and changes to the Accountant's Review Copy. Then you can merge the Accountant's Review Copy with your original company data. This permits you to continue using QuickBooks to record transactions at the same time your accountant reviews and makes changes to your records.

To create an accountant's review copy of Fearless Painting Service:

Step 1: Insert a removable disk.

Step 2: Click **File** on the Menu Bar.

Step 3: Select **Accountant's Review**, then select **Create Accountant's Copy**....

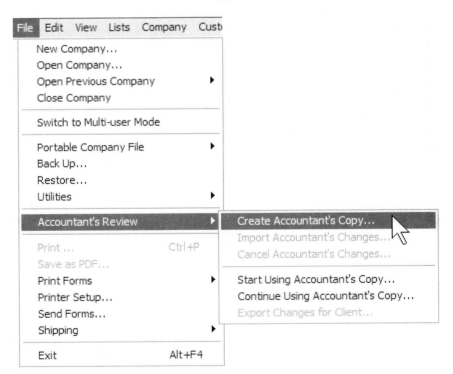

Step 4: When the message appears that QuickBooks must close all windows to prepare an accountant's copy, click **OK**.

Step 5: When the following window appears:

- Select Save in: **QuickBooks 2006**.
- Enter Filename: **[your name] Chapter 12**.
- Select Save as Type: **Accountant Transfer File (*.QBX)**.
- Click **Save**.

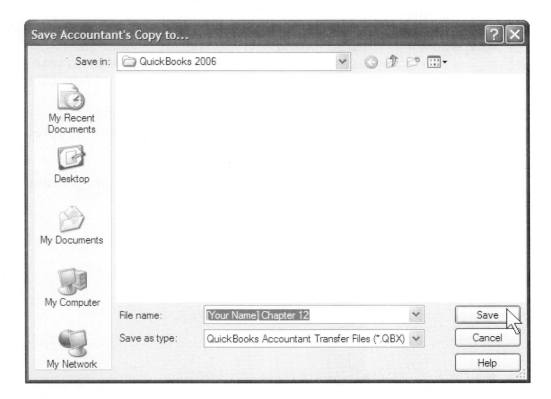

QuickBooks will create a copy of your QuickBooks company file for your accountant's temporary use. After the accountant has made necessary adjustments to the accountant's review copy, the accountant's copy is then merged with your QuickBooks company data file, incorporating the accountant's changes into your company's records.

SAVE CHAPTER 12

Save Chapter 12 as a portable QuickBooks file to the location specified by your instructor.

Step 1: If necessary, insert a removable disk.

Step 2: From the menu bar, click **File | Portable Company File | Create File**.

Step 3: When the *Close and Reopen* window appears, click **OK**.

Step 4: When the following *Create Portable Company File* window appears, enter the filename: **[your name] Chapter 12** and the appropriate location. Then click **Save**.

Step 5: Click **OK** after the portable file has been created successfully.

Step 6: Close the company file by clicking **File** (Menu), **Close Company**.

ASSIGNMENTS

> **NOTE: See the Quick Reference Guide in Part 3 for step-by-step instructions to frequently used tasks.**

EXERCISE 12.1:
QUICKBOOKS PREMIER REMOTE ACCESS

This feature is available with the QuickBooks Premier version. QuickBooks Remote Access permits you to access your QuickBooks company data from remote locations.

Step 1: If you have QuickBooks Premier, from the **File** menu, select **Utilities | Remote Access**. If you have QuickBooks Pro software, use the Help index feature to search for Remote Access.

Step 2: Read about remote access. Summarize how remote access might be useful to a small business.

EXERCISE 12.2: WEB QUEST ASSIGNMENT

Not ready to file your tax return by April 15? File for a tax extension and postpone filing your tax return until mid August. File Form 4868 by April 15 and send a check for an estimate of the tax you owe to avoid penalties.

To learn more about filing for a tax extension:

Step 1: Learn more about filing for a tax extension at the IRS web site: www.irs.gov.

Step 2: 🖶 **Print** Form 4868 and instructions for filing a tax extension for a personal 1040 return and Schedule C.

CHAPTER 12 PRINTOUT CHECKLIST
NAME:_____DATE:_____

INSTRUCTIONS:
1. **CHECK OFF THE PRINTOUTS YOU HAVE COMPLETED.**
2. **STAPLE THIS PAGE TO YOUR PRINTOUTS.**

☑ ***PRINTOUT CHECKLIST – CHAPTER 12***
☐ Profit and Loss Budget Overview
☐ Estimate
☐ Invoice Nos. 11 and 12
☐ Deposit Summary
☐ Customer Balance Detail
☐ Profit and Loss Statement
☐ Invoice No. 13
☐ Audit Trail Report

☑ ***PRINTOUT CHECKLIST – EXERCISE 12.1***
☐ QuickBooks Remote Access

☑ ***PRINTOUT CHECKLIST – EXERCISE 12.2***
☐ IRS Form 4868 and Instructions

COMPANY PROJECT 12.1

PROJECT 12.1:
NEW BEGINNINGS LAWN CARE REPORTS

SCENARIO

New Beginnings Lawn Care needs to prepare a budget for 2009.

> Project 12.1 is a continuation of Project 9.1. Project 9.1 must be completed before starting Project 12.1.

TASK 1: OPEN PORTABLE COMPANY FILE

To open the portable company file (.QBM) file, convert the portable file to a regular company file with a .QBW extension as follows:

Step 1: From the menu bar, click **File | Portable Company File | Open File**.

Step 2: Identify the filename and location for the portable company file:

- Click the **Browse** button to find the location of the portable company file on the hard drive or removable media.

- Select the file: **[your name] Project 9.1.QBM**.

Step 3: Identify the name and location of the new company file (.QBW) file to use for completing Project 12.1:

- Filename: **[your name] Project 12.1**. The **.QBW** extension should appear automatically based upon your Windows settings.

- Location: **C:\Program Files\Intuit\QuickBooks 2006**. This is the location of the .QBW file on the hard drive of your computer. Click the Browse button to specify another location.

Step 4: Click **Open** to open the portable company file.

Step 5: Click **Cancel** when the *Create a Backup* window appears.

Step 6: If prompted, enter your **User Name** and **Password**, then click **OK**.

Step 7: Click **OK** when the QuickBooks sample company message appears.

Step 8: Change the company name to: **[your name] Project 12.1 New Beginnings Lawn Care.**

TASK 2: BUDGET, EXPORT TO EXCEL

Prepare a budget for New Beginnings Lawn Care for the year 2009.

Step 1: Prepare a Profit & Loss Budget Overview for New Beginnings Lawn Care for the year 2009 using the following information:

- January sales are expected to be $800. Sales are expected to increase by 2 percent each month.

- Gasoline and supplies for January are budgeted at $60. These costs are expected to increase by 1 percent each month.

Step 2: Memorize the P&L Budget Overview for New Beginnings Lawn Care for the year 2009.

Step 3: **Export** the P&L Budget Overview to Excel software.

Step 4: **Print** the P&L Budget Overview for New Beginnings Lawn Care for the year 2009 from Excel.

TASK 3: MEMORIZE REPORTS, EXPORT TO EXCEL

Prepare the following reports for New Beginnings Lawn Care for the year 2008.

▤ Profit and Loss, Standard

▤ Balance Sheet, Standard

▤ Statement of Cash Flows

Step 1: Memorize each report.

Step 2: 🖶 **Print** the reports.

Step 3: **Export** the reports to Excel software.

TASK 4: SAVE PROJECT 12.1

Save Project 12.1 as a portable QuickBooks file to the location specified by your instructor.

Step 1: If necessary, insert a removable disk.

Step 2: From the menu bar, click **File | Portable Company File | Create File**.

Step 3: When the *Close and Reopen* window appears, click **OK**.

Step 4: When the following *Create Portable Company File* window appears, enter the filename: **[your name] Project 12.1** and the appropriate location. Then click **Save**.

Step 5: Click **OK** after the portable file has been created successfully.

Step 6: Close the company file by clicking **File** (Menu), **Close Company**.

PROJECT 12.1 PRINTOUT CHECKLIST

NAME: _____ DATE: _____

INSTRUCTIONS:
1. *CHECK OFF THE PRINTOUTS YOU HAVE COMPLETED.*
2. *STAPLE THIS PAGE TO YOUR PRINTOUTS.*

- ☑ *PRINTOUT CHECKLIST – PROJECT 12.1*
- ☐ Budget
- ☐ Profit & Loss, Standard
- ☐ Balance Sheet, Standard
- ☐ Statement of Cash Flows

PART 3
QUICK REFERENCE GUIDE

The Quick Reference Guide contains step-by-step instructions for commonly used QuickBooks tasks.

CHART OF ACCOUNTS

CUSTOMER TRANSACTIONS

VENDOR TRANSACTIONS

EMPLOYEE TRANSACTIONS

BANKING TRANSACTIONS

ENTRIES

REPORTS

MICROSOFT OFFICE AND QUICKBOOKS

CORRECTING ERRORS

QUICKBOOKS SOFTWARE

INSTALL QUICKBOOKS SOFTWARE

To install QuickBooks software, follow the directions that accompany the software.

DISPLAY QUICKBOOKS PRODUCT INFORMATION

1. With the company file open, hold down the **Crtl** key and the **1** key at the same time to display the *Product Information* window.
2. The Product field at the top of the window lists the version (QuickBooks Pro Version 2006) and the maintenance release (e.g., R3P).
3. Click **OK** to close the *Product Information* window.

UPDATE QUICKBOOKS SOFTWARE

1. Back up your company file. (From the **File** menu, select **Back Up**.)
2. Establish your Internet connection.
3. From the **Help** menu, select **Update QuickBooks**.
4. Click the **Options** tab.
5. If you would like QuickBooks to automatically update each time you connect to the Internet, select **Yes** for Automatic Update.
6. To download an update, click the **Update Now** tab. Click the **Get Updates** button. When asked if you want to update QuickBooks, click **Yes**.

SINGLE-USER AND MULTI-USER MODES

1. If you are in multi-user mode, to switch to single-user mode, from the **File** menu, select **Switch to Single-User Mode**. Click **OK**.
2. If you are in single-user mode, to switch to multi-user mode, from the **File** menu, select **Switch to Multi-User Mode**. Click **OK**.

3. To set multi-user as the default mode for a specific company file, from the **File** menu, select **Open Company**. When the *Open A Company* window appears, in the lower left corner of the window, check: **Open file in multi-user mode**.

COMPANY COMMANDS

START QUICKBOOKS SOFTWARE

1. Click **Start** | **Programs** | **QuickBooks Pro** | **QuickBooks 2006**.

2. If necessary, close the *QuickBooks Learning Center* window to begin using QuickBooks.

SET UP NEW COMPANY

1. Click **File** (menu) | **New Company**.

2. Follow the onscreen instructions to complete the EasyStep Interview to set up a new company. Also see Chapter 8.

SAVE PORTABLE COMPANY FILE (.QBM)

To save a portable QuickBooks company file to the hard drive or removable drive:

1. After starting QuickBooks Software, click **File** (menu) | **Portable Company File** | **Create File**.

2. Enter the company filename and location.

3. Click **Save**.

OPEN PORTABLE COMPANY FILE (.QBM)

To open a QuickBooks company file that is on the hard drive or a removable drive:

1. After starting QuickBooks Software, click **File** (menu) | **Portable Company File** | **Open File**.

2. Select the portable company filename (.QBM) and location to open.

3. Enter the new QuickBooks working filename (.QBW) and location.

4. Click **Open**.

CHANGE COMPANY NAME

1. Click **Company** (menu) | **Company Information.**

2. Enter the new company name.

3. Click **OK**.

BACK UP COMPANY FILE (.QBB)

4. Click **File** (menu) | **Backup.**

5. Select location of backup file and backup filename.

6. Click **Save**.

Also, see Chapter 1.

RESTORE COMPANY FILE (.QBB)

1. Click **File** (menu) | **Restore.**

2. Select location of backup file and backup filename.

3. Select location and name of restored file.

4. Click **OK**.

OPEN COMPANY FILE (.QBW)

To open a QuickBooks company file that is on the hard drive (C:) or that has been restored to the C: drive:

1. After QuickBooks Software is open, click **File** (menu bar) | **Open Company**.

2. Select the company file and location.

3. Click **OK**.

CLOSE QUICKBOOKS COMPANY FILE (.QBW)

1. Click **File** on the menu bar.
2. Click **Close Company**.

EXIT QUICKBOOKS SOFTWARE

1. Click **File** on the menu bar.
2. Click **Exit**.

HELP FEATURE

1. Click **Help** (menu bar) | **QuickBooks Help** | **Index**.
2. Type in the keyword you are seeking.
3. Click **Display**.

CHART OF ACCOUNTS

ENTER NEW ACCOUNTS

1. From the **Company** section of the Home page, click the **Chart of Accounts** icon.
2. **Right-click** to display the popup menu. Select **New**.
3. Enter **Type of Account, Account Number, Name, Description,** and **Tax Line**.
4. Click **Next** to enter another account.
5. Click **OK** to close the *New Account* window.

ENTER BEGINNING BALANCES

1. If the account has a beginning balance, when entering the new account, from the *New Account* (or *Edit Account*) window, enter the **Opening Balance** and the **As Of Date** for the beginning balance.
2. Click **OK**.

PRINT CHART OF ACCOUNTS

1. From the **Report Center**, select: A**ccountant & Taxes** | **Account Listing**.
2. Click **Print**.

CUSTOMER TRANSACTIONS

ENTER CUSTOMER INFORMATION

1. Click the **Customer Center** on the Navigation Bar.
2. Click the **New Customer & Job** button.
3. Enter customer information.
4. Click **Next** to enter another customer or click **OK** to save and close the window.

INVOICE CUSTOMERS

1. From the **Customer** section of the Home page, click the **Invoices** icon.
2. Enter invoice information.
3. Click **Print** to print the invoice.
4. Click **Save & New** to enter another invoice or **Save & Close** to close the window.

RECEIVE CUSTOMER PAYMENTS

1. From the **Customer** section of the Home page, click the **Receive Payments** icon.

2. Enter receipt information.

3. Click **Save & New** to enter another receipt or **Save & Close** to close the window.

DEPOSIT CUSTOMER PAYMENTS

1. From the **Banking** section of the Home page, click the **Record Deposits** icon.

2. Enter deposit information.

3. Click **Save & New** to enter another deposit or **Save & Close** to close the window.

VENDOR TRANSACTIONS

ENTER VENDOR INFORMATION

1. From the **Vendor Center**, click the **New Vendor** button.

2. Enter vendor information.

3. Click **Next** to enter another vendor or click **OK** to save and close the window.

ENTER ITEMS

1. From the **Company** section of the Home page, click the **Items & Services** icon.

2. **Right-click** to display the popup menu. Select **New**.

3. Enter inventory item information.

4. To enter another item, click **Next**.

5. When finished, click **OK**.

CREATE PURCHASE ORDERS

1. After entering the inventory items, to record the purchase of inventory, from the **Vendor** section of the Home page, click **Purchase Orders**.

2. Enter **purchase information**.

3. To enter another purchase order, click **Save & New**.

4. When finished, click **Save & Close**.

RECEIVE ITEMS

1. From the **Vendor** section of Home page, click **Receive Inventory.**

2. Select **Receive Inventory with Bill** or **Receive Inventory without Bill**.

3. Select the vendor. If asked if you want to match against outstanding purchase orders, click **Yes**.

4. Enter the remaining information.

5. To enter another item received, click **Save & New**.

6. When finished, click **Save and Close**.

ENTER BILLS AGAINST INVENTORY

1. From the **Vendor** section of the Home page, click **Enter Bills Against Inventory**.

2. Select the vendor and choose the Item Receipt that corresponds to the bill.

3. Enter the remaining information.

4. To enter another bill, click **Save & New**.

5. When finished, click **Save and Close.**

PAY BILLS

1. From the **Vendor** section of the Home page, click **Pay Bills**.

2. Select **Show all bills**.

3. Select bills to pay.

4. Click **Pay & Close**.

PRINT CHECKS

1. From the **File** menu, click **Print Forms | Checks**.

2. Select **Bank Account**.

3. Enter **First Check Number**.

4. Select checks to print.

5. Click **OK**.

6. Select **Type of Check**.

7. Click **Print**.

EMPLOYEE TRANSACTIONS

ENTER EMPLOYEE INFORMATION

1. From the **Employee Center**, click the **New Employees** button.

2. Enter **employee information**.

3. Click **Next** to enter another employee or click **OK** to save and close the window.

TRACK TIME

1. From the **Employee** section of the Home page, click **Use Weekly Timesheet**.

2. Select **Employee Name**.

3. Select **Week**.

4. Enter time worked (if needed, select customer and service item).

5. To enter another timesheet, click **Save & New**.

6. Click **Print** to print the timesheets.

7. When finished, click **Save and Close**.

PAY EMPLOYEES

1. From the Employee Navigator, click **Pay Employees**.
2. Enter **Check Date** and **Pay Period Ends**.
3. Select **Employees**.
4. Select **Enter hours and preview check before creating**.
5. Click **Create.**
6. Continue until all the paychecks have been created. Then click **Print Paychecks**.
7. Click **Print** to print the paychecks.

BANKING TRANSACTIONS

WRITE CHECKS

1. From the Banking section of the Home page, click **Write Checks**.
2. Select **Bank Account.**
3. Enter **Check Date** and remaining check information.
4. Enter **Account** and **amount**.
5. Select **To be printed** if check will be printed.
6. Click **Print** to print the checks.

MAKE DEPOSITS

1. From the Banking section of the Home page, click **Record Deposits**.
2. Select **Bank Account.**
3. Enter **Date** and deposit information.
4. Click **Print** to print the deposit summary.
5. Click **Save & Close.**

RECONCILE BANK STATEMENT

1. From the Banking section of the Home page, click **Reconcile**.
2. Select **Bank Account.**
3. Enter **Statement Date** and **Ending Balance**.
4. Enter **Service Charges** and **Interest Earned**.
5. Click **Continue**.
6. Check deposits and checks that appear on the bank statement.
7. Click **Reconcile Now**.

ENTRIES

JOURNAL ENTRIES

1. From the **Company** menu, select **Make General Journal Entries**.
2. Enter **Date**, **Entry Number**, **Accounts**, and **Debit and Credit** amounts.
3. Click **Save & New** to enter another journal entry.
4. Click **Save & Close** to close the *Make General Journal Entries* window.

ADJUSTING ENTRIES

1. From the Banking Navigator, click the **Make Journal Entry** icon.
2. Enter **Date, Entry Number (ADJ #), Accounts,** and **Debit and Credit** amounts.
3. Click **Save & New** to enter another journal entry.
4. Click **Save & Close** to close the *Make General Journal Entries* window.

CORRECTING ENTRIES

To correct an error, make two entries.

1. Eliminate the effect of the incorrect entry by making the opposite journal entry.

   For example, assume the Cash account should have been debited for $200.00 and the Professional Fees account credited for $200.00. However, the following incorrect entry was made instead.

Debit	Cash	2,000.00
Credit	Professional Fees	2,000.00

   To eliminate the effect of the incorrect entry, make the following entry:

Debit	Professional Fees	2,000.00
Credit	Cash	2,000.00

2. After eliminating the effect of the incorrect entry, make the correct entry that should have been made initially.

Debit	Cash	200.00
Credit	Professional Fees	200.00

CLOSING

Before closing a fiscal period, prepare adjusting entries and print all reports needed. To close the fiscal period:

1. From the Home page, click **Customize home page and set preferences**.

2. From the *Preferences* window, select | **Accounting** | **Company Preferences.**

3. Under Closing Date, enter the **Date Through Which Books Are Closed**.

4. Click **OK**.

REPORTS

PRINT TRIAL BALANCE

1. From the **Report Center**, select: **Accountant & Taxes**.
2. Under the Account Activity section, select: **Trial Balance**.
3. Select **Dates**.
4. Click **Print**.

PRINT GENERAL JOURNAL

1. From the **Report Center**, select: **Accountant & Taxes**.
2. Under the Account Activity section, select: **Journal**.
3. Select **Dates**.
4. Click **Print**.

PRINT GENERAL LEDGER

1. From the **Report Center**, select: **Accountant & Taxes**.
2. Under the Account Activity section, select: **General Ledger**.
3. Select **Dates**.
4. Click **Print**.

PRINT INCOME STATEMENT

1. From the **Report Center**, select: **Company & Financial**.
2. Under the Profit & Loss (income statement) section, select: **Standard**.
3. Select **Dates**.
4. Click **Print**.

PRINT BALANCE SHEET

1. From the **Report Center**, select: **Company & Financial**.
2. Under the Balance Sheet & Net Worth, select: **Standard**.
3. Select **Dates**.
4. Click **Print**.

MICROSOFT OFFICE AND QUICKBOOKS

PREPARE MICROSOFT WORD CUSTOMER LETTERS

1. From the **Customer Center**, click the **Word** icon.
2. From the drop-down list, select: **Prepare Customer Letters**.
3. Complete the onscreen steps to prepare a customer letter.

PREPARE MICROSOFT WORD COLLECTION LETTERS

1. From the **Customer Center**, click the **Word** icon.
2. From the drop-down list, select: **Prepare Collection Letters**.
3. Complete the onscreen steps to prepare a collection letter.

IMPORT DATA FROM MICROSOFT EXCEL

To import lists of customers, vendors, accounts, or items from Microsoft Excel into QuickBooks:

1. Back up the QuickBooks company file.
2. From the **File** menu, select: **Utilities | Import | Excel Files**.
3. From the *Import a File* window, click **Set up Import** tab.
4. Select the **import file** and **mapping**.
5. Click the **Preference** tab. Select how to handle duplicates and errors.
6. Click **Preview**. Make appropriate corrections.
7. Click **Import**.

Another way to import data from Excel is from the specific Center. For example, to import the customer list from Excel:

1. From the **Customer Center**, click the **Excel** button.
2. Select: **Import from Excel**.
3. From the *Import a File* window, click **Set up Import** tab.
4. Select the **import file** and **mapping**.
5. Click the **Preference** tab. Select how to handle duplicates and errors.
6. Click **Preview**. Make appropriate corrections.
7. Click **Import**.

EXPORT DATA TO MICROSOFT EXCEL

You can export data to Microsoft Excel for customer customers, vendors, inventory items, transactions, payroll summary and reports. For example, to export customer data to Excel:

1. Click the **Customer Center**.
2. Display the **Customer List**. If necessary, use the View drop-down menu to filter the customer list.
3. Click the **Excel** button. Select **Export Customer List**.
4. Select **a new Excel workbook**. Click **Export**.
5. When the Excel file opens, click **File | Save As** to save the Excel file.

EXPORT REPORTS TO MICROSOFT EXCEL

To export reports to Microsoft Excel:

1. Using the **Report Center**, display the desired report.
2. Click the **Export** button at the top of the report window.
3. Select **a new Excel workbook**. Click **Export**.
4. When the Excel file opens, click **File | Save As** to save the Excel file.

CORRECTING ERRORS

QuickBooks provides a number of ways to correct errors. Often how you correct an error in QuickBooks depends upon *when* you discover the error.

For example, if you make an error when you are entering information into an onscreen check form, you can correct the error using the Backspace key. However, if you do not discover the error until after the check is saved, to correct the error, you should void the check and prepare a new check.

CORRECTING ERRORS BEFORE DOCUMENT IS SAVED

In general, errors detected before the document is saved can be corrected in one of the following ways:

1. **Backspace key:** Deletes characters to the left of the cursor in the current field you are entering.

2. **Delete key:** Deletes characters to the right of the cursor.

3. **Undo command:** Before you press the *Enter* key, you can undo typing on the current line.

4. **Clear button:** On some onscreen forms, a Clear button appears in the lower right corner of the window. Clicking this button clears all fields on the screen.

5. **Revert command (Edit menu):** Reverts the entire screen back to its original appearance.

BACKSPACE

> The Backspace key erases the character to the *left* of the cursor. The Delete key erases the letter to the *right* of the cursor.

The Backspace key is used to correct errors that occur when you are entering data. For example, if you mistype a company name on a check, you can use the Backspace key to delete the incorrect letters. Then enter the correct spelling.

Assume you need to write a check to Davis Business Associates for professional services performed for your company.

To use the Backspace key to correct an error on a check:

1. With Rock Castle Construction Company file open, click **Write Checks** in the Banking section of the Home page to display the *Write Checks* window.

> Use the data file for any of the Chapter 1 through 7 company files.

2. When the *Write Checks* window appears:

   - Select **To be printed**.
   - Select from the *Pay to the Order of* drop-down list: **Davis Business Associates**.
   - Type the street address: **1234 Brentwodo**.

3. The correct address is 1234 Brentwood. Press the **backspace** key **twice** to erase "**do**."

> Davis Business Associates should automatically appear in the Address field.

4. Type "**od**" to finish entering Brentwood.

UNDO

The Undo command can be used to undo typing before you press the Enter key.

To use the Undo command:

> You can only use the **Undo** command *before* you press the Enter key.

1. With the same *Write Checks* window still open and the check for Davis Business Associates displayed, type the city and state for the Davis address: **Bayshore, CA**. Do not press Enter.

2. After you type the address, Mr. Castle tells you the address is San Diego, CA, not Bayshore. To use the undo command, click **Edit** on

the menu bar. Then click **Undo Typing**. Bayshore, CA, will be deleted.

3. Next, enter the correct city and state: **San Diego, CA**.

The Undo command is useful if you want to delete an entire line of typing.

CLEAR

A Clear button is usually located in the lower right corner of an unsaved onscreen form. If you start entering data and want to clear all the fields in the onscreen form, click the **Clear** button.

After an onscreen form has been saved, the Clear button changes to a Revert button.

The Clear command also appears on the Edit menu. This command can be used before a document, such as a check, has been saved.

To illustrate, assume that you decide to wait to pay Davis Business Associates until they complete all the work they are performing for you. Therefore, you want to erase everything that you have entered on the check.

> The Revert button permits you to revert the onscreen form back to its appearance when you opened the saved onscreen form. This feature can be used before the onscreen form has been resaved.

To use the Clear function:

1. With the *Write Checks* window still open and the check for Davis Business Associates displayed, click **Edit** on the menu bar.

2. Click **Clear**. The *Write Checks* window returns to its original appearance with blank fields. The information you entered about Davis Business Associates has been erased.

The Clear command on the Edit menu and the Clear button on the onscreen form perform the same function: both clear the contents of an onscreen form that has not yet been saved.

CORRECTING ERRORS ON SAVED DOCUMENTS

Once a document has been saved, you can use one of three approaches to correct the error:

1. **Display** the document, correct the error, then save the document again.

2. **Void** the erroneous document, then create a new document.

3. **Delete** the erroneous document, then create a new document.

ENTER CORRECTIONS IN SAVED ONSCREEN FORM

To enter corrections in a saved onscreen form, complete three steps:

1. Display the erroneous onscreen form. For example, display an incorrect invoice in the *Create Invoices* window.

2. Correct the error by entering changes directly in the onscreen form.

3. Save the onscreen form.

Note: You cannot correct deposits using this approach. If you attempt to make changes to a saved deposit, you will receive a warning that you must delete the deposit and then reenter the appropriate information.

> **TIP:** If the correction involves a check (Write Checks, Pay Bills, or Create Paychecks), display the check in the *Write Checks* window by clicking **Previous** or use the **Find** command on the **Edit** menu.

VOID

The Void command will void a document and remove its effect from your accounting records. For example, if you void a check, the check amount is no longer deducted from your checking account. However, the check will still appear in your QuickBooks records, but is labeled Void.

To void a document in QuickBooks, first display the document on your screen. Then select **Edit** from the menu bar. The Edit menu will change depending upon the document that has been opened. For example, if you open a check, the Edit menu will display "Void Check." If you open an invoice, then the Edit menu will display "Void Invoice."

To void a check in QuickBooks:

1. With the *Write Checks* window open, enter the following information for Davis Business Associates:

Date	12/15/2007
Check Amount	$200.00
Account	Professional Fees

2. Click **Save & Close** to save the check.

3. Next, you decide to void the check and pay Davis Business Associates at a later time. Display the check for Davis Business Associates on 12/15/2007 for $200.

4. Click **Edit** on the menu bar.

5. Click **Void Check**.

> Notice that VOID now appears in the Memo field of the check and the amount of the check has been changed to $0.00.

The voided check will remain in your QuickBooks records but the amount of the check will not be deducted from your checking account.

To void an invoice:

1. Open any invoice.

2. Click **Edit** (menu).

> Notice that the Edit menu now displays Void Invoice instead of Void Check.

3. If you wanted to void the invoice, you would click Void Invoice. For this activity, close the Edit menu by clicking anywhere outside the Edit drop-down menu.

DELETE

The difference between the Delete command and the Void command is that when the Delete command is used, the document is deleted and completely removed from your QuickBooks records. The document is no longer displayed in the QuickBooks records.

When the Void command is used, the document's effect upon your accounts is removed from your accounting records, but the voided document still appears in the QuickBooks records marked "VOID".

When the Delete command is used, the document is removed from your accounting records. The audit trail maintains a record of all changes made to your QuickBooks records, including deleted documents, but the document itself does not appear in your QuickBooks system.

To delete the Davis Business Associates' check:

1. Display the voided check to Davis Business Associates.

2. With the check displayed on your screen, click **Edit** (menu).

3. Click **Delete Check** to delete the check. Now this check will no longer appear in your QuickBooks accounting records.

4. Click **OK** when asked if you are sure you want to delete the check.

5. Close the *Write Checks* window.

The Delete command removes the document from your records. If you want to maintain a record of the document but simply remove its effect from your records, use the Void command. The Void command provides a better trail of changes made to your accounting records.

NOTES:

REAL WORLD QUICKBOOKS PROJECT

SCENARIO

Appendix A provides an opportunity to use experiential learning with QuickBooks. This appendix contains a framework for developing a QuickBooks project for a real small business or nonprofit organization. The milestones for project development are similar whether for a small business or not-for-profit organization; however, the specifics of the project, such as the accounts used, may differ.

The Real World QuickBooks Project consists of the following seven milestones:

Milestone 1: Develop a proposal. In this milestone, you will identify a real world user (either a small business or a nonprofit organization) that needs assistance in establishing an accounting system using QuickBooks. After identifying the user, gather information from the user and develop a plan for a QuickBooks accounting system that will meet the user's needs.

Milestone 2: Develop a prototype or sample QuickBooks accounting system for the user. Set up a company in QuickBooks with a sample chart of accounts for the user to review. After obtaining approval of the chart of accounts from the user and your instructor, enter beginning balances for the accounts.

Milestone 3:   Develop sample QuickBooks lists for customers, vendors, items, and employees. Obtain user and instructor approval for the lists and enter the list information.

Milestone 4:   Enter sample transactions to test the prototype.

Milestone 5:   Identify the reports that the user needs and then create memorized reports using QuickBooks.

Milestone 6:   Develop documentation for the project including instructions for future use.

Milestone 7:   Present the final project first to your class and then to the user.

Appendix A
Learning Objectives

Appendix A contains guidelines and tips to complete the following seven milestones for a Real World QuickBooks Project:

INTRODUCTION

The Real World QuickBooks Project is divided into 7 milestones. Each milestone should be reviewed by your instructor before you proceed to the next milestone. In addition, the QuickBooks Project Approval form should be signed by the project user as each step is completed and approved.

MILESTONE 1: PROPOSAL

For Milestone 1, complete the following steps to develop a project proposal:

Step 1: Identify a real world QuickBooks project.

Step 2: Gather project information.

Step 3: Write the project proposal.

IDENTIFY PROJECT

The first step is to identify an actual user who needs a QuickBooks accounting system. The user can be either a small business or a not-for-profit organization. For example, the user can be a friend or relative who operates a small business and needs a computerized accounting system. Some colleges have Service Learning Coordinators who assist in matching student volunteers with charitable organizations needing assistance.

GATHER PROJECT INFORMATION

IMPORTANT! All information the user shares with you is confidential information that you should not share with anyone else. If you need to share information with your instructor, ask the user's permission first.

After identifying the user, the next step is to interview the user to determine specific accounting needs. Communication is extremely important to the process of designing and developing a successful accounting system. Listening to the user's needs and then communicating to the user the possible solutions are part of the ongoing development process. If users are not familiar with accounting or QuickBooks, they may not be able to communicate all of their needs. This requires you to gather enough information from the user to identify both the need and the solution.

Create a checklist to use when gathering information from the user.

A sample checklist follows:

❑	Organization Name
❑	Type of Business (Industry)
❑	Chart of Accounts Information
❑	Customer List Information
❑	Vendor List Information
❑	Employee List Information
❑	Item List Information
❑	Types of Transactions to Be Recorded
❑	Types of Reports Needed
❑	Users of the QuickBooks System

Before the interview, review all seven milestones of the project to identify the types of information you need. For example, when gathering information for the customer list, what customer fields does the user need?

WRITE PROPOSAL

After gathering information from the user, write a proposal that describes your plan for designing and developing your project. The proposal is a plan of what you intend to accomplish and how you will accomplish it.

Your proposal should have a professional appearance and tone that communicates to your client your competency and your enthusiasm for his or her project. Components of the proposal include:

1. **Cover Letter.** The cover letter provides an opportunity for you to thank the client for the opportunity to work together on this QuickBooks project, provide a brief introduction about yourself, summarize the main points in your proposal, and provide your contact information if the client has questions.

2. **Proposal Cover Page.** Include the project name, your name, course name and number, and the date.

3. **Proposal Report.** Include the following headings and sections:

   - **Overview and Objective.** Briefly describe the user organization and operations. Identify the user's requirements and needs of a computerized accounting system. For example, the user needs accounting records for tax purposes. Evaluate the feasibility of meeting the organization's needs with QuickBooks and the objectives of this project.

   - **Scope of Services.** Outline the services that you will provide for the client. What accounting features of QuickBooks will be implemented? Accounts receivable? Accounts payable? Specify the services you will provide the client. Will you provide implementation and setup? Conversion assistance?

   - **Client Responsibilities.** Clearly specify any responsibilities or information that the client will need to provide.

- **Cost/Benefit Analysis.** Provide a summary of the costs associated with the project that the client might expect to occur. Provide information about the benefits that might be expected, including financial and nonfinancial benefits. For example, estimated time that the client might save in maintaining accounting records.

- **Timeline.** Identify and list the major tasks involved in completing the project. Include a timeline with completion dates for each task. See the sample format below.

Task	Projected Completion Date
1._____	_____
2._____	_____
3._____	_____
4._____	_____
5._____	_____
6._____	_____
Etc._____	_____

- **Summary.** Provide a short summary including any disclaimers or remaining challenges. End the proposal on a positive, upbeat note.

Submit the proposal to both the user and your instructor. Obtain approval from both the user and your instructor. Ask the user to sign off on the proposal using the approval form that appears on a following page.

TIP: When creating the Chart of Accounts, refer to the tax form the organization will use. Obtain copies of tax forms at www.irs.gov.

MILESTONE 2:
COMPANY SETUP AND CHART OF ACCOUNTS

In this milestone, you will set up a prototype or sample company for the user to review and revise.

Step 1: Based on the information collected from the user, prepare a chart of accounts for the company.

Step 2: Submit the chart of accounts to your instructor for review and recommendations.

TIP: Nonprofits use fund accounting. Use subaccounts or the class tracking preference for fund accounting.

Step 3: Have the user review the chart of accounts and make recommendations. Ask the user to sign off on the chart of accounts using the approval form.

Step 4: After obtaining approval from both the user and instructor, enter beginning balances for the accounts.

MILESTONE 3: CUSTOMER, VENDOR, EMPLOYEE, AND ITEM LISTS

After the chart of accounts has been approved, proceed to developing lists for the user.

Step 1: After consulting with the user, list the customer information (fields) needed for each customer. If necessary, create user-defined fields in QuickBooks to accommodate the user's needs.

Step 2: List the information needed by the organization for each vendor. Create any user-defined fields that are needed for vendors.

Step 3: List the employee information needed by the organization for each employee. Determine any payroll items needed to accurately record payroll.

Step 4: Determine the items (inventory, non-inventory, and service items) required to meet the organization's needs. List the information needed for each item.

Step 5: After obtaining approval for the lists from the user and your instructor, enter information into the customer, vendor, employee, and item lists. Enter year-to-date information for employee payroll if applicable.

P: For ideas on how to stomize QuickBooks for ur specific company, click elp, **Using QuickBooks r Your Type of** usiness.

MILESTONE 4: TRANSACTIONS

Complete the following steps for Milestone 4.

Step 1: Determine the types of transactions the user will enter in QuickBooks (for example: cash sales, credit card sales, purchase orders).

Step 2: Enter sample transactions in QuickBooks. Obtain the user and instructor's approval of the results.

Step 3: Modify forms as needed to meet the user's needs. For example, if the user needs a Date column on the invoice, customize the invoice by following the instructions in Project 9.1.

Step 4: After obtaining the user's approval for transactions, create memorized transactions for the transactions that will be repeated periodically.

It is important that you and the user reach an agreement regarding what you will complete before you turn the project over to the user. Discuss with the user whether you will be entering only a few sample transactions or entering all transactions for the year to date. For example, if entering all transactions is too time consuming, you may agree that you will enter only sample transactions and the user will enter the real transactions after you submit the final project.

MILESTONE 5: MEMORIZED REPORTS

Complete the following steps for Milestone 5:

Step 1: Determine which reports the user needs. Review Chapters 4, 5, 6, and 7 to obtain information about the different reports that QuickBooks can generate. You may need to make the user aware of the reports that are available in QuickBooks and then let the user select the reports he/she would find useful.

Step 2: Obtain user and instructor approval for the reports.

Step 3: After obtaining approval concerning the reports, create and memorize the reports using QuickBooks.

MILESTONE 6: DOCUMENTATION AND USER INSTRUCTIONS

Create documentation for the user. Include a history of the project development as well as instructions that the user will need. For example, instructions regarding how and when to back up and restore company files are essential. Providing instructions on how to use memorized transactions and memorized reports is also advisable.

TIP: Provide the user with instructions for using QuickBooks Help feature.

An easy way to provide the user with adequate instructions is to recommend existing training materials to the user and then simply reference pages in the training materials. For example, if the user obtains a copy of this book, you may wish to reference pages of the text for each task the user will be performing.

MILESTONE 7: PRESENTATION

There are three parts to this milestone:

Step 1:   Make any final changes to your project.

Step 2:   Make the project presentation to your class.

Step 3:   Make a project presentation to the user.

The presentation to your instructor and classmates is practice for the final presentation to the user. You may want to ask your classmates for suggestions you can incorporate into your final presentation for the user.

A suggested outline for the project presentation follows:

1. History and Overview. Provide background about the user and the user's needs as an introduction for your presentation.

2. Demonstration. If the classroom has projection equipment, demonstrate your QuickBooks project. Display memorized transactions and memorized reports, and list information for the class to view. *Remember to use test/sample data for the class presentation instead of actual user data that is confidential.*

3. Examples. Present examples of the documentation and user instructions you are providing the client (see Milestone 6).

4. Cost/Benefit and Advantages/Disadvantages. Briefly present advantages and disadvantages of using QuickBooks for this particular project as well as associated costs and benefits.

5. Summary. Present concluding remarks to summarize the major points of your presentation.

6. Questions and Answers. Provide classmates or the user an opportunity to ask questions about the project. In preparing for your presentation, you will want to anticipate possible questions and prepare appropriate answers.

TIP: Be prepared for users to ask if they may call you if they need assistance in the future. Adequate user instructions (Milestone 6) are essential in minimizing the user's future dependence on you.

QuickBooks® Project Approval

Milestone	Approved by:	Date
1. Proposal	_____	_____
2. Company Setup and Chart of Accounts	_____	_____
3. Lists: Customer, Vendor, Item, and Employee	_____	_____
4. Transactions	_____	_____
5. Memorized Reports	_____	_____
6. Documentation	_____	_____
7. Final Presentation	_____	_____

Comments
1. Proposal:
2. Company Setup and Chart of Accounts:
3. Lists: Customer, Vendor, Item, and Employee:
4. Transactions:
5. Memorized Reports:
6. Documentation:
7. Final Presentation:

APPENDIX B
QUICKBOOKS ⚡ ONLINE FEATURES

In Appendix B, you will learn the following online features of QuickBooks:

INTRODUCTION

Online features available in QuickBooks 2006 include:

1. Online Banking.

2. Online Billing.

3. Online Resources.

If you have access to online banking services, you can complete the following Online Banking section.

ONLINE BANKING

QuickBooks permits you to use online banking. First, you must set up online banking with a participating financial institution and then you can bank online using an Internet connection.

QuickBooks offers an Online Banking feature so that you can conduct banking transactions online using the Internet. To use Online Banking with QuickBooks, you must complete the following steps to set up Online Banking:

Step 1: Obtain Internet access through an Internet Service Provider (ISP) or Local Area Network (LAN).

Step 2: Have an account with a financial institution that offers online banking services. (Note: Your financial institution may charge a fee for online banking services.)

To view a list of financial institutions providing online banking services, from the **Banking** menu select **Online Banking | Available Financial Institutions**.

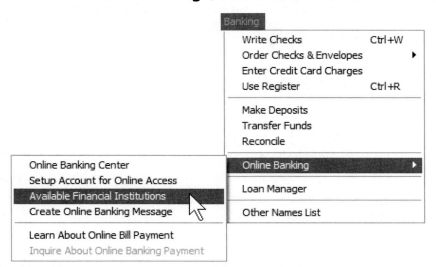

Step 3: Obtain a PIN/password from your financial institution for online banking.

Step 4: Enable accounts using QuickBooks Online Banking Setup Interview:

- From the **Banking** menu, select **Online Banking | Setup Account for Online Access.** Click **Yes** if asked if you want to continue.

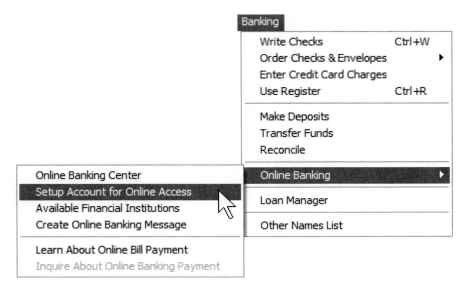

Step 5: Click **Next** and follow the onscreen instructions to Apply for Online Banking Services and then Enable Accounts.

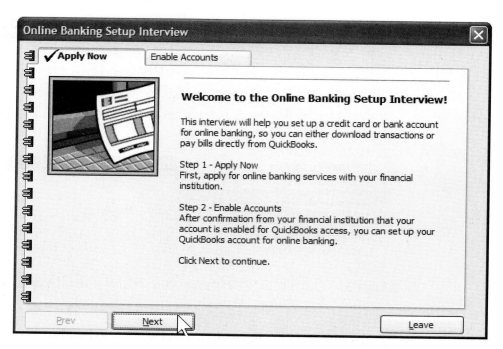

Step 6: Click **Leave** to close the Online Banking Setup Interview if you are not setting up your online account at this time.

VIEW ONLINE ACCOUNT BALANCES

After your QuickBooks account is set up for online banking, you can use two different online banking features:

1. Online account access permits you to download transaction information about your account from your financial institution and view your online account balance.

2. Online payment permits you to pay your bills online. Online payment services, such as those offered by Intuit, allow you to pay bills online for a fee.

If you have set up your QuickBooks accounts for online banking, to use the online account access feature:

Step 1: From the Banking section of the Home page, click the **Online Banking** icon to display the *Online Banking Center*.

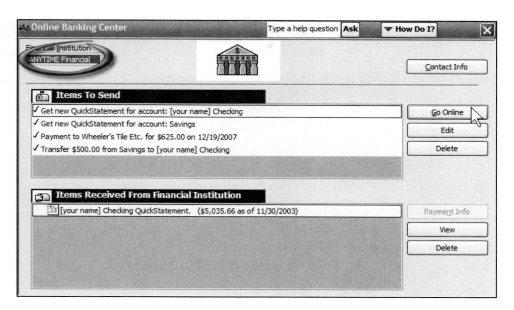

Step 2: Select Financial Institution: **ANYTIME Financial**.

Step 3: Normally, you would click **Go Online** to download transactions that have occurred in your account since your last download. Your Checking QuickStatement should appear under Items Received From Financial Institution.

Step 4: Select your **Checking QuickStatement**, then click **View**, to view your online account balance.

RECONCILE ONLINE BANK ACCOUNTS

To reconcile online bank accounts:

Step 1: With the *Match Transactions* window open from Step 4 above, select the **Show Register** checkbox.

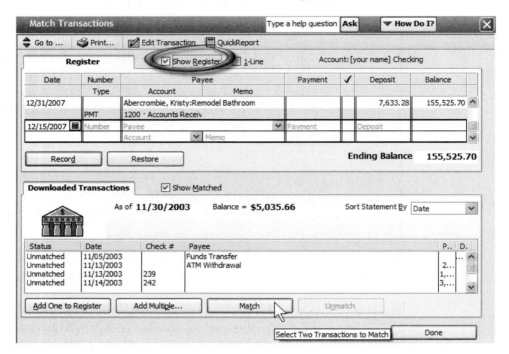

Step 2: Next, click **Match** to match downloaded transactions on the QuickStatement to transactions recorded in your QuickBooks accounts.

- Matched transactions: downloaded transactions that match transactions recorded in your QuickBooks accounts.

- Unmatched transactions: downloaded trans-actions that do not match your QuickBooks records. Unmatched transactions result when: (1) the transaction has not been entered in your QuickBooks records, or (2) the transaction has been entered in your QuickBooks records but the amount or check number does not match.

Step 3: Adjust your QuickBooks records to account for any unmatched transactions. Check for incorrect amounts or check numbers and make corrections as needed to your records. Enter any unmatched and unrecorded transactions in your QuickBooks records as follows:

- Record unmatched transactions in your QuickBooks account register (Click the **Record** button on *the Match Transactions* window), or

- Enter the unmatched transactions in the *Pay Bills* or *Make Deposits* windows.

Step 4: Reconcile your bank statement. When you receive your paper bank statement, reconcile your statement using the Banking *Reconcile* window. From the Banking *Reconcile* window, click the **Matched** button to mark matched online transactions from Step 2 as cleared.

ONLINE BILLING

In QuickBooks Pro and Premier 2006, you can E-mail invoices to customers. See Chapter 4 for instructions about how to E-mail invoices for online billing.

If you sign up for QuickBooks Online Billing, your customers can pay you electronically. To learn more about how to use QuickBooks to accept online customer payments, see Chapter 4 or click Add QuickBooks services in the Customize section of the Home page.

ONLINE RESOURCES

See the textbook website (listed on the back cover of the textbook) for links to useful online resources and websites.

NOTES:

INDEX